Thoughts On Pakistan

B R Ambedkar

THOUGHTS ON PAKISTAN

BY

B. R. AMBEDKAR

M.A., Ph.D., D.Sc., Barrister-at-Law

Member of the R. T. C.

Ex-Principal Government Law College, Bombay.

Fellow, University of Bombay.

" More brain, O Lord, more brain ! or we shall mar
Utterly this fair garden we might win."

BOMBAY

THACKER AND COMPANY LIMITED
RAMPART ROW

1941

OTHER BOOKS BY THE AUTHOR

Problem of the Rupee.

Evolution of Provincial Finance in British India.

Small Holdings in India.

Caste in India.

Annihilation of Caste.

Federation v/s. Freedom.

INSCRIBED TO THE MEMORY

OF

RAMU

As a token of my appreciation
of her goodness of heart, her
nobility of mind and her purity
of character and also for the
cool fortitude and readiness to
suffer along with me which she
showed in those friendless days
of want and worries which fell
to our lot.

Printed by Kashiram Vishram Savadkar at The Bharat Bhushan
Printing Press, 57 Vincent Road, Dadar, Bombay—14 and
Published by C. E. Murphy for Thacker and Company
Limited, Rampart Row, Bombay.

TABLE OF CONTENTS

To the reader I may say that the report was submitted to the Executive Council of the I. L. P. in August last and is printed as it then stood. Owing to want of time I have not been able to make it as uptodate in some respects as I would have liked to do. But I am sure that such omissions are trivial and do not in the least detract from the value of the book such as it is. On the other hand I believe that the value of the book is greatly enhanced by the 14 Appendices and 3 Maps which form an important accompaniment to the book. I would beg of the reader to pay more attention to the solution of the issues raised and less to my skill or rather want of it as a literary craftsman. Let him take to heart the warning which Carlyle gave to Englishmen of his generation. He said :

The Genius of England no longer soars Sunward, world-defiant, like an Eagle through the storms, " mewing her mighty youth ", ... : the Genius of England — much like a greedy Ostrich intent on provender and a whole skin . . . . . ; with its Ostrich-head stuck into . . . . . whatever sheltering Fallacy there may be, and *so* awaits the issue. The issue has been slow ; but it now seems to have been inevitable. No Ostrich, intent on gross terrene provender and sticking its head into Fallacies, but will be awakened one day — in a terrible *a posteriori* manner if not otherwise ! Awake before it comes to that. Gods and men bid us awake ! The Voices of our Fathers, with thousandfold stern monition to one and all, bid us awake."

This warning, I am convinced, applies to Indians in their present circumstances as it once did to Englishmen and Indians, if they pay no heed to it, will do so at their peril.

Now a word for those who have helped me in the preparation of this Report. In this I have been assisted by Mr. M. G. Tipnis, D.C.E., (Kalabhuwan, Baroda) and Mr. Chagganlal Modi, the former in preparing the maps and the latter in typing the manuscript. I wish to express my gratitude to both for their work which they have done purely as a labour of love. Thanks are also due in a special measure to my friends Mr. B R. Kadrekar and Mr. K. V. Chitre for their labours in undertaking the most uninteresting and dull task of correcting the proofs and supervising the printing.

28th December 1940.
    ' Rajagrah '   B. R. Ambedkar,
Dadar, Bombay, 14.

INTRODUCTION

The Muslim League's Resolution on Pakistan has called forth different reactions. There are some who look upon it as a case of political measles to which a people in the infancy of their conscious unity and power are very liable. Others have taken it as a permanent frame of the Muslim mind and not merely as a passing phase and have in consequence been greatly perturbed.

The question is undoubtedly controversial. The issue being vital there is nothing unusual if in the controversy raised by it a dispassionate student finds more stupification and less understanding, more heat and less light, more redicule and less seriousness. Some confess that this demand for partitioning India into two political entities with separate national interests staggers their imagination, others are so choked with a sense of righteous indignation at this wanton attempt to break the unity of a country, which it is claimed has stood as one for centuries, that their rage prevents them from giving expression to their thoughts. Others think that it need not be taken seriously. They treat it as a trifle and try to destroy it by shooting into it similies and metaphors. "You don't cut your head to cure your headache," "you don't cut a baby into two because two women are engaged in fighting out a claim as to who its mother is," are some of the metaphors which are used to prove the absurdity of Pakistan.

My position in this behalf is definite if not singular. I do not think the demand for Pakistan is the result of mere political distemper, which will pass away with efflux of time. As I read the situation it seems to me that it is a characteristic in the biological sense of the term which the Muslim body politic has developed in the same manner as an organism develops a characteristic. Whether it will survive or not in the process of natural selection must depend upon the forces that may become operative in the struggle for existence between Hindus and Musalmans.

Secondly, I am not staggered by Pakistan ; I am not indignant about it ; nor do I believe that it can be smashed by shooting into it similies and metaphors. Those who believe in shooting it by similies should remember that nonsense is nonetheless nonsense because it is in rhyme, and that a metaphor is no argument though it be sometimes the gunpowder to drive one home and imbed it in the memory. I believe that it would be neither wise nor possible to reject summarily a scheme if it has behind it the sentiment if not the passionate support of 90 p. c. Muslims of India. I have no doubt that the only proper attitude to Pakistan is to study it in all its aspects, to understand its implications and to form an intelligent judgment about it.

With all this, a reader is sure to ask : Is this book on Pakistan seasonable in the sense that one must read it, as one must eat the fruits of the season to keep himself in health ? If it is seasonable, is it readable ? These are natural queries and an author, whose object is to attract readers, may well make use of the usual introduction to meet them.

As to the seasonableness of the book there can be no doubt. The way of looking at India by Indians themselves must be admitted to have undergone a complete change during the last 20 years. Referring to India Prof. Arnold Toynbee wrote in 1915 :——

" British Statesmanship in the nineteenth century regarded India as ' Sleeping Beauty ', whom Britain had a prescriptive right to woo when she awoke ; so it hedged with thorns the garden where she lay, to safeguard her from marauders prowling in the desert without. Now the princess is awake, and is claiming the right to dispose of her own hand, while the marauders have transformed themselves into respectable gentlemen diligently occupied in turning the desert into a garden too, but grievously impeded by the British thorn-hedge. When they politely request us to remove it, we shall do well to consent, for they will not make the demand till they feel themselves strong enough to enforce it, and in the tussle that will follow if we refuse, the sympathies of the Indian princess will not be on our side. Now that she is awake, she wishes to walk abroad among her neighbours; she feels herself capable of rebuffing without our countenance any blandishments or threats they may offer her, and she is becoming as weary as they of the thorn-hedge that confines her to her garden.

" If we treat her with tact, India will never wish to secede from the spiritual brotherhood of the British Empire, but it is inevitable that she should lead a more and more independent life of her own, and follow the example of Anglo-Saxon Commonwealths by establishing direct relations with her neighbours...."

Although the writer is an Englishman, the view expressed by him in 1915 was the view commonly held by all Indians irrespective of caste or creed. Now that India the " Sleeping Beauty " of Prof. Toynbee is awake, what is the view of the Indians about her ? On this question there can be no manner of doubt that those, who have observed this Sleeping Beauty behave in recent years, feel she is a strange being quite different from the angelic Princess that she was supposed to be. She is a mad maiden having a dual personality, half human, half animal, always in convulsions because of her two natures in perpetual conflict. If there is any doubt about her dual personality it has now been dispelled by the Resolution of the Muslim League demanding the cutting up of India into two, Pakistan and Hindustan, so that these conflicts and convulsions due to a dual personality being bound in one may cease for ever, and so freed from each other, may dwell in separate homes congenial to their respective Hindu and Muslim cultures.

It is beyond question that Pakistan is a scheme which will have to be taken into account. The Muslims will insist upon the scheme being considered. The British will insist upon some kind of settlement being reached between the Hindus and Muslims before they consent to any devolution of political power. There is no use blaming the British for insisting upon such a settlement as a condition precedent to transfer of power. The British cannot consent to settle power upon an aggressive Hindu majority and make it its heir, leaving it to deal with the minorities at its sweet pleasure. That would not be ending imperialism. It would be creating another imperialism. The Hindus therefore cannot avoid coming to grips with Pakistan much as they would like to do.

If the scheme of Pakistan has to be considered, and there is no escape from it, then there are certain points which must be borne in mind.

The first point to note is that the Hindus and Muslims must decide the question themselves. They cannot invoke the aid of any one else. Certainly they cannot expect the British to decide it for them. From the point of view of the Empire it matters very little to the British whether India remains one undivided whole, or is partitioned into two divisions, Pakistan and Hindustan, or into twenty linguistic fragments as planned by the Congress, so long as all of them are content to live within the Empire. The British need not interfere for the simple reason that they are not affected by such territorial divisions.

Further if the Hindus are hoping that the British will use force to put down Pakistan, that is impossible. In the first place coercion is no remedy. The futility of force and resistance was pointed out by Burke long ago in his speeches relating to coercion of the American Colonies. His memorable words may be quoted not only for the benefit of the Hindu Mahasabha but for the benefit of all. This is what he said :

"The use of force alone is temporary. It may endure a moment but it does not remove the necessity of subduing again : a nation is not governed which is perpetually to be conquerred. The next objection to force is its uncertainty. Terror is not always the effect of force, and an armament is not a victory. If you do not succeed you are without resource ; for conciliation failing, force remains ; but force failing, no further hope of reconciliation is left. Power and Authority are sometimes bought by kindness, but they can never be begged as alms by an impoverished and defeated violence. A further objection to force is that you impair the object by your very endeavours to preserve it. The thing you fought for (to wit the loyalty of the people) is not the thing you recover, but depreciated, sunk, wasted and consumed in the contest".

Coercion, as an alternative to Pakistan, is therefore unthinkable.

Again the Muslims cannot be deprived of the benefit of the principle of self-determination. The Hindu Nationalists, who rely on self-determination and ask how Britain can refuse India what the conscience of the world has conceded to the smallest of the European nations, cannot in the same breath ask the British to deny it to other minorities. The Hindu Nationalist, who hopes that Britain will coerce the Muslims into abandoning Pakistan, forgets that the right of nationalism to freedom from an aggressive foreign imperialsim and the right of a minority to freedom from an aggressive majority's nationalism are not two different things ; nor does the former stand on a more sacred footing than the latter. They are merely two aspects of the struggle for freedom and as such equal in their moral import. Nationalists, fighting for freedom from aggressive imperialism, cannot well ask the help of the British imperialists to thwart the right of a minority to freedom from the nationalism of an aggressive majority. The matter must therefore be decided upon by the Muslims and the Hindus alone. The British cannot decide the issue for them. This is the first important point to note.

The essence of Pakistan is the opposition to the establishment of one Central Government having supremacy over the whole of India. Pakistan contemplates two Central Governments, one for Pakistan and another for Hindustan. This gives rise to the second important point which Indians must take note of. That point is that the issue of Pakistan shall have to be decided upon before the plans for a new constitution are drawn and its foundations are laid. If there is to be one Central Government for India the design of the constitutional structure would be different from what it would be if there is to be one Central Government for Hindustan and another for Pakistan. That being so, it will be most unwise to postpone the decision. Either the scheme should be abandoned and another substituted by mutual agreement or it should be decided upon. It will be the greatest folly to suppose that if Pakistan is buried for the moment it will never raise its head again. I am sure, burying Pakistan is not the same thing as burying the ghost of Pakistan. So long as the hostility to one Central Government for India, which is the ideology underlying Pakistan, persists the ghost of Pakistan will be there casting its ominous shadow upon the political future of India. Neither will it be prudent to make some kind of a make-shift arrangement for the time being leaving the permanent solution to some future day. To do so would be something like curing the symptoms without removing the disease. But as it often happens in such cases, the disease is driven in, thereby making certain its recurrence, perhaps in a more virulent form.

I feel certain that whether India should have one Central Government is not a matter which can be taken as settled ; it is a matter in issue and although it may not be a live issue now, some day it will be so.

The Muslims have openly declared that they do not want to have any Central Government in India and they have given their reasons in most unambiguous terms. They have succeeded in bringing into being 5 provinces which are predominently Muslim in population. In these provinces they see the possibility of Muslims forming a Government and they are anxious to see that the independence of the Muslim Governments in these provinces is preserved. Actuated by these considerations the Central Government is an eye-sore to the Muslims of India. As they visualize the scene they see their Muslim Provinces made subject to a Central Government predominently Hindu and endowed with powers of supervision over and even of interference in, the administration of these Muslim Provinces. The Muslims feel that to accept one Central Government for the whole of India is to consent to place the Muslim Provincial Governments under a Hindu Central Government and to see the gain, secured by the creation of Muslim Provinces, lost by subjecting them to the Hindu Government at the Centre. The Muslim way of escape from this tyranny of a Hindu Centre is to have no Central Government in India at all.*

But are the Mussalmans alone opposed to the existence of a Central Government? What about the Hindus? There seems to be a silent premise underlying all political discussions that are going on among the Hindus that there will always be in India a Central Government as a permanent part of her political constitution. How far such a premise can be taken for granted is more than I can say. But I may point out that there are two factors which are dormant for the present but which some day may become dominant and turn the Hindus away from the idea of a Central Government.

First is the cultural antipathy between the Hindu Provinces. The Hindu Provinces are by no means a happy family. It cannot be pretended that the Sikhs have any tenderness for the Bengalees or the Rajputs for the Madrasis. The Bengalee loves only himself. The Madrasi is bound by his own world. As to the Maratha, who does not recall that the Marathas, who set out to destroy the Muslim Empire in India, became a menace to the rest of the Hindus whom they harassed and kept under their yoke for nearly a century? The Hindu Provinces have no common traditions and no interests to bind them. On the other hand the differences of language, race, and the conflicts of the past have been the most powerful forces tending to divide them. It is true that the Hindus are getting together and the spirit moving them to become one united nation is working on them. But it must not be forgotten that they have not yet become a nation. They are in the process of becoming a nation and before the process is completed there may be a set-back which may destroy the work of a whole century.

*This point of view was put forth by Sir Mohamed Iqbal at the Third Round Table Conference.

In the second place there is the financial factor. It is not sufficiently known what is costing the people of India to maintain the Central Government and the proportionate burden each Province has to bear.

The total Revenue of British India comes to Rs. 1,94,64,17,926 per annum. Of this sum the amount, raised by the Provincial Governments from Provincial sources, comes annually to Rs. 73,57,50,125 and that raised by the Central Government from central sources of Revenue comes to Rs 1,21,06,67,801 This will show what the Central Government costs the people of India. When one considers that the Central Government is concerned only with maintaining peace and does not discharge any functions which have relation to the progress of the people, it should cause no surprise if people begin to ask whether it is necessary that they should pay annually such an enormous price to purchase peace. In this connection it must be borne in mind that the people in the Provinces are literally starving and there is no source left to the Provinces to increase their revenue.

This burden of maintaining the Central Government, which the people of India have to bear, is most unevenly distributed over the different Provinces The sources of Central Revenues are (1) Customs, (2) Excise, (3) Salt, (4) Currency, (5) Post and Telegraph, (6) Income Tax and (7) Railways. It is not possible from the accounts published by the Government of India to work out the distribution of the three sources of central revenue, namely Currency, Post and Telegraph and Railways. Only the revenue raised from other sources can be so worked out Province by Province. The result is shown in the following table :—

	Provinces	Revenue raised by Provincial Government from Provincial sources.	Revenue raised by Central Government from central sources.
		Rs.	Rs.
1	Madras	16,13,44,520	9,53,26,745
2	Bombay	12,44,59,553	22,53,44,247
3	Bengal	12,76,60,892	23,79,01,583
4	U. P.	12,79,99,851	4,05 53,030
5	Bihar	5,23,83,030	1,54,37,742
6	C. P. & Berar	4,27,41,280	31,42,682
7	Assam	2,58,48,474	1,87,55,967
8	Orissa	1,81,99,823	5,67,346
9	Punjab	11,35,86,355	1,18.01,385
10	N. W. F.	1,80,83,548	9,28,294
11	Sind	3,70,29,354	5,66,46,915

It will be seen from this table that the burden of maintaining the Central Government is not only heavy but falls unequally upon the different Provinces. The Bombay Provincial Government raises Rs. 12,44,59,553 ; as against this the Central Government raises Rs. 22,53,44,247 from Bombay. The Bengal Government raises Rs. 12,76,60,892 ; as against this the Central Government raises Rs. 23,79,01,583 from Bengal. The Sind Government raises Rs. 3,70,29,354 ; as against this the Central Government raises Rs. 5,66,46,915 from Sind. The Assam Government raises nearly Rs. $2\frac{1}{2}$ crores ; but the Central Government raises nearly Rs. 2 crores from Assam. While such is the burden of the Central Government on these Provinces the rest of the Provinces contribute next to nothing to the Central Government. The Punjab raises Rs. 11 crores for itself but contributes only Rs. 1 crore to the Central Government. In the N. W. F. the Provincial Revenue is Rs. 1,80,83,548 ; its total contribution to the Central Government however is only Rs. 9,28,294. U. P. raises Rs. 13 crores but contributes only Rs. 4 crores to the Centre. Bihar collects Rs. 5 crores for itself ; she gives only $1\frac{1}{2}$ crores to the Centre. C. P. and Berar levy a total of 4 crores and pay to the Centre 31 lakhs.

This financial factor has so far passed without notice. But time may come when even to the Hindus, who are the strongest supporters of a Central Government in India, the financial considerations may make a greater appeal than what purely patriotic considerations do now. So it is possible that some day the Muslims for communal considerations and the Hindus for financial considerations may join hands to abolish the Central Government.

If this were to happen it is better if it happens before the foundation of a new constitution is laid down. If it happens after the foundation of the new constitution, envisaging one Central Government, were laid down, it would be the greatest disaster. Out of the general wreck not only India as an entity will vanish, but it will not be possible to save even the Hindu unity. Because as I have pointed out there is not much cement even among the Hindu Provinces, and once that little cement which exists is lost, there will be nothing with which to build up even the Hindu Unity. It is because of this that Indians must decide, before preparing the plans and laying the foundations, for whom the constitutional structure is to be raised and whether it is temporary or permanent. After the structure is built as one whole, on one single foundation, with girders running through from one end to the other and if thereafter a part is to be severed from the rest, the knocking out of the rivets will shake the whole building and produce cracks in other parts of the structure which are intended to remain as one whole. The danger of cracks is greater if the cement which binds them is, as in the case of India, of a poor quality. If the new constitution is designed for India as one whole and a structure is raised on that basis and thereafter the question of separation of Pakistan from Hindustan is raised and the Hindus have to yield, the alterations that may become necessary to give effect to this severance may bring about the collapse of the whole structure. The desire of the Muslim Provinces may easily infect the Hindu Provinces and the spirit of disruption generated by the Muslim Provinces may cause all round disintegration.

History is not wanting in instances of disruption of constitutions after they were established. There is the instance of the Southern States of the American Union. Natal has always been anxious to get out from the Union of South Africa and Western Australia recently applied, though unsuccessfully, to secede from the Australian Commonwealth.

In these cases actual disruption has not taken place and where it did it was soon healed. Indians however cannot draw comfort that fortune will show them the same good turn. In the first place it would be futile to entertain the hope that if a disruption of the Indian Constitution took place by the Muslim Provinces separating from the Hindu Provinces, it would be possible to win back the seceding provinces as was done in the U. S. A. after the Civil War. Secondly if the new Indian Constitution is a Dominion Constitution, even the British may find themselves powerless to save the Constitution from such a disruption, if it takes place after its foundations are laid. It seems to be therefore imperative that the issue of Pakistan should be decided upon before the new Constitution is devised.

If there can be no doubt that Pakistan is a scheme which Indians will have to resolve upon at the next revision of the Constitution and if there is no escape from deciding upon it then it, would be a fatal mistake if the people approached it without a proper understanding of the question. The ignorance of some of the Indian Delegates to the Round Table Conference of constitutional law, I remember, led Mr. Garvin of the Observer to remark that it would have been much better if the Simon Commission,

2

instead of writing a report on India, had made a report on constitutional problems of India and how they were met by the constitution of the different countries of the world. Such a report I know was prepared for the use of the delegates who framed the Constitution of South Africa. This is an attempt to make good that deficiency and as such I believe it will be welcomed as a seasonable piece.

I would deal with the second question namely whether the book is readable. Augustine Birrell has given a warning to all writers when he said :—

"Cooks, warriors, and authors must be judged by the effects they produce; toothsome dishes, glorious victories, pleasant books, these are our demands. We have nothing to do with ingredients, tactics, or methods. We have no desire to be admitted into the kitchen, the council, or the study. The cook may use her saucepans how she pleases, the warrior place his men as he likes the author handle his material or weave his plot as best he can, when the dish is served we only ask, Is it good ? when the battle has been fought, Who won ? when the book comes out, Does it read ?

"Authors ought not to be above being reminded that it is their first duty to write agreeably. Some very disagreeable men have succeeded in doing so, and there is therefore no need for any one to despair. Every author, be he grave or gay, should try to make his book as ingratiating as possible. Reading is not a duty, and has consequently no business to be made disagreeable. Nobody is under any obligation to read any other man's book. "

I take note of the warning. But I am not worried about it That may well apply to other books but not to a book on Pakistan. Every Indian must read a book on Pakistan, if not this, then some other, if he wants to help his country to stear a clear path.

If my book does not read well, i.e., its taste be not good, the reader will find two things in it which, I am sure, are good.

First thing he will find is that the ingredients are good. There is in the book material which may be helpful and to gain access to which he will have to labour a great deal. Indeed the reader will find that the book contains an epitome of India's political and social history during the last twenty years which it is necessary for every Indian to know.

The second thing he will find is that there is no partisanship. The aim is to expose the scheme of Pakistan in all its aspects and not to

advocate it. The aim is to explain and not to convert. It would however be an idle pretence for me to say that I have no views on Pakistan.
Views I have. Some of them are expressed, others may have to be
gathered. Two things however may well be said about my views. In
the first place wherever they are expressed they have been reasoned
out. Secondly, whatever the views, they have certainly not the fixity
of a popular prejudice. They are really thoughts and not views.
In other words I have an open mind, though not an empty mind. A
person with an open mind is always the subject of congratulations. While
this may be so, it must at the same time be realized that an open mind
may also be an empty mind and that such an open mind, if it is a happy
condition, it is also a very dangerous condition for a man to be in. A disaster may easily overtake a man with an empty mind. For such a person
is like a ship without a ballast and without a rudder. It can have no direction. It may float but may also a suffer shipwreck against a rock for want
of direction. While aiming to help the reader by placing before him all
the material relevant and important, the reader will find that I have not
sought to impose my views on him. I have placed before him both sides
of the question and have left him to form his own opinion on it.

The reader may complain that I have been provocative in stating
the relevent facts I am conscious that such a charge may be levelled
against me. I apologize freely and gladly for the same. My excuse is
that I have no intention to hurt. I had only one purpose that is to
force the attention of the indifferent and the casual reader upon the issue
that is dealt with in the book. I ask the reader to put aside any irritation
that he may feel with me and concentrate his thoughts on this tremendous
issue : Which is to be, Pakistan or no Pakistan ?

PART I

MUSLIM CASE FOR PAKISTAN

The Muslim Case for Pakistan is sought to be justified on the following grounds :—

(i) *What the Muslims are asking for is the creation of administrative areas which are ethnically more homogeneous.*

(ii) *The Muslims want these homogeneous administrative areas which are predominently Muslim to be constituted into separate states*

   (a) *because the Muslims by themselves constitute a separate nation and desire to have a national home, and*

   (b) *because experience shows that the Hindus want to use their majority to treat the Musalmans as though they were second-class citizens in an alien State.*

This part is devoted to the exposition of these grounds.

CHAPTER I

WHAT DOES THE LEAGUE DEMAND ?

On the 26th of March 1940 Hindu India was startled to attention as it had never been before. On that day the Muslim League at its Lahore Session passed the following Resolution :—

" 1. While approving and endorsing the action taken by the Council and the Working Committee of the All-India Muslim League as indicated in their resolutions dated the 27th of August, 17th and 18th of September and 22nd of October 1939 and 3rd of February 1940 on the constitutional issue, this Session of the All-India Muslim League emphatically reiterates that the Scheme of Federation embodied in the Government of India Act, 1935, is totally unsuited to, and unworkable in the peculiar conditions of, this country and is altogether unacceptable to Muslim India.

" 2. It further records its emphatic view that while the declaration dated the 18th of October 1939 made by the Viceroy on behalf of his Majesty's Government is reassuring in as far as it declares that the policy and plan on which the Government of India Act, 1935, is based will be reconsidered in consultation with the various parties, interests and communities in India, Muslim India will not be satisfied unless the whole constitutional plan is reconsidered *de novo* and that no revised plan would be acceptable to the Muslims unless it is framed with their approval and consent.

" 3. Resolved that it is the considered view of this Session of the All-India Muslim League that no constitutional plan would be workable in this country or acceptable to the Muslims unless it is designated on the following basic principle, viz. that geographically contiguous units are demarcated into regions which should be so constituted with such territorial readjustments as may be necessary, that the areas in which the Muslims are numerically in a majority as in the North Western and Eastern Zones of India should be grouped to constitute "Independent States" in which the Constituent Units shall be autonomous and sovereign ;

That adequate, effective and mandatory safeguards should be specifically provided in the constitution for minorities in these units and in the regions for the protection of their religious, cultural, economic, political, administrative and other rights, and interests in consultation with them ; and in other parts of India where the Musalmans are in a minority, adequate, effective and mandatory safeguards shall be specifically provided in the constitution for them and other minorities for the protection of their religious, cultural, economic, political, administrative and other rights and interests in consultation with them.

" This Session further authorizes the Working Committee to frame a scheme of Constitution in accordance with these basic principles, providing for the assumption finally by the respective regions of all powers such as defence, external affairs, communication, customs, and such other matters as may be necessary. "

What does this resolution contemplate ? A reference to para. 3 of the Resolution will show that the Resolution contemplates that the areas in which Muslims predominate shall be incorporated into Independent States. In concrete terms it means that Punjab, North Western Frontier, Baluchistan and Sind in the North-West and Bengal in the East will instead of remaining as the Provinces of

British India shall be incorporated as independent states outside of British India. This is the sum and substance of the Resolution of the Muslim League.

Does the Resolution contemplate that these Muslim Provinces after being incorporated into states will remain each an independent sovereign state or will they be joined together into one constitution as members of a single state, federal or unitary ? On this point the Resolution is rather ambiguous if not self-contradictory. It speaks of grouping the zones into "Independent States in which the Constituent Units shall be autonomous and sovereign". The use of the terms "Constituent Units" indicates that what is contemplated is a Federation. If that is so then the use of the word "sovereign" as an attribute of the Units is out of place. Federation of Units and sovereignty of Units are contradictions. It may be that what is contemplated is a confederation. It is, however, not very material for the moment whether these Independent States are to form into a federation or confederation. What is important is the basic demand, namely that these areas are to be separated from India and formed into Independent States.

The Resolution is so worded as to give the idea that the scheme adumbrated in it is a new one. But there can be no doubt that the Resolution merely resuscitates a scheme which was put forth by Sir Mahomed Iqubal in his Presidential address to the Muslim League at its Annual Session held at Lucknow in December 1930. The Scheme was not then adopted by the league. It was, however, taken up by one Mr. Rehmat Ali who gave it the name, Pakistan, by which it is known. Mr. Rehmat Ali, M.A., LL.B., founded the Pakistan Movement in 1933. He divided India into two, namely *Pakistan* and *Hindustan* His Pakistan included Punjab, N. W. F., Kashmir, Sind and Baluchistan. The rest to him was *Hindustan.* His idea was to have an "Independent and separate Pakistan" composed of five Moslem Provinces in the North as an independent state. The proposal was circulated to members of the Round Table Conference but never officially put forth. But it seems an attempt was made privately to obtain the consent of the British Government. They, however, declined to consider it

3

because they imagined that this was a " revial of the old Muslim Empire."*

The League has only enlarged the original scheme of Pakistan. It has sought to create one more Muslim State in the East to include the Muslims in Bengal and Assam.   Barring this it expresses in its essence and general outline the scheme put forth by Sir Mahomed Iqubal and propogated by Mr. Rahmat Ali.   There is no name given to this new Muslim State in the East.   Until it is christained with a name the whole scheme may be spoken of by the name, Pakistan.

The Scheme not only called Hindu India to attention; it has shocked Hindu India.   Now it is natural to ask what is there that is new or shocking in this Scheme.

II

Is the idea of linking up of the provinces in the North-West a shocking idea ?   If so let it be remembered that the linking of these provinces is an age old project put forth by successive Viceroys, Administrators and Generals.   Of the Pakistan Provinces in the North-West, the Punjab and N. W. F. constituted a single province ever since the Punjab was conquered by the British in 1849.   The two continued to be a single province till 1901.   It was in 1901 that Lord Curzon broke up their unity by creating the present two provinces out of what was originally one single province.   As to the linking up of the Punjab with Sind there can be no doubt that had the conquest of Sind followed and not preceded the conquest of Punjab it would have been incorporated into the Punjab for the two are not only contiguous but are connected by a single river which is the most natural tie between them.   But although Sind was joined to Bombay, because in the absence of the Punjab it was the only base from which it could be governed, still the idea of disconnecting Sind from Bombay and joining it to the Punjab was not given up and

---

Halide Edib—" Inside India, " p. 355.

projects in that behalf were put forth from time to time. It was first put forth during the Governor Generalship of Lord Dalhousie ; but for financial reasons, it was not sanctioned by the Court of Directors. After the Mutiny the question was reconsidered, but owing to the backward state of communications, along the Indus, Lord Canning refused to give his consent.   In 1876 Lord Northbrook was of the opinion that Sind should be joined to the Punjab.   In 1877 Lord Lytton, who succeeded Northbrook, sought to create a trans-Indus province, consisting of the six frontier districts of the Punjab and of the trans-Indus districts of Sind.   This would have included the six Frontier districts of the Punjab namely, Hazara, Peshawar, Kohat, Bannu (except the Cio-Indus tracts), Dera Ismail Khan (with the same exception), Dera Gazi Khan, and trans-Indus Sind (with the exception of Karachi). Lytton also proposed that Bombay should receive the whole or part of the Central Provinces, in order to compensate it for the loss of trans-Indus Sind.   These proposals were not acceptable to the Secretary of State.   During the Viceroyalty of Lord Lansdowne (1888-94) the same was revived in its original form, namely the transfer of Sind to the Punjab, but owing to the formation of the Baluchistan Agency Sind had ceased to be a frontier district and the idea which was military in its motive lost its force and Sind remained without being incorporated in the Punjab.   Had the British not acquired Baluchistan and had Lord Curzon not thought of carving out the N. W. F. out of the Punjab, we would have witnessed long ago the creation of Pakistan as an Administrative Unit.

With regard to the claim for the creation of a national Muslim State in Bengal again there is nothing new in it.   It will be recalled by many that in 1905 the Province of Bengal and Assam was divided by the then Viceroy, Lord Curzon into two provinces . (1) Eastern Bengal and Assam with Dacca as its capital and (2) Western Bengal with Calcutta as its capital.   The newly created province of Eastern Bengal and Assam included Assam and the following districts of the old Province of Bengal and Assam : (1) Dacca, (2) Mymansingh, (3) Faridpur, (4) Backergunge, (5) Tippera, (6) Naokhali, (7) Chittagong, (8) Chittagong Hill Tracts, (9) Rajashahi, (10) Dinajpur, (11) Jalpaiguri, (12) Rangpur, (13) Bogra, (14) Pabna and (15) Malda.   Western Bengal included rest of the districts of the old Province of Bengal and Assam with the addition of the district of Sambalpur which was transferred from C. P. to Western Bengal.

This division of one province into two, which is known in Indian history as the Partition of Bengal, was an attempt to create a Muslim State in Eastern Bengal inasmuch as the new province of Eastern Bengal and Assam was, barring parts of Assam, a predominantly Muslim area. But the partition was abrogated in 1911 by the British who yielded to the Hindus, who were opposed to it and did not care for the wishes of the Muslims, as they were too weak to make them felt Had the partition of Bengal remained intact the Muslim state in Eastern Bengal, instead of being a new project, would now have been 35 years old.*

III

Is the idea of separation of Pakistan from Hindustan shocking? If so, let me recall a few facts which are relevant to the issue and which form the basic principles of Congress policy It will be remembered that as soon as Mr. Gandhi captured the Congress he did two things to popularize it.   First thing he did was to introduce Civil Disobedience.

Before Mr. Gandhi there were two political parties in India contending for power, the Liberals and the Terrorists of Bengal. In both the conditions for admission were extremely difficult.   In the Liberal Party the condition for admission was not merely education but a high degree of learning.   Without first establishing a reputation for study one could never hope to obtain admission to the Liberal Party.   It effectively excluded the uneducated from the path to a political career.   The Terrorists had prescribed the hardest test conceivable.   Only those, who were prepared to give their lives not in the sense of dedicating it but in the sense of shedding it, could

---

*Government of India Gazette Notification No. 2832, dated 1st September 1905.   The two Provinces became separate administrative Units from 16th October 1905.

become members of their organization. No knave could therefore get an entry in the terrorists, organization. Civil disobedience does not require learning. It does not call for the shedding of life. It is an easy middle way for that large majority who have no learning and who do not wish to undergo the extreme penalty and at the same time obtain the fame and notoriety of being patriots. It is this middle path which made the Congress more popular than the Liberal Party or the Terrorist Party.

The second thing Mr Gandhi did was to introduce the principle of Linguistic Provinces. In the constitution that was framed by the Congress under the inspiration and guidance of Mr. Gandhi, India was to be divided into the following Provinces with the language and head quarters as given below :—

Province.	Language	Head Quarters.
Ajmere-Merwara	Hindustani	Ajmere.
Andhra	Telugu	Madras.
Assam	Assamese	Gauhati.
Bihar	Hindustani	Patna.
Bengal	Bengali	Calcutta.
Bombay (City)	Marathi-Gujarati	Bombay.
Delhi	Hindustani	Delhi.
Gujarat	Gujarati	Ahmedabad.
Karnatak	Kannada	Dharwar.
Kerala	Malyalam	Calicut.
Mahakosal	Hindustani	Jubbulpore.
Maharashtra	Marathi	Poona.
Nagpur	Marathi	Nagpur.
N. W. F.	Pushtu	Peshawar.
Punjab	Punjabi	Lahore.
Sindh	Sindhi	Karachi.
Tamil Nadu	Tamil	Madras.
United Provinces	Hindustani	Lucknow.
Utkal	Oriya	Cuttok.
Vidarbha (Berar)	Marathi	Akola.

In this distribution there is no attention paid to considerations of area, population or revenue. The thought that every administrative unit must be capable of supporting and supplying a minimum standard of civilized life, for which it must have sufficient area, sufficient population and sufficient revenue has no place in this scheme of distribution of areas for provincial purposes. The dominant factor is language, unmitigated by any other consideration. No thought is given to the fear that it might introduce a disruptive force in the already loose structure of the Indian social life. The scheme was no doubt put forth with the sole object of winning the people to the Congress by appealing to their local patriotism. The idea of linguistic provinces has come to stay and the demand for giving effect to it has become so insistent and irresistible that the Congress when it came into power was forced to put it into effect. Orissa was separated from Bihar. Andhra is demanding separation from Madras. Karnatak is asking for separation from Maharashtra. The only linguistic province that is not demanding separation from Maharashtra is Gujarat. Or rather Gujarat has given up for the moment the idea of separation. That is probably because Gujarat has realized that union with Maharashtra is, politically as well as commercially, a better investment.

Be that as it may, the fact remains that separation on linguistic basis is now an accepted principle with the Congress. It is no use saying that the separation of Karnatak and Andhra is based on linguistic difference and that the claim to separation of Pakistan is based on cultural difference. This is a distinction without difference. Linguistic difference is simply another name for cultural difference.

Now if there is nothing shocking in the separation of Karnatak and Andhra what is there to shock in the demand for the separation of Pakistan ? If it is disruptive in its effect it is no more disruptive than the separation of Hindu provinces such as Karnatak from Maharashtra or Andhra from Madras. Pakistan is merely another manifestation of a cultural unit demanding freedom for the growth of its own distinctive culture.

CHAPTER II

A NATION CALLING FOR A HOME

That there are factors, administrative, linguistic or cultural, which are the predisposing causes behind these demands for separation, is a fact which is admitted and understood by all. Nobody minds these demands and many are prepared to concede them. But the Hindus say that the Muslims are going beyond the idea of separation and the questions are asked what has led them to take this course ; why are they asking for partition, for an annulment of the tie by asking that Pakistan be legally divorced from Hindustan.

The answer is to be found in the declaration made by the Muslim League in its Resolution that the Muslims of India are a separate nation. It is this declaration by the Muslim League, which is both resented and rediculed by the Hindus.

The Hindu resentment is quite natural. Whether India is a nation or not has been the subject matter of controversy between the Anglo-Indians and the Hindu politicians ever since the Indian National Congress was founded. The Anglo-Indians were never tired of proclaiming that India was not a nation, that 'Indians' was only another name for the people of India. In the words of one Anglo-Indian "to know India was to forget that there is such a thing as India". The Hindu politicians and patriots were on the other hand equally persistent in their assertion that India is a nation. That the Anglo-Indians were right in their repudiation cannot be gainsaid. Even Dr. Tagore, the national poet of Bengal, agrees with them. But the Hindus never yielded on the point even to Dr. Tagore.

This was because of two reasons. Firstly the Hindu felt ashamed to admit that India was not a nation. In a world where nationality and nationalism were deemed to be special virtues in a people it was quite natural for the Hindus to feel, to use the language of Mr. H. G. Wells, that " it would be as improper for India to be without a nationality as it would be for a man to be without his clothes in a crowded assembly ". Secondly, he had realized that nationality had a most intimate connection with the claim for self-government. He knew that by the end of the 19th Century it had become an accepted principle that a people, who constituted a nation, were entitled on that account to self-government and that any patriot, who asked for self-government for his people, had to prove that they were a nation. The Hindu for these reasons never stopped to examine whether India was or was not a nation in fact. He never cared to reason whether nationality was merely a question of *calling* a people a nation or was a question of the people *being* a nation. He knew one thing, namely, he must maintain, even if he could not prove it, that India was a nation if he was to succeed in his demand for self-government for India.

In this assertion he was never contradicted by any Indian. The thesis was so agreeable that even serious Indian students of history came forward to write propagandist literature in support of it, no doubt out of patriotic motives. The Hindu social reformers, who knew that this was a dangerous delusion, could not openly contradict this thesis. For any one who questioned it was at once called a tool of the British bureaucracy and an enemy of the country. The Hindu politician was able to propagate his view for a long time. His opponent, the Anglo-Indian, had ceased to reply to him. His propaganda had almost succeeded. When it was about to succeed comes this declaration of the Muslim League—this rift in the lute. Just because it does not come from the Anglo-Indian it is a deadlier blow. It destroys the work which the Hindu politician has done for centuries If the Muslims in India are a separate nation then of course India is not a nation. This assertion cuts the whole ground from under the feet of the Hindu politicians. It is natural that they should feel annoyed by it and call it a stab in the back.

But stab or no stab, the point is, can the Musalmans be said to constitute a nation? Everything else is beside the point. This

raises the question.   What is a nation ?   Tomes have
on the subject.   Those who are curious may go through
and study the different basic conceptions that lie at the core of it,
as well as the different aspects of it.   But it is enough to know the
core of the subject and that can be set down in a very few words.
Nationality is a subjective psychological feeling.   It is a feeling of
a corporate sentiment of oneness which makes those who are charged
with it feel that they are kith and kin.   This national feeling is
a double edged feeling.   It is at once a feeling of fellowship for one's
own kith and a anti-fellowship feeling for those who are not one's
own kith.   It is a feeling of " consciousness of kind " which on the
one hand binds together those, who have it so strongly that it
overrides all differences arising out of economic conflicts or social
gradations and on the other, severs them from those who are not of
their kind.   It is a longing to belong to one's own group and
a longing not to belong to any other group.   This is the essence
of what is called a nationality and national feeling.

Now apply this test to the Muslim claim.   Is it or is it not
a fact that the Muslims of India are an exclusive group ?   Is it or
is it not a fact that they have a consciousness of kind ?   Is it or
is it not a fact that each Muslim is possessed by a longing to belong
to his own group and not any non-Muslim group ?

If the answer to these questions is in the affirmative then the
controversy must end and the Muslim claim that they are a nation
must be accepted without cavail.

What the Hindus must show is that notwithstanding some
differences there are enough affinities between Hindus and Musalmans to constitute them into one nation or to use plain language
which make the Muslims and Hindus long to belong together.

Hindus, who disagree with the Muslims—view that the Muslim
are a separate nation by themselves, rely upon certain features of
Indian social life and which seem to form the bonds of integra-
tion between Muslim society and Hindu society.

In the first place it is said that there is no difference of race
between Hindus and Muslims.   That the Punjabi Musalman and
the Punjabi Hindu, the U. P. Musalman and the U. P. Hindu,

, Musalman and the Bihar Hindu, the Bengal Musalman
and the Bengal Hindu, the Madras Musalman and Madras Hindu,
the Bombay Musalman and the Bombay Hindu are racially of one
stock.   Indeed there is more racial affinity between the Madras
Musalman and the Madras Brahmin than there is between the
Madras Brahmin and the Punjab Brahmin.   In the second place
reliance is placed upon linguistic unity between Hindus and Muslims.
It is said that the Musalmans have no common language of their
own which can mark them off as a linguistic group separate from
the Hindus.   On the contrary there is a complete linguistic unity
between the two.   In the Punjab both Hindus and Muslims speak
Punjabi.   In Sind both speak Sindhi.   In Bengal both speak
Bengali.   In Gujarat both speak Gujarati.   In Maharashtra both
speak Marathi.   So in every province.   It is only in towns that
the Musalmans speak Urdu and the Hindus speak the language
of the province.   But outside in the mofussil there is complete
linguistic unity between Hindus and Musalmans.   Thirdly, it is
pointed out that India is the land, which the Hindus and Musalmans
have now occupied together for centuries.   It is not exclusively the
land of the Hindus, nor is it exclusively the land of the Mahomedans.

Not only reliance is placed upon racial unity but reliance is
also placed upon certain common features in the social and cultural
life of the two communities.   It is pointed out that the social life
of many Muslim groups is honey-combed with Hindu customs. For
instance the *Avans* of the Punjab, though they are nearly all
Muslims, retain Hindu names and keep their geneologies in the
Brahmanic fashion.   Hindu surnames are also found among Muslims.
For instance the surname Chaudhari is a Hindu surname but is
common among Musalmans of U. P. and Northern India.   In the
matter of marriage certain groups of Muslims are Muslims in name
only.   They either follow the Hindu form of the ceremony alone or
perform the ceremony first by Hindu rites and then call the Kazi
and have it performed in the Muslim form.   In some sections of
Muslims the law applied is Hindu Law in the matter of marriage,
guardianship and inheritance.   This was so even in the Punjab and
the N. W. F.   In the social sphere the caste system is alleged to be
as much a part of Muslim society as it is of Hindu society.   In the

religious sphere it is pointed out that many Muslim *pirs* had Hindu disciples; and similarly some Hindu *Yogis* have had Muslim *chelas.* Reliance is placed on instances of friendship between saints of the rival creeds.   At Girot, in the Punjab, the tombs of two ascetics, Jamali Sultan and Diyal Bhawan, who lived in close amity during the early part of the nineteenth century, stand close to one another, and are reverenced by Hindus and Musalmans alike.   Bawa Fathu, a Muslim Saint, who lived about 1700 A. D. and whose tomb is at Ranital in the Kangra District, received the title of prophecy by the blessing of a Hindu Saint, Sodhi Guru Gulab Singh.   On the other hand, Baba Shahana, a Hindu Saint whose cult is observed in the Jang District, is said to have been the *Chela* of a Muslim pir who changed the original name, Mihra, of his Hindu follower, into Mir Shah.

Now all this, of course, is true.   That a large majority of the Muslims belong to the same race as the Hindus is beyond question. That all Mahomedans do not speak a common tounge, that many speak the same language as the Hindus cannot be denied.   That there are certain social customs which are common to both cannot be gainsaid.   That certain religious rites and practices are common to both is also a matter of fact.   But the question is : can all this support the conclusion that the Hindus and Mahomedans on account of them constitute one nation or these things have fostered in them a feeling that they long to belong to each other ?   Such a conclusion would be nothing short of an utter delusion.

There are many flaws in the Hindu argument.   In the first place what are pointed out as common features are not the result of a conscious attempt to adopt or adapt each others' ways and manners to bring about social fusion.   On the other hand this uniformity is the result of certain purely mechanical causes.   They are partly due to incomplete conversions.   In a land like India where the majority of the Muslim population has been recruited from caste and out-caste Hindus the Muslimization of the convert was not complete and effectual, either from fear of revolt or because of the method of persuation or insufficiency of preaching due to insufficiency of priestly stuff. There is therefore little wonder if great sections of the Muslim community here and there reveal their Hindu origin in their religious and social life.   Partly it is to be explained as the effect of common environment to which both Hindus and Muslims have been subjected for centuries.   A common environment is bound to produce common reactions and constantly reacting in the same way to the same environment is bound to produce a common type.   Partly are these common features to be explained as the remnants of a period of religious amalgamation between Hindus and Muslims inaugurated by the Emperor Akbar, the result of a dead past which has no present and no future.

As to the argument based on unity of race, unity of language and occupation of a common county the matter stands on a different footing.   If these considerations were decisive in making or unmaking a nation the Hindus would be right in saying that by reason of race, community of language and habitant the Hindus and Musalmans form one nation.   As a matter of historical experience neither race, nor language nor country has sufficed to mould a people into a nation.   The argument is so well put by Renan that it is impossible to improve upon his language.   Long ago in his famous essay on Nationality Renan observed :—

" that race must not be confounded with nation.   The truth is that it is no pure race ; and that making politics depend upon ethnographical analysis, is allowing it to be borne upon a Chimera... Racial facts, important as they are in the begining, have a constant tendency to lose their importance.   Human history is essentially different Zoology.   Race is not everything, as it is in the sense of rodents and felines. "

Speaking about language Renan points out that —

" Language invites re-union ; it does not force it.   The United States and England, Spanish America and Spain, speak the same languages and do not form single nations.   On the contrary, Switzerland owes her stability to the fact that she was founded by the assent of her several parts, counts three or four languages. In man there is something superior to language, – will.   The will of Switzerland to be united, in spite of the variety of her languages, is a much more important fact than a similarity of language, often obtained by persecution ".

As to common country Renan argued that :—

" it is no more the land than the race that makes a nation. The land provides a *substratum,* the field of battle and work ;

man provides the soul ; man is everything in the formation of that sacred thing which is called a people. Nothing of material nature suffices for it "

Having shown that race, language, country do not suffice to create a nation Renan raises in a pointed manner the question, what more then is necessary to constitute a nation ? His answer may be given in his own words :—

"A nation is a living soul, a spiritual principle. Two things, which in truth are but one, constitute this soul, this spiritual principle. One is in the past, the other in the present. One is the common possession of a rich heritage of memories , the other is the actual consent, the desire to live together, the will to preserve worthily the undivided inheritance which has been handed down. Man does not improvise. The nation, like the individual, is the outcome of a long past of efforts, and sacrifices, and devotion. Ancestor-worship is therefore, all the more legitimate ; for our ancestors have made us what we are. A heroic past, great men, glory,—I mean glory of the genuine kind,—these form the social capital, upon which a national idea may be founded. To have common glories in the past, a common will in the present , to have done great things together, to will to do the like again,—such are the essential conditions for the making of a people. We love in proportion to the sacrifices we have consented to make, to the sufferings we have endured. We love the house that we have built, and will hand down to our descendant. The Spartan hymn, " We are what you were ; we shall be what you are ", is in its simplicity the national anthem of every land.

" In the past an inheritance of glory and regrets to be shared, in the future a like ideal to be realised , to have suffered, and rejoiced, and hoped together ; all these things are worth more than custom houses in common, and frontiers in accordance with strate- gical ideas ; all these can be understood in spite of diversities of race and language. I said just now, 'to have suffered together' for indeed, suffering in common is a greater bond of union than joy. As regards national memories, mournings are worth more than triumphs ; for they impose duties, they demand common effort ".

Are there any common historical antecedents which the Hindus and Muslims can be said to share together as matters of pride or as matters of sorrow ? That is the crux of the question. That is the question which the Hindus must answer, if they wish to maintain, that Hindus and Musalmans together form a nation. Now so far as this aspect of their relationship is concerned they have been just two armed battalions warring against each other. There was no common cycle of participation for a common achivement. Their past is a past of mutual destruction—a past of mutual animosities, both in the political as well as in the religious fields. As Bhai Parmanand points out in his pamphlet called " The Hindu National Movement ":— " In history the Hindus revere the memory of Prithi Raj, Partap, Shivaji and Be-ragi Bir who fought for the honour and freedom of this land (against the Muslims), while the Mahomedans look upon the invaders of India, like Muhammad bin Qusim and rulers like Aurangzeb as their national heroes ". In the religious field Hindus draw their inspirations from the Ramayan, Mahabharat, and the Geeta. The Musalman on the other hand derive their inspiration from the Quaran and the Hadis. Thus, the things that divide are far more vital than the things which unite In depending upon certain common features of Hindu and Mahomedan social life, in relying upon common language, common race and common country the Hindu is mistaking what is accidental and superficial for what is essential and fundamental. The political and religious antagonisms divide the Hindus and Musalmans far more deeply than the so-called common things able to bind them together. The prospects might perhaps be different if the past of the two communities can be forgotten by both. Renan points out the importance of forgetfulness as a factor in building up a nation :—

" Forgetfulness, and I shall even say historical error, form an essential factor in the creation of a nation , and thus it is that the progress of historical studies may often be dangerous to the nationality. Historical research, in fact, brings back to light the deeds of violence that have taken place at the commencement of all political formations, even of those the consequences of which have been most beneficial. Unity is ever achieved by brutality. The union of Northern and Southern France was the result of an extermination, and of a reign of terror that lasted for nearly a hundred years. The king of France who was, if I may say so, the ideal type of a secular crystalliser, the king of France who made the most perfect national unity in existence, lost his prestige when seen at too close a distance. The nation that he had formed cursed him ; and today the knowledge of what he was worth, and what he did, belonges only to the cultured.

" It is by contrast that these great laws of the history of Western Europe become apparent. In the undertaking which the king of France, in part by his justice, achieved so admirably, many countries came to disaster. Under the crown of St. Stephen, Magyars and Slave have remained as distinct as they were eight hundred years ago. Far from combining the different elements in its dominious, the house of Hapsburg has held them apart and often opposed to one another. In Bohemia, the Czech element and the German element are superimposed like oil and water in a glass. The Turkish policy of separation of nationalities according to religion has had much graver results. It has brought about the ruin of the East. Take a town like Smyrna or Salonica ; you will find there five or six communities each with its own memories, and possessing among them scarcely anything in common. But the essence of the nation is, that all its individual members should have things in common ; and also, that all of them should hold many things in oblivion. No French citizen knows whether he is a Burgundian, and Alan, or a Visgoth ; every French citizen ought to have forgotten St. Bartholomew, and the massacres of the South in the thirteenth century. There are not ten families in France able to furnish proof of a French origin ; and yet, even if such a proof were given, it would be essentially defective, in consequence of a thousand unknown crosses, capable of deranging all genealogical systems ".

The pity of it is that the two Communities can never forget or obliterate their past. Because their past is imbedded in their religion, for each to give up its past is to give up its religion. To hope for this is to hope in vain.

In the absence of common historical antecedents the Hindu view that Hindu and Musalmans form one nation falls to the ground. To maintain it is to keep up a hallucination. There is no such longing between the Hindus and Musalmans to belong together as there is among the Musalmans of India.

It is no use saying that this claim of the Musalmans being a nation is an after-thought of their leaders. As an accusation it is true. The Muslims were hitherto quite content to call themselves a community. It is only recently that they have begun to style themselves a nation. But an accusation, attacking the motives of a person, does not amount to a refutation of his thesis. To say that because the Muslims once called themselves a community, they are, therefore, now debarred from calling themselves a nation is to misunderstand the mysterious working of the psychology of national feeling. Such an argument presupposes that wherever there exist a people, who possess the elements that go to the making up of a nation there *must* be manifested that sentiment of nationality which is their natural consequence and that if they fail to manifest it for some time then that is to be used as evidence showing the unreality of the claim of being a nation, if made afterwards. There is no historical support for such a contention. As Prof. Toynbee points out .—

> " it is impossible to argue *a priori* from the presence of one or even several of these factors to the existence of a nationality , they may have been there for ages and kindled no response and it is impossible to argue from one case to another ; precisely the same group of factors may produce nationality here, and there have no effect. "

This is probably due to the fact, as pointed out by Prof. Barker, that it is possible for nations to exist and even to exist for centuries, in unreflective silence and that the spiritual essence of a national life may exist without the members of a nation being aware of its presence. Some such thing has no doubt happened in the case of the Musalmans. They were not aware of the fact that there existed for them the spiritual essence of a national life. This explains why the sense of nationality dawned upon them so late. But it does not mean that the spiritual essence of a national life did not exist at all.

It is no use contending that there are cases where a sense of nationality exists but there is no desire for a separate national existence. Cases of the French in Canada, of the English in South Africa, may be cited as cases in point. It must be admitted that there do exist cases, where people are aware of their nationality, but this awareness does not produce in them that passion which is called nationalism. In other words, there may be nations conscious of themselves but without being charged with nationalism. On the basis of this reasoning it may be urged that the Musalmans may hold that they are a nation but they need not on that account demand a separate national existence; why can they not be content with the position which the French occupy in Canada and the English occupy in South Africa ?   Such a position is quite a sound position. It must, however, be remembered that such a position can only be taken by way of pleading with the Muslims not to insist on partition.   It is no argument against their claim for partition if they insist upon it.

But lest pleading should be mistaken for refutation it is necessary to draw attention to two things.   Firstly there is a difference between nationality and nationalism.   They are two different psychological states of the human mind.   Nationality means "consciousness of kind, awareness of the existence of that tie of kinship".   Nationalism means "the desire for a separate national existence for those who are bound by this tie of kinship."   Secondly it is true there cannot be nationalism without the feeling of nationality being in existence.   But it is important to bear in mind that the converse is not always true.   The feeling of nationality may be present and yet the feeling of nationalism may be quite absent.   That is to say nationality does not in all cases produce nationalism.   For nationality to flame into nationalism two conditions must exist.   First there must arise the "will to live as a nation." Nationalism is the dynamic expression of that desire.   Secondly there must be a territory which nationalism could occupy and make it a state as well as a cultural home of the nation.   Without such a territory nationalism, to use Lord Acton's phrase, would be a "soul as it were wandering in search of a body in which to begin life over again and dies out finding none".   The Muslims have developed a "will to live as a nation."   For them nature has found a territory which they can occupy and make it a state as well as a cultural home for the new born Muslim nation.   Given these favourable conditions there should be no wonder if the Muslims say that they are not content to occupy the position which the French choose to occupy in Canada or the English choose to occupy in South Africa : that they shall have a national home which they can call their own.

5

CHAPTER III

ESCAPE FROM DEGRADATION

" What justification have the Musalmans of India for demanding the partition of India and the establishment of separate Muslim States ? Why this issurrection ? What grievances have they ? "—ask the Hindus in a spirit of righteous indignation.

Any one who knows history will not fail to realize that it has now been a well established principle that nationalism is a sufficient justification for the creation of a national state. As the great historian Lord Acton points out :—

"In the old European System, the rights of nationalities were neither recognized by Governments nor asserted by the people. The interest of the reigning families, not those of the nations, regulated the frontiers, and the administration was conducted generally without any reference to popular desires. Where all liberties were suppressed, the claims of national independence were necessarily ignored, and a princess, in the words of Fenelon, carried a monarchy in her wedding portion."

Nationalities were at first listless. When they became conscious—

"They first rose against their conquerors in defence of their legitimate rulers. They refused to be governed by usurpers. Next came a time when they revolted because of the wrongs inflicted upon them by their rulers. The insurrections were provoked by particular grievances justified by definite complaints. Then came the French Revolution which effected a complete change. It taught the people to regard their wishes and wants as the supreme criterion of their right to do what they liked to do with themselves. It proclaimed the idea of the sovereignty of the people uncontrolled by the past and uncontrolled by the existing state. This text taught by the French Revolution became an accepted dogma of all liberal thinkers. Mill gave it his support. "One hardly knows" says Mill "what any division of the human race should be freed to do, if not to determine with which of the various collective bodies of human beings they choose to associate themselves".

He even went so far as to hold that—

"It is in general a necessary condition of free institutions that the boundaries of governments should coincide in the main with those of nationalities."

Thus history shows that the theory of nationality is imbedded in the democratic theory of the sovereignty of the will of a people. This means the demand by a nationality for a national state does not require to be supported by any list of grievances. The will of the people is enough to justify it.

But if grievances must be cited in support of their claim then the Muslims say that they have them in plenty. They may be summed up in one sentence—namely that constitutional safeguards have failed to save them from the tyranny of the Hindu majority.

At the Round Table Conference the Muslims presented their list of safeguards, which were formulated in the well-known fourteen points. The Hindu representatives at the Round Table Conference would not consent to them. There was an impasse. The British Government intervened and gave what is known as "the Communal decision." By that decision the Muslims got all their fourteen points. There was much bitterness amongst the Hindus against the Communal Award. But the Congress did not take part in the hostility that was displayed by the Hindus generally towards it although it did retain the right to describe it as anti-national and to get it changed with the consent of the Muslims. So careful was the Congress not to wound the feelings of the Muslims that when the Resolution was moved in the Central Assembly condemning the Communal Award the Congress, though it did not bless it, remained neutral neither opposing nor supporting it. The Mahomedans were well justified in looking upon this Congress attitude as a friendly gesture.

The victory of the Congress at the polls in the Provinces, where the Hindus are in a majority, did not disturb the tranquility of the Musalmans. They felt they had nothing to fear from the Congress and the prospects were that the Congress and the Muslim League would work the constitution in partnership. But two years and seven months of the Congress Government in the Hindu Provinces have completely disillusioned them and have made them the bitterest enemies of the Congress. The Deliverance Day celebration held on the 22nd December 1939 shows the depth of their resentment. What is worse, their bitterness is not confined to the Congress. Musalmans who at the Round Table Conference joined in the demand for Swaraj are today the most ruthless opponents of Swaraj.

What has the Congress done to annoy the Muslims so much? The Muslim League has asserted that under the Congress regime the Muslims were actually tyrannized and oppressed   Two Committees appointed by the League are said to have investigated and reported on the matter.   But apart from these matters which require to be examined by an impartial tribunal, there are undoubtedly two things which have produced the clash   (1) The refusal by the Congress to recognize the Muslim League as the only representative body of the Muslims. (2) The refusal by the Congress to form Coalition Ministries in Congress Provinces.

On the first question, both the Congress and the League are adamant   The Congress is prepared to accept the Muslim League as one of the many Muslim political organizations such as the Ahrar Party, National Muslims and Jamait-ul-Ulema.   But it will not accept the Muslim League as the only representative body of the Muslims. The Muslim League on the other hand is not prepared to enter into any talks unless the Congress accepts it as the only representative body of the Musalmans of India   The Hindus stigmatize this claim of the League as an extravagant one and try to ridicule it.   The Muslims may say that if the Hindus would only stop to inquire how treaties between nations are made they would realize the stupidity of their view.   It may be argued that when a nation proceeds to make a treaty with another nation it recognizes the Government of the latter as fully representing it.   Now in no country does the Government of the day represent the whole nation.   A Government of the day only represents a majority. But nations do not refuse to settle their disputes because the Governments which represent them do not represent the whole people.   It is enough if each Government represents a majority of its citizens.   This analogy, the Muslims may contend, must apply to the Congress—League quarrel on this issue.   The League may not represent the whole body of Muslims. But if it represents a majority of them then the Congress should have no compunction to deal with it for the purpose of effecting a settlement of the Hindu-Moslem question. Of course it is open to the Government of a country not to recognize the Government of another country where there is more than one body claiming to be the Government. Similarly the Congress may not recognize the League. But then it must recognize either the National Muslims or the Ahrars or the Jamiat-ul-Ulema and fix the terms of settlement between the two communities. Of course, it must act with the full knowledge as to which is more likely to be repudiated by the Muslims—an agreement with the League or an agreement with the other Muslim parties. The Congress must deal with one or the other. To deal with neither is not only stupid but mischievous. This attitude of the Congress only serves to annoy the Muslims and to exasperate them. The Muslims rightly interpret this attitude of the Congress as an attempt to create divisions among them with a view to cause confusion in their ranks and weaken their front.

On the second issue, the Muslim demand has been that in the cabinets there shall be included Muslim Ministers who have the confidence of the Muslim members in the Legislature. They expected that this demand of theirs would be met by the Congress if it came in power. But they were sorely disappointed. With regard to this demand the Congress took a legalistic attitude. The Congress agreed to include Muslims in their cabinets provided they resigned from their parties, joined the Congress and signed the Congress pledge. This was resented by the Muslims on three grounds.

In the first place, they regarded it as a breach of faith. The Muslims say that this demand of theirs is in accordance with the spirit of the Constitution. At the Round Table Conference it was agreed that the cabinets shall include representatives of the minority communities. The minorities insisted that a provision to that effect should be made a part of the statute. The Hindus on the other hand desired that the matter should be left to be regulated by convention. A *via media* was found. It was agreed that the provision should find a place in the Instrument of Instructions to the Governors of the Provinces and an obligation should be imposed upon him to see that effect was given to the convention in the formation of the cabinets.

The Musalmans did not insist upon making this provision a part of the statute because they depended upon the good faith of the Hindus. But this agreement was broken by a party which had given the Muslims to understand that towards them its attitude would be not only correct but considerate.

In the second place, the Muslims felt that the Congress view was a perversion of the real scope of the convention. They rely upon the text of the clause* in the Instrument of Instructions and argue that the words "member of a minority community" in it can have only one meaning, namely, a person having confidence of the community. The position taken by the Congress is in direct contradiction with the meaning of this clause and is indeed a covert attempt to break all other parties in the country and to make the Congress the only political party in the country. The demand for signing the Congress pledge can have no other intention. This attempt to establish a totalitarian state may be welcome to the Hindus. But it meant the political death of the Muslims as a free people.

This resentment of the Muslims was considerably aggravated when they found the Governors, on whom the obligation was imposed to see that effect was given to the convention, declined to act. Some Governors declined because they were helpless by reason of the fact that the Congress was the only majority party which could produce a stable Government, that a Congress Government was the only government possible and that there was no alternative to it except suspending the constitution. Other Governors declined because they became active supporters of the Congress Governments and showed their partisanship by praising the Congress or by wearing Khadi which is the official party dress of the Congress. Whatever be the reasons the Muslims discovered that an important safeguard had failed to save them.

---

* "In making appointments to his Council of Ministers our Governor shall use his best endeavours to select his Ministers in the following manner, that is to say, to appoint in consultation with the person who in his judgment is most likely to command a stable majority in the Legislature those persons (including so far as practicable members of important minority communities) who will best be in a position collectively to command the confidence of the Legislature. In so acting he shall bear constantly in mind the need for fostering a sense of joint responsibility among his Ministers."

The Congress reply to these accusations by the Muslims are mainly two. In the first place, they say that coalition cabinets are inconsistent with collective responsibility of the cabinet. This the Musalmans refuse to accept as an honest plea. The English people were the first and the only people, who made it a principle of their system of Government. But even there it has been abandoned since. The English Parliament debated the issue and came to the conclusion that it was so sacrosanct as could not be departed from nor a departure from it affected the efficiency or smooth working of the governmental machine. Secondly, as a matter of fact there was no collective responsibity in the Congress Government. It was a Government by departments. Each Minister was independent of the other and the Prime Minister was just a Minister. For the Congress to talk about collective responsibiliy was just really impertinent. The plea was even dishonest, because it is a fact that in provinces where the Congress was in a minority they did form coalition Ministries without asking the Minister from other parties to sign the Congress pledge. The Muslims are entitled to ask that if coalition is bad it must be bad in all places, how can it be good in one place and bad in another?

The second reply of the Congress is that even if they have to take Muslim Ministers in their cabinet who have not the confidence of the majority of the Muslims, they have not failed to protect their interests. Indeed they have done everything to advance the interests of the Muslims. This no doubt rests on the view Pope held of government when he said—

" With forms of Government let fools contend ;
What is administered best is best "

But the Congress High Command seem to have misunderstood what the main contention of the Muslims and the Minorities has been. Their quarrel is not on the issue whether the Congress has or has not done any good to the Muslims and the Minorities. Their quarrel is on an issue which is totally different. Are the Hindus to be a ruling race and the Muslims and other minorities to be subject races under Swaraj ? That is the issue involved in the demand for coalition ministries. On that the Muslims and other minorities have taken a definite stand. They are not prepared to accept the position of subject races.

That the ruling community has done good to the ruled is quite beside the point and is no answer to the contention of the minority communities that they refuse to be treated as a subject people. The British have done many good things in India for the Indians. They have improved their roads, constructed canals on more scientific principles, effected their transport by Railways, carried their letters by penny post, flashed their messages by lightening, improved their currency, regulated their weights and measures, corrected their notions of geography, astronomy and medicine and stopped their internal quarrels and effected some advancement in their material conditions. But because of these acts of good government did any-body on that account ask the Indian people to remain grateful to the British and give up their agitation for self-government ? Or because of these acts of social uplift did the Indians on that account give up their protest against being treated as a subject race by the British ? The Indians did nothing of the kind. They refused to be satisfied with these good deeds and continued to agitate for their right to rule themselves. This is as it should be. For, as was said by Curran, the Irish Patriot, no man can be grateful at the cost of his self respect, no woman can be grateful at the cost of her chastity and no nation can be grateful at the cost of its honour. To do otherwise is to show that one's philosophy of life is just what Carlyle called ' pig philosophy '. The Congress High Command does not seem to realize that the Muslim and the other minorities care more for the recognition of their self respect at the hands of the Congress than for mere good act on the part of the Congress. Men who are conscious of their being are not pigs who care only for fattening food. They have their pride which they will not yield even for gold. In short " life is more than the meat ".

It is no use saying that the Congress is not a Hindu body A body which is Hindu in its composition is bound to reflect the Hindu mind and support Hindu aspirations. The only difference between the Congress and the Hindu Maha Sabha is that the latter is crude in its utterance and brutal in its actions while the Congress is politic and polite. But apart from this difference of fact there is no other difference between the Congress and the Hindu Maha Sabha.

Similarly it is no use saying that the Congress does not recognize the distinction between rulers and ruled. If this is so the Congress

6

must prove its *bona fides* by showing its readinesss to recognize the other communities as free and equal partners. What is the test of such recognition ? It seems to me that there can be only one—namely agreeing to share power with the *effective* representatives of the minority communities. Is the Congress prepared for it ? Every one knows the answer. The Congress is not prepared to share power with a member of a community who does not owe allegiance to the Congress. Allegiance to Congress is a condition precedent to sharing power. It seems to be a rule with the Congress that it allegiance to Congress is not forthcoming from a community then that community must be excluded from political power.

Exclusion from political power is the essence of the distinction between ruling race and subject race and inasmuch as the Congress maintained this principle it must be said that this distinction was enforced by the Congress while it was in the saddle. The Musalmans may well complain that they have already suffered enough and that this reduction to the position of a subject race is like the proverbial last straw. Their decline and fall in India began ever since the British occupation of the country. Every change, executive, administrative or legal, introduced by the British has inflicted a series of blows upon the Muslim Community. The Muslim rulers of India had allowed the Hindus to retain their law in civil matters. But they had abrogated the Hindu criminal law and had made the Muslim criminal law the law of the state applicable to all Hindus as well as Muslims. The first thing the British did was to displace gradually the Muslim criminal law by another of their making until the process was finally completed by the enactment of Macauley's Penal Code. This was the first blow to the prestige and position of the Muslim Community in India. This was followed by the abridgement of the field of application of the Shariat or the Muslim Civil Law. Its application was restricted to matters concerning personal relations such as marriage and inheritance and then only to the extent permitted by the British. Side by side came the abolition in 1837 of Persian as the official language of the Court and of the general administration and the substitution of the English and the vernaculars in place of Persian. Then came the abolition of the Quazis who during the Muslim rule administered the Shariat. In their places were apppointed law officers and judges who might be of any religion but who got the right of interpreting Muslim law and whose decisions became binding on Muslims. These were severe blows to the Muslims. As a result the Muslims found their prestige gone, their laws replaced, their language shelved and their education shorn of its monetary value. Along with these came more palpable blows in the shape of annexation of Sind and Oudh and the Mutiny. The last particularly affected the higher classes of Muslims who suffered enormously by the extensive confiscation of property inflicted upon them by the British as a punishment for their suspected complicity in the Mutiny. By the end of the Mutiny the Musalmans, high and low, were brought down by these series of events to the lowest depths of broken pride, black dispair and general penuary. Without prestige, without education and without resurces the Muslim were left to face the Hindus. The British, pledged to neutrality, were indifferent to the result of the struggle between the two communities. The end is that the Musalmans are completely worsened in the struggle. By the British conquest a complete political revolution has taken place between the relative position of the two communities. For 600 years the Musalmans had been the masters of Hindus. The British occupation brought them down to the level of the Hindus. From masters to fellow subjects was degradation enough. But a change from the status of fellow subjects to that of subjects of the Hindus is really humiliation. Is it unnatural, ask the Muslims, if they seek an escape from so intolerable a position by the creation of separate national States in which the Muslims can find a peaceful home and in which the conflicts between a ruling race and a subject race can find no place to plague their lives ?

PART II

HINDU CASE AGAINST PAKISTAN

There seem to be three reasons present to the mind of the Hindus who are opposing this scheme of Pakistan. They are as under :—

    1   Because it involves the breaking-up of the unity of India.

    2. Because it weakens the defences of India.

    3. Because it fails to solve the communal problem.

Is there any substance in these objections ? This Part is concerned with an examination of the validity of these objections.

CHAPTER IV

BREAK-UP OF UNITY

Before the Hindus complain about the destruction of the unity of India let them make certain that the unity they are harping upon does exist. What unity is there between Pakistan and Hindustan ?

Those Hindus who maintain the affirmative chiefly rely upon the fact that the areas which the Muslims want to be separated from India have always been a part of India. Historically this is no doubt true. Not only was this area a part of India when Chandragupta was the ruler ; it was also a part of India when Hwen Thasang, the Chinese pilgrim visited India in the 7th Century A D. In his diary Hwen Thasang has recorded that India was divided into 5 divisions or to use his language there were 'five Indies '* (1) Northern India, (2) Western India, (3) Central India, (4) Eastern India and (5) Southern India and that these five divisions contained 80 kingdoms. According to Hwen Thasang Northern India comprised the Punjab proper, including Kashmir and the adjoining hill states with the whole of Eastern Afghanistan beyond the Indus, and the present Cis-Satlej States to the West of the Sarasvati river. Thus in Northern India there were not only included the districts of Kabul, Jallabad, Peshwar, Gazni and Banu, but they were all subject to the ruler of Kapisa, who was a Hindu Kshatriya and whose capital was most probably at Charikar, 27 miles from Kabul. In the Punjab proper the hilly districts of Taxila, Singhapura, Urasa Punch and Rajaori, were subject to the Raja of Kashmir ; while the whole of the plains, including Multan and Shorkot were dependent

---

* Cunninghams' Ancient Geography of India. (Ed. Majumdai) pp. 13-14.
The writers of the Puranas divided India into 9 divisions.

on the ruler of Taki or Sangala, near Lahore. Such was the extent of the northern boundary of India at the time when Hwen Thasang came on his pilgrimage. But as Prof. Toynbee points out.

"We must be on our guard against 'historical sentiment', that is, against arguments taken from conditions which once existed or were supposed to exist, but which are no longer real at the present moment. They are most easily illustrated by extreme examples. Italian newspapers have discribed the annexation of Tripoli as recovering the soil of the Fatherland because it was once a province of the Roman Empire ; and the entire region of Macedonia is claimed by Greek Chauvinists on the one hand, because it contains the site of Pella, the cradle of Alexander the Great in the fourth century B. C. and by Bulgarians on the other, because Ohhrida, in the opposite corner, was the capital of the Bulgarian Tzardom in the tenth century A. D. though the drift of time has burried the tradition of the latter almost as deep as the achievements of the 'Emathian Conqueror' on which the modern Greek nationalists insists so strongly. "

The same logic applies here. Here also agruments are taken from conditions which once existed but which are no longer real and which omit to take into consideration later facts which history has to record during practically one thousand years—after the return of Hwen Thasang.

It is true that when Hwen Thasang came, not only Punjab but what is now Afghanistan was part of India and further the people of Punjab and Afghanistan were either Vedic or Buddhists by religion. But what has happened since Hwen Thasang left India ?

The most important thing that has happened is the invasion of India by the Muslim hordes from the North-west. The first Muslim invasion of India was by the Arabs who were led by Mahommad bin Quasim. It took place in 711 A. D. and resulted in the conquest of Sind. This first Muslim invasion did not result in a permanent occupation of the country because the Caliphate of Bagdad by whose order and command the invasion had taken place was obliged to withdraw* its direct control from this distant province of Sind by the

---

*Sind was reoccupied by Mohammed Ghori.

middle of the 9th century A. D.   But soon after this withdrawal there began a series of terrible invasions by Muhamad of Gazni in 1001 A. D. Muhamad died in 1030 A D.   But within the short span of 30 years he invaded India 17 times.   He was followed by Mahommed Ghori who began his carreer as an invader in 1173.   He was killed in 1206. For thirty years had Muhamad of Gazni ravaged India and for thirty years Mahommed Ghori harried the same country in the same way.   Then followed the incursions of the Mogal hordes of Chingiz Khan.   They first came in 1221.   They then only wintered in India but did not enter it.   Twenty years after they marched on Lahore and sacked it.   Of their inroads the most terrible was under Taimur in 1398.   Then comes on the scene a new invader in the person of Babar who invaded India in 1526.   The invasions of India did not stop with that of Babar.   There occurred two more invasions.   In 1738 Nadirshah's invading host swept over Punjab like a flooded river "furious as the ocean"   He was followed by Ahmadsha Abdalli who invaded India in 1761, smashed the forces of the Marathas at Panipat and crushed for ever the attempt of the Hindus to gain the ground which they had lost to their Muslim invaders.

These Muslim invasions* were not undertaken merely out of lust for loot or conquest.   There was another object behind them. The expedition against Sind by Mahommad bin Quasim was of a punitive character and was undertaken to punish Raja Dahir of Sind who had refused to make restitution for the seizure of an Arab ship at Debul, one of the sea-port towns of Sind.   But there is no doubt that striking a blow at the idolatry and polytheism of Hindus and establishing Islam in India was also one of the aims of this expedition.   In one of his despatches to Hajjaj, Mahommad bin Quasim is quoted to have said :—

"The nephew of Raja Dahir, his warriors and principle officers have been dispatched, and the infidels converted to Islam or destroyed.   Instead of idol-temples, mosques and other places of worship have been created, the Khutbah is read, the call to prayers is raised, so that devotions are performed at stated hours. The Takbir and praise to the Almighty God are offered every morning and evening."

*What follows regarding the objects and methods of the Muslim invaders has been taken almost verbatim from " Indian Islam " by Dr. Tirus especially the quotations.

After receiving the above dispatch, which had been forwarded with the head of the Raja, Hajjaj sent the following reply to his general :—

" Except that you give protection to all, great and small alike, make no difference between enemy and friend.   God says, " Give no quarter to infidels but cut their throats."   Then know that this is the command of the great God.   You shall not be too ready to grant protection, because it will prolong your work.   After this give no quarter to any enemy except those who are of rank."

Muhamad of Gazni also looked upon his numerous invasions of India as the waging of a holy war.   A Utbi the historian of Muhamad in describing his raids writes :—

" He demolished idol temples and established Islam.   He captur-ed .... cities, killed the polluted wretches, destroying the idolators, and gratifying Muslims.   ' He then returned home and promulgated accounts of the victories obtained for Islam. ...... and vowed that every year he would undertake a holy war against Hind."

Mahommed Ghori was actuated by the same holy zeal in his invasions of India.   Hasan Nizami the historian describes his work in the following terms :—

' He purged by his sword the land of Hind from the filth of infidelity and vice, and freed the whole of that country from the thorn of God-plurality and the impurity of idol-worship, and by his royal vigour and intrepidity left not one temple standing.'

Timur has in his Memoir explained what led him to invade India.   He says :—

" My object in the invasions of Hindustan is to lead a campaign against the infidels, to convert them to the true faith according to the command of Mahammad (on whom and his family be the bless-ing and peace of God), to purify the land from the defilement of misbelief and polytheism, and overthrow the temples and idols, whereby we shall be *Ghazis* and *Mujhkids*, companions and soldiers of the faith before God."

These invasions of India by Muslims were as much invasions of India as they were wars among the Muslims themselves.   This fact has remained hidden because the invaders are all lumped together as Muslims without distinction.   But as a matter of fact they were Tartars, Afghans and Mongols. Mahomed of Gazni was a Tartar, Mahomed of Ghori was an Afghan, Timur was a Mongol, Baber was a Tartar, Nadirshah and Ahmedshah Abdali were Afghans. In invading India the Afghan was out to destroy the Tartar and the Mongol was out to destroy both the Tartar as well as the Afghan   They were not a loving family cemented by the feeling of Islamic brotherhood. They were deadly rivals of one another and their wars were often wars of mutual extermination. What is however important to bear in mind is that with all their internecine conflicts they were all united by one common objective and that was to destroy the Hindu faith.

The methods adopted by the Muslim invaders of India are not less significant for the subsequent history of India than the object of their invasions.

Muhammad Bin Quassim's first act of religious zeal was forcibly to circumcise the Brahmins of the captured city of Debul ; but on discovering that they objected to this sort of conversion, he then proceeded to put all above the age of 17 to death, and to order all others, with women and children, to be led into slavery. The temple of the Hindus was looted, and the rich booty was divided equally among the soldiers, after one-fifth, the legal portion for the government, had been set aside.

Mahomed of Gazni from the first adopted those plans that would strike terror into the hearts of the Hindus. After the defeat of Raja Jaipal in A. D. 1001 Mahomed ordered that Jaipal " be paraded about in the streets so that his sons and chieftains might see him in that condition of shame, bonds and disgrace ; and that the fear of Islam might fly abroad through the country of the infidels.

" The slaughtering of 'infidels' seemed to be one thing that gave Mahomed particular pleasure. In one attack on Chand Rai, in A. D. 1019, many infidels were slain or taken prisoners, and the Muslims paid no regard to booty until they had satiated themselves with the slaughter of the infidels and worshippers of the sun and fire.' The historian naively adds that the elephants of the Hindu armies came to Mahmud of their own accord, leaving idols, preferring the service of the religion of Islam."

Not infrequently the slaughter of the enemy gave a great setback to the indigenous culture of the Hindus, as in the conquest of Bihar by Muhammad Bakhtyar Khilji. When he took a certain place, the Tabaquat-i-Nasiri informs us that

"great plunder fell into the hands of the victors. Most of the inhabitants were Brahmins with shaven heads. They were put to death. Large numbers of books were found.........but no one could explain their contents as all the men had been killed the whole fort and city being a place of study.

"Of the destruction of temples and the desecration of idols we have an abundance of evidence. Muhammad bin Quassim carried out his plan of destruction systematically in Sind, we have seen, but he made an exception of the famous temple at Multan for purposes of revenue, as this temple was a place of resort for pilgrims, who made large gifts to the idol. Nevertheless while he thus satisfied his avarice by letting the temple stand, he gave vent to his malignity by having a piece of cow's flesh tied around the neck of the idol.

"Minhaj-as-Siraj further tells how Mahmud became widely known for having destroyed as many as a thousand temples, and of his great feat in destroying the temple of Somnath and carrying off its idol, which he asserts was broken into four parts. "One part he deposited in the Jami Masjid of Gazni, one he placed at the entrance of the royal palace, the third he sent to Mecca, and the fourth to Medina."

It is said by Lane Poole that Mahomed of Gazni "who had vowed that every year should see him wage a holy war against the infidels of "Hindustan" could not rest from his idol-breaking campaign so long as the temple of Somnath remained inviolate. It was for this specific purpose that he, at the very close of his career, undertook his arduous march across the desert from Multan to Anhalwara on the coast, fighting as he went, until he saw at last the famous temple.

"There, a hundred thousand pilgrims were wont to assemble, a thousand Brahmins served the temple and guarded its treasures, and hundreds of dancers and singers played before its gates. Within stood the famous linga, a rude pillar stone adorned with gems and lighted by jewelled condelbra which were reflected in rich hangings, embroidered with precious stones like stars, that decked the shrine ...Its ramparts were swarmed with incredulous Brahmins,

mocking the vain arrogance of foreign infidels whom the God of
Somnath would assuredly consume. The foreigners, nothing daunted,
scaled the walls ; the God remained dumb to the urgent appeals of
his servants ; fifty thousand Hindus suffered for their faith and the
sacred shrine was sacked to the joy of the true believers. The great
stone was cast down, and its fragments were carried off to grace
the coqueror's palace. The temple gates were set up at Gazni and
a million pounds' worth of treasure rewarded the iconoclast.''*

Muhammad Ghori one of the enthusiastic successors of Mahmud
of Gazni, in his conquest of Ajmir

"destroyed pillars and foundations of the idol-temples, and built
in their stead mosques and colleges, and the precepts of Islam and
the customs of the law were divulged and established. At Delhi,
the city and its vicinity were freed from idols and idol worship, and
in the sanctuaries of the images of the gods mosques were raised by
the worshippers of the one God.''

Qutb-ud-Din Aybak also is said to have destroyed nearly
a thousand temples, and then raised mosques on their foundations.
The same author states that he built the Jami Masjid, Delhi, and
adorned it with the stones and gold obtained from the temples
which had been demolished by elephants, and covered it with
inscriptions (from the Quran) containing the divine commands.
We have further evidence of this harrowing process having been
systematically employed from the inscription extant over the
eastern gateway of this same mosque at Delhi, which relates that
the materials of 27 idol temples were used in its construction.

"Ala-ud-Din, in his zeal to build n second Minar to the Jami
Masjid, to rival the one built of Qutb-ud-din, is said by Amir Khusru
not only to have dug stones out of the hills, but to have demolished
temples of the infidels to furnish a supply. In his consequents of
South India the the destruction of temples was carried out by
"Ala-ud-Din" as it had been in the north by his predecessors.

"The Sultan Firoz Shah, in his Futuhat, graphically relates how
he treated Hindus who had dared to built new temples. When
they did this in the city (Delhi) and the environs, in opposition to

---

*"Medieval India."

the law of the Prophet, which declares that such are not to be tolerated, under Divine guidance I destroyed these edifices, I killed these leaders of infidelity and punished others with stripes, until this abuse was entirely abolished and where infidels and idolaters worshipped idols, Musalmans now by God's mercy perform their devotions to the true God."

Even in the reign of Shah Jahan we read of the destruction of the temples that the Hindus had started to rebuild, and the account of this direct attack on the piety of the Hindus is thus solemnly recorded in the Badhshah-namah :

"It had been brought to the notice of His Majesty, says the historian, that during the late reign (of Akbar) many idol-temples had been begun but remained unfinished at Benares, the great stronghold of infidelity.   The infidels were now desirous of completing them.   His Majesty, the defender of the faith, gave orders that at Benares and throughout all his dominions in every place all temples that had been begun should be cast down.   It was reported from the Province of Allahabad that 76 temples had been destroyed in the district of Benares."

It was left to Aurangzeb to make a final attempt to overthrow idolatory.   The author of Ma' athır ı-Alamgırı, dilates upon his efforts to put down Hindu teaching, and his destruction of temples in the following terms :—

"In April, A. D. 1669, Aurangzib learned that in the provinces of Thatta, Multan and Benares, but especially in the latter, foolish Brahmins were in the habit of expounding frivolous books in their schools, and that learners, Muslims as well as Hindus, went there from long distances.........The 'Director of the Faith' consequently issued orders to all the governors of provinces to destroy with a willing hand the schools and temples of the infidels ; and they were enjoined to put an entire stop to the teaching and practising of idolatrous worship.........

"Such invaders as Mahmud and Timur seem to have been more concerned with iconoclasm, the collection of booty, the enslaving of captives, and the sending of infidels to hell with the 'proselytizing sword' than they were with the conversion of them even by force. But when rulers were permanently established the winning of converts became a matter of supreme urgency.   It was a part of the state policy to establish Islam as the religion of the whole land."

"Qutb-ud-Din, whose reputation for desroying temples was almost as great as that of Mahmud, in the latter part of the twelfth century and early years of the thirteenth, must have frequently resorted to force as an incentive to conversion. One instance may be noted: when he approached Koil (Aligrah) in A. D. 1194, 'those of the garrison who were wise and acute were converted to Islam, but the others were slain with the sword'".

Further examples of extreme measures employed to effect a change of faith are all too numerous One pathetic case is mentioned in the time of the reign of Firuz Shah (A. D. 1351-1388). An old Brahmin of Delhi had been accused of worshipping idols in his house, and of even leading Muslim women to become infidels. He was sent for and his case placed before the judges, doctors, elders and lawyers. Their reply was that the provisions of the law were clear. The Brahmin must either become a Muslim or be burned The true faith was declared to him and the right course pointed out, but he refused to accept it. "Consequently he was burned by the order of the Sultan", and the commentator adds, "Behold the Sultan's strict adherence to law and rectitude, how he would not deviate in the least from its decrees."

"Not only was slaughter of the infidels and the destruction of their temples resorted to in earlier period of Islam's contact with India, but as we have seen, many of the vanquished were led into slavery. The dividing up of booty was one of the special attractions, to the leaders as well as to the common soldiers in these expeditions. Mahmud seems to have made the slaughter of infidels, the destruction of their temples, the capturing of slaves, and the plundering of the wealth of the people, particularly of the temples and the priests, the main object of his raids. On the occasion of his first raid he is said to have taken much booty , and half a million Hindus, 'beautiful men and women', were reduced to slavery and taken back to Ghazni."

When he later took Kanuaj, in A. D. 1017, he took so much booty and so many prisoners that 'the fingers of those who counted them would have tired.' The same authority describes how common Indian slaves had become in Ghazni and Central Asia after the campaign of A D. 1019.

"The number of prisoners may be conceived from the fact that each was sold for from two to ten dirhams. These were afterwards taken to Ghazni, and merchants came from far distant cities to purchase them ; . . . . . and the fair and the dark, the rich and the poor were commingled in one common slavery."

"In the year A. D. 1202, when Qutb-ud-Din captured Kalinjar, after the temples had been converted into mosques, and the very name of idolatry was annihilated, fifty thousand men came under the collar of slavery and the plain became black as pitch with Hindus."

Slavery was the fate of those Hindus who were caught in the din of war. But when there was no war the systematic abasement of the Hindus played no unimportant part in the methods adopted by the Muslim invaders. In the days of Alla-ud-Din at the beginning of the fourteenth century, the Hindus had in certain parts given the Sultan much trouble. So he determined to impose such taxes on them that they would be prevented from rising in rebellion.

"The Hindu was to be left unable to keep a horse to ride on, to carry arms, to wear fine clothes, or to enjoy any of the luxuries of life."

These edicts, says the historian of the period,

"were so strictly carried out that the chaukidars and khuts and muqaddims were not able to ride on horseback, to find weapon, to wear fine clothes, or to indulge in betel......No Hindu could hold up his head.........Blows, confinement in the stocks, imprisonment and chains were all employed to enforce payment."

"The payment of the jizyah by the Hindus continued throughout the dominions of the sultans, emperors, and kings in various parts of India with more or less regularity, though often the law was in force in theory only; since it depended entirely on the ability of the sovereign to enforce his demands. But, finally, it was abolished throughout the Mughul Empire in the ninth year of the enlightened Akbar's reign (A.D. 1665), after it had been accepted as a fundamental part of Muslim government policy in India for a period of more than eight centuries."

Lane Poole says that—

"the Hindu was taxed to the extent of half the produce of his land, and had to pay duties on all his buffaloes, goats, and other milch-cattle. The taxes were to be levied equally on rich and poor, at so much per acre, so much per animal. Any collectors or officers taking bribes were summarily dismissed and heavily punished with pincers, the rack, imprisonment and chains'

The new rules were strictly carried out, so that one **revenue officer** would string together 20 Hindu notables and enforce **payment by blows**. No gold or silver, not even the betel-nut, so cheering and stimulative to pleasures, was to be seen in a Hindu house, and the wives of the impoverished native officials were reduced to taking service in Muslim families. Revenue Officers came to be regarded as more deadly than the plague; and to be a government clerk was disgrace worse than death, in so much that no Hindu would marry his daughter to such a man."

All this was not the result of mere caprice or moral perversion. On the other hand what was done was in accordance with the ruling ideas of the leaders of Islam in their broadest aspects. These ideas were well expressed by the Kazi in reply to a question put by Sultan Alla-ud-Din wanting to know the legal position of the Hindus under Muslim law.

The Kazi said :—

" They are called payers of tribute, and when the revenue officer demands silver from them, they should without question, and with all humility and respect, tender gold. If the officer throws dirt in their mouths, they must without reluctance open their mouths wide to receive it.... . The due subordination of the Dhimmi is exhibited in this humble payment, and by this throwing of dirt into their mouths. The glorification of Islam is a duty, and contempt for religion is vain. God holds them in contempt, for he says, 'Keep them in subjection. To keep the Hindus in abasement is especially a religious duty, because they are the most inveterate enemies of the Prophet, and because the Prophet has commanded us to slay them, plunder them, and make them captive, saying, ' Convert them to Islam or kill them, and make them slaves, and spoil their wealth and property.' No doctor but the great doctor (Hanifah), to whose school we belong, has assented to the imposition of jizya on Hindus; doctors of other schools allow no other alternative but ' Death or Islam'."

Such is the story of this period of 762 years which elapsed between advent of Mahammud of Gazni and the return of Ahamadsha Abdali.

How far is it open for the Hindus to say that Northern India is part of Aryavarta ? How far is it open to the Hindus to say because

8

once it belonged to them, therefore it must remain for ever an integral part of India ?   Those who oppose separation and hold to the ' historic sentiment ' arising out of an ancient fact that Northern India including Afghanistan was once part of India and that the people of that area were either Buddhists or Hindus, must be asked whether the events of these 762 years of incessant Muslim invasions, the object with which they were launched and the methods adopted by these invaders to give effect to their object are to be treated as though they were matters of no account ?

Apart from other consequences which have flowed from them these invasions have in my opinion so profoundly altered the culture and character of the Northern areas which it is now proposed to be included in a Pakistan that there is not only no unity between that area and the rest of India but that there is as a matter of fact a real antipathy between the two.

The first consequence of these invasions was the breaking up of the unity of Northern India with the rest of India.   After his conquest of Northern India Mahomad of Gazni detached it from India and ruled it from Gazni.   When Mohammad Ghori came in the field as a conqueror he again attached it to India and ruled it from Lahore and then from Delhi.   Hakim, the brother of Akbar detached Kabul and Kandhar from Northern India.   Akbar again attached it to Northern India.   They remained attached until the death of Aurangzeb.   They were again detached by Nadirshah in 1738 and the whole of Northern India would have been severed from India had it not been for the check provided by rise of the Sikhs. Northern India therefore has been like a waggon which can be coupled or uncoupled according to the circumstances of the moment. If analogy is wanted the case of Alsace Lorraine could be cited. Alsace Lorraine was originally part of Germany, like the rest of Switzerland and the Low countries.   It continued to be so till 1680, when it was taken by France and incorporated into French territory. It belonged to France till 1871, when it was detached by Germany and made part of her territory.   In 1918 it was again detached from Germany and made part of France.   In 1940 it is detached from France and made part of Germany.

The methods adopted by the invaders have left behind them their aftermath. One aftermath is the bitterness between the Hindus and the Muslims which they have caused. This bitterness, between the two, is so deep-seated that a century of political life has not succeeded in assuaging it, nor making people forget it. Accompanied as the invasions were with the destruction of temples and forced conversions, with the spoilation of property, with the slaughter, enslavement and abasement of men, women and children, what wonder if the memory of these invasions has ever remained green, as a source of pride to the Muslims and as a source of shame to the Hindus? But these things apart, this north-west corner of India has been a theatre in which a stern drama has been played. Muslim hordes, in wave after wave, have surged down into this area and from thence scattered themselves in spray over the rest of India. These waves reached the rest of India in thin currents. In time, they also receded from their furthest marks. But while they lasted they left a deep deposit of Islamic culture over the original Aryan culture in this north-west corner of India which has given it a totally different colour, both in religious and political outlook. The Muslim invaders no doubt came to India singing a hymn of hate against the Hindus. But they did not merely sing their hymn of hate and go back burning a few temples on the way. That would have been a blessing. They were not content with so negative a result. They did a positive act, namely to plant the seed of Islam. The growth of this plant is remarkable. It is not a summer sappling. It is as great and as strong as an oak. Its growth is the thickest in Northern India. The successive invasions have deposited their silt more there than anywhere else, and have served as watering exercises of devoted gardeners. Its growth is so thick in Northern India that the remnants of Hindu and Buddhist culture are just shrubs. Even the Sikh axe could not fell this oak. Sikhs no doubt became the political masters of Northern India. But they did not gain back Northern India to that spiritual and cultural unity by which it was bound to the rest of India before Hwen Thasang. The Sikhs coupled it back to India. But it remains like Alsace Lorraine politically detachable and spiritually alien so far as the rest of India is concerned. It is only an unimaginative person who could fail to take notice of these facts or insist in the face of them that Pakistan means breaking up into two what is one whole.

What is the unity the Hindu sees between Pakistan and Hindustan ? If it is geographical unity then that is no unity. Geographical unity is unity intended by nature. But in building up a nationality on geographical unity it must be remembered that it is a case where Nature proposes and Man disposes. If it is unity in external things, such as ways and habits of life, that is no unity. Such unity is the result of exposure to a common environment. If it is administrative unity that again is no unity. The instance of Burma is in point. Arakan and Tennarsarim were annexed in 1826 by the treaty of Yendabu. Pegu and Martaban were annexed in 1852. Upper Burma was annexed in 1886. The administrative unity between India and Burma was forged in 1826. For over 110 years that administrative unity continued to exist. In 1937 the knot that tied the two together was cut asunder and nobody shed a tear over it. The unity between India and Burma was not less fundamental. If unity is to be of an abiding character it must be founded on a sense of kinship, in the feeling of being kindred. In short it must be spiritual. Judged in the light of these considerations, the unity between Pakistan and Hindustan is a myth. Indeed there is more spiritual unity between Hindustan and Burma than there is between Pakistan and Hindustan. And if the Hindus did not object to the severance of Burma from India it is difficult to understand how the Hindus can object to the severance of an area like Pakistan which, to repeat, is politically detachable from, socially hostile and spiritually alien to, the rest of India.

CHAPTER V

WEAKENING OF THE DEFENCES.

How will the creation of Pakistan affect the question of the Defence of Hindustan ? The question is not a very urgent one. For there is no reason to suppose that Pakistan will be at war with Hindustan immediately it is brought into being. But as the question is sure to be raised it is better to deal with it.

The question may be considered under three heads : (1) Question of Frontiers, (2) Question of Resources and (3) Question of Armed Forces

I

CONSIDERATIONS OF FRONTIERS

It is sure to be urged by the Hindus that Pakistan leaves Hindustan without a scientific frontier. The obvious reply, of course, is that the Musalmans cannot be asked to give up their right to Pakistan, because it adversely affects the Hindus in the matter of their boundaries But banter apart, there are really two considerations, which if taken into account, will show that the apprehensions of the Hindus in this matter are quite uncalled for.

In the first place, can any country hope to have a frontier which may be called scientific ? As Mr. Davies, the author of " North-West Frontier " observes .—

"It would be impossible to demarcate on the North-West of our Indian Empire a frontier which would satisfy ethnological, political and military requirements. To seek for a zone which traverses easily definable geographical features ; which does not violate ethnic considerations by cutting through the territories of closely related tribes ; and which at the same time serves as a political boundary, is utopian".

As a matter of history there has been no one scientific boundary for India and different persons have advocated different boundaries for India. The boundaries question has given rise to two policies, the " Forward " Policy and the " Back to the Indus " Policy. The " Forward " Policy had a greater and a lesser intent, to use the language of Sir George Macmunn. In its greater intent it meant active control in the affairs of Afghanistan as an *Etat Tampion* to India and the extension of Indian influence upto the Oxus. In its lesser intent it was confined to the absorption of the tribal hills between the administered territory (i.e. the Province of N.-W. F.) and Afghanistan as defined by the Durand line and the exercise of British control right up to that line. The greater intent of the Forward Policy, as a basis for a safe boundary for India, has long been abandoned. Consequently there remain three possible boundary lines to choose from : (1) the Indus River, (2) the present administrative boundry of the N.-W. F. and (3) the Durand Line. Pakistan will no doubt bring the boundary of Hindustan Back to the Indus, indeed behind the Indus, to the Sutlej. But this "Back to Indus" policy was not without its advocates. The greatest exponent of the Indus boundary was Lord Lawrence, who was stronlgy opposed to any forward move beyond the trans-Indus foot hills. He advocated meeting any invader in the valley of the Indus ; in his opinion it would be an act of folly and weakness to give battle at any great distance from our base ; and that the longer the distance an invading army has to march, through Afghanistan and the tribal country, the more harassed it would be. Others no doubt have pointed out that a river is a weak line of defence. But the principal reason for not retiring to the Indus boundary seems to lie elsewhere. Mr. Davies gives the real reason when he says that the—

"Back to Indus" cry becomes absurd when it is examined from the point of view of the inhabitants of the modern North-West Frontier Province. Not only would withdrawal mean loss of prestige, but it would also be a gross betrayal of those peoples to whom we have extended our beneficent rule."

In fact, it is no use insisting that any particular boundry is the safest, for the simple reason that geographical conditions are not decisive in the world to-day and modern technique has robbed natural frontiers of much of their former importance, even where they are mighty mountains, the broadest streams, or seas or deserts.

In the second place, it is always possible for nations with no natural boundaries to make good this defect. Countries are not wanting which have no natural boundaries. Yet all have made good the deficiencies of nature, by creating artificial fortifications as barriers, which can be far more impregnable than natural barriers. There is no reason to suppose that the Hindus will not be able to accomplish what other countries similarly situated have done. Given the resources, Hindus need have no fear for want of a naturally safe frontier.

II

QUESTION OF RESOURCES.

More important than the question of a scientific frontier, is the question of resources. If resources are ample for the necessary equipment, then it is always possible to overcome the difficulties created by an unscientific or a weak frontier. We must therefore consider the comparative resources of Pakistan and Hindustan. The following figures are intended to convey an idea of their comparative resources :—

Resources of Pakistan.

Provinces.	Area	Population	Revenues.*
			Rs.
N.-W. F.	13,518	2,425,003	1,90,11,842
Punjab	91,919	23,551,210	12,53,87,730
Sind	46,378	3,887,070	9,56,76,269
Baluchistan	54,228	420,648	. . .
Bengal	82,955	50,000,000	36,55,62,485
Total ..	288,998	80,283,931	60,56,38,326

Resources of Hindustan.

Provinces.	Area	Population	Revenues * Rs.
Ajmer-Merwara	2,711	560,292	21,00,000
Assam	55,014	8,622,251	4,46,04,441
Bihar	69,348	32,371,434	6,78,21,588
Bombay	77,271	18,000,000	34,98,03,800
C. P. & Berar	99,957	15,507,723	4,58,83,962
Coorg	1,593	163,327	11,00,000
Delhi	573	636,246	70,00,000
Madras	142,277	46,000,000	25,66,71,265
Orissa	32,695	8,043,681	87,67,269
U P.	206,248	48,408,763	16,85,52,881
Total	607,657	178,513,919	96,24,05,206

These are gross figures. They are subject to certain additions and deductions. Revenues derived by the Central Government from Railways, Currency and Post and Telegraphs are not included in these figures, as it is not possible to ascertain how much is raised from each Province. When it is done, certain additions will have to be made to the figures under revenue. There can be no doubt that the share form these heads of revenue that will be come to Hindustan will be much larger than the share that will go to Pakistan Just as additions will have to be made to these figures, so also deductions will have to be made from them. Most of these deductions will of course fall to the lot of Pakistan. As will be shown later some portion of the Punjab will have to be excluded from the scheme of Pakistan. Similarly some portion of Bengal will have to be excluded from the proposed Eastern Muslim State, although a district from Assam may have to be added to it. According to me 15 districts will have to be excluded from the Eastern Muslim State of Bengal and 13 districts of the Punjab shall have to be excluded from Pakistan. What would be the reduction in the area, population and revenue, that would result from the exclusion of these districts, there is no sufficient data available to enable any one to give an exact idea. One may however hazard the guess that so far as the Punjab and Bengal are

*Revenues include both Revenue raised by Provincial Governments in the Provinces from provincial sources & by the Central Government from Central Revenues.

concerned their revenues would be halved.   What is lost by Pakistan
by this exclusion, will of course be gained by Hindustan.   To put it
in concrete terms while the Revenues of Pakistan and the Eastern
Muslim State will be 60 crores *minus* 24 crores, i. e. 36 crores, the
Revenues of Hindustan will be about 96 crores *plus* 24 crores,
i. e. 120 crores.

The study of these figures, in the light of the observations
I have made, will show that the resources of Hindustan are far
greater than the resources of Pakistan, whether one considers the
question in terms of area, population or revenue.   There need,
therefore, be no apprehension on the score of resources.   Creation
of Pakistan will not leave Hindustan in a weakened condition.

III

QUESTION OF ARMED FORCES.

The defence of a country does not depend so much upon its
scientific frontier as it does upon its resources.   But more than
resources does it depend upon the fighting forces available to it.

What are the fighting forces available to Pakistan and to
Hindustan ?

The Simon Commission pointed out, as a special feature of
the Indian Defence Problem, that there were special areas which
alone offered recruits to the Indian Army and that there were other
areas which offered none or if at all very few.   The following table,
taken from the Report of the Commission, undoubtedly will come
as a most disagreeable surprise to many Indians, who think and care
about the defence of India.

	Areas of Recruitment.		Number of Recruits drawn.
1	N.-W. Frontier Province	...	5,600
2	Kashmir	...	6,500
3	Punjab	...	86,000
4	Baluchistan	...	300
5	Nepal	...	19,000

9

Areas of Recruitment.	Number of Recruits drawn.
6 United Provinces	16,500
7 Rajputana	7,000
8 Central India	200
9 Bombay	7,000
10 Central Provinces	100
11 Bihar & Orissa	300
12 Bengal	Nil
13 Assam	Nil
14 Burma	3,000
15 Hyderabad	700
16 Mysore	100
17 Madras	4,000
18 Miscellaneous	1,900
Total ...	158,200

The Simon Commission found that this state of affairs was natural to India, and in support of it, cited the following figures of recruitment from the different Provinces of India during the great war especially because "it cannot be suggested that any discouragement was offered to recruitment in any area" :—

Province.	Combatant Recruits Enlisted.	Non-combatant Recruits Enlisted.	Total.
Madras	51,223	41,117	92,340
Bombay	41,272	30,211	71,483
Bengal	7,117	51,935	59,052
United Provinces	163,578	117,565	281,143
Punjab	349,688	97,288	446,976
North-West Frontier	32,181	13,050	45,231
Baluchistan	1,761	327	2,088
Burma	14,094	4,579	18,673
Bihar & Orissa	8,576	32,976	41,552
Central Provinces	5,376	9,631	15,007
Assam	942	14,182	15,124
Ajmer-Merwara	7,341	1,632	8,973
Nepal	58,904	.	58,904
Total ...	742,053	414,493	1,156,546

This data reveals in a striking manner that the fighting forces available for the defence of India mostly come from area which are to be included in Pakistan. From this it may be argued, that without Pakistan, Hindustan cannot defend itself.

The facts brought out by the Simon Commission are of course beyond question. But they cannot be made the basis of a conclusion, such as is suggested by the Simon Commission, namely that only Pakistan can produce soldiers and that Hindustan cannot. That such a conclusion is quite untenable will be seen from the following considerations.

In the first place what is regarded by the Simon Commission as something peculiar to India is not quite so peculiar. What appears to be peculiar is not due to any inherent defect in the people. The peculiarity arises, because of the policy of recruitment followed by the British Government for years past. The official explanation of this predominance in the Indian Army of the men of the North-West is that they belong to the Martial Classes. But Mr. Chaudhari* has demonstrated by unimpeachable data, that this explanation is far from being true. He has shown that the predominance in the Army of the men of the North-West took place as early as the Mutiny of 1857, some 20 years before the theory of Martial and Non-martial Classes was projected in an indistinct form for the first time in 1879 by the Special Army Committee † appointed in that year, and that their predominance had nothing to do with their alleged fighting qualities but was due to the fact that they helped the British to suppress the Mutiny in which the Bengal Army was so completely involved. To quote Mr. Chaudhari :—

"The pre-Mutiny army of Bengal was essentially a Brahmin and Khattriya army of the Ganges basin. All the three Presidency Armies of those days, as we have stated in the first part of this

---

* See his series of Articles on " The Martial Races of India " published in the Modern Review for July 1930, September 1930, January 1931 and February 1931.

† The Questionnaire circulated by the Committee included the following question : " If an efficient and available reserve of the Indian Army is considered necessary for the safety of the Empire, should it not be recruited and maintained from those parts of the country which give us best soldiers, rather than amongst the weakest and least warlike races of India "? ....

article, were in a sense quite representative of the military potentialities of the areas to which they belonged, though none of them could, strictly speaking, be correctly described as national armies of the provinces concerned, as there was no attempt to draw upon any but the traditional martial elements of the population. But they all got their recruits mainly from their natural areas of recruitment, viz., the Madras Army from the Tamil and Telugu countries, the Bombay Army from Western India, and the Bengal Army from Bihar and U. P. and to a very limited extent from Bengal. There was no official restriction on the enrolment of men of any particular tribe, or caste or region, provided they were otherwise eligible. Leaving aside for the moment the practice of the Bombay and the Madras Armies, the only exception to this general rule in the Bengal Army was that which applied to the Punjabis and Sikhs, who, inspite of their magnificent military traditions, were not given a fair representation in the Army of Northern India. Their recruitment, on the contrary, was placed under severe restrictions by an order of the Government, which laid down that 'the number of Punjabis in a regiment is never to exceed 200, nor are more than 100 of them to be Sikhs'. It was only the revolt of the Hindustani regiments of the Bengal Army that gave an opportunity to the Punjabis to rehabilitate themselves in the eyes of the British authorities. Till then, they remained suspect and under a ban, and the Bengal Army on the eve of the Mutiny was mainly recruited from Oudh, North and South Bihar, especially the latter, principally Shahabad and Bhojpur, the Doab of the Ganges and Jumna and Rohilkhund. The soldiers recruited from these areas were mostly high-caste men, Brahmins of all denominations, Chhatrees, Rajputs and Ahirs. The average proportion in which these classes were enrolled in a regiment was: (1) Brahmin 7/24, (2) Rajputs $\frac{1}{4}$, Inferior Hindus $\frac{1}{6}$, Musalmans $\frac{1}{6}$, Punjabees $\frac{1}{8}$.

"To this army, the area which now-a-days furnishes the greatest number of soldiers—the Punjab, Nepal, N.W. F. Province, the hill tracts of Kumaon and Garhwal, Rajputana,—furnished very few recruits or none at all. There was practical exclusion in it of all the famous fighting castes of India,—Sikhs, Gurkhas, Punjabi Musalmans, Dogras, Jats, Pathans, Garhwalis, Rajputana Rajputs, Kumaonis, Gujars, all the tribes and septs, in fact, which are looked upon today as a tower of strength of the Indian Army. A single year and a single rebellion was, however, to change all this. The Mutiny, which broke out in 1857, blew up the old Bengal Army and brought into existence a Punjabized and barbarized army, resembling the Indian Army of to-day in broad lines and general proportions of its composition.

"The gap created by the revolt of the Hindustani regiments (of the Bengal Army) were at once filled up by Sikhs and other Punjabis, and hillmen eager for revenge and for the loot of the cities of Hindustan. They had all been conquered and subjugated by the British with the help of the Hindustani soldiers, and in their ignorance, they regarded the Hindustanis, rather than the handful of British, as their real enemies. This enmity was magnificently exploited by the British authorities in suppressing the Mutiny. When the news of the enlistment of Gurkhas reached Lord Dalhousie in England he expressed great satisfaction and wrote to a friend : ' Against the Oude Sepoys they may confidently be expected to fight like devils'. And after the Mutiny, General Mansfield, the Chief of the Staff of the Indian Army, wrote about the Sikhs : ' It was not because they loved us, but because they hated Hindustan and hated the Bengal Army that the Sikhs had flocked to our standard instead of seeking the opportunity to strike again for their freedom. They wanted to revenge themselves and to gain riches by the plunder of Hindustani cities. They were not attracted by mere daily pay, it was rather the prospect of wholesale plunder and stamping on the heads of their enemies. In short, we turned to profit the *espirit de corps* of the old Khalsa Army of Ranjit Singh, in the manner which for a time would most effectually bind the Sikhs to us as long as the active service against their old enemies may last '.

"The relations thus established were in fact to last much longer. The services rendered by the Sikhs and Gurkhas during the Mutiny were not forgotten and henceforward the Punjab and Nepal had the place of honour in the Indian Army."

That Mr. Chaudhari is right when he says that it was the Mutiny of 1857 which was the real cause of the preponderance in the Indian Army of the men of the North-West is beyond the possibility of doubt. Equally incontrovertible is the view of Mr. Chaudhari that this preponderance of the men of the North-West is not due to their native superiority in fighting qualities, as the same is amply borne out by the figures which he has collected, showing the changes in the composition of the Indian Infantry before the Mutiny and after the Mutiny.

CHANGES IN THE COMPOSITION OF THE INDIAN INFANTRY

Percentage of men from different Parts

Year.	North-West India.		North-East India U. P , Bihar	South India.	Burma.
	I. Punjab, N. W. F., Kashmir	II. Nepal, Garhwal, Kumaon.			
1856	Less than 10	Negligible	Not less than 90		Nil
1858	47	6	47		,,
1883	48	17	35	.	,,
1893	53	24	23	.	,,
1905	47	15	22	16	,,
1919	46	14.8	25·5	12	1·7
1930	58 5	22	11 0	5 5	3

These figures show that in 1856, one year before the Mutiny, the men from the North-West were a negligible factor in the Indian Army. But in 1858 one year after the Mutiny they had acquired a dominant position which has never received a set-back.

It will thus be seen that the distinction between martial and non-martial classes, which was put forth for the first time in 1879, as a matter of principle, which was later on insisted upon as a matter of serious consideration by Lord Roberts* and which was subsequently recognised by Lord Kitchner as a principle governing recruitment to the Indian Army had nothing to do with the origin of this preponderence of the men of the North-West in the Indian Army. No doubt, the accident that the people from North-West India had the good luck of being declared by the Government as belonging to the martial class, while most of the classes coming from the rest of India had the ill luck of being declared as belonging to the non-martial class, had important consequences. Being

---

* In his ' Forty-One Years ' he wrote · " Each cold season, I made long tours in order to acquaint myself with the needs and capabilities of the men of the Madras Army. I tried hard to discover in them those fighting qualities which had distinguished their forefathers during the wars of the last and the beginning of the present century . . . And I was forced to the conclusion that the ancient military spirit had died in them, as it had died in the ordinary Hindustani of Bengal and the Mahratta of Bombay, and that they could no longer with safety be pitted against warlike races, or employed outside the limit of Southern India."

regularly employed in the Army the people of North–West India came to look upon service in the army as an occupation with a security and a career which was denied to men from the rest of India. The large number of recruits drawn from North–West India therefore indicates nothing more than this—namely, owing to the policy of the British Government, Army has become their occupation and if people in other parts of India do not readily come forth to enlist in the Army the reason is that Government did not allow them to make service in the Army as their occupation. It must be noted that occupation tends to become hereditary and that the most difficult thing for a man to do is to take to a new occupation.

This division between martial and non-martial classes is of course a purely arbitrary and artificial distinction. It is as foolish as the Hindu theory of caste, making birth instead of worth the basis for recognition. At one time the Government insisted that the distinction they had adopted was a real distinction and that in terms of fighting qualities it meant so much fighting value. In fact, this was their justification for recruiting more men from the North-West of India. That this distinction has nothing to do with any difference in fighting qualities has now been admitted. Sir Phillip Chetwode,* late Commander-in-Chief of India, broadcasting from London on the constitution of the Indian Army, took pains to explain that the recruitment of a larger proportion of it from the Punjab did not mean that the people of the Peninsula were without martial qualities. Sir Phillip Chetwode explained that the reason why men of the North were largely recruited for the Indian Army was chiefly climatic, as the men from the South cannot stand the extremes of heat and cold of North India. No race can be permanently without martial spirit. Martial spirit is not a matter of native instinct. It is a matter of training and anybody can be trained to it.

But apart from this, there is enough fighting material in Hindustan besides what might be produced by special training. There are the Sikhs, about whose fighting qualities nothing need be said. There are the Rajputs who are even now included

---

*Indian Social Reformer, January 27th, 1940.

in the category of Martial classes. In addition to these there are the Marathas who have proved their calibre as a fighting race during the last European War. Even the people of the Madras Presidency can be depended upon for military purposes. Speaking of the Madrasis as soldiers, General Sir Frederick P. Haines, at one time Commander-in-Chief in India observed :—

> "It has been customary to declare that the Madras Army is composed of men physically inferior to those of the Bengal Army, and if stature alone be taken into consideration, this is true. It is also said that by the force of circumstances the martial feeling and the characteristics necessary to the real soldiers are no longer to be found in its ranks. I feel bound to reject the above assertions and others which ascribe comparative inefficiency to Madras troops. It is true that in recent years they have seen but little service ; for with the exception of the sappers, they have been specially excluded from all participation in work in the field. I cannot admit for one moment that anything has occurred to disclose the fact that the Madras Sepoy is inferior as a fighting man. The facts of history warrant us in assuming the contrary. In drill training and discipline, the Madras Sepoy is inferior to none ; while in point of health, as exhibited by returns, he compares favourably with his neighbours. This has been manifested by the sappers and their followers in the Khyber ; and the sappers are of the same race as the sepoys."

Hindustan need have therefore no apprehension regarding the supply of an adequate fighting force from among its own people. The sepration of Pakistan cannot weaken her in that respect.

The Simon Commission drew attention to three features of the Indian Army, which struck them as being special and peculiar to India. It pointed out that the duty of the Army in India was two-fold ; firstly, to prevent the independent tribes on the Indian side of the Afghan frontier from raiding the peaceful inhabitants of the plains below. Secondly, to protect India against invasion by countries lying behind and beyond this belt of unorganized territories. The Commission took note of the fact that from 1850 to 1922 there were 72 expeditions against the independent tribes, an average of one a year, and also of the fact that the countries behind and beyond this belt of unorganized territory lies the direction from which throughout the ages, the danger to India's territorial integrity has come " a quarter occupied by " States which according

to the Commission are not members of the League of the Nations "
and therefore, a great danger to India now than before. The
Commission insisted on emphasizing that these two facts constituted
a peculiar feature of the problem of military defence in India and
so far as the urgency and extent of the problem is concerned they
are "without parallel elsewhere in the Empire, and constituted
a difficulty in developing self-government which never arose in any
comparable degree in the case of the self-governing Dominions."

As a second unique feature of the Indian Army, the Commission observed —

"The Army in India is not only provided and organized to
ensure against external dangers of a wholly exceptional character:
it is also distributed and habitually used throughout India for the
purpose of maintaining or restoring internal peace. In all countries
...... the military is not normally employed in this way, and
certainly is not organized for this purpose. But the case of India
is entirely different. Troops are employed many times a year to
prevent internal disorder and, if necessary, to quell it. Police
forces, admirably organized as they are, cannot be expected in all
cases to cope with the sudden and violent outburst of a mob driven
frantic by religious frenzy. It is, therefore, well understood in
India both by the police and by the military—and, what is even
more to the point, by the public at large—that the soldiers may have
to be sent for ... This use of the Army for the purpose of maintaining or restoring internal order was increasing rather than diminishing, and that on these occasions the practically universal request
was for British troops. The proportion of the British to Indian
troops allotted to this duty has in fact risen in the last quarter of
a century. The reason of course is that the British soldier is a
neutral, and is under no suspicion of favouring Hindus against
Mahomedans or Mahomedans against Hindus . . . . . Inasmuch as
the vast majority of the disturbances which call for the intervention
of the military have a communal or religious complexion, it is
natural and inevitable that the intervention which is most likely to
be authoritative should be that which has no bias, real or suspected,
to either side. It is a striking fact in this connection that, while in
regular units of the Army in India as a whole British soldiers are
in a minority of about 1 to 2½, in the troops allotted for internal
security the preponderance is reversed, and for this purpose a

10

majority of British troops is employed—in the troops ear-marked for internal security the proportion is about eight British to seven Indian soldiers."

Commenting upon this feature of the Indian Army the Commission said :—

"When, therefore, one contemplates a future for India in which, in place of the existing Army organization, the country is defended and pacified by exclusively Indian units, just as Canada relies on Canadian troops and Ireland on Irish troops, it is essential to realize and bear in mind the dimensions and character of the Indian problem of internal order and the part which the British soldier at present plays (to the general satisfaction of the country-side) in supporting peaceful government."

The third unique feature of the Indian Army which was pointed out by the Simon Commission is the preponderance in it of the men from the North-West. The origin of this preponderance and the reasons underlying the official explanation given therefor have already been examined.

But there is one more special feature of the Indian Army to which the Commission made no referance at all. The Commission either ignored it or was not aware of it. But it is such an important feature that it overshadows all the three features to which the Commission refers, in its importance and in its social and political consequences.

It is a feature which, if widely known, will set many people furiously to think. It is sure to raise questions which may prove insoluable and which may easily block the path of India's political progress-questions of far greater importance and complexity than the question relating to Indianization of the Army.

This neglected feature relates to the communal composition of the Indian Army. Mr Chaudhari has collected the relevant data in his articles, already referred to, which throws a flood of light on this aspect of the Indian Army. The following table shows the proportion of soldiers serving in the Indian Infantry showing the area and the community from which they are drawn :—

CHANGES IN THE COMMUNAL COMPOSITION OF THE INDIAN ARMY

Area and Communities.	Percentage in 1914	Percentage in 1918.	Percentage in 1919.	Percentage in 1930.
I The Punjab, N. W. F and Kashmir.	47	46 5	46	58·5
1 Sikhs	19 2	17·4	15·4	13·58
2 Punjabi Musalmans	11 1	11 3	12·4	22·6
3 Pathans	6 2	5 42	4·51	6 35
II Nepal, Kumaon, Gharwal	15	18 9	14 9	22
1 Gurkhas	13 1	16 6	12 2	16 4
III Upper India	22	22 7	25·5	11
1 U. P Rajputs	6 4	6 8	7·7	2·55
2 Hindustani Musalmans	4 1	3 42	4·45	Nil.
3 Brahmins	1 8	1 86	2 5	Nil.
IV South India	16	11·9	12	5·5
1 Marathas	4·9	3·85	3 7	5 33
2 Madrasi Musalmans	3 5	2 71	2 13	Nil
3 Tamils	2 5	2	1·67	Nil.
V Burma				
1 Burmans	Nil	negligible.	1 7	3

This table brings out in an unmistakable manner the fact that the communal composition of the Indian Army has been undergoing a profound change. This change is particularly noticeable after 1919. The figures show a phenomenal rise in the strength of the Punjabi Musalman and the Pathan. They also show a substantial reduction of the Sikhs from the first to the third place ; by the degradation of the Rajputs to the fourth place and by the closing of the ranks to the U. P. Brahmins, the Madrasi Musalmans and the Tamilians.

A further analysis of the figures for 1930, which discloses the communal composition of the Indian Infantry and Indian Cavalry, has been made by Mr. Chaudhari in the following table.*

* This table shows the percentage of men of each eligible class in the Indian Infantry (82 active and 18 training battalions), the Indian Cavalry (21 regiments), and the 20 battalions of Gurkha Infantry. This table does not include the Indian personnel of (a) the 19 batteries of Indian Mountain Artillery, and (b) 3 regiments of Sappers and Miners, (c) the Indian Signal Corps, and (d) the Corps of Indian Pioneers, all of which are composed of different proportions of Punjabi Musalmans, Sikhs, Pathans, Hindustani Hindus and Musalmans, Madrasis of all classes and Hazra Afghans, either in class units or class companies. Except that some units in these arms of the service are composed of Madrasis and Hazras, now enrolled in other units of the Indian Army, the class composition of these units does not materially 'alter the proportion of the classes as given in the table. This table does not also include the Indian personnel attached to the British Infantry and Artillery units.

COMMUNAL COMPOSITION OF THE INDIAN ARMY IN 1930

	Class.	Districts	Percentag in Infantry.		Percentage in Cavalry.
			Excluding Gurkhas	Including Gurkhas	
1	Punjabi Musalman	Punjab	27	22 6	14 28
2	Gurkhas	Nepal	.	16·4	
3	Sikhs	Punjab	16 24	13 58	23 81
4	Dogras	North Punjab and Kashmir	11 4	9 54	9 53
5	Jats	Rajputana, U P Punjab.	9 5	7 94	19 06
6	Pathans	N W. F. Province	7 57	6 35	4 76
7	Marathas	Konkan	6·34	5·33	
8	Gharvalis	Garhwal	4 53	3 63	
9	U. P Rajputs	U P.	3 04	2 54	..
10	Rajputana Rajputs	Rajputana	2 8	2 35	.
11	Kumaonis	Kumaon	2 44	2 05	.
12	Gujars	N E Rajputana	1 52	1 28	
13	Punjabi Hindus	Punjab	1 52	1 28	
14	Ahirs	Do	1 22	1·024	
15	Musalmans, Rajputs, Ranghars.	Neighbourhood of Delhi	1 22	1 024	7·14
16	Kaimkhanis	Rajputana	.		4 76
17	Kachirs	Burma	1 22	1·024	
18	Chins	Do	1·22	1 024	
19	Karens	Do.	1 22	1·024	
20	Dekhani Musalmans	Deccan	.		4 76
21	Hindustani Musalmans	U P.	.	.	2 38

Reducing these figures in terms of communities we get the following per centage as it stood in 1930 :—

	Communities.	Percentage in Infantry.		Percentage in Cavalry.
		Excluding Gurkhas	Including Gurkhas.	
1	Hindus and Sikhs	60·55	50 554	61·92
2	Gurkhas	..	16·4	....
3	Muhammadans	35·79	29,974	30·08
4	Burmans	3·66	3·072	......

These figures show the communal composition of the Indian Army. The Musalmans according to Mr. Chaudhari formed 36% of the Indian Infantry and 30% of the Indian Cavalry.

These figures relate to the year 1930. We must now find out what changes have taken place since then in this proportion.

Now it is one of the most intriguing things in the Military history of India that no information is available on this point after 1930. It is impossible to know what is the proportion of the Muslims in the Indian Army at present. There is no Government publication from which such information can be gathered. In the past there was no dearth of publications giving this information. And it is very surprising that they should have now disappeared, or if they do appear, that they should cease to contain this information. Not only is there no Government Publication containing information on this point, but Government has refused to give any information on the point when asked by the members of the Central Legislative Assembly. The following questions and answers taken from the proceedings of the Central Legislative Assembly show how Government has been strenously combating every attempt to obtain information on the point .——

There was an interpellation on 15th Sept. 1938 when the following questions were asked and replies given ——

*Arrangements for the Defence of India.**

Q. 1360 : Mr. Badri Dutt Pande (on behalf of I dra Nath Chattopadhya.

(a)	x	x	x
(b)	x	x	x
(c)	x	x	x

(d) How many Indians have been recruited during 1937 and 1938 as soldiers and officers during 1937-38 for the Infantry and Cavalry respectively ? Amongst the soldiers and officers recruited, how many are Punjabi Sikhs, Pathans, Garhwalis, Mahrattas, Madrasis, Biharis, Bengalis and Hindustanis of the United Provinces and Gurkhas ?

* Legislative Assembly Debates, 1938 Vol. VI, page 2462

(e) If none but the Punjabi Sikhs, Pathans and Garhwalis have been recruited, is it in contemplation of the Honourable Member to recruit from all the Provinces for the defence of India and give them proper military training?

(f) Will the Defence Secretary be pleased to state if Provincial Governments will be asked to raise Provincial Regiments, trained and fully mechanised, for the defence of India? If not, what is his plan of raising an efficient army for the defence of India?

Mr. C. M. G. Ogilvie :—

(a) The Honourable Member will appreciate that it is not in the public interest to disclose the details of such arrangements.

(b) 5 cadets and 33 Indian apprentices were recruited for the Indian Air Force during 1937-38.

(c) During 1937-38, 5 Indians have already been recruited to commissioned ranks in the Royal Indian Navy, 4 will be taken by competitive examination in October, 1938, and 3 more by special examination of "Dufferin" cadets only. During the same period, 314 Indians were recruited to different non-commissioned categories in the Royal Indian

(d) During the year ending the 31st March 1938, 54 Indians were commissioned as Indian Commissioned officers. They are now attached to British units for training, and it is not yet possible to say what proportion will be posted to infantry and cavalry respectively.

During the same period, 961 Indian soldiers were recruited or cavalry, and 7970, for infantry. Their details by classes are not available at Army Headquarters and to call for them from the recruiting officers all over India would not justify the expenditure of time and labour involved.

(e) No.

(f) The reply to the first portion is in the negative. The reply to the second portion is that India already possesses an efficient army and so far as finances permit, every effort is made to keep it up-to date in all respects.

Mr. S. Satyamurti : With reference to the answers to clauses (*d*) and (*e*) of the question taken together, may I know whether the attention of Government has been drawn to statements made by many public men that the bulk of the army is from the Punjab and from one community ? Have Government considered those facts and will Government also consider the desirability of making the army truly national by extending recruitment to all provinces and communities, so as to avoid the danger present in all countries of a military dictatorship seizing political power ?

Mr. C. M. G. Ogilvie : I am not sure how that arises from this question, but I am prepared to say that provincial boundaries do not enter into government's calculations at all. The best soldiers are chosen to provide the best army for India and not for any province, and in this matter national considerations must come above provincial considerations. Where the bulk of best military material is found, there we will go to get it, and not elsewhere.

Mr. S Satyamurti · May I know whether the bulk of the army is from the Punjab and whether the Government have forgotten the experience of the brave exploits of men from my province not very long ago in the Indian Army, and may I know if Madrasis are practically kept out and many other provinces are kept out of the army altogether ?

Mr C. M. G. Ogilvie : Madras is not practically kept out of the army. Government gladly acknowledge the gallant services of the Madrasis in the army and they are now recruited to those Units where experience has proved them to be best. There are some 4,500 serving chiefly in the Sappers and Miners and Artillery.

Mr. S. Satyamurti : Out of a total of 120,000 ?

Mr. C. M. G. Ogilvie : About that.

Mr. S. Satyamurti : May I take it, that, that is a proper proportion, considering the population of Madras, the revenue that Madras pays to the Central exchequer, and the necessity of having a national army recruited from all the provinces ?

Mr. C. M. G. Ogilvie : The only necessity we recognise is to obtain the best possible army.

Mr. S. Satyamurti : May I know by what tests Government have come to the conclusion that provinces other than the Punjab cannot supply the best elements in the Indian Army ?

Mr. Ogilvie : By experience.

Dr. Sir Ziauddin Ahmad . May I ask if it is not a fact that all branches of Accounts Department are monopolised by the Madrasis and will Government immediately reduce the number in proportion to their numerical strength in India ?

Mr. Ogilvie : I do not see how that arises from this question either, but the Government are again not prepared to sacrifice efficiency for any provincial cause.

Indian Regiment consisting of Indians belonging to Different Castes.*

Q. 1078 : Mr. M. Anantrasayanam Ayyangar (on behalf of Mr. Manu Subedar) :

(a) Will the Defence Secretary state whether any experiment has ever been made under British rule of having an Indian regiment consisting of Indians recruited from different provinces and belonging to the different castes and sections, such as Sikhs, Mahrattas, Rajputs, Brahmins and Muslims ?

(b) If the reply to part (a) be in the negative, can a statement of Government's policy in this regard be made giving reasons why it has not been considered proper to take such action ?

(c) Is His Excellency the Commander-in-Chief prepared to take up this matter with His Majesty's Government ?

(d) Are Government aware that in the University Corps and in the Bombay Scout Movement, and in the Police Forces of the country, there is no separation by caste or creed?

Mr. C. M. G. Ogilvie :

(a) No.

(b) Government regard it as a fundamental principle of organization that Military Sub-Units, such as companies and squadrons, must be homogeneous.

(c) No, for the reason just mentioned.

(d) Yes.

Mr. S. Satyamurti : May I know the meaning which Government attach to the word "homogeneous"? Does it mean from the same province or the same community?

Mr. C. M. G. Ogilvie : It means that they must belong to the same class of persons.

Mr. S. Satyamurti. May I ask for some elucidation of this point? Do they make distinction between one class and another?

Mr. C. M. G. Ogilvie : Certainly.

Mr. S. Satyamurti. On what basis? Is it religious class or racial class or provincial class?

Mr. C. M. G. Ogilvie. Neither. It is largely racial class.

Mr. S. Satyamurti Which races are preferred and which are not preferred?

Mr. C. M. G. Ogilvie. I refer the Honourable Member to the Army List.

Recruitment to the Indian Army.*

Q. 1162. Mr. Brojendra Narayan Chaudhary · Will the Defence Secretary please state :—

(a) Whether the attention of Government has been drawn to the address of the Punjab's Premier, the Hon'ble, Sir Sikander Hyat Khan to his brother soldiers, in these words. . "No patriotic Punjabi would wish

---

* Legislative Assembly Debates 1938, Vol. VI, page 2754.

to impair Punjab's position of supremacy in the Army ",
as reported by the Associated Press of India in the Hindustan
Times of the 5th September 1938 ; and

(*b*) Whether it is the policy of Government to
maintain the supremacy of Punjabis in the army by
continuing to recruit the major portion from the Punjab ; or to
attempt recruitment of the Army from all the provinces
without racial or provincial considerations ?

Mr. C. M. G. Ogilvie :

(*a*) Yes.

(*b*) I refer the Honourable Member to replies I gave to
the supplementary questions arising from starred question
No. 1060 asked by Mr. Amarendra Nath Chattopadhyaya
on 15th Septemer 1938.

Mr. S. Satyamurti : With reference to the answer to part (*a*) of
the question, my Honourable friend referred to previous answers.
As far as I remember, they were not given after this statement
was brought before this House.   May I know if the Government
of India have examined this statement of the Punjab Premier,
" No patriotic Punjabi would wish to impair Punjab's position of
supremacy in the Army " ?   May I know whether Government
have considered the dangerous implications of this statement and
will they take steps to prevent a responsible Minister going about
and claiming provincial or communal supremacy in the Indian
Army, which ought to remain Indian first and Indian last ?

Mr. C. M. G. Ogilvie · I can only answer in exactly
the same words as I answered to a precisely similar question of the
Hon'ble Member on the 15th September last.   The policy of
Government with regard to the recruitment has been repeatedly
stated and is perfectly clear.

Mr. S. Satyamurti : That policy is to get the best material
and I am specifically asking my Honourable friend—I hope he
realises the implications of that statement of the Punjab Premier.
I want to know whether the Government have examined the
dangerous implications of any provincial Premier claiming

provincial supremacy in the Indian Army and whether they propose to take any steps to correct this dangerous misapprehension ?

Mr. C. M. G. Ogilvie . Government consider that there are no dangerous implications whatever but rather the reverse.

Mr. S. Satyamurti : Do Government accept the supremacy of any province or any community as desirable consideration, even if it is a fact, to be uttered by responsible public men and do not the Government consider that this will give rise to communal and provincial quarrels and jealousies inside the army and possibly a military dictatatorship in this country ?

Mr. C. M. G. Ogilvie · Government consider that none of these forebodings have any justification at all.

Mr. M. S Aney : Do the Government subscribe to the policy implied in the statement of Sir Sikander Hyat Khan ?

Mr. C. M. G. Ogilvie : Government's policy has been repeatedly stated and made clear.

Mr. M. S. Aney · Is it the policy that the Punjab should have its supremacy in the Army ?

Mr. C. M. G. Oiglivie The policy is that the best material should be recruited for the Army.

Mr. M. S. Aney : I again repeat the question. Is it the policy of Government that Punjab should have supremacy in the Army ?

Mr. M. G. Ogilvie : I have repeatedly answered that question. The policy is that the Army should get the best material from all provinces and Government are quite satisfied that it has the best material at present.

Mr. M. S. Aney : Is it not therefore necessary that Government should make a statement modifying the policy suggested by Sir Sikander Hyat Khan ?

Mr. C. M. G. Ogilvie : Government have no intention whatever of changing their policy in any particular.

Another interpellation took place on 23rd November 1938 when the question stated below was asked :——

*Recruitment to the Indian Army from the Central Provinces & Berar**

Q. 1402 : Mr. Govind V. Deshmukh : Will the Defence Secretary please state :——

(*a*) The Centres in the Central Provinces and Berar for recruiting men for the Indian Army ;

(*b*) The classes from which such men are recruited ;

(*c*) The proportion of the men from the C. P. & Berar in the Army to the total strength of the Army, as well as to the population of these provinces ; and

(*d*) The present policy of recruitment, and if it is going to be revised ; if not, why not ?

Mr. C. M. G. Ogilvie .

(*a*) There are no recruiting centres in the C. P. or Berar. Men residing in the C. P. are in the area of the Recruiting Officer, Delhi, and those of Berar in the area of the Recruiting officer, Poona.

(*b*) Mahrattas of Berar are recruited as a separate class. Other Hindus and Mussalmans who are recruited from the C. P. and Berar are classified as " Hindus " or " Musalmans ", and are not entered under any class denominaiion.

(*c*) The proportion to the total strength of the Army is .03 per cent and the proportion to the total male population of these provinces is .0004 per cent.

(*d*) There is at present no intention of revising the present policy, the reasons for which were stated in my reply to a supplementary question arising out of Mr Satyamurti's starred question No. 1060, on the 15th September 1938, and in answer to part (*a*) of started question No. 1086 asked by Mian Ghulam Kadir Muhammad Shahbau on the same date, and in the reply of His Excellency the Commander—in—Chief to the debates in the Council of State on the Honourable Mr. Sushil Kumar

Roy Chaudhary's Resolution regarding military training for Indians on the 21st February 1938 and on the Honourable Mr. P. N. Sapru's Resolution on the recruitment of all classes to the Indian Army in April, 1935.

This was followed by an intsrpellation on 6th Feb, 1939 When the below mentioned question was asked :—

Recruitment to the Indian Army*

Q. 129 . Mr. S. Satyamurti . Will the Defence Secretary be pleased to state :

(*a*) Whether Government have since the last answer on this question reconsidered the question of recruiting to the India Army from all piovinces and from all castes and communities ;

(*b*) Whether they have come to any conclusion ;

(*c*) Whether Government will categorically state the reasons as to why other provinces and communities are not allowed to serve in the army ; and

(*d*) What are the tests by which they have come to the conclusion that other provinces and other communities than those from whom recruitment is made to the Indian Army to day cannot come up to the standard of efficiency required of the Indian Army ?

Mr. C. M. G. Ogilvie .

(*a*) No.

(*b*) Does not arise.

(*c*) and (*d*) The reasons have been categorically stated in my replies to starred questions Nos. 1060 and 1086 of 15th September 1938, No. 1162 of 20th September 1938 and No. 1402 of 23rd November 1938 and also in the replies of His Excellency the Commander–in–Chief in the Council of State to the debates on the Honourable Mr. P. N. Sapru's Resolution regarding recruitment of all classes to the

---

*Legislative Assembly Debates, 1939 Vol. I, page 253.

Indian Army and the Honourable Mr. Sushil Kumar Roy Chaudhary's Resolution regarding Military training for Indians, on the 13th March, 1935, and 21st February 1938 respectively.

This obstinacy on the part of the Government of India in the matter of giving information on this most vital point has given rise to all sorts of speculation as to the present proportion of Muslims in the Indian Army. Some say that the proportion is between 60 and 70 p. c. Others say that it is somewhere in the neighbourhood of 50 p. c. Whether the first figure is true or the second is true the proportion must be high enough to cause alarm to the Hindus. There can be no other explanation of this secrecy so tenaciously maintained by Government. In the absence of exact information one could well adopt the latter figure as disclosing the true situation especially, on inquiry, it happens to be confirmed by those who are in a position to form some idea on the matter. If these facts are true, they are a flagrant violation of well established principles of British Army policy in India.

After the Mutiny, the British Government ordered two investigations into the organization of the Indian Army. First invesitgation was carried out by the Peel Commission which was appointed in 1859. The second investigation was undertaken by a body, called the Special Army Committee, which was appointed in 1879 and to which reference has already been made.

The principal question considered by the Peel Commission was to find out the weaknesses in the Bengal Army, which led to the Mutiny of 1857. The Peel Commission was told by witness after witness that the principal weakness in the Bengal Army which mutinied was that

" In the ranks of the regular Army men stood mixed up as chance might befall. There was no separating by class and clan into companies.........In the lines, Hindu and Mahomedan, Sikh and Poorbeah were mixed up, so that each and all lost to some extent their racial prejudice and became inspired with one common sentiment."*

---

*Mac Munn and Lovett – " The Armies of India " pp. 84-85 quoted by Chaudhari.

It was therefore proposed by Sir Jon Lawrence that in organizing the India Army care shouid be taken " to preserve that distinctiveness which is so valuable, and while it lasts, makes the Mahomedan of one country despise, fear or dislike the Mahomedan of another ; Corps should in future be provincial, and adhere to the geographical limits within which differences and rivalries are strongly marked. Let all races, Hindu or Mahomedan of one province be enlisted in one regiment and no others, and having created distinctive regiments, let us keep them so, against the hour of need. .... By the system thus indicated two great evils are avoided . firstly, that community of feeling throughout the native army and that mischievous political activity and intrigue which results from association with other races and travel in other Indian provinces."*

This proposal was supported by many military men before the Peel Commission and was recommended by it as a principle of Indian Army Policy. This principle is known as the principle of Class Composition.

The Special Army Committee of 1879 was concerned with quite a different problem What the problem was, becomes manifest fiom the questionnaire issued by the Committee. The questionnaire included the following question :—

"If the efficient and available reserve of the Indian Army is considered necessary for the safety of the Empire, should it not be recruited and maintained from those parts of the country which give us best soldiers, rather than among the weakest and least warlike races of India, due regard of course being had to the necessity of not giving too great strength or prominence to any particular race or religious group and with due regard to the safety of the Empire " ?

The principal part of the question is obviously the necessity or otherwise of "not giving too great strength or prominence to any particular race or religious group". On this question official opinion expressed before the Committee was unanimous.

---

* As quoted by Chaudhari,

Lt. General H. J. Warres, Commander-in-Chief of the Bombay Army stated :—

"I consider it is not possible to recruit the reserve of the Indian Army altogether from those parts of India which are said to produce best soldiers, without giving undue strength and prominence to the races and religions of these countries."

The Commander-in-Chief Sir Frederic P. Haines said :—

"Distinct in race, language and interests from the more numerous Army of Bengal, it is, in my opinion eminently politic and wise to maintain these armies (the Madras and Bombay Armies) as a counterpoise to it, and I would in no way diminish their strength in order that a reserve composed of what is called 'the most efficient fighting men whom it is possible to procure' may be established. If, by this it is meant to replace Sepoys of Madras and Bombay by a reserve of men passed through the ranks of the Bengal Army and composed of the same classes of which it is formed, I would say that any thing more unwise or more impolitic could hardly be conceived."

The Lt. Governor of the Punjab also shared this view. He too declared that he was "opposed to having one recruiting field for the whole armies" in India. "It will be necessary" he added, "for political reasons, to prevent preponderance of one nationality."

The Special Committee accepted this view and recommended that the composition of the Indian Army should be so regulated that there should be no predominance of any one community or nationality in the Army.

These two principles have been the governing principles of Indian Army policy. Having regard to the principle laid down by the Special Army Committee of 1879 the changes that have taken place in the communal composition of the Indian Army amount to a complete revolution. How this revolution was allowed to take place is beyond comprehension. It is a revolution which has taken place in the teeth of a well established principle. The principle was really suggested by the fear of the growing predominance of the men of the North-West in the Indian Army and was invoked with the special object of curbing that tendency. The principle was not only enunciated as a rule of guidance but was taken to be rigorously applied. Lord Roberts, who was opposed to this principle because it set a limit upon the recruitment of his pet men of the North-West, had to bow to this principle during his regime as the Commander-in-Chief of India. So well was the principle respected that when in 1903 Lord Kitchner entered upon the project of converting fifteen regiments of Madrasis into Punjabi regiments he immediately set up a counterpoise to the Sikhs and the Punjabi Musalmans by raising the proportion of Gurkhas and Pathans. As Sir George Arthur, his biographer says :—

> "The Government, mindful of the lesson taught by the Mutiny, was alive to the danger of allowing any one element in the Indian Army to preponderate unduly. An increase in the Punjabee infantry had as its necessary sequel a further recruitment of the valuable Gurkha material and the enlistment of more trans-border Pathans in the Frontier Militia."

That a principle, so unanimously upheld and so rigorously applied upto the period of the great war, should have been thrown to the wind after the Great War, without ceremony and without compunction and in a clandestine manner, is really beyond comprehension. What is the reason which has led the British to allow so great a preponderance of the Muslims in the Indian Army? Two explanations are possible. One is that the Musalmans really proved, in the Great War, that they were better soldiers than the Hindus. The second explanation is that the British have broken the rule and have given the Musalmans such a dominating position in the Army because they wanted to counter-act the forces of the Hindu agitation for wresting political power from the hands of the British.

Whatever be the explanation, two glaring facts stand out from the above survey. One is that the Indian Army today is predominantly Muslim in its composition. The other is that the Musalmans who predominate are the Musalmans from the Punjab and N. W. F. Such a composition of the Indian Army means that the Musalmans of the Punjab and the N. W. F. are made the sole defenders of India from foreign invasion. So patent has this fact become that the Musalmans of the Punjab and the N. W. F. are quite conscious of this proud position which has been assigned to them by the British for reasons best known to them. For, one often hears them say that they are the gate-keepers of India. The Hindus must consider the problem of the defence of India in the light of this crucial fact.

How far can the Hindus depend upon these gate-keepers to hold the gate and protect the liberty and freedom of India? The answer to this question must depend upon as to who comes to force the gate. It is obvious that there are only two foreign foes who are likely to force this gate at the North-West of India, Russia or Afghanistan, the borders of both of which touch the border of India. Which of them will invade India and when no one can definitely say. If the invasion came from Russia it may be hoped that these gate-keepers of India will be staunch and loyal enough to hold the gate and stop the invader. But suppose, the Afghans singly or in combination with other Muslim States march on India, will these gate-keepers stop the invader or will they open the gates and let him in? This is a question which no Hindu can afford to ignore. This is a question to which every Hindu must get a satisfactory answer, because it is the most crucial question.

Of course it is possible to say that Afghanistan will never think of invading India. But a theory is best tested by examining its capacity to meet the worst case. The loyalty and dependability of this Army of the Punjabi and N. W. F Muslims can only be tested by considering how it will behave in the event of an invasion by the Afghans. Will they respond to the call of the land of their birth or will they be swayed by the call of their religion, are questions which must be faced if ultimate security is to be obtained. Nor is it safe to seek to escape from these annoying and discomforting questions by believing that we need not worry about foreign invasion so long India is under the protection of the British. Such a complacent attitude is unforgiveable to say the least. In the first place the present war has shown that a situation may arise when Great Britain may not be able to protect India, although that is the time when India needs her protection most. Secondly, the efficiency of an institution must be tested under natural conditions and not under artificial conditions. The behaviour of the Indian Soldier under British control is artificial. His behaviour when he is under Indian control is its natural behaviour. British control does not allow much play to the natural instincts and natural sympathies of the men in the Army.

That is why the men in the Army behave so well. But that is an artificial and not a natural condition. That the Indian Army behaves well under British control is no guarantee of its good behaviour under Indian control. A Hindu must be satisfied that it will behave as well when British control is withdrawn.

The question how this army of the Punjabi and N. W. F. Muslims will behave if Afghanistan invades is a very pertinent and crucial question and must be faced, however unpleasant it may be to do so.

Some may say—why assume that the large proportion of Muslims in the army is a settled fact and that it cannot be unsettled. Those who can unsettle it are welcome to make what efforts they can. But so far as one can see, it is not going to be unsettled. On the contrary I should not be surprised if it was entered in the constitution, when revised, as a safeguard for the Muslim Minority. The Musalmans are sure to make this demand and as against the Hindus the Muslims somehow always succeed. We must, therefore, proceed on the assumption that the composition of the Indian Army will remain what it is at present. The basis remaining the same, the question to be pursued remains what it was : Can the Hindus depend upon such an army to defend the country against the invasion of Afghanistan ? Only the so-called Indian Nationalists will say yes to it. The boldest among the realists must stop to think before he can give an answer to the question. The realist must take note of the fact that the Musalmans look upon the Hindus as Kaffirs, who deserve more to be exterminated than protected. The realist must take note of the fact that while the Musalman accepts the European as his superior, he looks upon the Hindu as his inferior. It is doubtful how far a regiment of Musalmans will accept the authority of their Hindu officers if they were placed under them. The realist must take note that of all the Musalmans the Musalman of the North-West is the most disaffected Musalman, in his relation with the Hindus. The realist must take note that the Punjabi Musalman is fully susceptible to the propaganda in favour of Pan-Islamism. Taking note of all these considerations, there can be very little doubt that he would be a bold Hindu, who would say that in any invasion by Muslim countries, the Muslims in the Indian

Army would be loyal and that there is no danger of their going over to the invader. Even Theodore Morison*, writing in 1899, was of the opinion that—

"The views held by the Mahomedans (certainly the most aggressive and truculent of the peoples of India) are alone sufficient to prevent the establishment of an independent Indian Government. Were the Afghan to descend from the north upon an autonomous India, the Muhamedans, instead of uniting with the Sikhs and Hindus to repel him, would be drawn by all the ties of kinship and religion to join his flag".

And when it is recalled that in 1919 the Indian Musalmans who were carrying on the Khilafat movement actually went to the length of inviting the Amir of Afghanistan to invade India, the view expressed by Sir Theodore Morison acquires added strength and ceases to be a mere matter of speculation.

How this Army composed of the Muslims of the Punjab and N. W. F. will behave in the case of an invasion by Afghanistan is not the only question which the Hindus are called upon to consider. There is another and equally important question on which the Hindus must ponder. That question is · Will the Indian Government be free to use this army, whatever its loyalties, against the invading Afghans ? In this connection attention must be drawn to the stand taken by the Muslim League. It is to the effect that the Indian Army shall not be used against Muslim powers There is of course nothing new in this. This principle was enunciated by the Khilafat Committee long before the League. Apart from the question, with whom this principle first originated—the question remains how far the League will insist upon its being enforced. That the League has not succeeded in this behalf against the British Government does not mean that it will not succeed against an Indian Government. The chances are that it will, because, however unpatriotic the principle may be from the standpoint of the Hindus, it is most agreeable to the Muslim sentiment and the League may find a sanction for it in the general support of the Muslim community in India. If the Muslim League succeeds in enforcing this limitation upon India's right to use her fighting forces, what is going to be the position of the Hindus ? This is another question which the Hindus have to consider.

---

*Imperial rule in India, page 5.

If the shape of things to come is not going to be different from what it is, the Hindus will find themselves between the devil and the deep sea so far as the defence of India is considered, if India remains as one whole.   Having an army, they will not be free to use it because the League objects. Using it, it will not be possible to depend upon it because its loyalty is doubtful.   This is a position which is as pathetic as it is precarious   If the army continues to be dominated by the Muslims of the Punjab and N. W. F , the Hindus will have to pay them but will not be able to use them and even if they were free to use them against a Muslim invader they will find it hazardous to depend upon them.   If the League view prevails and India does not remain free to use her army against Muslim countries, then, even if the Muslims lose their predominance in the army, India on account of these military limitations, will have to remain on terms of sub-ordinate co-operation with Muslim countries on her border, as do, the Indian States under British paramountcy.

The Hindus have a difficult choice to make : to have a safe army on a safe border.   In this difficulty, what is the wisest course for the Hindus to pursue ?   Is it in their interest to insist that the Muslim India should remain part of India so that they may have a safe border, or is it in their interest to welcome its separation from India so that they may have a safe army ?   The Musalmans of this area are hostile to the Hindus   As to this there can be no doubt.   Which is then better for the Hindus   Should these Musalmans be *without and against or should they be within and against* ?   If the question is asked to any prudent man there will be only one answer, namely, that if the Musalmans are to be against the Hindus, it is better that they should be without and against, rather than within and against. Indeed it is a consummation devoutly to be wished that the Muslims should be without.   That is the only way of getting rid of the Muslim preponderance in the Indian Army.

How can it be brought about ?   Here again, there is only one way to bring it about and that is to support the scheme of Pakistan. Once Pakistan is created, Hindustan, having ample resources in men and money, can have an army which it can call its own and there will be no body to dictate as to how it should be used and against whom it should be used.   The defence of Hindustan far from being weakened by the creation of Pakistan, will be infinitely improved by it.

The Hindus do not seem to realize at what disadvantage they are placed from the point of view of their defence by their exclusion from the army. Much less do they know that strange as it may appear they are in fact purchasing this disadvantage at a very heavy price.

The Pakistan area which is the main recruiting ground of the present Indian Army contributes very little to the central exchequer as will be seen from the following figures :—

			Rs
Punjab	...	...	1,18,01,385
North West Frontier	...	...	9,28,294
Sind	...	...	5,86,46,915
Baluchistan	...	...	Nil
	Total	...	7,13,76,594

As against this the provinces of Hindustan contribute as follows :—

			Rs.
Madras	...	..	9,53,26,745
Bombay	...	...	22,53,44,247
Bengal*	...	...	12,00,00,000
U. P.	...	...	4,05,53,000
Bihar	...	...	1,54,37,742
C. P. & Berar	...	...	31,42,682
Assam	...	...	1,87,55,967
Orissa	...	...	5,67,346
	Total	...	51,91,27,729

The Pakistan Provinces, it will be seen, contribute very little. The main contribution comes from the Provinces of Hindustan. In fact it is the money contributed by the Provinces of Hindustan which enables the Government of India to carry out its activities in the Pakistan Provinces. The Pakistan Provinces are a drain of the Provinces of Hindustan. Not only do they contribute very little to the Central Government but they receive a great deal from the Central Government. The revenue of the Central Government

---

*Only ½ revenue is shown because nearly ½ population is Hindu.

amounts to Rs. 121 crores. Of this about Rs. 52 crores are annually spent on the army. In what area is this amount spent ? Who pays the bulk of this amount of Rs. 52 crores? The bulk of this amount of Rs. 52 crores which is spent on the army is spent over the Muslim army drawn from the Pakistan area. Now the bulk of this amount of Rs. 52 crores is contributed by the Hindu provinces and is spent on an army from which the Hindus, who pay for it, are excluded ! ! How many Hindus are aware of this tragedy ? How many know at whose cost this tragedy is being enacted ? Today the Hindus are not responsible for it because they cannot prevent it. Question is whether they will allow this tragedy to continue ? If they mean to stop it, then, the surest way of putting an end to it is to allow the scheme of Pakistan to take effect. To oppose it, is to buy a sure weapon of their own destruction. A safe army is better than a safe border.

CHAPTER VI

PAKISTAN AND COMMUNAL PEACE

Does Pakistan solve the Communal Question is a natural question which every Hindu is sure to ask. A correct answer to this question calls for a close analysis of what is involved in it. One must have a clear idea as to what is exactly meant, when Hindus and Muslims speak of the Communal Question. Without it, it will not be possible to say whether Pakistan does or does not solve the Communal Question.

It is not generally known that the Communal Question like the "forward policy" for the Frontier has a "greater" and a "lesser intent," and that in its lesser intent it means one thing and in its greater intent it means quite a different thing.

I

To begin with the Communal Question in its lesser intent. In its lesser intent the Communal Question relates to the representation of Hindus and Muslims in the Legislatures. Used in this sense, the question involves the settlement of two distinct problems :—

(1) The number of seats to be allotted to Hindus and Muslims in the different legislatures,

(2) The nature of the electorates through which these seats are to be filled in.

The Muslims at the Round Table Conference claimed :—

(1) That their representatives should be elected by separate electorates in all the Provincial as well as in the Central Legislatures.

13

(2) That they should be allowed to retain the weightage in representation given to Muslim minorities in those provinces in which they were a minority in the population, and that in addition they should be given in those provinces where they were a majority of the population, such as the Punjab, Sind, North-West Frontier Provinces and Bengal, a guaranteed statutory majority of seats.

The Hindus from the beginning objected to both these Muslim demands. They insisted on joint electorates for Hindus and Muslims in all elections to all the legislatures, Central and Provincial, and population ratio of representation for both minorities, Hindu and Muslim, wherever they may be, and raised the strongest objections to a majority of seats to any community being guaranteed by statute.

The Communal Award of His Majesty's Government settled this dispute by the simple, rough and ready method of giving the Muslims all that they wanted, without caring for the Hindu opposition. The Award allowed the Muslims to retain their weightages and their separate electorates, and in addition gave them the statutory majority of seats in those provinces where they were a majority in the population.

What is it in the Award which can be said to constitute a problem ? Is there any force in the objections of the Hindus to the Communal Award of His Majesty's Government ? This question must be considered carefully to find out whether there is substance in the objections of the Hindus to the Award.

First, as to their objection to the weightage to Muslim minorities in the matter of representation. Whatever may be the correct measure of allotting representation to minorities, the Hindus cannot very well object to the weightage given to Muslim minorities, because similar weightage has been given to Hindus in those provinces in which they are a minority and where there is sufficient margin for weightage to be allowed. The treatment of the Hindu minorities in Sind and the North-West Frontier Province is a case in point.

Second, as to their objection to a statutory majority. That again does not appear to be well founded. A system of guaranteed representation may be wrong and vicious and quite unjustifiable on theoretical and philosophical grounds. But considered in the light of circumstances such as those obtaining in India, the system of statutory majority appears to be inevitable. Once it is granted that a minority must be secured by law a certain minimum number of seats, that very provision gives rise, as a mere counterpart, to a system of statutory majority to the majority community. For, fixing the seats of the minority involves the fixation of the seats of the majority. There is therefore no escape from the system of statutory majority, once it is conceded that a minority is entitled to a minimum number of seats guaranteed by law. There is therefore no great force in the objections of the Hindus to a statutory majority of Muslims in the Punjab, N.-W. F. Province, Sind and Bengal. For even in Provinces where the Hindus are in majority and the Mahomedans are in minority, the Hindus have also got a statutory majority over the Muslims. There is thus a parity of position and to that extent there can be said to be no ground for complaint.

This does not mean that because the objections set forth by the Hindus have no substance, there are no real grounds for opposing the Communal Award. For there does exist a substantial ground of objection to the Communal Award, although, they do not appear to have been made the basis of attack by the Hindus.

This objection may be formulated in this wise in order to bring out its point. The Muslim minorities in the Hindu provinces insisted on separate electorates. The Communal Award gives them the right to determine that issue. This is really what it comes to when one remembers the usual position taken viz., that the Muslim minorities could not be deprived of their separate electorates without their consent, and the majority community of the Hindus has been made to abide by their determination. The Hindu minorities in Muslim provinces insisted that there should be joint electorates. Instead of conceding their claim, the Communal Award forced upon them the system of separate electorates to which they objected. If in the Hindu provinces the Muslim minorities are allowed the right of self-determination in the matter of electorates, the question arises : Why are not the Hindu minorities in the Muslim provinces given the right of self-determination in the matter of their electorates ? What is the answer to this question ? And, if there is no answer, then, there is undoubtedly a deep-seated inequity in the Communal Award of His Majesty's Government, which calls for redress.

It is no answer that the position of the Muslim minorities in the Hindu provinces, is not different from the position of the Hindu minorities in the Muslim provinces, inasmuch as in the former provinces also the Hindus will have a statutory majority based on separate electorates. A little scrutiny will show that there is no parity of position in these two cases. The separate electorates for the Hindu majorities in the Hindu provinces are not a matter of their choice. It is a consequence resulting from the determination of the Muslim minorities who claimed to have separate electorates for themselves. A minority in one set of circumstances may think that separate electorates would be a better method of self-protection and may have no fear of creating against itself and by its own action a statutory majority based on separate electorates for the opposing community. Another minority or for the matter of that the same minority in a different set of circumstances would not like to create by its own action and against itself a statutory majority based upon separate electorates and may, therefore, prefer joint electorates to separate electorates as a better method of self-protection Obviously the guiding principle, which would influence a minority, would be · Is the majority likely to use its majority in a communal manner and purely for communal purposes ? If it felt certain that the majority community is likely to use its communal majority for communal ends, it may well choose joint electorates, because it would be the only method by which it would hope to take away the communal cement of the statutory majority by influencing the elections of the representatives of the majority community in the legislatures. On the other hand, a majority community may not have the necessary communal cement, which alone would enable it to use its communal majority for communal ends, in which case a minority, having no fear from the resulting statutory majority and separate electorates for the majority community, may well choose separate electorates for itself. To put it concretely, the Muslim minorities in choosing separate electorates are not afraid of the separate electorates and the statutory majority of the Hindus, because they feel sure that by reason of their deep-seated differences of caste and race, the Hindus will never be able to use their majorities against the Muslims. On the other hand, the Hindu minorities in the Muslim provinces have no doubt that by reason of their social solidarity the Moslems will use their statutory majority to set into operation a " resolute Muslim Government ", after the plan proposed by Lord Salisbury for Ireland as a substitute for Home Rule ; with this difference, that Salisbury's Resolute Government was to last for twenty years only, while the Muslim Resolute Government is to last as long as the Communal Award stands. The situations therefore are not alike. The statutory majority of the Hindus based on separate electorates is the result of the choice made by the Muslim minority. The statutory majority of the Muslims based on separate electorates is something which is not the result of the choice of the Hindu minority. In one case, the Government of the Muslim minority by a Hindu communal majority is the result of the consent of the Muslim minority. In the other case, the Government of the Hindu minority by the Muslim majority is not the result of the consent of the Hindu minority, but is imposed upon it by the might of the British Government.

To sum up this discussion of the Communal Award, it may be said that " as a solution of the Communal Question in its " lesser intent ", there is no inequity in the Award because it gives weightage to the Muslim minorities in the Hindu Provinces If there is any inequity in it, it must be set off against the weightage given to the Hindu minorities in Muslim Provinces. Similarly, it may be said that there is no inequity in the Award because it gives a statutory majority to the Muslims in Provinces in which they are a majority. If there is any, the statutory majority resulting to the Hindus in Hindu Provinces from the limitation put upon the Muslim number of seats must be set off against it. But the same cannot be said in the matter of the electorates The Communal Award is inequitious inasmuch as, it accords unequal treatment to the Hindu and Muslim minorities in the matter of electorates. It grants the Muslim minorities in the Hindu Provinces the right of self-determination in the matter of electorates. But it does not grant the same right of self-determination in the matter of electorates to the Hindu minorities in the Muslim Provinces. In the Hindu Provinces the Muslim minority is allowed to choose the kind of electorates it wants and the Hindu majority is not permitted to have any say in the matter. But in the Muslim Provinces it is the Muslim majority which is allowed to choose the kind of electorates it prefers and the Hindu minority is not permitted to have any say in the matter. Thus, the Muslims in the Muslims Provinces, having been given both statutory majority and separate electorate as well, the Communal Award must be said to impose upon the Hindu minorities Muslim rule, which they can neither alter nor influence.

This is what constitutes the fundamental wrong in the Communal Award. That, this is a grave wrong, must be admitted. Certain political principles have now become axiomatic. One is, not to trust any one with unlimited political power. As has been well said,

"If in any state there is a body of men who possess unlimited political power, those over whom they rule can never be free. For, the one assured result of historical investigation is the lesson that uncontrolled power is invariably poisonous to those who possess it. They are always tempted to impose their cannon of good upon others, and in the end, they assume that the good of community depends upon the continuance of their power. Liberty always demands a limitation of political authority........."

The second principle is, that a King has no Divine Right to rule and so also a majority has no Divine Right to rule. A majority rule is only tolerated because it is for a limited period and subject to a right to have it changed. Secondly because, it is a rule of a political majority, i.e., a majority which has submitted itself to the sufferages of a minority and not a communal majority. If such is the limited scope of authority permissible to a political majority over a political minority, how can a communal minority be placed under perpetual subjection of a communal majority? To allow a communal majority to rule a minority without requiring the majority to submit itself to the sufferages of the minority, especially when the minority demands it, is to enact a perversion of democratic principles and to show a callous disregard for the safety and security of the Hindu minorities.

II

To turn to the Communal Question in its greater intent. What is it that the Hindus say is a problem ? In its greater intent the Communal Question relates to the deliberate creation of Muslim Provinces. At the time of the Lucknow Pact the Muslims only raised the Communal Question in its lesser intent. At the Round Table Conference the Muslims put forth, for the first time, the plan covered by the Communal Question in its greater intent. Before the Act of 1935 there were a majority of provinces in which the Hindus were in a majority and the Mahomedans in a minority. There were only three provinces in which Muslims were in a majority and the Hindus in a minority. They were the Punjab, Bengal and the North-West Frontier. Of these, the Muslim majority in the North-West Frontier was not effective, because there was no responsible government in that province, the Montagu–Chelmsford Scheme of Political Reforms not being extended to it. So, for all practical purposes there were only two provinces—the Punjab and Bengal—wherein the Muslims were in majority and the Hindus were in minority. The Muslims desired that the number of Muslim provinces should be increased. With this object in view they demanded that Sind should be separated from the Bombay Presidency, and created into a new self-governing province, and that the North-West Frontier Province, which was already a separate province, should be raised to the status of a self-governing province. Apart from other considerations, from a purely financial point of view, it was not possible to concede this demand. Neither Sind nor the N. W. F. were financially self-supporting. But in order to satisfy the Muslim demand the British Government went to the length of accepting the responsibility of giving an annual subvention to Sind* and N. W. F.† from the Central Revenues, so as to bring about a budgetory equilibrium in their finances and make them financially self-supporting.

These four provinces with Muslims in majority and Hindus in minority, which are now functioning as autonomous and

---

* Sind gets annual subvention of Rs. 1,05,00,000.
† N. W. F. gets annual subvention of Rs.1,00,00,000.

self-governing provinces were certainly not created for administrative convenience. They were not created for purposes of architectural symmetry—the Hindu provinces poised against the Muslim provinces. The scheme of the Muslim provinces was not a mere matter of pride to have Hindu minorities under Muslim majorities just as Hindu majorities had Muslim minorities under them. What was the underlying motive for this scheme of Muslim Provinces ? The Hindus say that the motive for the Muslim insistence, both on a statutory majority and separate electorates, was to enable the Muslim in the Muslim Provinces to mobilize and make effective Muslim power in its exclusive form and to the fullest extent possible. Asked what could be the purpose of having the Muslim political power mobilized in this fashion, the Hindus answer that it was done to give in the hands of the Muslims of the Muslim Provinces an effective means to tyrannize their Hindu minorities in case the Muslim minorities in the Hindu Provinces were tyrannized by their Hindu majorities. Thinking that the Hindu majority will tyrannize the Muslim minority in the Hindu provinces, the scheme gave the Mahomedan majorities a handle to tyrannize the Hindu minorities in the five Mahomedan provinces. It thus became a system of protection against blast by counter-blast, against terror by terror and eventually against tyranny by tyranny. The plan is undoubtedly, a dreadful one, involving the maintanance of justice and peace by retaliation, and providing an opportunity for the punishment of an innocent minority, Hindu in Mahomedan provinces and Mahomedan in Hindu provinces, for the sins of their co-religionists in other provinces. It is a scheme of communal peace through a system of communal hostages.

That the Muslims were aware from the very start, that the system of Communal Provinces was capable of being worked in this manner, is clear from the speech made by Maulana Abul Kalam Azad as President of the Muslim League Session held in Calcutta in 1927. In that speech the Maulana declared ·—

" That by the Lucknow Pact they had sold away their interests. The Delhi proposals of March last opened the door for the first time to the recognition of the real rights of Mussalmans in India. The separate electorates granted by the Pact of 1916 only ensured Muslim representation, but what was vital for the existence of the

community was the recognition of its numerical strength. Delhi
opened the way to the creation of such a state of affairs as would
guarantee to them in the future of India a proper share. Their
existing small majority in Bengal and the Punjab was only a census
figure, but the Delhi proposals gave them for the first time five
provinces of which no less than three (Sind, the Frontier Province
and Baluchistan) contained a real overwhelming Muslim majority.
If the Muslims did not recognise this great step they were not fit to
live. There would now be nine Hindu provinces against five
Muslim provinces, and whatever treatment Hindus accorded in
the nine provinces, Muslims would accord the same treatment to
Hindus in the five provinces. Was not this a great gain ? Was not
a new weapon gained for the assertion of Muslim rights ?"

That those in charge of these Muslim provinces know the
advantage of the scheme, and do not hesitate to put it to the
use for which it was intended, is clear from the recent speeches of
Mr. Fazl ul-Huq, the Prime Minister of Bengal.

That this scheme of Communal Provinces, which constitutes
the Communal Question in its larger intent, can be used as an
engine of communal tyranny there can be no doubt. The system
of hostages, which is the essence of the scheme of communal
provinces supported by separate electorates, is indeed insupportable on any ground. If this is the underlying motive of the demand
for the creation of more Muslim provinces, then no doubt, the
system resulting from it is a vicious system

This analysis leaves no doubt that the communal statutory
majority based on separate communal electorates and communa
provinces, especially constituted to enable the statutory majority
to tyrannize the minority are, undoubtedly, the two evils which
compose what is called, ' the Communal Problem '.

For the existence of this problem the Hindus hold the
Muslims responsible and the Muslims hold the Hindus responsible
Hindus accuse Muslims of contumacy. Muslims accuse Hindus
of meanness. Both, however, forget that the communal problem
exists not because Muslims are extravagant and insolent in their
demands and Hindus are mean and grudging in their concessions.
It exists and will exist wherever a hostile majority is brought face

14

to face against a hostile minority.   Controversies relating to separate vs joint electorates, controversies relating to population ratio vs weightage are all inherent in a situation where a minority is pitted against a majority.   The best solution of the communal problem is not to have two communities facing each other, one a majority and the other a minority, wound up steel-frame of a single government.

How far does Pakistan approximate to this ideal solution of the Communal Question ?

The answer to this question is quite obvious.   If the scheme of Pakistan is to follow the present boundaries of the Provinces in the North-West and in Bengal, then certainly it does not eradicate the evils which lie at the heart of the Communal Question.   It retains the very elements which give rise to it, namely the pitting of a minority against a majority.   The rule of Hindu minorities by Muslim majorities and the rule of Muslim minorities by Hindu majorities is the crying evil of the present situation.   This very evil will reproduce itself in Pakistan if the provinces marked out for it are incorporated into it as they are, i. e., with the boundaries drawn as at present.   Besides this, the evil which gives rise to the Communal Question in its larger intent, will not only remain as it is but will assume a new malignity.   Under the existing system, the power centered in the Communal Provinces to do mischief to their hostages is limited by the power which the Central Government has over the Provincial Governments.   At present the hostages are at least within the pale of a Central Government which is Hindu in its composition and which has power to interfere for their protection.   But when Pakistan becomes a Muslim state with full sovereignty over internal and external affairs it would be free from the control of the Central Government to which the Hindu minorities could appeal.   There will be no authority which could interfere on their behalf to curb this power of mischief.   So that, the position of the Hindus in Pakistan may easily become the position of the Armenians under the Truks or of the Jews in Tsarist Russia, or in Nazi Germany.   Such a scheme would be intolerable and the Hindus may well say that they cannot agree to Pakistan and leave their co-religionist as a helpless prey to the fanaticism of a Muslim National State.

III

This, of course, is a very frank statement of the consequences which will flow from giving effect to the scheme of Pakistan. But care must be taken to locate the source of these consequences. Do they flow from the scheme of Pakistan itself or do the flow from the boundaries that accompany it ? If the evils flow from the scheme itself, i.e., if they are inherent in it, then of course it is unnecessary for any Hindu to waste his time in considering it. He may be well justified in summarily dismissing it. On the other hand if the evils are not inherent in the scheme but are the result of the boundaries accompanying it, then Pakistan reduces itself to a mere question of changing the boundaries.

A study of the question amply supports the view that the evils of Pakistan are not inherent in it, but that they are the results of the boundaries, which accompany it. That the source of these evils is only boundaries, becomes clear if one studies the distribution of population. The reasons why these evils will be reproduced within Pakistan in the North-West and in the Muslim State in the East is because, with the present boundaries, they do not become single ethnic states. They remain mixed states composed of a Muslim majority and a Hindu minority as before. The evils are the evils which are inseparable from a mixed state. If Pakistan is made a single unified ethnic state, the evils will automatically vanish. There will be no question of separate electorates within Pakistan, because in such a homogenous Pakistan there will be no majorities to rule and no minorities to be protected. Similarly, there will be no majority of one community to hold, in its possession, a minority of an opposing community.

The question therefore is one of demarkation of boundaries and reduces itself to this Is it possible for the boundaries of Pakistan to be so fixed, that instead of producing a mixed state composed of majorities and minorities, with all the evils attendant upon it, Pakistan will be an ethnic state composed of one homogenous community namely Muslims ? The answer is that in a large part of the area affected by the project of the League, a homogenous state can be created by merely shifting the boundaries but in the rest homogeneity can be produced only by shifting the population.

In this connection I invite the reader to study carefully the figures given in the Appendices I, II, III showing the distribution of the population in the areas affected, and also the maps showing how new boundries can create homogeneous Muslim states.

Taking the Punjab, two things must be noted :—

(i) There are certain districts in which the Musalmans predominate. There are certain districts which the Hindus predominate. There are very few in which the two are, more or less, evenly distributed ;

(ii) The districts in which the Muslims predominate and the districts in which the Hindus predominate are not interspersed. The two sets of districts form two separate areas.

For the formation of the Eastern Muslim State in Bengal one has to take into consideration the distribution of population in both the Provinces of Bengal and Assam. Here also four things are clear :

(i) In Bengal there are some districts in which the Muslims predominate. In others the Hindus predominate.

(ii) In Assam also there are some districts in which the Muslims predominate. In others the Hindus predominate.

(iii) Districts in which the Muslims predominate and those in which the Hindus predominate are not interspersed. They form separate areas.

(iv) The districts of Bengal and Assam in which the Muslims predominate are contiguous.

Given these facts, it is perfectly possible to create homogenous Muslim States out of the Punjab, Bengal and Assam by drawing their boundaries in such a way that the areas which are predominantly Hindu shall be excluded. That this is possible is shown by the maps given in the appendix.

In the North-West Frontier and Sind the situation is rather hard. How the matter stands in the N. W. F. and Sind may be seen by an examination of the data given in the appendices numbering IV to VII. As may be seen from the appendices there are no districts in which the Hindus in N. W. F. and Sind are concentrated. They are scattered and bits of them are to be found in almost every district of the two provinces. Appendices IV, V, VI and VII shows that the Hindus in Sind and N. W. F. are mostly congregated in urban areas of the Districts.   In Sind the Hindus outnumber the Muslims in most of the towns, while the Muslims outnumber the Hindu in villages.   In the N. W. F. the Muslims outnumber the Hindus in towns as well as in the villages.

The case of the N W. F. and Sind therefore differs totally from the case of the Punjab and Bengal   In the Punjab and Bengal owing to the natural segregation of the Hindus and Muslims in different areas it is possible to create a homogenous State by merely altering their boundaries, involving the shifting of the population in a very small degree.   But in the N W. F. and Sind owing to the scattered state of the Hindu population alteration of boundaries cannot suffice for creating a homogeneous state   There is the only one remedy and that is to shift the population.

Some scoff at the idea of the shifting and exchange of population.   But those who scoff can hardly be aware of the complications which a minority problem gives rise to and the failures attendant upon almost all the efforts made to sooth there relations.   The constitutions of the post-war states, as well as the older states in Europe which had a minority problem, proceeded on the assumption that constitutional safeguards for minorities should suffice for their protection and the constitutions of most of the new states with majorities and minorities were studded with long lists of fundamental rights and safeguards to see that they were not violated by the majorities.   What was the experience ?   Experience showed that safeguards did not save the minorities.   Even after safeguards the same old policy of exterminating the minorities continued to hold the field.   But, at long last, when the States realized that even this ruthless war had failed to solve the problem of minorities they agreed that the best way to solve it was for each to exchange its alien minorities within, its border, for its own which was without its border with a view to bring about homogeneous States. This is what happened in Turkey, Greece and Bulgaria.   Those who scoff at the idea of transfer of population will do well to study the history of the minority problem, as it arose between Turkey, Greece and Bulgaria.   If they do, they will find that after trying all possible methods of solving the problem it was agreed between these countries that the only effective way of solving it was to exchange population.

The task undertaken by the three countries was by no means a minor operation. It involved the transfer of some 20 million people from one habitat to another. But undaunted, the three shouldered the task and carried it to a successful end. That is because they felt that the considerations of communal peace must outweigh every other consideration.

That the transfer of minorities is the only lasting remedy for communal peace is beyond doubt. If that is so, there is no reason why Hindus and Muslims should keep on trading in safeguards which have proved so unsafe. That, if small countries with limited resources like Greece, Turkey and Bulgaria were capable of such an undertaking, there is no reason to suppose that what they did cannot be accomplished by Indians. After all, the population involved is inconsiderable and it would be a height of folly to give up a sure way to communal peace because some obstacles in it require to be removed.

There is one point of criticism to which so far no reference has been made. As it is likely to be urged I propose to deal with it here. It is sure to be asked, how will Pakistan affect the position of Muslims that will be left in Hindustan ? The question is natural because the scheme of Pakistan does seem to concern itself with Muslim majorities who do not need protection and abandons the Muslim minorities who do. But the point is who can raise it ? Surely not the Hindus. Only the Muslims of Pakistan or the Muslims of Hindustan can raise it. The question was put to Mr. Rehmat Ali, the protagonist of Pakistan and this is the answer given by him :—

"How will it affect the position of the forty five million Muslems in Hindustan proper ?"

"The truth is that in this struggle their thought has been more than a wrench to me. They are the flesh of our flesh and the soul of our soul. We can never forget them ; nor they, us. Their present position and future security is, and shall ever be, a matter of great importance to us. As things are at present, Pakistan will not adversely affect their position in Hindustan. On the basis of population (one Muslem to four Hindus), they will still be entitled to the same representation in legislative as well as administrative fields which they possess now. As to the future, the only effective guarantee we can offer is that of reciprocity, and, therefore, we solemnly undertake to give all those safeguards to non-Muslim minorities in Pakistan which will be conceded to our Muslim minority in Hindustan.

"But what sustains us most is the fact that they know we are proclaiming Pakistan in the highest interest of the 'Millet'. It is as much theirs as it is ours. While for us it is a national citadel, for them it will ever be a moral anchor. So long as the anchor holds, everything is or can be made safe. But once it gives way, all will be lost."

The answer given by the Muslims of Hindustan is equally clear. They say "we are not weakened by the separation of Muslims into Pakistan and Hindustan. We are better protected by the existence of separate Islamic States on the Eastern and Western border of Hindustan than we are by their submersion in Hindustan. Who can say that they are wrong? Has it not been shown that Germany as an outside state was better able to protect the Sudeten Germans in Czechoslovakia than the Sudetens were able to do themselves?*

Be that as it may, the question does not concern the Hindus. The question that concerns the Hindus is How far does the creation of Pakistan remove the communal question from Hindustan? That is a very legitimate question and must be considered. It must be admitted that by the creation of Pakistan Hindustan is not freed of the communal question. While Pakistan can be made a homogenous state by redrawing its boundaries, Hindustan must remain a composite state. The Musalmans are scattered all over Hindustan—though they are mostly congregated in towns–and no ingenuity in the matter of redrawing of boundaries can make it homogeneous. The only way to make Hindustan homogenous is to arrange for exchange of population. Until that is done, it must be admitted that even with the creation of Pakistan the problem of majority vs. minority will remain in Hindustan as before and will continue to produce disharmony in the body politic of Hindustan.

* The leaders of the Muslims League seem to have studied deeply Hitler's bullying tactics against Czechoslovakia in the interest of the Studeten Germans and also learned the lessons which those tactics teach. See their threatening speeches in the Karachi session of the League held in 1937.

Admitting that Pakistan is not capable of proving a complete solution of the Communal Problem within Hindustan, does it follow that the Hindus on that account should reject Pakistan ? Before the Hindus draw any such hasty conclusion they should consider the following effects of Pakistan.

First consider the effect of Pakistan on the magnitude of the Communal Problem. That can be best gauged by reference to the Muslim population as it will be grouped within Pakistan and Hindustan.

Muslim Population in Pakistan		Muslim Population in Hindustan	
1. Punjab	13,332,460	1 Total Muslim Population in British India (Excluding Burma and Aden)	66,442,766
2 N W F	2,227,303		
3. Sind	2,830,800	2 Muslim Population grouped in Pakistan and Eastern Bengal State	47,897,301
4. Baluchistan	405,309		
5. Eastern Bengal Muslim State —		3 Balance of Muslims in British Hindustan.	18,545,465
(1) Eastern Bengal	27,497,624		
(11) Sylhet	1,603,805		
Total	47,897,301		

What do these figures indicate ? What they indicate is, that the Muslims that will be left in British Hindustan will be only 18,545,465 and the rest 47,897,301 forming a vast majority of the total Muslim population will be out of it and will be the subjects of Pakistan and the Eastern Muslim States. This distribution of the Muslim population, in terms of the communal problem means, that while without Pakistan the communal problem involves $6\frac{1}{2}$ crores of Muslims, after Pakistan it will involve only 2 crores of Muslims. Is this to be no consideration for Hindus who want communal peace ? To me it seems that if Pakistan does not solve the communal problem in Hindustan it enormously reduces its proportion and makes it of minor significance and much easier of peaceful solution.

In the second place, let the Hindus consider the effect of Pakistan on the communal representation in the Central Legislature. The following table gives the distribution of seats in the Central Legislature as prescribed under the Government of India Act and as it would be if Pakistan came into being.

Name of the Chamber	Distribution of Seats			Distribution of seats.		
	I.—As at present.			II.—After Pakistan.		
	Total seats,	Non-Muslim (Hindu) Territorial seats.	Muslim Territorial seats.	Total seats	Non-Muslim (Hindu) Territorial seats	Muslim Territorial seats.
Council of State.	150	75	49	126	75	25
Federal Assembly.	250	105	82	211	105	43

To bring out clearly the quantitative change in the communal distribution of seats which must follow the establishment of Pakistan the above figures are reduced to percentages in the table that follows —

Name of the Chamber	...on of seats present		Distribution of seats II.—After Pakistan	
	Percentage of Muslim seats to total seats	Percentage of Muslim seats to Hindu seats	Percentage of Muslim seats to total seats	Percentage of Muslim seats to Hindu seats.
Council of State	33	66	25	33 1/3
Federal Assembly	33	80	21	40

From this table one can see what vast changes must follow the establishment of Pakistan. Under the Government of India Act the ratio of Muslim seats to the total is $33°/_0$ in both the chambers, but to the Hindu seats the ratio is 66 p.c. in the Council of State and. 80 p.c. in the Assembly—almost a position of equality with the Hindus. After Pakistan the ratio of Muslim seats to total seats falls from 33 1/3 p.c. to 25 p.c. in the Council and to 21 p.c. in the Assembly, while the ratio to Hindu seats falls from 66 p.c. to 33 1/3 p.c in the Council and from 80 p.c. to 40 p.c. in the Assembly. The figures assume that the weightage given to the Muslims will remain the same even after Hindustan is separated from Pakistan. If the present weightage to Muslims is cancelled or reduced there would be further improvement in the representation of the Hindus

15

But assuming that no change in weightage is made, is this a small gain to the Hindus in the matter of representation at the Centre? To me it appears that it is a great improvement in the position of the Hindus at the Centre, which would never come to them, if they oppose Pakistan.

These are the material advantages of Pakistan. There is another which is psychological. The Muslims, in Southern and Central India, draw their inspiration from the Muslims of the North and the East. If after Pakistan there is communal peace in the North and the East, as there should be, there being no majorities and minorities therein, the Hindus may reasonably expect communal peace in Hindustan. This severance of the bond between the Muslims of the North and the East and the Muslims of Hindustan is another gain to the Hindus of Hindustan.

Thus, taking into consideration these effects of Pakistan, it cannot be disputed that if Pakistan does not wholly solve the communal problem within Hindustan it does free the Hindus from the turbulence of the Muslims as predominant partners. It is for the Hindus to say whether they will reject such a proposal simply because it does not offer a complete solution. Some gain is better than much harm.

IV

One last question and this discussion of Pakistan in relation to communal peace may be brought to a close. Will the Hindus and Muslims of the Punjab and Bengal agree to redraw the boundaries of their provinces to make the scheme of Pakistan as flawless as it can be made?

As for the Muslims they ought to have no objection to redrawing the boundaries. If they do object then it must be said that they do not understand the nature of their own demand. This is quite possible, since the talk that is going on among Muslim protagonists of Pakistan is of a very loose character. Some speak of Pakistan as a Muslim National State, others speak of it as a Muslim National Home. Neither care to know whether there is any difference between a National State and a National Home. But there can be no doubt that there is a vital difference between the two. What that difference is was discussed at great length at the time of constituting in Palestine a Jewish national home. It seems that a clear conception of what this difference is, is necessary, if the likely Muslim opposition to the redrawing of the boundaries is to be overcome.

According to a leading authority :—

"A National Home connotes a territory in which a people, without receiving the rights of political sovereignty has nevertheless a recognised legal position and receives the opportunity of developing its moral, social, and intellectual ideals."

The British Government itself, in its basic statement on Palestine policy issued in 1922, thus defined its conception of the national home :—

"When it is asked what is meant by the development of the Jewish national home in Palestine, it may be answered that it is not the imposition of a Jewish nationality upon the inhabitants of Palestine as a whole, but the further development of the existing Jewish Community, with the assistance of Jews in other parts of the world, in order that it may become a centre in which the Jewish people as a whole may take, on grounds of religion and race, an interest and a pride. But in order that this community should have the best prospect of free development and provide a full opportunity for the Jewish people to display its capacities, it is essential that it should know that it is in Palestine as of right and not on sufferance. This is the reason why it is necessary that the existence of a Jewish National Home in Palestine should be internationally guaranteed, and that it should be formally recognized to rest upon ancient historic connection."

From this it will be clear that there is an essential difference between a National Home and a National State. The difference consists in this : In the case of a National Home the people who constitute it do not receive the right of political sovereignty over the territory and the right of imposing their nationality on others also living in that territory. All that they get, is a recognized legal position guaranteeing them the right to live as citizens and freedom to maintain their culture. In the case of a National State, people constituting it, receive the rights of political sovereignty with the right of imposing their nationality upon the rest.

This difference is very important and it is in the light of this that one must examine their demand for Pakistan. What do the Muslims want Pakistan for? If they want Pakistan to create a National Home for Muslims then there is no necessity for Pakistan. In the Pakistan Provinces they already have their National Home with the legal right to live and advance their culture If they want Pakistan to be a National Muslim State then they are claiming the right of political sovereignty over the territory included in it. This they are entitled to do. But the question is should they be allowed to retain within the boundaries of these Muslim States Non-Muslim minorities as their subjects with a right to impose upon them the nationality of these Muslim States. No doubt such a right is accepted to be an accompaniment of political sovereignty. But it is equally true that in all mixed States this right has become a source of mischief in modern times. To ignore the possibilities of such mischief in the creation of Pakistan and the Eastern Muslim State, will be to omit to read the bloody pages of recent history on which have been recorded the atrocities, murders, plunders and arsons committed by the Turks, Greeks, Bulgars, and the Czechs against their minorities. It is not possible to take away this right from a state of imposing its nationality upon its subjects because it is incidental to political sovereignty. But it is possible not to provide any opportunity for the exercise of such a right. This can be done by allowing the Muslims to have National Muslim States but to make such states strictly homogeneous, strictly ethnic states. Under no circumstances can they be allowed to carve out mixed states composed of Muslims opposed to Hindus, with the former superior in member to the latter.

This is probably not contemplated by the Muslims who are the authors of Pakistan It was certainly not contemplated by Sir M Iqbal, the originator of the scheme. In his Presidential address to the Muslim League in 1930 he expressed his willingness to agree to " the exclusion of Ambala Division and perhaps of some other districts where non-Muslims predominate " on the ground that such exclusion " will make it less extensive and more Muslim in population ". On the other hand it may be that those who are putting forth the Scheme of Pakistan do contemplate that it will include the Punjab and Bengal within their present boundaries. To them it must become clear, that to insist upon the present boundaries is sure to antagonize even those Hindus who have an open mind on the question. Hindus can never be expected to consent to the inclusion of the Hindus in a Muslim State deliberately created for the preservation and propagation of the Muslim faith and Muslim culture. Not only Hindus will oppose but Muslims will be found out. For, Muslims, if they insist upon the retention of the present boundaries, will open themselves to the accusation that behind their demand for Pakistan there is something more sinister than a mere desire to create a National Home or a National State, namely to perfect the scheme of Hindu hostages in Muslim hands by increasing the balance of Muslim majorities against Hindu minorities in the Muslim areas.

So much for considerations which ought to weigh with the Muslims in the matter of changing the provincial boundaries to make Pakistan as far as possible a purely ethnic state, free from the complications of majorities and minorities.

Now as to the considerations which ought to weigh with the Hindus of the Punjab and Bengal. This is a more difficult of the two parties to the question. In this connection it is enough to consider the reaction of the high caste Hindus only. For it is they who guide the Hindu masses and form Hindu opinion. Unfortunately the high caste Hindus are bad as leaders. They have a trait of character which often leads the Hindus to disaster. This trait is formed by their acquisitive instinct and aversion to share with others the good things of life. They have a monopoly of education and wealth and with wealth and education they have captured the State. To keep this monopoly to themselves has been the ambition and goal of their life. Charged with this selfish idea of class domination they take every move to exclude the lower classes of Hindus from wealth, education and power, the surest and the most effective being the preparation of scriptures, inculcating upon the minds of the lower classes of Hindus that their duty in life was only to servs the higher classes. In keeping this monopoly in their own hands, and excluding the lower classes from any share in it, the high caste Hindus have succeeded for a long time and beyond measure. It is only recently that the lower class Hindus rose in revolt against this monopoly by starting the Non–Brahmin Parties in the Madras and the Bombay Presidencies and C. P. Notwithstanding the high caste *Hindus* have successfuly maintained their privileged position. This attitude of keeping education, wealth and power as a close preserve for themselves and refusing to share it, which the high caste Hindus have developed in their relation with the lower classes of Hindus, is sought to be extended by them to the Muslims. They want to exclude the Muslims from place and power as they have done the lower class Hindus. This trait of the high caste Hindus is the key to understand their politics.

Two illustrations reveal this trait of theirs. The Hindus in 1929 opposed the separation of Sindh from Bombay Presidency before the Simon Commission, strenuously and vehemently. But in 1915 the Hindus of Sind put forth the opposite plea and wanted Sind to be separated from Bombay. The reason in both the cases was the same. In 1915 there was no representative Government in Sind, which if there was would be undoubtedly a Muslim Government. The Hindus advocated separation because in the absence of a Muslim Government they could obtain jobs in Government in a greater and greater degree. In 1929 they objected to separation of Sind because they knew that a separate Sind will be under a Muslim Government, and a Muslim Government was sure to disturb their monopoly and displace them to make room for Muslim candidates. The opposition of the Bengali Hindus to the Partition of Bengal is another illustration of this trait of the high caste Hindus. The Bengali Hindu had the whole of Bengal, Bihar, Orissa, Assam and even U. P. for his pasture. He had captured the civil service in all these Provinces. The partition of Bengal meant a diminution in the area of this pasture: It meant that the Bengali Hindu was to be ousted from Eastern Bengal to make room for the Bengali Musalmans who had so far no place in the civil service of Bengal. The opposition to the partition of Bengal on the part of the Bengali Hindus was due principally to their desire not to allow the Bengali Musalmans to take their places in Eastern Bengal. Little did the Bengali Hindus dream that by opposing partition and at the same time demading Swaraj he was preparing the way for making the Musalmans the rulers of both Eastern as well as Western Bengal.

These thoughts occur to one's mind because one fears that the high caste Hindus blinded by their hereditary trait might oppose Pakistan for no other reason except that it limits the field for their self-seeking careers. Among the many reasons that might come in the way of Pakistan one need not be surprised if one of them happens to be the selfishness of the high caste Hindus.

There are two alternatives for the Hindus of the Punjab and Bengal and they may be asked to face them fairly and squarely. The Muslims in the Punjab number 13,332,460 and the Hindus with Sikhs and the rest number 11,392,732. The difference is only 1,939,728. This means that the Muslim majority in the Punjab is only a majority of 8 p. c. Given these facts, which is better ? To oppose Pakistan by refusing to redraw the boundaries and allow the Muslim majority of 54 p. c. to rule the Hindu minority of 46 p. c or to redraw the boundaries, to allow Muslims and Hindus to be under separate national states, and thus rescue the whole body of Hindus from the terrors of the Muslim rule ?

The Muslims in Bengal number 27,497,624 and the Hindus number 21,570,407. The difference is only of 5,927,217. This means that the Muslim majority in Bengal is only a majority of 12 p.c. Given these facts, which is better ? To oppose the creation of a National Muslim State out of Eastern Bengal and Sylhet by refusing to redraw the boundaries and allow the Muslim Majority of only 12 p.c. to rule the Hindu minority of 44 p. c.; or to consent to redraw the boundaries, to have Muslims and Hindus placed under separate National States, and thus rescue the 44 p. c. of Hindus from the horrors of Muslim rule ?

Let the Hindus of Bengal and the Punjab consider which alternative they should prefer. It seems to me that the moment has come when the high caste Hindus of Bengal and the Punjab should be told that if they propose to resist Pakistan, because it cuts off a field for gainful employment, 'they are committing the greatest blunder.

The time for successfully maintaining in their own hands a monopoly of place and power is gone. They may cheat the lower order of Hindus in the name of nationalism. But they cannot cheat the Muslim majorities in Muslim Provinces and keep their monopoly of place and power. The determination to live under a Muslim majority and to hope to gain more than your share may be a very courageous thing. But it is certainly not a wise thing Because, the chances are that you will lose all. On the other hand, if the Hindus of Bengal and the Punjab agree to separate, true, they will not get more, but they will certainly not lose all.

PART III

WHAT, IF NOT PAKISTAN.

Having stated the Muslim case for Pakistan and the Hindu case against it, it is necessary to turn to the alternatives to Pakistan, if there be any. In forming one's judgement on Pakistan, one must take into account the alternatives to it. Either there is no alternative to Pakistan : or there is an alternative to Pakistan, but it is worse than Pakistan. Thirdly, one must also take into consideration what would be the consequences, if neither Pakistan nor its alternative is found acceptable to the parties concerned. The relevant data having a bearing on these points is presented in this part under the following heads :—

(1) Hindu alternative to Pakistan.

(2) Muslim alternative to Pakistan.

(3) Lessons from abroad.

CHAPTER VII

HINDU ALTERNATIVE TO PAKISTAN.

Thinking of the Hindu alternative to Pakistan, the scheme that at once comes to one's mind is the one put forth by the late Lala Hardyal in 1925 It was published in the form of a statement which appeared in the *Pratap* of Lahore.   In this statement, which he called his political testament, Lala Hardyal said :—*

" I declare that the future of the Hindu race, of Hindustan and of the Punjab, rests on these four pillars . (1) Hindu Sangathan, (2) Hindu Raj, (3) Shuddhi of Moslems, and (4) Conquest and Shuddhi of Afghanistan and the frontiers.   So long as the Hindu nation does not accomplish these four things, the safety of our children and great-grand-children will be ever in danger, and the safety of the Hindu race will be impossible.   The Hindu race has but one history, and its institutions are homogeneous.   But the Musalmans and Christians are far removed from the confines of Hinduism, for their religions are alien and they love Persian, Arab and European institutions.   Thus, just as one removes foreign matter from the eye, Shuddhi must be made of these two religions. Afghanistan and the hilly regions of the frontier were formerly part of India, but are at present under the domination of Islam ...... Just as there is Hindu religion in Nepal, so there must be Hindu institutions in Afghanistan and the frontier territory ; otherwise it is useless to win Swaraj For, mountain tribes are always warlike and hungry. If they become our enemies, the age of Nadirshah and Zamanshah will begin anew.   At present English officers are protecting the frontiers ; but it cannot always be......If Hindus want to protect themselves, they must conquer Afghanistan and the frontiers and convert all the mountain tribes."

* See *Times of India* dated 25-7-1925, " Through Indian Eyes "

I do not know how many Hindus would come forward to give their support to this scheme of Lala Hardyal as an alternative to Pakistan.

In the first place Hindu Religion is not a proselytising religion. Maulana Mahomed Ali was quite right when, in the course of his address as President of the Congress, he said :—

"Now, this has been my complaint for a long time against Hinduism, and on one occasion, lecturing at Allahabad in 1907. I had pointed out the contrast between Musalmans and Hindus, by saying that the worst that can be said of a Muslim was that he had a tastelessness which he called a dish fit for kings, and wanted all to share it with him, thrusting it down the throats of such as did not relish it and would rather not have it, while his Hindu brother who prided himself on his cookery, retired into the privacy of his kitchen and greedily devoured all that he had cooked, without permitting even the shadow of his brother to fall on his food, or sparing even a crumb for him. This was said not altogether in levity ; and in fact, I once asked Mahatma Gandhi to justify this feature of his faith to me."

What answer the Mahatma gave to his question Mr Mahomed Ali did not disclose. The fact however is that however much the Hindus may wish, Hindu religion cannot become a missionary religion like Islam or Christianity   It is not that the Hindu religion was never a missionary religion. On the contrary it was once a missionary religion—indeed must have been a missionary religion, otherwise it is difficult to explain how it could have spread over an area so vast as the Indian continent.* But once a missionary religion the Hindu religion perforce ceased to be a missionary religion after the time when the Hindu society developed its system of castes. For, caste is incompatible with conversion. To be able to convert a stranger to its religion, it is not enough for a community to offer its creed. It must be in a position to admit the convert to its social life and to absorb and assimilate him among its kindred. It is not possible for the Hindu Society to satisfy this prerequisite of effective conversion. There is nothing to prevent a Hindu, with a missionary zeal, to proceed to convert an alien to the Hindu faith.

* On the question whether the Hindu Religion was a missionary Religion and if it was why it ceased to be so, see my essay on *Caste and Conversion* in the Annual Number of the Telgu Samachar for 1926.

But before he converts, he is bound to be confronted with the question ;   What is to be the caste of the convert ?   This is not an easy question to answer.   According to the Hindus, for a person to belong to a caste he must be born in it.   A convert is not born in a caste, therefore he belongs to no caste.   This is also an important question   More than political or religious, man is a social animal.   He may not have, need not have, religion ; he may not have, need not have, politics.   He must have society ; he cannot do without society.   But, for Hindus to be without caste, is to be without society.   And, where there is no society for the covert there can be no conversion.   So long as Hindu society is fragmented in autonomous and autogenic castes, Hindu religion cannot be a missionary religion.   The conversion of the Afghans and the frontier tribes to Hinduism is therefore an idle dream.

In the second place, Lala Hardyal's scheme must call for financial resources the immensity of which it is hardly possible to compute   Who can furnish the funds necessary for the conversion of the Afghans and the frontier tribesmen to Hinduism ?   The Hindus, having ceased to convert others to their faith for a long time, have also lost the zeal for conversion.   Want of zeal is bound to affect the question of finances.   Further, Hindu society being moulded in the cast of the *Chaturvarna* wealth has, from very ancient times, been most unevenly distributed.   It is only the Baniya who is the heir to wealth and property among the Hindus.   There are of course the landlords who are the creation of foreign invaders or native rebels, but they are not as numerous as the Baniya.   The Baniya is money-mad and his pursuits are solely for private gain. He knows no other use of money except to hold it and to transmit it to his descendants. Spread of religion or acquisition and promotion of culture do not interest him.   Even decent living has no place in his budget.   This has been his tradition for ages.   If money is excepted, he is much above the brute in the conception and manner of life.   Only one new service, on the expenditure side, has found a place in his budget.   That service is politics.   This has happened since the entry of Mr. Gandhi as a political leader. That new service is the support of Gandhian politics.   Here again the reason is not love of politics.   The reason is to make private gain out of public affairs. What hope that such men will spend. money on such bootless cause as the spread of Hindu religion among the Afghans and Frontier Tribes ?

Thirdly, there is the question of facilities for conversion that may be available in Afghanistan. Lala Hardyal evidently thought that it is possible to say in Afghanistan, with the same impunity as in Turkey, that the Koran is wrong or that is out of date Only one year before the publication of his political testament by Lala Hardyal i. e. in 1924 one Niamatulla—a follower of Mirza Ghulam Ahamed of Quadiyan — who claimed to be the messiah and Mahdi and a prophet of a sort—was stoned to death* at Kabul by the order of the highest ecclesiastical tribunal of Afghanistan. The crime of this man was as reported by a Khilafat paper, that he was professing and preaching ideas and beliefs inconsistent with Islam and Shariat. This man, says the same paper, was stoned to death according to the agreeing judgements of the first Sharai (cannon) Court, the central Appellate Court and the Ulema and Divines of the final Appellate Committee of the Ministry of Justice. In the light of these difficulties the scheme must be said to be wild in its conception and is sure to prove ruinous in its exccecution. It is adventurous in character and is too fantastic to appeal to any reasonable men except perhaps some fanatical Arya Samajists of the Punjab.

II

The stand taken by the Hindu Mahasabha has been defined by Mr. V. D. Savarkar, the president of the Sabha, in his presidential addresses at the annual sessions of the Sabha As defined by him the Hindu Maha Sabha is against Pakistan and proposes to resist it by all means. What these means are we do not know. It may however be said that force, coercion and resistance are only negative alternatives and only Mr. Savarkar and the Hindu Maha Sabha can say how far these means will succeed.

---

* See Report in Times of India 27-11-24 " Through Indian Eyes "

It would however not be fair to Mr. Savarkar to say that he has only a negative attitude towards the claim put forth by the Muslims of India.   For, he has put forth his positive proposals in reply to them.

To understand his positive proposals, one must grasp some of his basic conceptions.   Mr. Savarkar lays great stress on a proper understanding of the terms, Hinduism, Hindutva and Hindudom He says—*

"In expounding the Ideology of the Hindu movement, it is absolutely necessary to have a correct grasp of the meaning attached to these three terms   From the word "Hindu" has been coined the word "Hinduism" in English.   It means the schools or system of Religion the Hindus follow. The second word "Hindutva" is far more comprehensive and refers not only to the religious aspects of the Hindu people as the word "Hinduism" does but comprehends even their cultural, linguistic, social and political aspects as well.   It is more or less akin to "Hindu Polity" and its nearly exact translation would be "Hinduness".   The third word "Hindudom" means the Hindu people spoken of collectively.   It is a collective name for the Hindu World, just as Islam denotes the Moslem World."

Mr. Savarkar takes it as a gross misrepresentation to say that the Hindu Maha Sabha is a religious body.   In refutation of this misrepresentation Mr Savarkar says —†

"It has come to my notice that a very large section of the English educated Hindus holds back from joining the Hindu Maha Sabha......under the erroneous idea that it is an exclusively Religious organization-something like a Christian Mission. Nothing could be far from truth. The Hindu Maha Sabha is not a Hindu Mission. It leaves Religious questions regarding theism, monotheism, Pantheism or even atheism to be discussed and determined by the different Hindu schools of religious persuations. It is not a Hindu Dharma Maha Sabha,—but a Hindu-National Maha Sabha. Consequently by its very constitution it is debarred to associate itself exclusively as a partisan with any particular religious school or sect even within the Hindu fold. As a national Hindu body it will of course propagate and defend the National Hindu Church comprising each and all religions of Hindusthani origin against any non-Hindu attack or

* Speech at the Calcutta Session of the Hindu Maha Sabha held in December 1939, page 14
† Ibid page 25

encroachment.   But the sphere of its activity is far more comprehensive than that of an exclusively religious body.   The Hindu Maha Sabha indentifies itself with the National life of Hindudom in all its entirety, in all its social, economical, cultural and above all political aspects and is pledged to protect and promote all that contributes to the freedom, strength and glory of the Hindu Nation; and as an indispensable means to that end to attain Purna Swarajya, absolute political Independence of Hindusthan by all legitimate and proper means."

Mr. Savarkar does not admit that the Hindu Maha Sabha is started to counteract the Muslim League and that as soon as the problems arising out of the Communal Award are solved to the satisfaction of both Hindus and Musalmans the Hindu Maha Sabha will vanish   Mr. Savarkar insists that the Hindu Maha Sabha must continue to function even after India becomes politically free. He says :—*

" .... Many a superficial critic seems to fancy that the Maha Sabha was only contrived to serve as a make-weight, as a re-action checkmating the Moslem League or the anti-Hindu policy of the present leaders of the Congress and will be out of court or cease automatically to function as soon as it is shorned of this spurious excuse to exist.   But if the aims and object of the Maha Sabha mean anything it is clear that it was not the outcome of any frothy effusion, any fussy agitation to remove a grievance here or oppose a seasonal party there.   The fact is that every organism whether individual or social which is living and deserves to survive throws out offensive and defensive organs as soon as it is brought to face adversely changing environments.   The Hindu Nation too as soon as it recovered and freed itself from the suffocating grip of the pseudo-Nationalistic ideology of the Congress brand developed a new organ to battle in the struggle for existence under the changed conditions of modern age. This was the Hindu Maha Sabha. It grew up of a fundamental necessity of the National life and not of any ephemeral incident.   The constructive side of its aims and objects make it amply clear that its mission is as abiding as the life of the Nation itself.   But that apart, even the day to day necessity of adapting its policy to the ever changing political currents make it incumbent on Hindudom to have an exclusively Hindu organization independent of any moral or intellectual servility or subservience to any non-Hindu or jointly representative institution, to guard Hindu interest and save them from being

---

* Ibid pages 24—27.

jeopardised. It is not so only under the present political subjection of Hindustan but it will be all the more necessary to have some such exclusively Hindu organization, some such Hindu Maha Sabha in substance whether it is identical with this present organization or otherwise to serve as a watchtower at the gates of Hindudom for at least a couple of centuries to come, even after Hindustan is partially or wholly free and a National Parliament controls its political destiny.

Because, unless something altogether cataclysmic in nature upsets the whole political order of things in the world which practical politics cannot envisage today, all that can be reasonably expected in immediate future is that we Hindus may prevail over England and compel her to recognise India as a self-governing unit with the status contemplated in the West Minster Statute. Now a National Parliament in such a self-governing India can only reflect the electorate as it is, the Hindus and the Moslems as we find them, their relations a bit bettered, perhaps a bit worsened. No realist can be blind to the probability that the extra-territorial designs and the secret urge goading on the Moslems to transform India into a Moslem state may at any time confront the Hindustani state even under self-government either with a Civil War or treacherous overtures to alien invaders by the Moslems. Then again there is every likelihood that there will ever continue at least for a century to come a danger of fanatical riots, the scramble for services, legislative seats, weightages out of proportion to their population on the part of the Moslem minority and consequently a constant danger threatening internal peace. To checkmate this probability which if we are wise we must always keep in view even after Hindustan attains the status of a self-governing country, a powerful and exclusive organization of Hindudom like the Hindu Maha Sabha will always prove a sure and devoted source of strength, a reserve force for the Hindus to fall back upon to voice their grievances more effectively than the joint Parliament can do, to scent danger ahead, to warn the Hindus in time against it and to fight out if needs be any treacherous design to which the joint state itself may unwittingly fall a victim.

The History of Canada, of Palestine, of the movement of the Young Turks will show you that in every state where two or more such conflicting elements as the Hindus and Moslems in India happen to exist as constituents, the wiser of them has to keep its exclusive organization in tact, strong and watchful to defeat any attempt at betrayal or capture of the National State by the opposite party ; especially so if that party has extra-territorial affinities, religious or cultural, with alien bordering states."

17

Having stated what is Hindustan, and what is Hindu Maha Sabha, Mr. Savarkar next proceeds to define his conception of Swaraj. According to Mr. Savarkar—*

" Swaraj to the Hindus must mean only that in which their "Swatva", their "Hindutva" can assert itself without being overloaded by any non-Hindu people, whether they be Indian Territorials or extra-Territorials—some Englishmen are and may continue to be territorially born Indians. Can therefore, the overlordship of these Anglo-Indians be a "Swarajya" to the Hindus ? Aurangajeb or Tipu were hereditary Indians, nay, were the sons of converted Hindu mothers. Did that mean that the rule of Aurang jeb or Tipu was a "Swarajya" to the Hindus ? No ! although they were territorially Indians they proved to be the worst enemies of Hindudom and therefore, a Shivaji, a Gobindsingh, a Pratap or the Peshwas had to fight against the Moslem domination and establish real Hindu Swarajya."

As part of his Swaraj Mr. Savarkar insists upon two things.

First, the retention of the name Hindustan as the proper name for India.†

The name " Hindustan " must continue to be the appellation of our country. Such other names as India, Hind etc. being derived from the same original word Sindhu may be used but only to signify the same sense-the land of the Hindus, a country which is the abode of the Hindu Nation. Aryavarta, Bharat-Bhumi and such other names are of course the ancient and the most cherished epithets of our Mother Land and will continue to appeal to the cultured elite In this insistence that the Mother Land of the Hindus must be called but " Hindusthan, " no encroachment or humiliation is implied in connection with any of our non-Hindu countrymen. Our Parsee and Christian countrymen are already too akin to us culturally and are too patriotic and the Anglo-Indians too sensible to refuse to fall in line with us Hindus on so legitimate a ground. So far as our Moslem countrymen are concerned it is useless to conceal the fact that some of them are already inclined to look upon this molehill also as an insuperable mountain in their way to Hindu-Moslem unity. But they should remember that the Moslems do not dwell only in India nor are the Indian Moslems the only heroic remnats of the Faithful in Islam. China has crores of Moslems, Greece, Palestine and even

* *Ibid* page 18
† *Ibid* pages 19-20

Hungary and Poland have thousands of Moslems amongst their nationals. But being there a minority, only a community, their existence in these countries has never been advanced as a ground to change the ancient names of these countries which indicate the abodes of those races whose overwhelming majority owns the land. The country of the Poles continues to be Poland and of the Greecians as Greece. The Moslems there did not or dared not to distort them but are quite content to distinguish themselves Polish Moslems or Greecian Muslims or Chinese Moslems when occasion arises. So also our Moslem countrymen may distinguish themselves nationally or territorially whenever they want, as "Hindusthanee Moslems" without compromising in the least their separateness as a Religious or Cultural entity. Nay, the Moslems have been calling themselves as "Hindusthanis" ever since their advent in India, of their own accord.

"But if inspite of it all some irascible Moslem sections amongst our countrymen object even to this name of our Country, that is no reason why we should play cowards to our own conscience. We Hindus must not betray or break up the continuity of our Nation from the Sindhus in Rugvedic days to the Hindus of our own generation which is implied in "Hindustan," the accepted appellation of our Mother Land. Just as the land of the Germans is Germany, of the English England, of the Turks Turkisthan, of the Afghans Afghanisthan—even so we must have it indelibly impressed on the map of the earth for all times to come a "Hindustan"—the land of the Hindus.

Second is the retention of Sanskrit as sacred language, Hindi as national language and Nagari as the script of Hindudom.*

The Sanskrit shall be our "देवभाषा," our sacred language and the "Sanskrit Nishtha" Hindi, the Hindi which is derived from Sanskrit and draws its nourishment from the latter, is our "राष्ट्रभाषा" our current national language—besides being the richest and the most cultured of the ancient languages of the world, to us Hindus the Sanskrit is the holiest tongue of tongues. Our scriptures, history, philosophy and culture have their roots so deeply imbedded in the Sanskrit literature that it forms veritably the brain of our Race. Mother of the majority of our mother tongues, she has suckled the rest of them at her breast. All Hindu languages current today whether derived from Sanskrit or grafted on to it can only grow and flourish

---

* *Ibid.*, pages 21, 22, 23.

on the sap of life they imbibe from Sanskrit. The Sanskrit language therefore must ever be an indispensable constituent of the classical course for Hindu youths.

In adopting the Hindi as the National tongue of Hindudom no humiliation or any invidious distinction is implied as regards other provincial tongues. We are all as attached to our provincial tongues as to Hindi and they will all grow and flourish in their respective spheres. In fact some of them are today more progressive and richer in literature. But nevertheless, taken all in all the Hindi can serve the purpose of a National Pan-Hindu Language best. It must also be remembered that the Hindi is not made a National Language to order. The fact is that long before either the English or even the Moslems stepped in India the Hindi in its general form had already come to occupy the position of a National tongue throughout Hindustan. The Hindu pilgrim, the tradesman, the tourist, the soldier, the Pandit travelled up and down from Bengal to Sind and Kashmere to Rameshwar by making himself understood from locality to locality through Hindi. Just as the Sanskrit was the National language of the Hindu intellectual world even so Hindi has been for at least a thousand years in the past the National Indian Tongue of the Hindu communality.........

By Hindi we of course mean the pure "Sanskrit Nistha" Hindi, as we find it for example in the "Satyartha Prakash" written by Maharsi Dayanand Saraswati How simple and untainted with a single unnecessary foreign word is that Hindi and how expressive withal ! It may be mentioned in passing that Swami Dayanandji was about the first Hindu leader who gave conscious and definite expression to the view that Hindi should be the Pan-Hindu National language of India. "This Sanskrit Nistha" Hindi has nothing to do with that hybrid, the so-called Hindusthani which is being hatched up by the Wardha scheme. It is nothing short of a linguistic monstrosity and must be ruthlessly suppressed. Not only that but it is our bounden duty to oust out as ruthlessly all unnecessory alien words whether Arabian or English, from every Hindu tongue—whether provincial or dilectical ....

" ...... Our Sanskrit alphabetical order is phonetically about the most perfect which the world has yet devised and almost all our current Indian scripts already follow it. The Nagari Script too follows this order. Like the Hindi language the Nagari Script too has already been current for centuries all over India amongst the Hindu literary circles for some two thousands years at any rate in the past and was even popularly nick-named as the "Shastri Lipi" the script of our Hindu Scriptures......It is a matter of common knowledge that if Bengali or Gujarathi is printed in Nagari it is more or less understood by readers in several other provinces. To have only one common language throughout Hindustan at a stroke is impracticable and unwise. But to have the Nagari script as the only common script throughout Hindudom is much more feasible. Nevertheless, it should be borne in mind that the different Hindu scripts current in our different provinces have a future of their own and may flourish side by side with the Nagari. All that is immediately done indispensable in the common interest of Hindudom as a whole is that the Nagari Script must be made a compulsary subject along with the Hindi language in every school in the case of Hindu students."

What is to be the position of the Non-Hindu minorites under the Swaraj as contemplated by Mr. Savarkar? On this question this is what Mr. Savarkar has to say :—*

"When once the Hindu Maha Sabha not only accepts but maintains the principles of " one man one vote " and the public services to go by merit alone added to the fundamental rights and obligations to be shared by all citizens alike irrespective of any distinction of Race or Religion...... any further mention of minority rights is on principle not only unnecessary but self-contradictory. Because it again introduces a consciousness of majority and minority on Communal basis. But as practical politics requires it and as the Hindu Sanghatanists want to relieve our non-Hindu country-men of even a ghost of suspicion, we are prepared to emphasise that the legitimate rights of minorities with regard to their Religion, Culture, and Language will be expressly guaranteed : on one condition only that the equal rights of the majority also must not in any case be encroached upon or abrogated. Every minority may have seperate schools to train up their children in their own tongue, their own religious or cultural institutions and can receive Government help also for these,—but always in proportion to the taxes they pay into the common exchequer. The same principle must of course hold good in case of the majority too.

Over and above this, in case the constitution is not based on joint electorates and on the unalloyed National principle of one man one vote, but is based on the communal basis then those minorities who wish to have seperate electorate or reserve seats will be allowed

---

* *Ibid* page 4.

to have them,—but always in proportion to their population and provided that it does not deprive the majority also of an equal right in proportion to its population too.

That being the position assigned to the minorities Mr. Savarkar concludes* that under his scheme of Swaraj—

    " .... The Moslem minority in India will have the right to be treated as equal citizens, enjoying equal protection and civic rights in proportion to their population. The Hindu majority will not encroach on the legitimate rights of any non-Hindu minority. But in no case can the Hindu majority resign its right which as a majority it is entitled to exercise under any Democratic and legitimate constitution. The Moslem minority in particular has not obliged the Hindus by remaining in minority and therefore, they must remain satisfied with the status they occupy and with the legitimate share of civic and political rights that is their proportionate due. It would be simply preposterous to endow the Moslem minority with the right of exercising a practical veto on the legitimate rights and previleges of the majority and call it a "Swarajya". The Hindus do not want a change of masters, are not going to struggle and fight and die only to replace an Edward by an Aurangajeb simply because the latter happens to be born within Indian borders, but they want henceforth to be masters themselves in their own house, in their own Land."

And it is because he wants his Swaraj to bear the stamp of being a Hindu Raj that Mr. Savarkar wants that India should have the appellation of Hindustan.

This structure has been reared by Mr. Savarkar on two propositions which he regards as fundamental.

First is that the Hindus are a nation by themselves. He enunciates this proposition with great elaboration and vehemance. Says† Mr. Savarkar .—

    "In my Presidential speech at Nagpur I had, for the first time in the history of our recent politics pointed out in bold relief that the whole Congress ideology was vitiated *ab initio* by its unwitted assumption that the territorial unity, a common habitat, was the only factor that constituted and ought to and must constitute

---

*Ibid page 16.
†Ibid pages 14-17.

a Nation. This conception of a Territorial Nationality has since then received a rude shock in Europe itself from which it was imported wholesale to India and the present War has justified my assertion by exploding the myth altogether. All Nations carved out to order on the Territorial design without any other common bond to mould each of them into a national being have gone to lack and ruin, tumbled down like a house of cards. Poland and Czechoslovakia will ever serve as a stern warning against any such efforts to frame heterogeneous peoples into such hot-potch Nations, based only on the shifting sands of the conception of Territorial Nationality, not cemented by any Cultural, Racial or Historical affinities and consequently having no common will to incorporate themselves into a Nation. These treaty-Nations broke up at the first opportunity they got · German part of them went over to Germany, the Russian to Russia, Czechs to Czechs, and Poles to Poles. The cultural, linguistic, historical and such other organic affinities proved stronger than the territorial one. Only those Nations have persisted in maintaining their National unity and identity during the last three to four centuries in Europe which had developed Racial, Linguistic, Cultural and such other organic affinities in addition to their Territorial unity or even at times inspite of it and consequently willed to be homogeneous National units— such as England, France, Germany, Italy, Portugal etc.

Judged by any and all of these tests which go severally and collectively to form such an homogeneous and organic Nation, in India we Hindus are marked out as an abiding Nation by ourselves. Not only we own a common Father Land, a Territorial unity, but what is scarcely found anywhere else in the world we have a common Holy Land which is identified with our common Father Land. This Bharat Bhumi, this Hindustan, India is both our पितृभू and पुण्यभू. Our patriotism therefore is doubly sure. Then we have common affinities Cultural, Religious, Historical, Linguistic, and Racial which through the process of countless centuries of association, and assimilation moulded us into a homogeneous and organic Nation and above all induced a will to lead a corporate and common National Life. The Hindus are no treaty Nation—but an organic National Being.

On more pertinent point must be met as it often misleads our Congresssite Hindu brethern in particular. The homogeneity that wellds a people into a National Being does not only imply the total absence of all internal differences, Religious, Racial or Linguistic of sects and sections amongst themselves. It only means that they differ more from other people as a National unit than they differ

amongst themselves.   Even the most unitarian Nations of today—say
the British or the French cannot be free from any religious, linguistic,
cultural, racial or other differences, sects or sections or even some
antipathies existing amongst themselves.   National homogeneity
connotes oneness of a people in relation to the contrast they present
to any other people as a whole.

We Hindus, inspite of thousand and one differences within our fold
are bound by such religious, cultural, historical, racial, linguistic and
other affinities in common as to stand out as a definitely homogeneous,
people as soon as we are placed in contrast with any other non-Hindu
people—say the English or Japanese or even the Indian Moslems.
That is the reason why today we the Hindus from Kashmere to
Madras and Sindh to Assam will to be a Nation by ourselves".........

The second proposition on which Mr Savarkar has built up his
scheme relates to the definition of the term Hindu.   According to
Mr. Savarkar a Hindu is a person :—

"... who regards and owns this Bharat Bhumi, this land from the
Indus to the Seas, as his Father Land as well as his Holy Land;—
i.e., the land of the origin of his religion, the cradle of his Faith.

The followers therefore of Vaidicism, Sanatanism, Jainism.
Buddhism, Lingaitism, Shikhism, the Arya Samaj, the Brahmosamaj,
the Devasamaj, the Prarthana Samaj and such other religions of Indian
origin are Hindus and constitute Hindudom, i.e., Hindu people
as a whole.

Consequently the so-called aboriginal or hill-tribes also are Hindus :
because India is their Father Land as well as their Holy Land of
whatever form of Religion or worship they follow.

This definition therefore, should be recongnized by the Government
and made the test of Hindutva in enumerating the population of
Hindus in the Government census to come.   The definition rendered
in Sanskrit stands thus :—

$$\text{॥ आसिंधु सिंधु पर्यंता यस्य भारत भूमिका ॥}$$
$$\text{॥ पितृभू : पुण्यभूश्चैव स वै हिंदुरितिस्मृतः ॥ १ ॥}$$

This definition of the term Hindu has been framed with great
care and caution.   It is designed to serve two purposes which
Mr. Savarkar has in view.   Firstly, to exclude from it Muslims,
Christians, Parsis and Jews by introducing the recognition of India

as a holy land in the qualifications required for being a Hindu. Secondly to include Bhuddists, Jains, Sikhs, etc. by not insisting upon belief in the sanctity of the Vedas as an element in the qualifications.

Such is the alternative of Mr. Savarkar and the Hindu Maha Sabha. As must have been noticed, the scheme has some most important features.

One is, the categorical assertion that the Hindus are a nation by themselves. This of course means that the Muslims are a separate nation by themselves. That this is his view Mr. Savarkar does not leave it to be inferred. He insists upon it in no uncertain terms and with the most absolute emphasis he is capable of. Speaking at the Hindu Maha Sabha Session held at Ahmedabad in 1937, Mr. Savarkar said—

"Several infantile politicians commit the serious mistake in supposing that India is already welded into a harmonious nation, or that it could be welded thus for the mere wish to do so. These our well-meaning but unthinking friends take their dreams for realistics. That is why they are impatient of communal tangles and attribute them to communal organizations. But the solid fact is that the so-called communal questions are but a legacy handed down to us by centuries of a cultural, religious and national antagonism between the Hindus and the Muslims. When time is ripe you can solve them; but you cannot suppress them by merely refusing recognition of them. It is safer to diagnose and treat deep-seated disease than to ignore it. Let us bravely face unpleasant facts as they are. India cannot be assumed today to be an unitarian and homogeneous nation, but on the contrary these are two nations in the main, the Hindus and Muslims in India."

Strange as it may appear Mr. Savarkar and Mr. Jinnah instead of being opposed to each other on the one nation *versus* two nations issue are in complete agreement about it. Both agree, not only agree but insist that there are two nations in India—one the Muslim nation and the other the Hindu nation. They differ only as the terms and conditions on which the two nations should live.

18

Mr. Jinnah says that India should be cut up into two, Pakistan and Hindustan, the Muslim nation to occupy Pakistan and the Hindu nation to occupy Hindustan. Mr. Savarkar on the other hand insists that, although there are two nations in India, India shall not be divided into two parts, one for Muslims and the other for the Hindus; that the two nations shall dwell in one country and shall live under the mantle of one single constitution; that the constitution shall be such that the Hindu nation will be enabled to occupy a predominant position that is due to it and the Muslim nation made to live in the position of subordinate co-operation with the Hindu nation. In the struggle for political power between the two nations the rule of the game, which Mr. Savarkar prescribes, is to be one man one vote, be the man Hindu or Muslim. In his scheme a Muslim is to have no advantage which a Hindu does not have. Minority is to be no justification for privilege and majority is to be no ground for penalty. The state will guarantee Muslim Religion and Muslim Culture. But the state will not guarantee the Muslims any defined measure of political power in the form of secured seats in the Legislature or in the Administration and if such guarantee is insisted upon by the Muslims* such guaranteed quota is not to exceed there proportion to the general population. Thus, Mr. Savarkar would even strip the Muslim nation of all the political privileges it has secured so far by confiscating their weightages.

This alternative of Mr. Savarkar to Pakistan has, about it, a frankness, boldness and definiteness which distinguishes it from the irritating vagueness and indefiniteness which characterizes the Congress declarations about minority rights. Mr. Savarkar's scheme has at least the merit of telling the Muslims, thus far, and no further. The Muslims know where they are with regard to the Hindu Maha Sabha. On the other hand, with the Congress the Musalmans find themselves nowhere because the Congress has been treating the Muslims and the minority question as a game in diplomacy if not in duplicity.

At the same time it must be said that Mr. Savarkar's attitude is illogical if not queer. Mr. Savarkar admits that the Muslims are a separate nation. He concedes that they have a right to cultural

* It should be noted that Mr Savarkar is not opposed to separate electorates for the Muslims. It is not clear whether he is in favour of separate electorates for Muslims even where they are in a majority.

autonomy.   He allows them to have a national flag.   Yet the opposes the demand of the Muslim nation for a separate national home.   If he claims a national home for the Hindu nation how can he refuses the claim of the Muslim nation for a national home ?

If would not have been a matter of much concern if inconsistency was the only fault of Mr. Savarkar.   But Mr. Savarkar in advocating his scheme is really creating a most dangerous situation for safety and security of India.   History records two ways as being open to a major nation to deal with a minor nation when they are citizens of the same country and are subject to the same constitution   One way is to destroy the nationality of the minor nation and to assimilate it and absorb it into the major nation, so as to make one nation out of two   This is done by denying to the minor nation any right to language, religion or culture and by seeking to enforce upon it the language, religion and culture of the major nation.   The other way is to divide the country and to allow the minor nation a separate, autonomous and sovereign existence, independent of the major nation.   Both these ways were tried in Austria and Turkey, the second after the failure of the first.

Mr Savarkar adopts neither of these two ways.   He does not propose to suppress the Muslim nation.   On the contrary he is nursing and feeding it by allowing it to retain its religion, language and culture, elements which go to sustain the soul of a nation.   At the same time he does not consent to divide the country so as to allow the two nations to become separate, autonomous states each sovereign in its own territory.   He wants the Hindus and Muslims to live as two separate nations in one country, each maintaining its own religion, language and culture. One can understand and even appreciate the wisdom of the theory of suppression of the minor nation by the major nation because the ultimate aim is to bring about one nation.   But one can not follow the advantage of the theory which says that there must ever be two nations but that there shall be no divorce between them.   One can justify this attitude only if the two nations were to live in friendly intercourse as equal partners with mutual respect and accord.   But that is not to be, because Mr. Savarkar will not allow the Muslim nation to be coequal in authority with the Hindu nation.   He wants the Hindu nation to be the dominant nation and the Muslim nation to be the servient nation. Why should Mr. Savarkar, after sowing this seed of enmity between the Hindu nation and the Muslim nation, want that they should live under one constitution and occupy one country, it is difficult to explain.

One cannot give Mr. Savarkar the credit for having found a new way. What is difficult to understand is that he should believe that his way is the right way. Mr. Savarkar has taken old Austria and old Turkey as his model and pattern for his scheme of Swaraj. He sees that in Austria and Turkey there lived one major nation *juxta posed* to other minor nations bound by one constitution with the major nation dominating the minor nations and argues that if this was possible in Austria and Turkey, why should it not be possible for Hindus to do the same in India.

That Mr. Savarkar should have taken old Austria and old Turkey as his models to build upon is really very strange. Mr. Savarkar does not seem to be aware of the fact that old Austria and old Turkey are no more. Much less does he seem to know the forces which have blown up old Austria and old Turkey to bits. If Mr. Savarkar instead of studying the past—of which he is very fond and very proud—were to devote more attention to the present he would have learnt that old Austria and old Turkey came to ruination for insisting upon maintaining the very scheme of things which Mr. Savarkar has been advising his " Hindudom " to adopt namely, to establish a Swaraj in which there will be two nations under the mantle of one single constitution in which the major nation will be allowed to hold the minor nation in subordination to itself.

The history of the disruption of Austria, Czechoslovakia, and Turkey is of the utmost importance to India and the members of the Hindu Maha Sabha will do well to peruse the same I need say nothing here about it because I have collected the lessons to be drawn from their fateful history in another chapter. Suffice it to say that the scheme of Swaraj formulated by Mr. Savarkar will give the Hindus an empire over the Muslims and thereby satisfy their vanity and their pride in being an imperial race. But it can never ensure a stable and peaceful future for the Hindus, for the simple reason that the Muslims will never yield willing obedience to so dreadful an alternative.

III

Mr. Savarkar is quite unconcerned about the Muslim reaction to his scheme. He formulates his scheme and throws it in the face of the Muslims with the covering letter 'take it or leave it'. He is not perturbed by the Muslim refusal to join in the struggle for Swaraj. He is quite conscious of the strength of the Hindus and the Hindu Maha Sabha and proposes to carry on the struggle in the confident hope that alone and unaided the Hindus will be able to wrest Swaraj. Mr. Savarkar is quite prepared to say to the Musalmans -

"If you come, with you, if you don't, without you ; and if you oppose, inspite of you—the Hindus will continue to fight for their national freedom as best as they can."

Not so Mr. Gandhi. At the very commencement of his career as a political leader of India when Mr. Gandhi startled the people of India by his promise to win Swaraj within six months Mr. Gandhi said that he can perform the miracle only if certain conditions were fulfilled. One of these conditions was the achievement of Hindu-Moslem unity. Mr. Gandhi is never tired of saying that there is no Swaraj without Hindu-Moslem unity. Mr. Gandhi did not merely make this slogan the currency of Indian politics but he has strenuously worked to bring it about. Mr. Gandhi, it may be said, began his career as a political leader of India with the manifesto dated 2nd March 1919 declaring his intention to launch Satyagraha against the Rowlett Act and asking those who desired to join him to sign the Satyagraha pledge. That campaign of Satyagraha was a short-lived campaign and was suspended by Mr. Gandhi on 18th April 1919. As a part of his programme Mr. Gandhi had fixed* the 6th March 1919 to be

* See his Manifesto dated 23rd March 1919.

observed all over India as a day of protest against the Rowlett Act. Mass meetings were to be held on that day and Mr. Gandhi had prescribed that the masses attending the meetings should take a vow in the following terms :—

"With God as witness, we Hindus and Mahomedans declare that we shall behave towards one another as children of the same parents, that we shall have no differences, that the sorrows of each shall be the sorrows of the other and that each shall help the other in removing them. We shall respect each other's religion and religious feelings and shall not stand in the way of our respective religious practices. We shall always refrain from violence to each other in the name of religion."

There was nothing in the campaign of Satyagraha against the Rowlett Act which could have led to any clash between Hindus and Muslims. Yet Mr. Gandhi asked his followers to take the vow. This shows how intent he was from the very beginning upon Hindu-Muslim unity

The Mahomedans started the Khilafat movement in 1919. The objective of the movement was twofold ; to preserve the Khilafat and to maintain the integrity of the Turkish Empire. Both these objectives were insupportable. The Khilafat could not be saved simply because the Turks in whose interest this agitation was carried on did not want the Sultan. They wanted a Republic and it was quite unjustifiable to compel the Turks to keep Turkey a Monarchy when they wanted to convert it into a republic. It was not open to insist upon the integrity of the Turkish Empire because it meant the perpetual subjection of the different nationalities to the Turkish rule and particularly of the Arabs, especially when it was agreed upon all hands that the doctrine of self-determination should be made the basis of the peace settlement.

The movement was started by the Mahomedans. But it was taken up by Mr. Gandhi with a tenacity and faith which must have surprised many Mahomedans themselves. There were many people who doubted the ethical basis of the Khilafat movement and tried to disuade Mr. Gandhi from taking any part in a movement the ethical basis of which was so questionable. But Mr. Gandhi had so completely persuaded himself of the justice of the Khilafat agitation that he refused to yield to their advice. Time and again he argued that the cause was just and it was his duty to join. The position taken up by him may be summed up in his own words.*

"(1) In my opinion, the Turkish claim is not only not immoral and unjust, but it is highly equitable, if only because Turkey wants to retain what is her own. And the Mahomedan manifesto has definitely declared that whatever guarantees may be necessary to be taken for the protection of the non-Muslim and non-Turkish races, should be taken so as to give the Christians theirs and the Arabs their self-government under the Turkish suzerainty;

(2) I do not believe the Turk to be weak, incapable or cruel. He is certainly disorganised and probably without good generalship. The argument of weakness, incapacity and cruelty one often hears quoted in connection with those from whom power is sought to be taken away. About the alleged massacres a proper commission has been asked for, but never granted. And in any case security can be taken against oppression;

(3) I have already stated that, if I were not interested in the Indian Mahomedans, I would not interest myself in the welfare of the Turks any more than I am in that of the Austrians or the Poles. But I am bound as an Indian to share the sufferings and trials of fellow-Indians. If I deem the Mahomedan to be my brother, it is my duty to help him in his hour of peril to the best of my ability, if his cause commends itself to me as just;

(4) The fourth refers to the extent Hindus should join hands with the Mahomedans. It is therefore a matter of feeling and opinion. It is expedient to suffer for my Mahomedan brother to the utmost in a just cause and I should therefore travel with him along the whole road so long as the means employed by him are as honourable as his end. I cannot regulate the Mahomedan feeling. I must accept his statement that the Khilafat is with him a religious question in the sense that it binds him to reach the goal even at the cost of his own life."

Mr. Gadhi not only agreed with the Muslims in the Khilafat cause but acted as their guide and their friend. The part played by Mr. Gandhi in the Khilafat agitation and the connection between the Khilafat agitation and the non-co-operation movement has

* Young India 2nd June 1920.

become obscured by the reason of the fact that most people believed that it was the Congress who initiated the non-cooperation and that was initiated for the sake of winning Swaraj. That such a view should prevail is quite understandable because most people content themselves with noting the connection between the non-cooperation movement and the special session of the Congress held at Calcutta on 7th and 8th September 1920. But any one who cares to go behind September 1920 and examine the situation as it then stood will find that this view is not true. The truth is that the Non-cooperation has its origin in the Khilafat agitation and not in the Congress movement for Swaraj. that it was started by the Khilafatists to help Turkey and only adopted by the Congress: that Swaraj was not its primary object, but its primary object was Khilafat and that Swaraj was added as a secondary object, to induce the Hindus to join in it.

The Khilafat movement may be said to have begun on the 27th October 1919 when the day was observed as the Khilafat Day all over India. On the 23rd November 1919 the First Khilafat Conference met at Delhi. It was at this session that the Muslims considered the feasibility of Non-cooperation as a means of compelling the British Government to redress the Khilafat wrong. On the 10th March 1920 Khilafat Conference met at Calcutta and decided upon Non-cooperation as the best weapon to further the object of their agitation.

On the 9th June 1920 the Khilafat Conference met at Allahabad and unanimously reaffirmed their resolve to resort to Non-cooperation and appointed an Executive Committee to enforce and lay down a detailed programme. On 22nd June 1920 the Muslims sent a message to the Viceroy stating that they will start Non-cooperation if the Turkish grievances were not redressed before 1st August 1920. On the 30th June 1920 the Khilafat Committee meeting held at Allahabad resolved to start Non-cooperation, after a month's notice to the Viceroy. Notice was given on the 1st August 1920 and the Non-cooperation commenced on 31st August 1920. This short resume shows that the Non-cooperation was started by the Khilafat Committee and all that the Congress special session at Calcutta did was to adopt what the Khilafat Conference had already done and that too not in the interest of Swaraj but in the interest of helping the Musalmans in furthering the cause of Khilafat.   This is clear from the perusal of the Congress Resolution[*] passed at the special session held at Calcutta.

Although the Non-cooperation movement was launched by the Khilafat Committee and merely adopted by the Congress primarily to help the Khilafat cause the person who suggested it to the Khilafat Committee and who identified himself with the Committee and took the responsibility for giving effect to it and who brought about its adoption by the Congress was Mr. Gandhi.

At the first Khilafat Conference held at Delhi on 23rd November 1919 Mr. Gandhi was present.   Not only Mr. Gandhi was present but it was he who advised the Muslims to adopt Non-co-operation as a method of forcing the British to yield to their demands regarding the Khilafat   The joining of Mr. Gandhi in the Khilafat movement is full of significance.   The Muslims were anxious to secure the support of the Hindus in the cause of Khilafat. At the Conference held on 23rd November 1919 the Muslims had invited the Hindus.   Again on 3rd June 1920 a joint meeting of the Hindus and the Khilafatist Muslims was held at Allahabad.

---

* "In view of the fact that on the Khilafat question both the Indian and Imperial Governments have signally failed in their duty towards the Muslims of India and the Prime Minister has deliberately broken his pledged word given to them, and that it is the duty of every non-Muslim Indian in every legitimate manner to assist his Muslim brother in his attempt to remove the religious calamity that has overtaken him ;

"And in view of the fact that, in the matter of the events of the April of 1919, both the said Governments have grossly neglected or failed to protect the innocent people of the Punjab and punish officers guilty of unsoldierly and barbarous behaviour towards them, and have exonerated Sir Michael O'Dwyer who proved himself directly responsible for most of the official crimes and callous to the sufferings of the people placed under his administration, and that the debate in the House of Lords betrayed a woeful lack of sympathy with the people of India, and systematic terrorism and frightfulness adopted in the Punjab, and that the latest Viceregal pronouncement is proof of entire absence of repentance in the matters of the Khilafat and the Punjab.

"This Congress is of opinion that there can be no contentment in India without redress of the two aforementioned wrongs, and that the only effectual means to vindicate national honour and to prevent a repetition of similar wrongs in future is the establishment of Swarajya.

"This Congress is further of opinion that there is no course left open for the people of India but to approve of and adopt the policy of progressive non-violent Non-co-operation inaugurated by Mahatma Gandhi, until the said wrongs are righted and Swarajya is established."

Mrs. Annie Besant says   "It will be remembered that Mr. Gandhi, in March 1920, had forbidden the mixing up of Non-co-operation in defence of the Khilafat with other questions ; but it was found that the Khilafat was not sufficiently attractive to Hindus", so at the meeting of the All-India Congress Committee held at Benares on May 30 and 31, the Punia Atrocities and the deficiencies of the Reforms Act were added to the provocative causes *The Future of Indian Politics*, page 250.

This meeting was attended among others by Sapru, Motilal Nehru and Annie Besant. But the Hindus were hesitant in joining the Muslims. Mr. Gandhi was the only Hindu who joined the Muslims. Not only did he show courage to join them, but also he kept step with them, nay-led them. On 9th June 1920 when the Khilafat Conference met at Allahabad and formed an Executive Committee to prepare a detailed programme of Non-co-operation and give effect to it, Mr. Gandhi was the only Hindu on that Executive Committee. On the 22nd June 1920 the Muslims sent a massage to the Viceroy that they will start Non-Co-operation if the Turkish grievances were not redressed before 1st August 1920 On the same day Mr. Gandhi also sent a letter to the Viceroy explaining the justice of the Khilafat cause, the reasons why he has taken up the cause and the necessity of satisfying the Muslims. Later he went headlong and took the lead out of the hands of the Khilafatists. For instance the notice given to the Viceroy on the 1st August 1920 that Non-co-operation will be started on the 31st August was given by Mr. Gandhi and not by the Khilafatists. Again when Non-co-operation was started by the Khilafatists on the 31st August 1920 Mr. Gandhi was the first to give a concrete shape to it by returning his medal. After inaugurating the Non-co-operation movement as an active member of the Khilafat Committee Mr. Gandhi next directed his energy to the cause of persuading the Congress to adopt Non-co-operation and strengthen the Khilafat movement With that object in view Mr. Gandhi travelled the country between the 31st August and 1st September 1920 in the company of the Ali Brothers who were the founders of the Khilafat movement impressing upon the people the necessity of Non-co-operation. People could notice the disharmony in the tune in this propaganda tour. As the Modern Review pointed out "Reading between the lines of their speeches, it is not difficult to see that with one of them the sad plight of the Khilafat in distant Turkey is the central fact, while with the other the attainment of Swaraj here in India is the object in view." This dichotomy * of interest did not augur well for the

---

* Mr. Gandhi repudiated the suggestion of the Modern Review and regarded it as "cruelest cut". Dealing with the criticism of the Modern Review in his Article in Young India for 20th October 1921 Mr. Gandhi said "I claim that with us both the Khilafat is the central fact, with Maulana Mahomed Ali because it is his religion, with me because, in laying down my life for the Khilafat, I ensure safety of the cow, that is my religion, from the Musalman knife,"

success of the ultimate purpose. None the less Mr. Gandhi succeeded in carrying the Congress with him in support of the Khilafat cause.*

The effect of its taking up the Khilafat cause upon the dimensions of the Congress was tremendous. The Congress was really made great and powerful not by the Hindus but by the Muslims. After this Resolution the Muslims who were outside it trooped in the Congress and the Congress Hindus in turn welcomed them. Swami Shradhanand has recorded† his impressions of the Congress Session which he attended after the Muslims came into it in the following terms :—

" On sitting on the dias (Lucknow Congress platform) the first thing that I noticed, was that the number of Moslem delegates was proportionately fourfold of what it was at Lahore in 1893. The majority of Moslem delegates had donned gold, silver and silk emroidered chogas (flowing robes) over their ordinary course suits of wearing apparel. It was rumoured that these 'chogas' had been put by Hindu moneyed men for Congress Tamasha. Of some 433 Moslem delegates only some 30 had come from outside, the rest belonging to Lucknow City. And of these the majority was admitted free to delegates seats, board and lodging. Sir Syed Ahmad's Anti-Congress League had tried in a public meeting to disuade Moslems from joining the Congress as delegates. As a countermove the Congress people lighted the whole Congress camp some four nights before the session began and advertised that that night would be free. The result was that all the "Chandul Khanas" of Lucknow were emptied and a huge audience of some thirty thousand Hindus and Moslems was addressed from half a dozen platforms. It was then that the Moslem delegates were elected or selected. All this was admitted by the Lucknow Congress organisers to me in private.

"A show was being made of the Moslem delegates. A Moslem delegate gets up to second a resolution in Urdu. He begins : Hozarat, I am a Mahomedan delegate." Some Hindu delegate gets up and calls for three cheers for Mahomedan delegates and the response is so enthusiastic as to be beyond description."

---

* The Resolution of Non-co-operation was carried by 1886 votes against 884. The late Mr. Tairsee once told me that a large majority of the delegates were no others than the taxi drivers of Calcutta who were paid to vote for the Non co-operation resolution.

† Liberator, 22nd April 1926.

For this hilarious if ephemeral unity credit must of course go to. Mr. Gandhi.

When the Musalmans in 1919 approached the Hindus for participation in the Non-co-operation movement which the Muslims desired to start for helping Turkey and the Khilafat the Hindus were found to be divided in three camps. One was a camp of those who were opposed to non-co-peration in principle. A second camp consisted of those Hindus who were prepared to join the Muslims in their campaign of non-co-operation provided the Musalmans agreed to give up Cow Slaughter. A third group consisted of Hindus who feared that the non-co-operation of the Mahomedans might be extended by them to inviting the Afghans to invade India in which case the movement instead of resulting in Swaraj might result in the subjection of India to Muslim Raj.

Mr. Gandhi did not care for those Hindus who were opposed to joining the Muslims in the Non-co-operation movement. But with regard to the others he told them that their attitude was unfortunate. To those Hindus who wanted to give their support on the condition that the Muslims give up cow killing Mr. Gandhi said :—*

" I submit that the Hindus may not open the Goraksha question here. The test of friendship is assistance in adversity, and that too, unconditional assistance. Co-operation that needs consideration is a commercial contract and not friendship. Conditional co-operation is like adulterated cement which does not bind. It is the duty of the Hindus, if they see the justice of the Mahomedan cause, to render co-operation. If the Mahomedans feel themselves bound in honour to spare the Hindus' feelings and to stop cow-killing, they may do so, no matter whether the Hindus co-cperate with them or not. Though therefore, I yield to no Hindu in my worship of the cow, I do not want to make the stopping of cow-killing a condition precedent to co-operation. Uncondititional co-operation means the protection of the cow. "

To those Hindus who feared to join the non-co-operation movement for the reasons that Muslims may invite the Afghans to invade India Mr. Gandhi said :—†

" It is easy enough to understand and justify the Hindu caution. It is difficult to resist the Mahomedan position. In my opinion, the

---
* Young India, 10th December 1919.
† Young India, 9th June 1920.

best way to prevent India from becoming the battle ground between the forces of Islam and those of the English is for Hindus to make Non-co-operation a complete and immediate success, and I have little doubt that, if the Mahomedans remain true to their declared intention and are able to exercise self-restraint and make sacrifices, the Hindus will "play the game" and join them in the campaign of Non-co-operation. I feel equally certain that Hindus will not assist Mahomedans in promoting or bringing about an armed conflict between the British Government and their allies, and Afghanistan. British forces are too well organised to admit of any successful invasion of the Indian frontier. The only way, therefore, the Mahomedans can carry on an effective struggle on behalf of the honour of Islam is to take up Non-co-operation in real earnest. It will not only be completely effective if it is adopted by the people on an extensive scale, but it will also provide full scope for individual conscience. If I cannot bear an injustice done by an individual or a corporation and I am directy or indirecty instrumental in upholding that individual or corporation, I must answer for it before my Maker; but I have done all that is humanly possible for me to do consistently with the moral code that refuses to injure even the wrong-doers, if I cease to support the injustice in the manner described above. In applying therefore such a great force, there should be no haste, there should be no temper shown. Non-co-operation must be and remain absolutely a voluntary effort. The whole thing, then, depends upon Mahomedans themselves. If they will but help themselves, Hindu help will come and the Government, great and mightly though it is, will have to bend before this irresistible force. No Government can possibly withstand the bloodless opposition of a whole nation."

Unfortunately the hope of Mr. Gandhi that 'no Government can possibly withstand the bloodless opposition of a whole nation' did not come true. Within a year of the starting of the Non-co-operation movement Mr. Gandhi had to admit* that the Musalmans had grown impatient and that—

"In their impatient anger, the Musalmans ask for more energetic and more prompt action by the Congress and Khilafat organisations. To the Musalmans, Swaraj means, as it must mean, India's ability to deal effectively with the Khilafat question. The Musalmans therefore decline to wait if the attainment of Swaraj means indefinite delay or a programme that may require the Musalmans of India to become impotent witnesses of the extinction of Turkey in European waters.

It is impossible not to sympathise with this attitude. I would gladly recommend immediate action if I could think of any effective course. I would gladly ask for postponement of Swaraj activity if thereby we could advance the interest of the Khilafat. I could gladly take up measures outside Non-co-operation, if I could think of any in order to assuage the pain caused to the millions of the Musalmans.

But, in my humble opinion, attainment of Swaraj is the quickest method of righting the Khilafat wrong. Hence it is that for me that the solution of the Khilafat question is attainment of Swaraj and *Vice Versa*. The only way to help the afflicted Turks is for India to generate sufficient power to be able to assert herself. If she cannot develop that power in time, there is no way out for India and she must resign herself to the inevitable. What can a paralytic do to stretch forth a helping hand to a neighbour but to try to cure himself of his paralysis ? Mere ignorant, thoughtless and angry outburst of violence may give vent to pent-up rage but can bring no relief to Turkey".

The Musalmans were not in a mood to listen to the advice of Mr. Gandhi. They refused to worship the principle of non-violence. They were not prepared to wait for Swaraj. They were in a hurry to find the most expeditious means of helping Turkey and saving the Khilafat. And the Muslims in their impatience did exactly what the Hindus feared they would do, namely-invite the Afghans to invade India How far the Khilafatists had proceeded in their negotiations with the Amir of Afghanistan it is not possible to know. But that such a project was entertained by them is beyond question. It needs no saying that the project of an invasion of India was the most dangerous project and every sane Indian would dissociate himself from so mad a project. What part Mr. Gandhi played in this project it is not possible to discover. But he did not certainly dissociate himself from it. On the contrary his misguided zeal for Swaraj and his obsession on Hindu-Moslem nnity as the only means of achieving it led him to support the project. Not only did he advise* the Amir not to enter into any treaty with the British Government but declared—

" I would, in a sense, certainly assist the Amir of Afghanistan if he waged war against the British Government. That is to say,

* Young India dated 4th May 1921.

I would openly tell my countrymen that it would be a crime to help a government which had lost the confidence of the nation to remain in power ".

Can any sane man go so far for the sake of Hindu-Moslem unity ? But Mr. Gandhi was so attached to Hindu-Moslem unity that he did not stop to enquire what he was really doing in this mad endeavour. So anxious was Mr. Gandhi in laying the foundations of Hindu-Moslem unity well and truly that he did not forget to advise his followers regarding the National Cries. In an Article in Young India of 8th September 1920 Mr. Gandhi said :—

"During the Madras tour, at Bezwada I had occasion to remark upon the national cries and I suggested that it would be better to have cries about ideals than men. I asked the audience to replace Mahtma Gandhi-ki-Jai and Mahomed Ali-Shoukat Ali-ki-Jai by Hindu-Musalman-ki-Jai. Brother Shaukat Ali, who followed, positively laid down the law. In spite of the Hindu-Muslim unity, he had observed that, if Hindus shouted Bande Mataram, the Muslims rang out with Allaho Akbar and *vice versa*. This, he rightly said jarred on the ear and still showed that the people did not act with one mind. There should be therefore only three cries recognised. Allaho Akbar to be joyously sung out by Hindus and Muslims showing that God alone was great and no other. The second should be Bande Mataram (Hail Motherland) or Bharat Mata-ki-Jai (Victory to Mother Hind) The third should be Hindu-Musalman-ki-Jai without which there was no victory for India, and no true demonstration of the greatness of God. I do wish that the newspapers and public men would take up the Maulana's suggestion and lead the people only to use the three cries. They are full of meaning. The first is a prayer and confession of our littleness and therefore a sign of humility. It is a cry in which all Hindus and Muslims should join in reverence and prayerfulness. Hindus may not fight shy of Arabic words, when their meaning is not only totally inoffensive but even ennobling. God is no respecter of any particular tongue. Bande Mataram, apart from its wonderful associations, expresses the one national wish the rise of India to her full height. And I should prefer Bande Mataram to Bharat Mata-ki-Jai, as it would be a graceful recognition of the intellectual and emotional superiority of Bengal. SinceI ndia can be nothing without the union of the Hindu and the Muslim heart, Hindu-Musalman-ki-Jai is a cry which we may never forget.

There should be no discordance in these cries. Immediately some one has taken up any of the three cries, the rest should take it up and not attempt to yell out their favourite. Those who do not wish to join may refrain, but they should consider it a breach of etiquette to interpolate their own when a cry has already been raised. It would be better too, always to follow out the three cries in the order given above."

These are not the only things Mr. Gandhi has done to build up Hindu-Moslem unity. He has never called the Muslims to account even when they have been guilty of gross crimes against Hindus.

It is a notorious fact that many prominent Hindus who had offended the religious susceptibilities of the Muslims either by their writings or by their part in the Shudhi movement have been murdered by some fanatic Musalman. First to suffer was Swami Shradhanand, who was shot by Abdul Rashid on the 23rd December 1926 when he was lying in his sick bed. This was followed by the murder of Lala Nanakchand, a prominent Arya Samajist of Delhi. Rajpal the author of the Rangila Rasool was stabbed by Ilamdin on the 6th April 1929 while he was sitting in his shop. Nathuramal Sharma was murdered by Abdul Qayum in September 1934 who stabbed him to death in the Court of the Judicial Commissioner of Sind where he was seated in Court awaiting the hearing of his appeal against his conviction under Section 195, I. P. C. for the publication of a pamphlet on the history of Islam.

Kanna, the Secretary of the Hindu Sabha was severely assaulted in 1938 by the Mahomedans after the Session of the Hindu Maha Sabha held in Ahmedabad and very narrowly escaped death.

This is of course a very short list and is capable of being expanded. But whether the number of prominent Hindus killed by fanatic Muslims is large or small matters little. What matters is the attitude of those who count towards these murderers. The murderers of course paid the penalty of law where law is enforced. But the leading Moslems never condemned these criminals. On the contrary they were hailed as religious martyrs and agitation was carried on for showing clemency to them. As an illustration of this attitude one may refer to Mr. Barkat Alli, a barrister of Lahore, who argued the appeal of Abdul Qayum. He went to the length of saying that

Qayum was not guilty of murder of Nathuramal because his act was justifiable by the law of the Koran.   This attitude of the Moslems is quite understandable.   What is not understandable is the attitude of Mr. Gandhi.

Mr. Gandhi has been very punctilious in the matter of condemning any and every act of violence and has forced the Congress much against its will to condemn it.   But Mr. Gandhi has never protested against such murders : nor the Muslims have ever been in the habit of condemning.*   Has he ever called upon the leading Muslims to condemn them ?   He has kept silent over them.   Such an attitude can be explained only on the ground that Mr. Gandhi was anxious to preserve Hindu-Moslem unity and did not mind the murders of a few Hindus if it could be achieved by sacrificing their lives.

This attitude to excuse the Muslims any wrong lest it should injure the cause of unity is well illustrated by what Mr. Gandhi had to say in the matter of the Mopla riots.

The blood-curling atrocities committed by the Moplas in Malabar against the Hindus were indescribable.   All over Southern India, a wave of horrified feeling had spread among the Hindus of every shade of opinion, which was intensified when certain Khilafat leaders were so misguided as to pass resolutions of " Congratulations to the Moplas on the brave fight they were conducting for the sake of religion ".   Any person could have said that this was too heavy a price for Hind-Moslem unity.   But Mr. Gandhi was so much obsessed by the necessity of establishing Hindu-Moslem unity that he was prepared to make light of the doings of the Moplas and the Khilafatists who were congratulating them.   He spoke of the Mopalas as the " brave God-fearing Moplas who were fighting for what they consider as religion and in a manner which they consider as religious ".   Speaking of the Muslim silence over the Mopla atrocities Mr. Gandhi told the Hindus :—

" The Hindus must have the courage and the faith to feel that they can protect their religions in spite of such fanatical eruptions. A

---

* It is reported that for earning merit for the soul of Abdur Rashid, the murderer of Swami Shradhanand, in the next world the students and professors of the famous theological college at Deoband finished five complete recitations of the Koran and had planned to finish D. V. a lakh and a quarter recitations of Koranic verses..   Their prayer was " God Almighty may give the marhoom (i.e. Rashid) a place in the 'a' ala-e-illeeyeen (the summit of the seventh heaven)—Times of India, 30-11-27 *Through Indian Eyes* columns.

20

verbal disapproval by the Mussalmans of Mopla madness is no test of Mussalman friendship. The Mussalmans must naturally feel the shame and humiliation of the Moplah conduct about forcible conversions and looting, and they must work away so silently and effectively that such thing might become impossible even on the part of the most fanatical among them. My belief is that the Hindus as a body have received the Mopla madness with equanimity and that the cultured Mussalamans are sincerely sorry of the Mopla's perversion of the teaching of the Prophet ".

The Resolution* passed by the Working Committee of the Congress on the Mopla atrocities shows how careful the Congress was not to hurt the feelings of the Musalmans.

"The Working Committee places on record its sense of deep regret over the deeds of violence done by Moplas in certain areas of Malabar, these deeds being evidence of the fact that there are still people in India who have not understood the message of the Congress and the Central Khilafat Committee, and calls upon every Congress and Khilafat worker to spread the said message of non-violence even under the gravest provocation throughout the length and breadth of India."

"Whilst, however, condemning violence on the part of the Moplas, the Working Committee desires it to be known that the evidence in its possession shows that provocation beyond endurance was given to the Moplas and that the reports published by and on behalf of the Government have given a one-sided and highly exaggerated account of the wrongs done by the Moplas and an understatement of the needless destruction of life resorted to by the Government in the name of peace and order.

"The Working Committee regrets to find that there have been instances of so-called forcible conversion by some fanatics among the Moplas, but warns the public against believing in the Government and inspired versions. The Report before the Committee says :

"The families which have been reported to have been forcibly converted into Mahomedanism lived in the neighbourhood of Manjeri. It is clear that conversions were forced upon Hindus by a fanatic gang which was always opposed to the Khilafat and Non-co-operation movement and there were only three cases so far as our information goes."

---

* The resolution says that there were only three cases of forcible conversion !! In reply to a question in the Central Legislature (Debates 16th January 1922) Sir William Vincent replies "The Madras Government report that the number of forcible conversions probably runs to thousands but that for obvious reasons it will never be possible to obtain anything like an accurate estimate",

The following instances of the silence of Mr. Gandhi over the cases of Muslim intransigence are recorded by Swami Shradhanand in his weekly journal called the ' Liberator '. Writing in the issue of 30th September 1926 about Muslims and Untouchability, the Swamiji said :—

" As regards the removal of untouchability it has been authoritatively ruled several times that it is the duty of Hindus to expatiate for their past sins and non-Hindus should have nothing to do with it. But the Mahomedan and the Christian Congressmen have openly revolted against the dictum of Gandhi at Vaikom and other places. Even such an unbiased leader as Mr. Yakub Hassan, presiding over a meeting called to present address to me at Madras, openly enjoined upon Musalmans the duty of converting all the untouchables in India to Islam."

But Mr. Gandhi said nothing by way of remostrance either to the Muslims or to the Christians.

In his issue of July 1926 the Swami writes :—

" There was another prominent fact to which I drew attention of Mahatma Gandhi. Both of us went together one night to the Khilaphat Conference at Nagpur. The Ayats (verses) of the Quoran recited by the Maulanas on that occasion, contained frequent references to Jihad against, and killing, the Kaffirs. But when I drew his attention to this phase of the Khilafat movement, Mahatmaji smiled and said, "They are alluding to the British Buraucracy." In reply I said that it was all subversive of the idea of nonviolence and when the reversion of feeling came the Mahomedan Maulanas would not refrain from using these verses against the Hindus."

The Swami's third instance relates to the Mopla Riots. Writing in the Liberator of 26th August 1926 the Swami says :—

" The first warning was sounded when the question of condemning the Moplas for their atrocities on Hindus came up in the Subjects Committee. The original resolution condemned the Moplas wholesale for the killing of Hindus and burning of Hindu homes and the forcible conversion to Islam. The Hindu members themselves proposed amendments till it was reduced to condemning only certain individuals who had been guilty of the above crimes. But some of the Moslem leaders could not bear this even. Maulana Fakir and other Maulanas, of course, opposed the resolution and there was no wonder. But I was surprised, an out and out Nationalist like

Maulana Hasrat Mohani opposed the resolution on the ground that the Mopla country no longer remained Dar-ul-Aman but became Dar-ul-Harab and as they suspected the Hindus of collusion with the British enemies of the Moplas. Therefore, the Moplas were right in presenting the Quoran or sword to the Hindus. And if the Hindus became Mussalmans to save themselves from death, it was a voluntary change of faith and not forcible conversion—Well, even the harmless resolution condemning some of the Moplas was not unanimously passed but had to be accepted by a majority of votes only. There were other indications also, showing that the Musalmans considered the Congress to be existing on their sufferance and if there was the least attempt to ignore their idiosyncrasies the superficial unity would be scrapped asunder."

The last one refers to the burning of the foreign cloth started by Mr. Gandhi. Writing in the Liberator of 13th August 1926 the Swamiji says :—

"While people came to the conclusion, that the burning of foreign cloth was a religious duty of Indians and Messrs. Das, Nehru and other topmost leaders made bon-fire of cloth worth thousands, the Khilafat Musalmans got permission from Mahatmaji to *send all foreign cloth for the use* of the Turkish brethren. This again was a great shock to me. While Mahatmaji stood adamant and did not have the least regard for Hindu feelings when a question of principle was involved, for the Moslem dereliction of duty, there was always a soft corner in his heart."

In the history of his efforts to bring about Hindu-Moslem unity mention must be made of two incidents. One is the Fast which Mr. Gandhi underwent in the year 1924. It was a fast of 21 days. Before undertaking the fast Mr. Gandhi explained the reasons for it in a statement from which the following extracts are taken .

" The fact that Hindus and Musalmans, who were only two years ago apparently working together as friends, are now fighting like cats and dogs in some places, shows conclusively that the non-co-operation they offered was not non-violent. I saw the symptoms in Bombay, Chauri Chaura and in a host of minor cases. I did penance then. It had its effects *protants*. But this Hindu-Muslim tension was unthinkable. It became unbearable on hearing of the Kohat tragedy. On the eve of my departure from Sabarmati for Delhi, Sarojini Devi wrote to me that speeches and homilies on peace would not do. I must find out an effective remedy. She was right in saddling the responsibility on me. Had, not been instrumental in bringing into being the vast energy of the people ?   I must find the remedy if the energy proved self-destructive.

I was violently shaken by Amethi, Sambhal and Gulbarga.   I had read the reports about Amethi and Sambhal prepared by Hindu and Musalman friends.   I had learnt the joint finding of Hindu and Musalman friends who went to Gulbarga.   I was writing in deep pain and yet I had no remedy.   The news of Kolhat set the smoulding mass aflame.   Something had got to be done.   I passed two nights in restlessness and pain.   On Wednesday I knew the remedy. I must do penance.

" It is a warning to the Hindus and Mussulmans who have professed to love me.   If they have loved me truly and if I have been deserving of their love, they will do penance with me for the grave sin of denying God in their hearts.

" The penance of Hindus and Mussulmans is not fasting but retracing their steps.   It is true penance for a Mussulmans to harbour no ill-will for his Hindu brother and an equally true penance for a Hindu to harbour none for his Mussulman brother.

" I did not consult friends-not even Hakim Saheb who was closeted with me for a long time on Wednesday-not Maulana Mahomed Ali under whose roof I am enjoying the privilege of hospitality.

" But was it right for me to go through the fast under a Mussulman roof ?   (Gandhi was at the time the guest of Mr. Mahomed Ali at Delhi).   Yes, it was.   The fast is not born out of ill-will against a single soul.   My being under a Mussalman roof ensures it against any such interpretation.   It is in the fitness of things that this fast should be taken up and completed in a Mussalman house.

" And who is Mahomed Ali ?   Only two days before the fast we had a discussion about a private matter in which I told him what was mine was his and what was his was mine.   Let me gratefully tell the public that I have never received warmer or better treatment than under Mohomed Ali's roof.   Every want of mine is anticipated. The dominant thought of every one of his household is to make me and mine happy and comfortable.   Doctors Ansari and Abdur Rehman have constituted themselves my medical advisers.   They

examine me daily. I have had many a happy occasion in my life.
This is no less happy than the previous ones. Bread is not everything. I am experiencing here the richest love. It is more than
bread for me.

"It has been whispered that by going so much with Mussulman
friends, I make myself unfit to know the Hindu mind. The Hindu
mind is myself. Surely I do not live amidst Hindus to know the
Hindu mind when every fibre of my being is Hindu. My Hinduism
must be a very poor thing if it cannot flourish under influences the
most adverse. I know instictively what is necessary for Hinduism
But I must labour to discover the Mussulman mind. The closer I
come to the best of Mussulmans, the juster I am likely to be in my
estimate of the Mussulmans and their doings. I am striving to
become the best cement between the two communities. My longing
is to be able to cement the two with my blood, if necessary. But,
before I can do so, I must prove to the the Mtssalmans that I love
them as well as I love the Hindus My religion teaches me to love
all equally. May God help me to do so ! My fast among other
things is meant to qualify me for achieving that equal and selfless
love. "

The fast produced Unity Conferences. But the Unity
Conferences produced nothing except pious resolutions which were
broken as soon as they were announced

The other incident to be noted is the part Mr. Gandhi played
in the Communal settlement. He offered the Muslims a blank
cheque. The blank cheque only served to exasperate the Muslims
as they interpreted it as an act of evasion. He opposed the separate
electorates at the Round Table Conference. When they were given
to the Muslims by the Communal Award Mr. Gandhi and the
Congress did not approve of it. But when it came to voting upon it
they took the strange attitude of neither approving it nor opposing it.

Such is the history of Mr. Gandhi's efforts to bring about Hindu-
Moslem unity What fruits did these efforts bear ? To be able to
answer this question it is necessary to examine the relationship between
the two communities during 1920—40 the years during which
Mr. Gandhi laboured so hard to bring about Hindu-Moslem Unity.
The relationship is well described in the Annual Reports on the
affairs of India submitted year by year to Parliament by the

Government of India under the old Government of India Act.   It is on these reports* that I have drawn for the facts recorded below.

Beginning with the year 1920 there occurred in that year in Malabar what is known as the Mopla Rebellion.   It was the result of the agitation carried out by two Muslim organizations, the Khuddam-i-Kaba (servants of the Mecca Shrine) and the Central Khilafat Committee.   Agitators actually preached the doctrine that India under the British Government was Dar-ul-Haral and that the Muslims must fight against it and if they could not they must carry out the alternative principle of *Hijrat*   The Moplas were suddenly carried off their feet by this agitation.   The outbreak was essentially a rebellion aginst the British Government.   The aim was to establish the kingdom of Islam by overthrowing the British Government. Knives, swords and spears were secretly manufactured, bands of desperados collected for an attack on the British authority   On August 20th a severe encounter took place between the Moplas and British forces at Pirunangdi.   Roads were blocked, telegraph lines cut, and the railway destroyed in a number of places   As soon as the administration had been paralysed the Moplas declared that Swaraj had been established   A certain Ali Musaliar was proclaimed Raja, Khilafat flags were flown, and Ernad and Walluranad were declared Khilafat Kingdoms.   As a rebellion against British Government it was quite understandable   But what baffled most was the treatment accorded by the Moplas to the Hindus of Malabar.   The Hindus were visited by a dire fate at the hands of the Moplas.   Massacres forcible conversions, descration of temples, foul outrages upon women, such as ripping open pregnant women, pillage, arson and destruction— in short, all the accompaniments of brutal and unrestrained barbarism, were perpetrated freely by the Moplas upon the Hindus until such time as troops could be hurried to the task of restoring order through a difficult and extensive tract of the country   This was not a Hindu-Moslem riot.   This was just a Barthalomeio   The number of Hindus who were killed, wounded or converted is not known.   But the number must have been enormous.

In the year 1921-22 communal jealousies did not subside.   The Muharram Celebrations had been attended by serious riots both in

---

*The series is known as " India in 1920 " & so on.

Bengal and in the Punjab. In the latter province in particular, communal feeling at Multan reached very serious heights, and although the casualty list was comparatively small, a great deal of damage to property was done.

Though the year 1922-23 was a peaceful year the relations between the two communities were strained throughout 1923-24. But in no locality did this tension produce such tragic consequences as in the city of Kohat. The immediate cause of the trouble was the publication and circulation of a pamphlet containing a verulently Anti-Islamic poem. Terrible riots broke out on the 9th and 10th of September 1924, the total casualties being about 155 killed and wounded. House property to the estimated value of Rs. 9 lakhs was destroyed, and a large quantity of goods were looted. In the event, the whole Hindu population evacuated Kohat City. After protracted negotiations, an agreement of reconciliation was concluded between the two communities Government giving an assurance that, subject to certain reservations, the prosecutions pending against persons concerned in rioting should be dropped. With the object of enabling the sufferers to restart their businesses and rebuild their houses, Government sanctioned advances, to be free of interest in certain instances, amounting to Rs. 5 lakhs. But even after settlement had been reached and evacuees had returned to Kohat there was no peace and throughout 1924-25 the tension between the Hindu and Musalman masses in various parts of the country increased to a lamentable extent. In the summer months there was a distressing number of riots. In July severe fighting broke out between Hindus and Musalmans in Delhi, which was accompanied by serious casualties. In the same month there was a bad outbreak at Nagpur. August was even worse. There were riots at Lahore, at Lucknow, at Moradabad, at Bhagalpur and Nagpur in British India ; while a severe affray took place at Gulbarga in the Nizam's Dominions. September-October saw severe fighting at Lucknow, Shahajahanpur, Kankinarah and at Allahabad. The most terrible outbreak of the year being the one that took place at Kohat and which was accompanied by murder, arson and loot.

In 1925-26 the antagonism between Hindus and Muslims became wide spread. Very significant features of the Hindu-Muslim rioting, which took place during this year were its wide distribution and its occurrence, in some cases, in small villages, Calcutta, the United Provinces, the Central Provinces and the Bombay Presidency were all scenes of riots, some of which led to regrettable losses of life. Certain minor and local Hindu festivals, which occurred at the end of August, gave rise to communal trouble in Calcutta, in Berar, in Gujarat in the Bombay Presidency, and in the United Provinces. In some of these places there were actual clashes between the two communities, but elsewhere, notably at Kankinarah—one of the most thickly populated jute mill centres of Calcutta—serious rioting was prevented by the activity of the police. In Gujarat, Hindu-Muslim feeling was running high in these days and was marked by at least one case of temple desecration. The important Hindu festival of Ramlila, at the end of September, gave rise to acute anxiety in many places, and at Aligarh, an important place in the United Provinces, its celebration was marked by one of the worst riots of the year. The riot assumed such dangerous proportions that the police were compelled to fire to restore order, and five persons were killed, either by the police or by rioters. At Lucknow the same festival gave rise at one time to a threatening situation, but the local authorities prevented actual rioting. October saw another serious riot at Sholapur in the Bombay Presidency. There, local Hindus were taking a car with Hindu idols through the city, and when they came near the mosque, a dispute arose between them and certain Muslims, which developed into a riot.

A deplorable rioting started in Calcutta in the beginning of April in an affray outside a mosque between Muslims and some Arya Samajists and continued to spread until April 5th, though there was only one occasion on which the police or military were faced by a crowd which showed determined resistance, namely, on the evening of the 5th April, when fire had to be opened. There was also a great deal of incendiarism and in the first three days of incendiarism Fire Brigade had to deal with 110 fires. An unprecedented feature of the riots was the attacks on temples by Muslims and on Mosques by Hindus which naturally led to intense bitterness. There were 44 deaths and 584 persons were injured. There was a certain amount of looting and business was suspended, with great economic loss to Calcutta.

21

Shops began to reopen soon after the 5th, but the period of tension was prolonged by the approach of a Hindu festival on the 13th of April, and of the Id on the 14th. The Sikhs were to have taken out a procession on the 13th, but Government were unable to give them the necessary license. The apprehensions with regard to the 13th and 14th of April, fortunately, did not materialise and outward peace prevailed until the 22nd April when it was abruptly broken as a result of a petty quarrel in a street which restarted the rioting. Fighting between mobs of the two communities, generally on a small scale, accompanied by isolated assaults and murders continued for six days. During this period there were no attacks on the temples or mosques and there was little arson or looting. But there were more numerous occasions on which the hostile mobs did not immediately disperse on the appearance of the police and on 12 occasions it was necessary to open fire. The total number of casualties during this second phase of the rioting was 66 deaths and 391 injured. The dislocation of business was much more serious during the first riots and the closing of Marwari business houses was not without an effect on European business firms. Panic caused many of the markets to be wholly or partially closed and for two days the meat supply was practically stopped. So great was the panic that the removal of refuse in the disturbed area was stopped Arrangements were, however, made to protect supplies, and the difficulty with the municipal scavengers was overcome as soon as the municipality, had applied to the police for protection. There was a slight extension of the area of rioting but no disturbances occurred in the mill area around Calcutta. Systematic raiding of the portions of the disturbed area, the arrest of hooligans, the seizure of weapons and the reinforcement of the police by the deputation of British soldiers to act as special police officers had the desired effect, and the last three days of April, in spite of the continuance of isolated assaults and murders, witnessed a steady improvement in the situation. Isolated murders were largely attributable to hooligans of both communities and their persistence during the first as well as the second outbreak induced a general belief that these hooligans were hired assassins. Another equally persistent feature of the riots, namely the distribution of inflammatory printed leaflets by both sides' together with the employment of hired roughs, encouraged the belief that money had been spent to keep the fight going.

The year 1926-27 was one continuous period of Communal riots. Since April 1926 every month witnessed affrays more or less serious between partizans of the two communities and only two months passed without actual rioting in the legal sense of the word. The examination of the circumstances of these numerous riots and affrays shows that they originated either in utterly petty and trivial disputes between individuals, as, for example, between a Hindu shopkeeper and a Muhammadan customer, or else the immediate cause of trouble was the celebration of some religious festival or the playing of music by Hindu processionists in the neighbourhood of Muhammadan places of worship One or two of the riots, indeed, were due to nothing more than strained nerves and general excitement. Of these the most striking example occurred in Delhi on June 24th when the bolting of a pony in a crowded street gave the impression that a riot had started, upon which both sides immediately attacked each other with brickbats and staves.

Including the two outbursts of rioting in Calcutta during April and May 1926, 40 riots took place during the twelve months ending with April 1st 1927, resulting in the deaths of 197 persons and in injuries more or less severe to 1,598 others. These disorders were wide-spread, but Bengal, the Punjab, and the United Provinces were the parts of India most seriously affected. Bengal suffered most from rioting, but on many occasions during the year, tension between Hindus and Muhammadans was high in the Bombay. Presidency including its outlying division, Sind. Calcutta remained uneasy throughout the whole of the summer. On June 1st a petty dispute developed into a riot in which forty persons were hurt After this, there was a lull in overt violence until July 15th on which day fell an important Hindu religious festival. During its celebration the passage of a procession with bands playing in the neighbourhood of certain mosques resulted in a conflict in which 14 persons were killed and 116 injured. The next day saw the beginning of the important Muhammadan festival of Mohorrum. Rioting broke out on that day and after a lull, was renewed on the 19th, 20th, 21st and 22nd. Isolated assaults and cases of stabbing occurred on the 23rd, 24th and 25th. The total ascertained casualties during this period of rioting were 28 deaths and 226 injured. There were further riots in Calcutta on the 15th September and 16th October and on the latter day there was also rioting in the adjoining city of Howrah, during which one or two persons were killed and over 30 injured. The April and May riots had been greatly aggravated by incendiarism, but, happily, this feature was almost entirely absent from the later disorders and during the July riots, for example, the Fire Brigade was called upon to deal with only four incendiary fires.

Coming to the year 1927-28 the following facts stare us in the face. Between the beginning of April and the end of September 1927, no fewer than 25 riots were reported. Of these 10 occurred in the United Provinces, six in the Bombay Presidency, to 2 each in the Punjab, the Central Provinces, Bengal, and Bihar and Orissa, and one in Delhi. The majority of these riots occurred during the celebration of a religious festival by one or other of the two communities, whilst some arose out of the playing of music by Hindus in the neighbourhood of mosques or out of the slaughter of cows by Muhammadans. The total casualties resulting from the above disorders were approximately 103 persons killed and 1,084 wounded.

By far the most serious riot reported during the year was that which took place in Lahore between the 4th and 7th of May 1927. Tension between the two communities had been acute for some time before the outbreak, and the trouble when it came was precipitated by a chance collision between a Muhammadan and two Sikhs. The disorder spread with lightning speed and the heavy casualty list—27 killed add 272 injured—was largely swollen by unorganised attacks on individuals. Police and troops were rushed to the scene of rioting and quickly made it impossible for clashes on a big scale to take place between hostile groups Casual assassinations and assaults were reported, however, for two or three days longer before the streets and lanes of Lahore became safe for solitary passersby.

After the Lahore riot in May there was a lull of two months in inter-communal rioting, if we except a minor incident which happened about the middle of June in Bihar and Orissa ; but July witnessed no fewer than eight riots of which the most serious occurred in Multan in the Punjab, on the occasion of the annual Muharram celebrations. Thirteen killed and twenty-four wounded was the toll taken by this riot. But August was to see worse rioting still. In that month, nine riots occurred, two of them resulting in heavy loss of life. In a riot in Bettiah a town in Bihar and Orissa, arising out of a dispute over a religious procession, eleven persons were killed and over a hundred injured, whilst the passage of a procession in front of a mosque in Bareilly in the United Provinces was the occasion of rioting in which fourteen persons were killed and 165 were injured. Fortunately this proved to be the turning point in inter-communal trouble during the year, and September witnessed only 4 riots One of these, however, the riot in Nagpur in the Central Provinces on September 4th, was second only to the Lahore riot in seriousness and in the damage which it occasioned. The spark which started the fire was the trouble in connection with a Muhammadan procession, but the materials for the combustion had been collecting for some time. Nineteen persons were killed and 123 injured were admitted to hospital as a result of this riot, during the course of which many members of the Muhammadan community abandoned their homes in Nagpur.

A feature of Hindu-Muhammadan relations during the year which was hardly less serious than the riots was the number of murderous outrages committed by members of one community against persons belonging to the other. Some of the most serious of these outrages were perpetrated in connection with the agitation relating to *Rangila Rasul* and *Risala Vartman* two publications containing most scurrrilous attack on the Prophet Muhammed and as a result of them, a number of innocent persons lost their lives, sometimes in circumstances of great barbarity. In Lahore a series of outrages against individuals led to a state of great excitement and insecurity during the summer of 1927.

The excitement over the *Rangila Rasul** case had by now travelled far from its original centre and by July had begun to

_____

* *Rangila Rasul* was written in reply to *Sitaka Chmala* a pamphlet written by a Musalman alleging that Sita wife of Rama the hero of Ramayana was a prostitute.

produce unpleasant repercussions on and across the North-West Frontier. The first signs of trouble in this region became apparent early in
June, and by latter part of July the excitement had reached its height .
On the British side of the border, firm and tactful handling of the situation by the local authorities averted any serious breach of the peace.
Economic boycott of Hindus was freely advocated in the British
frontier districts, especially in Peshawar, but this movement met with
little success, and although Hindus were maltreated in one or two
villages, the arrest of the culprits, together with appropriate action
under the Criminal Law, quickly restored order. Across the border
however, the indignation aroused by these attacks on the Prophet
gave rise to more serious consequences. The frontier tribesmen are
acutely sensitive to the appeal of religion and when a well-known
Mullah started to preach against the Hindus among the Afridis and
Shinwaris in the neighbourhood of the Khybar Pass, his words fell
on fruitful ground. He called upon the Afridis and Shinwaris to
expel all Hindus living in their midst unless they declared in
writing that they dissociated themselves from the doings of their
co-religionists down country. The first to expel their Hindu
neighbours were two clans of the Khybar Afridis, namely, the
Kukikhel and Zakkakhel, on the 22nd of July. From these, the
excitement spread among their Shinwari neighbours who gave their
Hindu neighbours notice to quit a few days later. However, after
the departure of some of the Hindus the Shinwaris agreed to allow
the remainder to stay on. Some of the Hindus on leaving the
Khyber were roughly handled. In two cases stones were thrown,
though happily without any damage resulting. In a third affair
a Hindu was wounded and a large amount of property carried off,
but this was recovered by Afridi Khassadars in full, and the culprits
were fined for the offence. Thereafter arrangements were made for
the picketing of the road for the passage of any Hindus evacuating
tribal territory. Under pressure from the Political Agent, an Afridi
jirga decided towards the end of July to suspend the Hindu boycott
pending a decision in the Risala Vartman case. In the following
week, however, several Hindu families, who had been living at
Landi Kotal at the head of the Khyber Pass moved to Peshawar
refusing to accept the assurances of the tribal chiefs but leaving one

person from each family behind to watch over their interests. All told, between four hundred and four hundred and fifty Hindus, men, women and children, had come into Peshwar by the middle of August, when the trouble was definitely on the wane. Some of the Hindus were definitely expelled, some were induced to leave their homes by threats, some left from fear, some no doubt from sympathy with their neighbours. Expulsion and voluntary exodus from tribal territory were alike without parallel. Hindus had lived there for more generations than most of them could record as valued and respected, and, indeed, essential members of the tribal system, for whose protection the tribesmen had been jealous, and whose blood feuds they commonly made their own. In all, about 450 Hindus left the Khyber during the excitement , of thess about 330 had returned to their homes in tribal territory by the close of the year 1927. Most of the remainder had decided to settle, at any rate for the present, amid the more secure conditions of British India.

The year 1928-29 was comparatively more peaceful than the year 1927-28. His Excellency Lord Irwin, by his speeches to the Central Legislature and outside the walls of the latter, had given a strong impetus to the attempts to find some basis for agreement between the two communities on those questions of political importance which are at least contributory causes of the strained relations between them. Again, the issues arising out of the Statutory Commission's enquiry have, to a large extent, absorbed the energy and attention of the different communities, with the result that less importance has been attached to local causes of conflict, and more importance to the broad question of constitutional policy. Moreover, the legislation passed during the autumn session of the Indian Legislature in 1927 penalising the instigation of inter-communal hostility by the press, had some effect in improving the inter-communal position. But the year was not altogether free from Communal disturbances The number of riots during the 12 months ending with March 31st, 1929, was 22. But though the number of riots is comparatively small, unfortunately, the casualties, which were swelled heavily by the Bombay riots, were very serious, no fewer than 204 persons having been killed and

nearly a thousand injured. Of these, the fortnight's rioting in
Bombay accounts for 149 killed and 739 injured Seven of these
22 riots, or roughly one third of them, occurred on the day of the
celebration of the annual Muhammadan festival of *Bakr-i-Id* at the
end of May.   The celebration of this festival is always a dangerous
time in Hindu-Muslim relations because part of the ceremony
consists in animal sacrifice, and when cows are the animals chosen,
the slightest tension between Hindus and Muslims is apt to produce
an explosion   Of the *Bakr-i-Id* riots only two were serious and both
of them took place in the Punjab.   In a village of the Ambala
District ten people were killed and nine injured in a riot, whilst the
other riot referred to here, that which took place in Softa village of
Gurgaon District in the Southern Punjab, attained considerable
notoriety because of its sensational features.   The village of Softa is
about 27 miles south of Delhi, and is inhabited by Muslims.   This
village is surrounded by villages occupied by Hindu cultivators who,
on hearing that the Muslims of Softa intended to sacrifice a cow on
'Id Day' objected to the sacrifice of the particular cow selected on the
ground that it had been accustomed to graze in fields belonging to
the Hindu cultivators.   The dispute over the matter assumed
a threatening aspect and the Superintendent of Police of the district
accordingly went with a small force of police, about 25 men in all,
to try to keep peace.   He took charge of the disputed cow and
locked it up, but his presence did not deter the Hindu cultivators
of a few neighbouring villages from collecting about a thousand
people armed with pitchforks, spears and staves, and going to Softa.
The Superintendent of Police and an Indian Revenue official, who
were present in the village, assured the crowd that the cow, in
connection with which the dispute had arisen would not be sacrificed,
but this did not satisfy the mob which threatened to burn the whole
village if any cow was sacrificed, and also demanded that the cow
should be handed over to them.   The Superintendent of Police
refused to agree to this demand, whereupon the crowd became
violent and began to throw stones at the police and to try to get
round the latter into the village.   The Superintendent of Police
warned the crowd to disperse, but to no effect.   He, therefore,
fired one shot from his revolver as a further warning, but the crowd

still continued to advance and he had to order his party of police to fire. Only one volley was fired at first, but as this did not cause the retreat of the mob two more villages had to be fired before the crowd slowly dispersed, driving off some cattle belonging to the village.

While the police were engaged in this affair a few Hindu cultivators got into Softa at another place and tried to set fire to the village. These were, however, driven away by the police after they had inflicted injuries on three or four men. In all 14 persons were killed and 33 injured in this affair. The Punjab Government deputed a judicial officer to enquire into this affair. His report, which was published on July the 6th, justified the action of the police in firing on the mob and recorded the opinion that there was no reason to suppose that the firing was excessive or was continued after the mob had desisted from its unlawful aggression. Had the police not opened fire, the report proceeds, their own lives would have been in immediate danger, as also would the lives of the people of Softa. Lastly, in the opinion of the officer writing the report, had Softa village been sacked there would certainly have been within 24 hours a communal conflagration of such violence in the surrounding country-side that a very large number of casualties must have been entailed.

The riots of Kharagpur, an important railway centre not far from Calcutta, also resulted in serious loss of life. Two riots took place at Kharagpur, the first on the occasion of the Muharram celebration at the end of June and the second on the 1st September 1928 when the killing of a cow was the signal for trouble to begin. In the first riot 15 were killed and 21 injured, while in the second riot the casualties were 9 killed and 35 wounded. But none of these riots are to be compared with the long outbreak in Bombay from the beginning to the middle of February, when, as we have seen, 149 persons were killed and well over 700 injured.

During the year 1929-30 communal riots, which had been so conspicuous and deplorable a feature of public life during the preceding years, were very much less frequent. Only 12 were of sufficient importance to be reported to the Government of India,

22

and of these only the disturbances in the City of Bombay were really serious.   Starting on the 23rd of April they continued sporadically until the middle of May, and were responsible for 35 deaths and about 200 other casualties.   An event which caused considerable tension in April was the murder at Lahore of Rajpal, whose pamphlet "*Rangila Rasul*", containing a scurrilous attack on the Prophet of Islam, was responsible for much of the communal trouble in previous years, and also for a variety of legal and political complications. Fortunately, both communities showed commendable restraint at the time of the murder, and again on the occasion of the execution and funeral of the convicted man , and although feelings ran high no serious trouble occurred.

Coming to the year 1930-31 there occurred innumerable communal disturbances mostly due to the Muslim opposition to the Civil Disobedience movement started by the Congress in that year. Among the various riots and disturbances the majority of which arose out of events connected with Congress activities were the following   In July, 8th, 9th and 10th, there were disturbances in Rangpur (Bengal), Vellore (Madras), and Lahore , and on the 11th, disturbances occurred in Bombay and Etah (United Provinces). On the 17th, there was a riot in Madura (Madras) and a disturbance in Amroati (Central Provinces); and there were disturbances in Jubbulpore (Central Provinces) and in Calcutta on the 19th On the 23rd a riot occurred in Shikarpur (Sind) and on the following day a disturbance in Ludhiana (Punjab).   In August, there were disturbances in Bombay on the 2nd, in Champaran District (Bihar) on the 12th, in Amritsar on the 14th, in Karachi on the 22nd, and in Kaira District (Bombay) on the 31st.   On the 24th, a party of police was attacked in Betul District (Central Provinces) by Gond tribesmen who had been breaking the Forest Law at the instigation of the Congress.   In September, on the 1st and 2nd, there were disturbances in Khulna District (Bengal) and in Karachi, and on the 4th there was an affray between the police and agriculturists who had been incited by Congress workers to defy the Government in Satara District (Bombay).   A riot occurred in Bulandshahr District (United Provinces) on the 12th, and a disturbance in Raipur (Central Provinces) on the 16th.   On the 25th there was a serious riot near Panvel (Bombay) as a result of incidents not dissimilar to those which provoked the clash with the police in Satara District three weeks previously. A disturbance occurred in Moradabad on the 26th, and there was trouble in Gopinathpore (Bengal) and Raipur (Central Provinces) on the 30th. There was no serious rioting during October, but disturbances occurred near Cawnpore on the 2nd, in Midnapore District (Bengal) on the 3rd, in Roorkee (United Provinces) and near Tamluk (Bengal) on the 4th, in the Bhandara and Seoni Districts of the Central Provinces on the 6th and 10th respectively, in Tippera District (Bengal) on the 17th, near Nasik (Bombay) on the 19th, in Dinajpur District (Bengal) on the 22nd, in Moradabad on the 24th, in Bombay on the 26th, near Chandausi (United Provinces) on the 28th, and in Delhi on the 29th Disturbances also took place in Bombay on the 5th and 7th of November, and there was a riot in the Santal Parganas (Bihar and Orissa) on the 10th/12th. The persistent refusal of the majority of Muslims to participate in the Civil Disobedience caused some increase in communal tension during this period, and several serious Hindu-Muslim riots occurred, of which perhaps the worst were those which took place in and around Sukkur in Sind between the 4th and 11th of August and affected over a hundred villages. The outbreak in the Kishoreganj subdivision of Mymensingh District (Bengal) on the 12th/15th of July was also on a large scale. In addition, there were communal disturbances on the 3rd of August in Ballia (United Provinces), on the 6th of September in Nagpur, and on the 6th/7th September in Bombay; and a Hindu-Christian riot broke out near Tiruchendur (Madras) on the 31st of October. On the 12th of February, in Amritsar, an attempt was made to murder a Hindu cloth merchant who had defied the picketers, and a similar outrage which was perpetrated the day before in Benares had very serious consequences. In this instance the victim was a Muslim trader, and the attack proved fatal ; as a result, since Hindu-Moslem relations throughout most of Northern India were by this time very strained, a serious communal riot broke out and continued for five days, causing great destruction of property and numerous casualties. Among the other communal clashes during this period were the riots at Nilphamari (Bengal) on the 25th of January and at Rawalpindi on the 31st. The relations between Hindus and

Muslims throughout Northern India had markedly deteriorated during the first two months of 1931, and already, in February, there had been serious communal rioting in Benares.   This state of affairs was due chiefly to the increasing exasperation created among Muslims by the paralysis of trade and the general atmosphere of unrest and confusion that resulted from Congress activities.   In addition, the disappointment felt by certain Muslim delegates at the results of the Round Table Conference doubtless indirectly had some effect on the situation, and the increased importance which the Congress seemed to be acquiring as a result of the negotiations with the Government caused   the   community   serious   apprehensions,   in   view   of   the tyrannical and sometimes violent methods the supporters of the Civil Disobedience movement had been adopting in order to enforce their wishes.   The rioting in Benares, had been directly due to the murder of a Muslim trader who had defied the Congress picketers.   During March, the tension between the two communities, in the United Provinces at any rate, greatly increased.   Between the 14th and 16th there was serious rioting in the Mirzapur District, and on the 17th, trouble broke out in Agra and continued till the 20th.   On the 25th, when Congress workers endeavoured to induce Muslim shopkeepers in Cawnpore to close their premises in honour of the memory of Bhagat Singh, the Muslims resisted, and fighting thereupon extended throughout the city with extraordinary rapidity.   For at least two days the situation was altogether out of control, and the loss of life and destruction of property was appalling   This communal riot, which need never have occurred but for the provocative conduct of the adherents of the Congress, was the worst which India has experienced for many years.   The trouble moreover spread from the city to the neighbouring villages, where there were sporadic communal disturbances for several days afterwards.   There was also a communal riot in Dhanbad (Bengal) on the 28th, and in Amritsar District on the 30th ; and in many other parts of the country at this time the relations between members of the two communities were extremly strained.

In Assam the communal riot which occurred at Digboi in Lakhimpur District resulted in the deaths of one Hindu and three Muhammadans.   In Bengal among the very numerous cases of riots that occurred, mention may be made of the incident in Howrah on the 10th June, when the police were attacked by a mob while arresting persons accused of theft ; of three cases in Bakarganj District, when the police were violently assaulted while dischaiging their duties ; of the occurrence in Burdwan on the 9th of September, when a political prisoner who had been arrested on a warrant was forcibly rescued by a large number of villagers ; and of the communal riot which took place in the Asansol division during the Muharram festival.   In Bihar and Orissa there was a certain amount of communal tension during the year, particularly in Saran.   Altogether there were 16 cases of communal rioting and unlawful assembly.   During the Bakri-Id festival a clash occurred in the Bhabua sub-division of Shahabad.   Some 300 Hindus collected in the mistaken belief that a sacrifice of cattle had taken place.   The local officers had succeeded in pacifying them when a mob of about 200 Muhammadans armed with lathis, spears and swords, attacked the Hindus, one of whom subsequently died.   The prompt action of the police and the conciliation committee prevented a spread of the trouble.   The Muharram festival was marked by two small riots in Monghyr, the Hindus being the aggressors on one occasion and the Muhammadans on the other, and affrays also occurred between Muhammadans in Darbhanga and Muzaffarpur District, one man dying of injuries in the latter place.   In the Madras Presidency there were also several riots of a communal nature during the year and the relations between the two communities were in places distinctly strained.   The most serious disturbance of the year occurred at Vellore on the 8th of June, as a result of the passage of a Muhammadan procession with Tazias near a Hindu temple ; so violent was the conflict between members of the two communities that the police were compelled to open fire in order to restore order ; and sporadic fighting continued in the town during the next two or three days.   In Salem town, owing to Hindu-Muslim tension a dispute arose on the 13th of July, as to who had been the victor at a largely attended Hindu-Muslims wrestling match at Shevapet.   Another riot occurred in October at Kitchipalaiyam near Salem town ; the trouble arose from a few Muhammadans disturbing a street game played by some young Hindus.   Hindu-Muslim disturbances also arose in Polikal village, Kurnool District, on the 15th of March, owing to a dispute about the route of a Hindu procession, but the rioters were easily dispersed by a small force of police.   The factious quarrel between the Hindu and Christian Nadars at Pallipathu, in Tinnevelly District, culminated in a riot in which the Christians used a gun.   In the Punjab as regards rioting, there were 907 cases during the year as compared with 813 in 1929   Many of them were of a communal character, and the tension between the two principal communities remained acute in many parts of the Province.   In the United Provinces although communal tension in the Province during 1930 was not nearly so acute as during the first 3 months of 1931, and was for a while overshadowed by the excitement engendered by the Civil Disobedience movement, indications of it were fairly numerous, and the causes of disagreement remained as potent as ever   In Dehra Dun and Bulandshahr there were communal riots of the usual type, and a very serious riot occurred in Ballia City as a result of a dispute concerning the route taken by a Hindu procession, which necessitated firing by the police.   In Muttra, Azamgarh, Mainpuri and several other places riots also occurred.

Passing to the year 1931-32, the progress of constitutional discussions had a definite reaction in that it bred a certain nervous-ness among the Muslim and other minority communities as to their position under a constitution functioning on the majority principle. The first session of the Round Table Conference afforded the first " close-up " of the constitutional future   Until then the ideal of Dominon Status had progressed little beyond a vague and general conception, but the declaration of the Princes at the opening of the Conference had brought responsibility at the Centre, in the form of a federal government, within definite view.   The Muslims therefore felt that it was high time for them to take stock of their position. Within a few months this uneasiness was intensified by the Irwin-Gandhi settlement, which accorded what appeared to be a privileged position to the Congress, and Congress elation and pose of victory over the   Government did not tend to ease Muslim misgivings. Within three weeks of the " pact " occurred the savage communal riots at Cawnpore,   which significantly enough began with the attempts of Congress adherents to force Mahomedan shopkeepers to observe a *hartal* in memory of Bhagat Singh who was executed on 23rd March.   On the 24th March began the plunder of Hindu shops.   On the 25th there was a blaze.   Shops and temples were set fire to and burnt to cinders.   Disorder, arson, loot, murder, spread like wild fire.   Five hundred families abandoned their houses and took shelter in villages.   Dr. Ramchandra was one of the worse sufferers   All members of his family, including his wife and aged parents, were killed and their bodies thrown into gutters.   In the same slaughter Mr. Ganesh Shanker Vidyarthi lost his life.   The Cownpore Riots Inquiry Committee in its Report states that the riot was of unprecedented violence and peculiar atrocity, which spread with unexpected rapidity through the whole city and even beyond it.   Murders, arson and looting were wide-spread for three days, before the rioting was definitely brought under control. Afterwards it subsided gradually.   The loss of life and property was great   The number of verified deaths was 300, but the death roll is known to have been larger and was probably between four and five hundred.   A large number of temples and mosques were desecrated or burnt or destroyed and a very large number of houses were burnt and pillaged.

The year 1932-33 was relatively free from communal agitations and disturbances.   This welcome improvement was doubtless in some measure due to the suppression of lawlessness generally and the removal of uncertainty in regard to the position of Muslims under the new constitution.

But in 1933-34 throughout the country communal tension had been increasing and disorders which occurred not only on the occasion of such festivals as Holi, Id and Muharram, but also many resulting from ordinary incidents of every day life indicated that there had been a deterioration in communal relations since the year began.   Communal riots during Holi occurred at Benares and Cawnpore in the United Provinces, at Lahore in the Punjab, and at Peshawar.   Bakr-i-Id was marked by serious rioting at Ajodhya, in the United Provinces over cow sacrifice, also at Bhagalpore in Bihar and Orissa and at Cannanore in Madras.   A serious riot in the Ghazipur District of the United Provinces also resulted in several deaths.   During April and May there were Hindu-Muslim riots at several places in Bihar and Orissa, in Bengal, in Sind and Delhi, some of them provoked by very trifling incidents, as for instance, the unintentional spitting by a Muslim shopkeeper of Delhi upon a Hindu passer-by. The increase in communal disputes in British India was also reflected in some of the States where similar incidents occurred.

The position with regard to communal unrest during the months from June to October is indicative of little else than the normal deep-seated antagonism which has long existed between the two major communities. June and July months in which no Hindu or Muhammadan festival of importance took place, were comparatively free from riots, though the situation in certain areas of Bihar necessitated the quartering of additional police, and a long drawn-out dispute started in Agra. Muslims of this city objected to the noise of religious ceremonies in certain Hindu private houses which they said disturbed worshippers at prayers in a neighbouring mosque. Before the dispute was settled riots occurred on 20th July and again on 2nd September, in the course of which 4 persons were killed and over 80 injured. In Madras a riot on the 3rd September resulting in one death and injuries to 13 persons, was occasioned by a book published by Hindus containing alleged reflections on the Prophet ; during the same month minor riots occurred in several places in the Punjab and the United Provinces.

In 1934-35 serious trouble arose in Lahore on the 29th June as a result of a dispute between Muslims and Sikhs about a mosque situated within the precincts of a Sikh temple known as the Shahidganj Gurudwara. Trouble had been brewing for some time. Ill-feeling became intensified when the Sikhs started to demolish the mosque despite Muslim protests. The building had been in possession of the Sikhs for 170 years and has been the subject of prolonged litigation, which has confirmed the Sikh right of possession.

On the night of the 29th June a crowd of 3 or 4 thousand Muslims assembled in front of the Gurudwara. A struggle between this crowd and the Sikhs inside the Gurudwara was only averted by the prompt action of the local authorities. They subsequently obtained an undertaking from the Sikhs to refrain from further demolition.   But during the following week, while strenuous efforts were being made to persuade the leaders to reach an amicable settlement, the Sikhs under pressure of extremist influence again set about demolishing the mosque.   This placed the authorities in a most difficult position.   The Sikhs were acting within their legal rights.   Moreover the only effective method of stopping demolition would have been to resort to firing.   As the building was full of Sikhs and was within the precincts of a Sikh place of worship, this would not only have caused much bloodshed but, for religious reasons, would have had serious reactions on the Sikh population throughout the province.   On the other hand, inaction by Government was bound to cause great indignation among the Muslims, for religious reasons also ; and it was expected that this would show itself in sporadic attacks on the Sikhs and perhaps on the forces of Government.

It was hoped that discussions between leaders of the two communities would effect some rapprochment, but mischief-makers inflamed the minds of their co-religionists.   Despite the arrest of the chief offenders, the excitement increased.   The Government's gesture in offering to restore to the Muslims another mosque which they had purchased years ago proved unavailing.   The situation took a further turn for the worse on the 19th July and during the following two days the situation was acutely dangerous.   The central police station was practically besieged by huge crowds, which assumed a most menacing attitude.   Repeated attempts to disperse them without the use of firearms failed and the troops had to fire twice on the 20th July and eight times on the 21.   In all 23 rounds were fired and 12 persons killed.   Casualties, mostly of a minor nature, were numerous amongst the military and police.

As a result of the firing the crowds dispersed and did not re-assemble.   Extra police were brought in from other provinces and the military garrisons were strengthened.   Administrative control was re-established rapidly, but the religious leaders continued to fan the embers of the agitation.   Civil litigation was renewed and certain Muslim organisations framed some extravagant demands.

23

The situation in Lahore continued to cause anxiety up to the close of the year. On the 6th November a Sikh was mortally wounded by a Muslim. Three days later a huge Sikh-Hindu procession was taken out. The organisers appeared anxious to avoid conflict but none-the-less one serious clash occurred. This was followed by further rioting on the next day, but owing to good work by the police and the troops in breaking up the fights quickly, the casualties were small.

On the 19th March 1935 a serious incident occurred at Karachi after the execution of Abdul Quayum a Muslim who had murdered Nathuram at a Hindu alleged to have insulted Islam. Abdul Quayum's body was taken by the District Magistrate, accompanied by a police party, to be handed over to the deceased's family for burial outside the city ; A huge crowd, estimated to be about 25,000 strong, collected at the place of burial. Though the relatives of Abdul Quayum wished to complete the burial at the cemetery, the most violent members of the mob determined to take the body in procession through the city. The local authorities decided to prevent the mob entering, since this would have led to communal rioting. All attempts of the police to stop the procession failed, so a platoon of the Royal Sussex Regiment was brought up. It was forced to open fire at short range to stop the advance of the frenzied mob and to prevent itself from being overwhelmed. Forty seven rounds were fired by which 47 people were killed and 134 injured The arrival of reinforcements prevented further attempts to advance. The wounded were taken to the Civil Hospital and the body of Abdul Quayum was then interred without further trouble.

On 25th August 1935 there was a communal riot at Secunderabad.

In the year 1936 there were four communal riots. On the 14th April there occurred a most terrible riot at Firozabad in the Agra District. A Mahomedan procession was proceeding along the main bazar and it is alleged that bricks were thrown from the roofs of Hindu houses. This enraged the Mahomedans in the procession who set fire to the house of a Hindu Dr. Jivaram and the adjacent temple of Radha Krishna. The inmates of Dr. Jivaram's house perished in the fire in addition to 11 Hindus including 3 children who were burnt to death inside Dr. Jivaram's house. A second Hindu Muslim riot broke out in Poona in the Bombay Presidency on 24th April 1936. On the 27th April there occurred a Hindu-Moslem riot in Jamalpur in the Monghyr District. The fourth Hindu-Moslem riot of the year took place in Bombay on 15th October 1936.

The year 1937 was full of communal disturbances. On the 27th March 1937 there was a Hindu-Moslem riot at Panipat over the Holi procession and 14 persons were killed. On 1st May 1937 there occurred a communal riot in Madras in which 50 persons were injured. The month of May was full of communal riots which took place in C. P. and Punjab. The one that took place in Shikarpur in Sind caused great panic. On 18th June there was a Sikh-Muslim riot in Amritsar It assumed such proportions that British troops had to be called out to maintain order.

The year 1938 was marked by two communal riots one in Allahabad on 26th March and another in Bombay in April.

There were 6 Hindu-Moslem riots in 1939. On 21st January there was a riot at Asansol in which one was killed and 18 injured. It was followed by a riot in Cawnpore on the 11th February in which 42 were killed, 200 injured and 800 arrested. On the 4th March there was a riot at Benares followed by a riot at Cassipore near Calcutta on the 5th of March On 19th June there was again a riot at Cawnpore over the Rathajatra procession. A serious riot occurred on 20th November 1939 at Sukkur in which 21 were killed and 23 injured.

Who can deny that this record of rioting presents a picture which is grim in its results and sombre in its tone ? But being chronological in order the record might fail to give an idea of the havoc these riots have caused in any given province and the paralysis it has brought about in its social and economic life. To give an idea of the paralysis caused by the recurrence of riots in a province I have recast the record of riots for the Province of Bombay. As recast it reads thus :

Leaving aside the Presidency and confining oneself to the City of Bombay there can be no doubt that the record of the city is the blackest. The first Hindu-Moslem riot took place in 1893. This was followed by a long period of communal peace which lasted upto 1929. But the years that have followed have an appalling story to tell. From February 1929 to April 1938 a period of nine years there were no less than 10 communal riots. In 1929 there were two communal riots. In the first, 149 were killed and 739 were injured and it lasted for 36 days. In the second riot 35 were killed, 109 were injured and it continued for 22 days. In 1930 there were two riots. Details as to loss of life and its duration are not available In 1932 there were again two riots. First was a small one. In the second 217 were killed, 2,713 were injured and it went on for 49 days. In 1933 there was one riot, details about which are not available. In 1936 there was one riot in which 94 were killed, 632 were injured and it continued to rage for 65 days. In the riot of 1937, 11 were killed, 85 were injured and it occupied 21 days. The riot of 1938 lasted for $2\frac{1}{2}$ hours only but within that time 12 were killed and a little over 100 were injured. Taking the total period of 9 years and 2 months from February 1929 to April 1938 the Hindus and Muslims of the city of Bombay alone were engaged in a sanguinary warfare for 210 days during which period 550 were killed and 4,500 were wounded. This does not of course take into consideration the loss of property which took place through arson and loot.

V

Such is the record of Hindu-Moslem relationship from 1920 to 1940. Placed side by side with the frantic efforts were made by Mr. Gandhi to bring about Hindu-Moslem unity, the record makes a most painful and heart-rending reading. There would not be much exaggeration to say that it is a record of twenty years of civil war between Hindus and Muslims in India, interrupted by brief intervals of armed peace.

In this civil war men were, of course the principal victims. But women did not altogether escape molestation. It is perhaps not sufficiently known how much women have suffered in this communal hostilities. Data relating to the whole of India is not available. But some data relating to Bengal does exist.

On the 6th September 1932 questions were asked in the old Bengal Legislative Council regarding the abduction of women in the Province of Bengal. In reply, the Government of the day stated that between 1922 to 1927 the total number of women abducted was 568. Of these 101 were unmarried and 467 were married. Asked to state the community to which the abducted women belonged, it was disclosed that out of 101 unmarried women 64 were Hindus, 29 Muslims, 4 Christians and 4 non-descript and that out of 467 married women 331 were Hindus, 122 Muslims, 2 Christians and 12 non-descript. These figures relate to cases which were reported detected. They do not refer to cases which were either not reported or if reported were not detected. Usually, only about 10 p.c. of the cases are reported or detected and 90 p.c. go undetected. Applying this proportion to the facts disclosed by the Bengal Government, it may be said that about 35,000 women were abducted in Bengal during the short period of five years between 1922-27.

The attitude towards women folk is a good index of the friendly or unfriendly attitude between the two communities. As such the case which happened on 27-6-36 in the village of Govindpur in Bengal makes very instructive reading. The following account of it is taken from the opening speech* of the crown counsel when the trial of 40 Mahomedan accused began on the 10th August 1936. According to the prosecution :—

"There lived in Govindpur a Hindu by name Radha Vallabh. He had a son Harendra. There lived also in Govindpur a Muslim woman whose occupation was to sell milk. The local Musalmans of the village suspected that Harendra had illicit relationship with this Muslim milk woman. They resented that a Muslim woman should be in the keeping of a Hindu and they decided to wreck their vengeance on the family of Radha Vallabh for this insult.

---

* From the Report which appeared in the *Savadhan* a Marathi weekly of Nagpur in its issue of 25th August 1936.

A meeting of the Musalmans of Govindpur was convened and Harendra was summoned to attend this meeting. Soon after Harendra went to the meeting cries of Harendra were heard. It was found that Harendra was assaulted and was lying senseless in the field where the meeting was held. The Musalmans of Govindpur were not satisfied with this assault. They informed Radha Vallabh that unless he, his wife and his children embraced Islam the Musalmans will not feel satisfied for the wrong his son had done to them. Radha Vallabh was planing to send away to another place his wife and children. The Musalmans came to know of this plan. Next day when Kusum, the wife of Radha Vallabh, was sweeping the court yard of her house, some Mahomedans came, held down Radha Vallabh and some spirited away Kusum. After having taken her to some distance two Mahomedans by name Laker and Mahazar raped her and removed her ornaments. After some time she came to her senses and ran towards her home Her assailants again pursued her. She succeeded in reaching her home and locking herself in. Her Muslim assailants broke open the door caught hold of her and again carried her away on the road It was suggested by her assailants that she should be again raped on the street. But with the help of another woman by name Rajani, Kusum escaped and took shelter in the house of Rajani While she was in the house of Rajani the Musalmans of Govindpur paraded her husband Radha Vallabh in the streets in complete disgrace Next day the Musalmans kept watch on the roads to and from Govindpur to the Police station to prevent Radha Vallabh and Kusum from giving information of the outrage to the Police."

These acts of barbarism against women, committed without remorse, without shame and without condemnation by their fellow brethren show the depth of the antagonism which divided the two communities. The tempers on each side were the tempers of two warring nations. There was carnage, pillage, sacrilege and outrage of every species, perpetrated by Hindus against Musalmans and by Musalmans against Hindus—more perhaps by Musalmans against Hindus than by Hindus against Musalmans. Cases of arson have occurred in which Musalmans have set fire to the houses of Hindus in which the whole families of Hindus, men, women and children were roasted alive and consumed in the fire, to the great satisfaction of the Muslim spectators. What is ashtonishing is that these cold and deliberate acts of rank cruelty were not regarded as atrocities to be condemned but were treated as legitimate acts of warfare for which no apology was necessary. Enraged by these hostilities, the editor of the *Hindustan*—a Congress Paper—writing in 1926 used the following language to express the painful truth of the utter failure of Mr. Gandhi's efforts to bring about Hindu-Moslem unity. In words of utter dispair the editor said* . —

" There is an immence distance between the India of to-day and India a nation, between an uncouth reality which expresses itself in murder and arson and that fond fiction which is in the imagination of patriotic if self-deceiving men. To talk about Hindu-Moslem unity from a thousand platforms or to give it blazoning headlines is to perpetrate an illusion whose cloudy structure dissolves itself at the exchange of brick-bats and the desecration of tombs and temples. To sing a few pious hymns of peace and good will *a la Naidu*......will not benefit the country The President of the Congress has been improvising on the theme of Hindu-Moslem unity, so dear to her heart, with brilliant variations, which does credit to her genius but leaves the problem untouched. The millions in India can only respond when the unity song is not only on the tongues of the leaders but in the hearts of the millions of their countrymen."

Nothing I could say can so well show the futility of any hope of Hindu-Moslem unity. Hindu-Moslem unity up to now was at least in sight although it was like a mirage. Today it is out of sight and also out of mind. Even Mr. Gandhi has given up what, he perhaps now realizes, is an impossible task.

But there are others who notwithstanding the history of past twenty years believe in the possibility of Hindu-Muslim unity. This belief of theirs seems to rest on two grounds. Firstly, they believe in the efficacy of a Central Government to mould diverse set of peoples into one nation Secondly they feel that the satisfaction of Muslim demands will be a sure means of achieving Hindu-Muslim unity.

It is true that Government is a unifying force and that there are many instances where diverse people have become unified into one homogeneous people by reason of their being subjected to a single government. But the Hindus who are depending upon

---

* Quoted in " Through Indian Eyes " Columns of the Times of India, dated 16-8-26.

Government as a unifying force seem to forget that there are obvious limits to Government acting as a unifying force. The limits to Government working as a unifying force are set by the possibilities of fusion among the people. In a country where race, language and religion do not stand in the way of fusion Government, as a unifying force, is most effective. On the other hand in a country where race, language and religion put an effective bar against fusion Government, as a unifying force, can have no effect. If the diverse peoples in France, England, Italy and Germany became unified nations by reason of a common Government, it is because neither race, language nor religion obstructed the unifying process of Government. On the other hand if the people in Austria, Hungary, Czechoslovakia and Turkey failed to be unified, although under a common government, it is because race, language and religion were effective enough to counter and nullify the unifying effect of Government. No one can deny that race, language and religion have been too dominant in India to permit the people of India to be welded into a nation by the unifying force of a common Government. It is an illusion to say that the Central Government in India has moulded the Indian people into a nation. What the Central Government has done, is to tie them together, by one law and house them together in one place, as the owner of unruly animals does, by tying them in one rope and keeping them in one stable. All that the Central Government has done is to produce a kind of peace among Indians. It has not made them one nation.

It cannot be said that time has been too short for unification to take place. If one hundred and fifty years of life under a Central Government does not suffice, enternity will not suffice. For this failure the genius of the Indians alone is responsible. There is, among Indians no passion for unity, no desire for fusion. There is no desire to have a common dress. There is no desire to have a common language. There is no will to give up what is local and particular for something which is common and national. A Gujarati takes pride in being a Gujarati, a Maharashtriyan in being a Maharashtriyan, a Punjabi in being a Punjabi, a Madrasi in being a Madrasi and a Bengali prides in being a Bengali. Such is the mentality of the Hindus who accuse the Musalman of want of national

feeling when he says that I am a Musalman first and Indian afterwards. Can any one suggest that there exists anywhere in India
even among the Hindus an instinct or a passion that would put any
semblance of emotion behind their declaration " Civis Indianus
sum " or the smallest consciousness of a moral and social unity
which desires to give expression by sacrificing whatever is particular
and local in favour of what is common and unifying ? There is
no such consciousness and no such desire. Without such consciousness and without such desire to depend upon Government to bring
about unification is to deceive oneself.

Regarding the second it was no doubt the opinion of the Simon
Commission :—

"That the Communal riots were a manifestation of the anxieties
and ambitions aroused in both the communities by the prospect of
India's political future. So long as authority was firmly established
in British hands and self-government was not thought of, Hindu-
Moslem rivalry was confined within a narrower field. This was not
merely because the presence of a neutral bureaucracy discouraged
strife. A further reason was that there was little for members of one
community to fear from the predominance of the other. The
comparative absence of communal strife in the Indian States today
may be similarly explained. Many who are well acquainted with
conditions in British India a generation ago would testify that at that
epoch so much good feeling had been engendered between the two
sides that communal tension as a threat to civil peace was at
a minimum But the coming of the Reforms and the anticipation of
what may follow them have given new point to Hindu-Moslem
competition. The one community naturally lays claim to the rights
of a majority and relies upon its qualifications of better education and
greater wealth ; the other is all the more determined on those
accounts to secure effective protection for its members, and does not
forget that it represents the previous conquerors of the country. It
wishes to be assured of adequate representation and of a full share of
official posts."

Assuming that to be a true diagnosis, assuming that Muslim
demands are reasonable, assuming that the Hindus were prepared
to grant them—and these are all very big assumptions—it is a question
wheather a true union between Hindus and Muslims can take place

24

through political unity resulting from the satisfaction of Muslim political demands. Some people seem to think that it is enough if there is a political unity between Hindus and Muslims. I think this is the greatest delusion. Those who take this view seem to be thinking only of how to bring the Muslims to join the Hindus in their demands on the British for Dominion Status or Independence as the mood of the moment be. This, to say the least, is a very shortsighted view. How to make the Muslims join the Hindus in the latter's demands on the British is comparatively a very small question. In what spirit they will work the constitution? Will they work it only as aliens bound by an unwanted tie or will they work it as true kindreds, is the more important question. For working it as true kindreds, what is wanted is not merely political unity but a true union, of heart and soul, in other words social unity. Political unity is worth nothing, if it is not the expression of real union. It is as precarious as the unity between persons who without being friends become allies, as is now the case between Germany and Russia. Personally, I do not think that a permanent union can be made to depend upon the satisfaction of mere material interests. Pacts may produce unity But that unity can never ripen into union. A pact as a basis for a union is worse than usless. As its very nature indicates, a pact is separative in character. A pact cannot produce the desire to accommodate, it cannot instil the spirit of sacrifice, nor can it bind the parties to the main objective. Instead of accommodating each other, parties to a pact strive to get, as much as possible, out of each other. Instead of sacrificing for the common cause, parties to the pact are constantly occupied in seeing that the sacrifice made by one is not used for the good of the other. Instead of fighting for the main objective, parties to the pact are for ever engaged in seeing that in the struggle for reaching the goal the balance of power between the parties is not disturbed. Mr. Rennan spoke the most profound truth when he said :—

"Community of interests is assuredly a powerful bond between men. But nevertheless can interests suffice to make a nation? I do not believe it. Community of interests makes commercial treaties. There is a sentimental side to nationality; it is at once body and soul; a Zollverein is not a fatherland."

Equally striking is the view of James Bryce, another well-known student of history.   In the view of Bryce :—

"The permanance of an institution depends not merely on the material interests that support it, but on its conformity to the deep-rooted sentiment of the men for whom it has been made.   When it draws to itself and provides a fitting expression for that sentiment, the sentiment becomes thereby not only more vocal but actually stronger, and in its turn imparts a fuller vitality to the institution."

These observations of Bryce were made in connection with the foundation of the German Empire by Bismark who, according to Bryce, succeeded in creating a durable empire because it was based on a sentiment and that this sentiment was fostered—

". . . . most of all by what we call the instinct or passion or nationality, the desire of a people already conscious of a moral and social unity, to see such unity expressed and realized under a single government, which shall give it a place and name among civilized states."

Now what is it that produces this moral and social unity which gives permanance and what is it that drives people to see such unity expressed and realized under a single government which shall give it a place and name among civilized states ?

No one is more competent to answer this question than James Bryce.   It was just such a question which he had to consider in discussing the vitality of the Holy Roman Empire as contrasted with the Roman Empire.   If any Empire can be said to have succeeded in bringing about political unity among its diverse subjects it was the Roman Empire.   Paraphrasing for the sake of brevity the language of Bryce :—The gradual extension of Roman citizenship through the founding of colonies, first throughout Italy and then in the provinces ; the working of the equalized and equalizing Roman Law, the even pressure of the government on all subjects, the movements of population caused by commerce and the slave traffic, were steadily assimilating the various peoples   Emperors who were for the most part natives of the provinces cared little to cherish Italy or even after the days of the Antoninies, to conciliate Rome.   It was their policy to keep open for every subject a career by whose freedom they had themselves risen to greatness.   Annihilating distinctions of legal status among freemen, it completed the work which trade and literature and toleration to all beliefs but one were already performing. No quarrels of race or religions disturbed that calm, for all national distinctions were becoming merged in the idea of a Common Empire!

This unity produced by the Roman Empire was only a politica. unity. How long did this political unity last? In the words of Bryce :—

"Scarcely had this slowly working influences brought about this unity, when other influences began to threaten it. New foes assailed the frontiers ; while the loosening of the structure within was shewn by the long struggles for power which followed the death or deposition of each successive emperor. In the period of anarchy after the fall of Valerian, generals were raised by their armies in every part of the Empire, and ruled great provinces as monarchs apart, owning no allegiance to the possessor of the capital. The breaking-up of the western half of the Empire into separate kingdoms might have been anticipated by two hundred years, had the barbarian tribes on the borders been bolder, or had there not arisen in Diocletian a prince active and skillful enough to bind up the fragments before they had lost all cohesion, meeting altered conditions by new remedies. The policy he adopted of dividing and localizing authority recognized the fact that the weakened heart could no longer make its pulsations felt to the body's extremities. He parcelled out the supreme power among four monarchs, ruling as joint emperors in four capitals, and then sought to give it a factitious strength by surrounding it with an oriental pomp which his earlier predecessors would have scorned............... The prerogative of Rome was menaced by the rivalry of Nicomedia, and the nearer greatness of Milan."

It is therefore evident that political unity was not enough to give permanence and stability to the Roman Empire and as Bryce points out that "the breaking-up of the western half (of the Roman Empire) into separate kingdoms might have been anticipated by two hundred years had the barbarian tribes on the border been bolder, or had there not arisen in Diocletian a prince active and skillful enough to bind up the fragments before they had lost all cohesion, meeting altered conditions by new remedies." But the fact is that the Roman Empire which was tottering and breaking into bits and whose political unity was not enough to bind it together did last for several hundred years as one cohesive unit after it became the Holy Roman Empire. As Prof. Marvin points out* .—

"The unity of the Roman Empire was mainly political and military. It lasted for between four and five hundred years. The unity which supervened in the Catholic Church was religious and moral and endured for a thousand years."

The question is what made the Holy Roman Empire more stable than the Roman Empire could ever hope to be ? According to Bryce it was a common religion in the shape of Christianity and a common religious organization in the shape of the Christian Church which supplied the cement to the Holy Roman Empire and which was wanting in the Roman Empire. It was this cement which gave to the people of the Empire a moral and a social unity and made them see such unity expressed and realized under a single government.

Speaking of the unifying effect of Christianity as a common religion Bryce says :—

" It is on religion that the inmost and deepest life of a nation rests. Because Divinity was divided, humanity had been divided, likewise ; the doctrine of the unity of God now enforced the unity of man, who had been created in his image. The first lesson of Christianity was love, a love that was to join in one body those whom suspicion and prejudice and pride of race had hitherto kept apart. There was thus formed by the new religion a community of the faithful, a Holy Empire, designed to gather all men into its bosom, and standing opposed to the manifold polytheisms of the older world, exactly as the universal sway of the Caesors was contrasted with the innumerable kingdoms and city republics that had gone before it.............. "†

If what Bryce has said regarding the instability of the Roman Empire and the comparatively greater stability of its successor, the Holy Roman Empire, has any lesson for India and if the reasoning

---

* The unity of Western Civilization (4th Ed) page 27.

† The Christian Church did not play a passive part in the process of unification of the Roman Empire. It took a very active part in bringing it about. " Seeing one institution after another falling to pieces around her, seeing how countries and cities were being severed from each other by the erruption of strange tribes and the increasing difficulty of communication the Christian Church," says Bryce. " strove to save religious fellowship by strengthening the ecclesiastical organization, by drawing tighter every bond of outward union. Necessities of faith were still more powerful. Truth, it was said, is one, and as it must bind into one body all who hold it, so it is only by continuing in that body that they can preserve it. There is one Flock and one Shepherd."

of Bryce, that the Roman Empire was unstable because it had nothing more than political unity to rely on, and that the Holy Roman Empire was more stable, because it rested on the secure foundation of moral and social unity, produced by the possession of a common faith, is a valid reasoning and embodies human experience, then it is obvious that there can be no possibility of a union between Hindus and Muslims.   The cementing force of a common religion is wanting.   From a spiritual point of view Hindus and Musalmans are not merely two classes or two sects such as Protestants and Catholics or Shaivas and Vaishnavas.   They are two distinct species. In this view, neither Hindu nor Muslim can be expected to recognize that humanity is an essential quality present in them both, and that they are not many but one and that the differences between them are no more than accidents   For them Divinity is divided and with the division of Divinity their humanity is divided and with the division of humanity they must remain divided.   There is nothing to bring them in one bosom.

Without social union, political unity is difficult to be achieved. If achieved it would be as precarious as a summer sappling, liable to be uprooted by the gust of any hostile wind   With mere political unity, India may be a state.   But to be a state is not to be a nation and a state which is not a nation has small prospects of survival in the struggle for existence in these days when nationalism is the most dynamic force, seeking its ethical justification in the principle of self-determination for the distruction of all mixed states for which it is responsible.

CHAPTER VIII

MUSLIM ALTERNATIVE TO PAKISTAN.

I

The Hindus say they have an alternative to Pakistan. Have the Muslims also an alternative to Pakistan? The Hindus say yes, the Muslims say no. The Hindus believe that the Muslim proposal for Pakistan is only a bargaining manoeuveur put forth with the object of making additions to the communal gains already secured under the Communal Award. The Muslims repudiate the suggestion. They say there is no equivalent to Pakistan and therefore they will have Pakistan and nothing but Pakistan. It does seem that the Musalmans are devoted to Pakistan and are determined to have nothing else and that the Hindus in hoping for an alternative are merely indulging in wishful thinking. But assuming that the Hindus are shrewd enough in divining what the Muslim game is, will the Hindus be ready to welcome the Muslim alternative to Pakistan? The answer to the question must of course depend upon what the Muslim alternative is.

What is the Muslim alternative to Pakistan? No one knows. Muslims, if they have any, have not disclosed it and perhaps will not disclose it till the day when the rival parties meet to revise and settle the terms on which Hindus and Muslims are to associate with each other in the future. To be forewarned is to be forearmed. It is therefore necessary for the Hindus to have some idea of the possible Muslim alternative to enable them to meet the shock of it; for the alternative cannot be better than the Communal Award and is sure to be many degrees worse.

In the absence of the exact alternative proposal one can only make a guess. Now one man's guess is as good as that of another and the party concerned has to choose on which of these he will rely. Among the likely guesses my guess is that the Muslims will put forth as their alternative some such proposal as the following :—

"That the future constitution of India shall provide ·

(i) That the Muslims shall have 50% representation in the Legislature, Central as well as Provincial, through separate electorates

(ii) That $\frac{1}{2}$ of the Executive in the Centre as well as in the Provinces shall consist of Muslims

(iii) That in the Civil Service 50% of the post shall be assigned to the Muslims.

(iv) That in the Fighting Forces the Muslim proportion shall be one half, both in the ranks and in the higher grades.

(v) That Muslims shall have 50% representation in all public bodies, such as councils and commissions, created for public purposes.

(vi) That Muslims shall have 50% representation in all international organizations in which India will participate.

(vii) That if the Prime Minister be a Hindu the Deputy Prime Minister shall be a Muslim.

(viii) That if the Commander-in-Chief be a Hindu, the Deputy Commander-in-Chief shall be a Muslim.

(ix) That no changes in the Provincial Boundaries shall be made except with the consent of 2/3rds of the Muslim members of the Legislature.

(x) That no action or treaty against a Muslim country shall be valid unless the consent of 2/3 rds of the Muslim Members of the Legislature is obtained.

(xi) That no law affecting the culture or religion or religious usage of Muslims shall be made except with the consent of 2/3 rds of the Muslim Members of the Legislature.

(xii) That the national language for India shall be Urdu.

(xiii) That no law prohibiting or restricting the slaughter of cows or the propagation of and conversion to Islam shall be valid unless it is passed with the consent of 2/3 rds of the Muslim Members of the Legislature.

(xiv) That no change in the constitution shall be valid unless the majority required for effecting such changes also includes a 2/3rd majority of the Muslim Members of the Legislature."

This guess of mine is not the result of imagination let loose. It is not the result of a desire to frighten the Hindus into an unwilling and hasty acceptance of Pakistan. If I may say so it is really an intelligent anticipation based upon available data coming from Muslim quarters

An indication of what the Muslim alternative is likely to be, is obtainable from the nature of the Constitutional Reforms which are contemplated for the Dominions of His Exalted Highness the Nizam of Hyderabad.

The Hyderabad scheme of Reforms is a novel scheme. It rejects the scheme of communal representation obtaining in British India. In its place is substituted what is called Functional Representation i.e. representation by classes and by professions. The composition

25

of the Legislature which is to consist of 70 members is to be as follows :—

Elected.			Nominated.			
Agriculture		12	Illakas ...		...	8
Patidars	8		Sarf-i-Khas	2		
Tenants	4		Paigahs	3		
Women		1	Peshkari	1		
Graduates		1	Salar Jung	1		
University		1	Samasthans	1		
Jagirdars		2				
Maashdars		1	Officials ...		.	18
Legal		2	Rural Arts and Crafts			1
Medical		2	Backward Classes		.	1
Western	1		Minor Unrepresented Classes.			3
Oriental	1		Others ...		..	6
Teaching ...		1				
Commerce ...		1				
Industries ...		2				
Banking ...		2				
Indigenous						
Co-operative and Joint Stock ...	1					
Organized Labour		1				
Harijan ...		1				
District Municipalities		1				
City Municipality		1				
Rural Boards ...		1				
Total		33			Total ...	37

Whether the scheme of functional representation will promote better harmony between the various classes and sections than communal representation does is more than doubtful. In addition to perpetuating existing social and religious divisions it may quite easily intensify class struggle by emphasizing class consciousness. The scheme appears innocuous but its real character will come out when every class will demand representation in proportion to its numbers. Be that as it may, functional representation is not the most significant feature of the Hyderabad scheme of Reforms. The most significant feature of the scheme is the proposed division of seats between Hindus and Musalmans in the new Hyderabad Legislature. Under the scheme as approved by H. E. H. the Nizam, communal representation is not altogether banished. It is retained along with functional representation. It is to operate through joint electorates. But there is to be equal representation for " the two majority communities " on every* elective body including the legislature and no candidate can succeed unless he secures 40 per cent. of the votes polled by members of his community. This principle of equal representation to Hindus and Muslims irrespective of their numbers† is not only to apply to every elective body but it is to apply to both elected as well as nominated members of the body.

In justification of this theory of equal representation it is stated that .—

" The importance of the Muslim community in the state, by virtue of its historical position and its status in the body politic, is so obvious that it cannot be reduced to the status of a minority in the Assembly."

Quite recently there have appeared in the press‡ the proposals formulated by one Mr. Mir Akbar Ali Khan calling himself the

*Besides the Central Legislature there are to be constituted under the Scheme of Reforms other popular bodies such as *Panchayats*, Rural Boards, Municipalities and Town Committees.

†The distribution of population of Hyderabad State (Excluding Berar) is according to the census of 1931 as followed —

Hindus	Untouchables	Muslims	Christians	Others	Total
96,99,615	24,73,230	15,34,666	1,51,382	5,77,255	1,44,36,148

‡See *Bombay Sentinel*, June 22nd, 1940 Mr. Mir Akbar Ali Khan says that he discussed his proposals with Mr. Srinivas Iyengar Ex-president of the Congress and the proposals published by him are really proposals as approved by Mr. Iyengar.

leader of the Nationalist Party as a means of settling the Hindu Moslem problem in British India.   They are as follows :—

(1) The future constitution of India must rest upon the broad foundation of adequate military defence of the country and upon making the people reasonably military minded.   The Hindus must have the same military mindedness as the Muslims.

(2) The present moment offers a supreme opportunity for the two communities to ask for the defence of India being made over to them.   The Indian Army must consist of an equal number of Hindus and Muslims and no regiment should be on a communal, as distinguished from regional basis

(3) The Governments in the Provinces and at the Centre should be wholly National Governments composed of men who are reasonably military-minded.   Hindu and Muslim Ministers should be equal in number in the Central as well as all provincial cabinets ; other important minorities might wherever necessary be given special representation. This scheme will function most satisfactorily with joint electorates, but in the present temper of the country separate electorates might be continued.   The Hindu Ministers must be elected by the Hindu members of the legislature and the Muslim Ministers by the Muslim members.

(4) The Cabinet is to be removable only on an express vote of no-confidence, against the Cabinet as a whole, by 2/3rds, which majority must be of Hindus and Muslims taken separately.

(5) The religion, language, script and personal law of each community should be safeguarded by a paramount constitutional check enabling the majority of members representing that community in the legislature placing a veto on any legislative or other measure affecting it.   A similar veto must be provided against any measure designed or calculated to affect adversely the economic well-being of any community.

(6) An adequate communal representation in the services must be agreed to as a practical measure of justice in administration and in the distribution of patronage.

If the proposals put forth by a Muslim leader of the Nationalist Party in Hyderabad State is any indication showing in what direction the mind of the Muslims in British India is running then here is a third basis in support of the guess I have made.

II

It is true that there was held in Delhi in the month of April 1940 a Conference of Muslims under the grandiloquent name of " The Azad Muslim Conference. " The Muslims who met in the Azad Conference were those who were opposed to the Muslim League as well as to the Nationalist Muslims. They were opposed to the Muslim League firstly, because of their hostility to Pakistan and secondly because like the League they did not want to depend upon the British Government for the protection of their rights.* They were also opposed to the Nationalist Musalmans (i. e. Congressites out and out) because they were accused of indifference to the cultural and religious rights of the Muslims.†

With all this the Azad Muslim Conference was hailed by the Hindus as a conference of friends. But the resolutions passed by the conference leave very little to choose between it and the League. Among the resolutions passed by the Azad Muslim Conference the following three bear directly upon the issue in question.

The first of these runs as follows —

" This conference, representative of Indian Muslims who desire to secure the fullest freedom of the country, consisting of delegates and

*Mufti Kifayat Ullah a prominent member of the conference in the course of his speech is reported to have said   " They had to demonstrate that they were not behind any other community in the fight for freedom   He wished to declare in clear terms that they did not rely on the British Government for the protection of their rights   They would themselves chalk out the safeguards necessary for the protection of their religious rights and would fight out any party, however powerful, that would refuse to accept those safeguards, as they would fight the Government for freedom (Prolonged cheers)   Hindustan Times, April 30,1940

†See the speeches of Maulana Hafizul Rehman and Dr. K. M. Ashraf in the same issue of the Hindustan Times.

representatives of every province, after having given its fullest and most careful consideration to all the vital questions affecting the interest of the Muslim community and the country as a whole declares the following :—

"India will have geographical and political boundaries of an individual whole and as such is the common homeland of all the citizens irrespective of race or religion who are joint owners of its resources. All nooks and corners of the country are hearths and homes of Muslims who cherish the historic eminence of their religion and culture which are dearer to them than their lives. From the national point of view every Muslim is an Indian. The common rights of all residents of the country and their responsibilities in every walk of life and in every sphere of human activity are the same. Indian Muslim by virtue of these rights and responsibilities, is unquestionably an Indian national and in every part of the country is entitled to equal privileges with that of every Indian national in every sphere of governmental, economic and other national activities and in public services ; For that very reason Muslims own equal responsibilities with other Indians for striving and making sacrifices to achieve the country's independence. This is a self-evident proposition, the truth of which no right thinking Muslim will question. This conference declares unequivocally and with all emphasis at its command that the goal of Indian Muslims is complete independence along with protection of their religion and communal rights, and that they are anxious to attain this goal as early as possible. Inspired by this aim they have in the past made great sacrifices and are ever ready to make greater sacrifices.

"The Conference unreservedly and strongly repudiates the baseless charge levelled against Indian Muslims by the agents of British Imperialism and others that they are an obstacle in the path of Indian freedom and emphatically declares that the Muslims are fully alive to their responsibilities and consider it inconsistent with their traditions and derogatory to their honour to lag behind others in the struggle for independence "

By this Resolution they repudiated the scheme of Pakistan Their second Resolution was in the following terms —

"This is the considered view of this conference that only that constitution for the future Government of India would be acceptable to the people of India which is framed by the Indians themselves elected by means of adult franchise. The constitution should fully safeguard all the legitimate interests of the Muslims in accordance with the recommendations of the Muslim Members of the Constituent Assembly.   The representatives of other communities or of an outside power would have no right to interfere in the determination of these safeguards."

By this Resolution the Conference asserted that the safeguards for the Muslims must be determined by the Muslims alone.

Their third Resolution was as under :—

" Whereas in the future constitution of India it would be essential, in order to ensure stability of government and preservation of security, that every citizen and community should feel satisfied this conference considers it necessary that a scheme of safeguards as regards vital matters mentioned below should be prepared to the satisfaction of the Muslims.

" This Conference appoints a board consisting of 27 persons.   This board, after the fullest investigation, consultation and consideration, make its recommendations for submission to the next session of this Conference, so that the Conference may utilise the recommendations as a means of securing a permanent national settlement to the communal question.   This recommendation should be submitted within two months.   The matters referred to the board are the following —

" 1.   The protection of Muslim culture, personal law and religious rights.

" 2.   Political rights of Muslims and their protection.

" 3   The formation of future constitution of India to be non-unitary and federal, with absolutely essential and unavoidable powers for the Federal Government.

" The provision of safeguards for the economic, social and cultural rights of Muslims and for their share in public services.

" The board will be empowered to fill up any vacancy in a suitable manner.   The board will have the right to co-opt other members. It will be empowered also to consult other Muslim bodies and if it considers, necessary, any responsible organisation in the country.   The 27 members of the board will be nominated by the president.

" The quorum for the meeting will be nine.

" Since the safeguards of the communal rights of different communities will be determined in the constituent assembly referred to in the resolution which this conference has passed, this conference considers it necessary to declare that Muslim members of this constituent assembly will be elected by Muslims themselves. "

We must await the Report of this Board to know what safeguards the Azad Muslim Conference will devise for the safety and protection of Muslims. But there appears no reason to hope that they will not be in favour of what I have guessed to be the likely alternative of the League for Pakistan. For it cannot be overlooked that the Azad Muslim Conference was a body of Muslims who were not only opposed to the Muslim League but were equally opposed to the Nationalist Muslims There is therefore no ground to trust that they will be more merciful to the Hindus than the League has been or will be.

Suppose my guess turns out to be correct it would be interesting to know what the Hindus will have to say in reply. Should they prefer such an alternative to Pakistan ? Or should they rather prefer Pakistan to such an alternative ? Those are questions which I must leave the Hindus and their leaders to answer. All I would like to say in this connection is that the Hindus before determining their attitude towards this question should note certain important considerations. In particular they should note that there is a difference between Macht Politic and Gravamin Politic ; that there is a difference between *communitas communitatum* and a nation of nations—; that there is a difference between safeguards to allay apprehensions of the weak and contrivances to satisfy the ambition for power by the strong : that there is a difference between providing safeguards and handing over the country. Further they should also note that what may with safety be conceded to Gravamin Politic may not be conceded to Macht Politic . What may be conceded with safety to a community may not be conceded to a nation and what may be conceded with safety to the weak to be used as a weapon of defence may not be conceded to the strong who may use it as a weapon of attack.

These are important considerations and if the Hindus overlook them they will do so at their peril. For the Muslim alternative is **really a frightful and dangerous alternative.**

CHAPTER IX

LESSONS FROM ABROAD

Hindus who will not yield to the demand of the Muslims for the division of India into Pakistan and Hindustan and would insist upon maintaining the geographical unity of India without counting the cost will do well to study the fate that has befallen other countries who like India were a nation of nations.

It is not necessary to review the history of all such countries. It is enough to recount here the story of two, Turkey and Czechoslovakia.

To begin with Turkey. The emergence of the Turks in history was due to the fact that they were driven away by the Mongols from their home in Central Asia, somewhere between 1230-40 A. D. which led them to settle in North-West Anatolia. Their career as the builders of the Turkish Empire began in 1326 with the conquest of Brusa. In 1360-61 they conquered Thrace from the Aegean to the Black Sea ; in 1361-62 the Byzantine Government of Constantinople accepted their supremacy. In 1369 Bulgaria followed suit. In 1371-72 Macedonia was conquered. In 1373 Constantinople definitely accepted Ottoman Sovereignty. In 1389 Servia was conquered. In 1430 Salonia and 1453 Constantinople, in 1461 Trebizond, in 1465 Quraman, in 1475 Kaffa and Tana were annexed

26

one after another. After a short lull, they conquered Mosul in
1514, Syria, Egypt, the Hiaz and the Yaman in 1516-17 and Belgrade
in 1521. This was followed in 1526 by a victory over the Hungarians
at Mohacz. In 1554 took place the first conquest of Bagdad and in
1639 second conquest of Bagdad. Twice they laid seige to Veinna,
first in 1529 and again in 1683 with a view to extend their conquest
beyond. But on both occasions they were repulsed with the result
that their expansion in Europe was completely checked for ever.
Still the countries they conquered between 1326 and 1683 formed
a vast empire. A few of these territories the Turks had lost to
their enemies thereafter, but taking the extent of the Turkish Empire
as it stood in 1789 on the eve of the French Revolution it comprised
(1) the Balkans, south of the Danub, (2) Asia Minor, the Levant
and the neighbouring islands (i e. Cyprus), (3) Syria and Palestine,
(4) Egypt and (5) North Africa from Egypt to Morocco.

The tale of the disruption of the Turkish Empire is easily told.
The first to break away *de facto* if not *de jure* was Egypt in 1769.
The next were the Christians in the Balkans. Bessarabia was taken by
Russia in 1812 after a war with Turkey. In 1812 Serbia rebelled with
the aid of Russia and the Turks were obliged to place Serbia under
a separate Government. In 1829 similar concessions were granted
to two other Danubian Provinces, Mo'davia and Wallachia. As a
result of the Greek war of Independence which lasted between 1822-29
Greece was completely freed from Turkish rule and Greek independence was recognised by the Powers in 1832. Between 1875-77 there
was turmoil amogst the Balkans. There was a revolt in Bosnia and
Herzegovina and the Bulgarians resorted to atrocities against the Turks,
to which the Turks replied with atrocities in equal measure. As
a result, Serbia and Montenegro declared war on Turkey and so did
Russia. By the Treaty of Berlin Bulgaria was given self-
government under Turkey and Eastern Rumania was to be ruled
by Turkey under a Christian Governor Russia gained Kars and
Batoum. Dobrudja was given to Rumania. Bosnia and Herzegovina
were assigned to Austria for administration and England occupied
Cyprus. In 1881 Greece gained Thessaly and France occupied
Tunis. In 1885 Bulgaria and Eastern Roumalia were united into
one state.

The story of the growth and decline of the Turkish Empire upto 1906 has been very graphically described by Mr. Lane Poole in the following words* :—

" In its old extent, when the Porte ruled not merely the narrow territory now called Turkey in Europe, but Greece, Bulgaria and Eastern Rumalia, Rumania, Serbia, Bosnia and Herzegovina, with the Crimea and a portion of Southern Russia, Egypt, Syria, Tripoli, Tunis, Algiers and numerous islands in the Mediterrenean, not counting the vast but mainly desert tract of Arabia, the total population (at the present time) would be over fifty millions, or nearly twice that of Europe without Russia. One by one her provinces have been taken away. Algiers and Tunis have been incorporated with France, and thus 175,000 square miles and five millions of inhabitants have transferred their alleigiance. Egypt is practically independent, and this means a loss of 500,000 miles and over six millions of inhabitants. Asiatic Turkey alone has suffered comparatively little diminution. This forms the bulk of her present dominions, and comprises about 680,000 square miles, and over sixteen millions of population. In Europe her losses have been almost as severe as in Africa where Tripoli alone remains to her. Serbia and Bosnia are administered by Austria and thereby nearly 40,000 miles and three and a half millions of peoples have become Austrian subjects. Wallachia and Moldavia are united in the independent kingdom of Rumania, diminishing the extent of Turkey by 46,000 miles and over five millions of inhabitants. Bulgaria is a dependent state over which the Porte has no real control and Eastern Rumalia has lately *de facto* become part of Bulgaria and the two contain nearly 40,000 square miles, and three millions of inhabitants. The kingdom of Greece with its 25,000 miles and two million population has long been separated from its parent. In Europe where the Turkish territory once extended to 230,000 miles, with a population of nearly 20 millions, it now reaches only the total of 66 thousand miles and a population

*Turkey - pages 363-64

of four and a half millions, it has lost nearly three fourths of its land, and about the same proportion of its people."

Such was the condition of Turkey in 1907. What has befallen her since then is unfortunately the worst part of her story. In 1908 taking advantage of the Revolution brought about by the young Turks, Austria annexed Bosnia and Herzegovina and Bulgaria declared her independece. In 1911 Italy took possession of Tripoli and in 1912 France occupied Morocco. Encouraged by the successful attack of Italy in 1912 Bulgaria, Greece, Serbia and Montenegro formed themselves into a Balkan League and declared war on Turkey. In this war known as the first Balkan War Turkey was completely defeated. By the treaty of London (1913) the Turkish territory in Europe was reduced to a narrow strip round Constantinople. But the treaty could not take effect because the victors could not agree on the distribution of the spoils of victory. In 1913 Bulgaria declared war on the rest of the Balkan League and Rumania declared war on Bulgaria in the hope of extending her territory. Turkey also did the same. By the Treaty of Bukharest (1913) which ended the second Balkan War Turkey recovered Adrianople and got Thrace from Bulgaria. Serbia obtained Northern Macedonia and Greece obtained Southern Macedonia (including Salonika), while Montenegro enlarged her territory at the expense of Turkey. By 1914 when the Great European War came on, the Balkans had won their independence from Turkey and the area in Europe that remained under the Turkish Empire was indeed a very small area round about Constantinople and her possessions in Asia. So far as the African Continent is concerned, the Sultan's power over Egypt and the rest of North Africa was only nominal ; for the European powers had established real control therein. In the Great War of 1914 the overthrow of Turkey was complete. All the provinces from the Mediterranean to the Persian Gulf were overrun, and the great cities of Bagdad, Jerusalem, Damascus and Alleppo were captured. In Europe the allied troops occupied Constantinople. The Treaty of Severes which brought the War with Turkey to a close sought to deprive her of all her outlying provinces and even of the fertile plains of Asia Minor. Greek claim for territory was generously allowed at the expense of Turkey in Macedonia, Thrace and Asia Minor and Italy was to receive Adalia and a large tract in the South. Turkey was to be deprived of all her Arab Provinces in Asia, Iraq, Syria, Palestine, Hedjaz and Nejd. There was left to Turkey only the capital, Constantinople and separated from this city, by a " neutral zone of the straits, " part of the barren plateau of Anatolia. The Treaty though accepted by the Sultan was fiercely attacked by the Nationalist Party under Kemal Pasha. When the Greeks advanced to occupy their new territory they were attacked and decisively beaten. At the end of the war with Greece which went on from 1920 to 1922 the Turks had reoccupied Smyrna. As the allies were not prepared to send armies to help the Greeks, they were forced to come to terms with the Nationalist Turks. At the Conference at Mudiania the Greeks agreed to revise the terms of the Treaty of Severes which was done by the Treaty of Lausaune in 1923 and which granted the demands of Turkey except in Western Thrace. The rest of the Treaty of Severes was accepted by the Turks which meant the loss of her Arab Provinces in Asia. Thus before the War of 1914 Turkey had lost all her Provinces in Europe. After the War she lost her Provinces in Asia. As a result of this dismemberment of the old Turkish Empire, what now remains of it is the small state called the Republic of Turkey with an area which is a minute fraction of the old Empire.*

II

Take the case of Czechoslovakia. It is the creation of the Treaty of Trainon which followed the European War of 1914. None of the peace treaties was more drastic in its terms than the Treaty of Trainon. Says Prof. Mackartney, " By it Hungary was not so much mutilated as dismembered. Even if we exclude Croatia, Slavonia, which had stood only in a federal relationship to the other lands of the Holy Crown—although one of eight hundred years' standing—Hungary proper was reduced to less than one

*The area of Turkey is 294,492 square miles exclusive of 3,708 square miles of lakes and swamps. The area of Turkey in Europe is only 9,257 square miles.

third (32·6 per cent.) of her prewar area, and a little over two fifth (41·6 per cent.) of her population. Territories and peoples formerly Hungarian were distributed among no less than seven states. " Of these states, there was one which did not exist before. It was a new creation. That was the state of Czechoslovakia.

The area of the Republic of Czechoslovakia was 54,244 square miles and the population was about 13,613,172. It included the territories formerly known as Bohemia, Moravia, Slovakia and Ruthenia. It was a composite state which included in its bosom three principal nationalities, (i) Czechs occupying Bohemia and Moravia (ii) Slovaks, occupying Slovakia and (iii) Ruthenians in occupation of Ruthenia.

Czechoslovakia proved to be a very short lived-state. It lived exactly for two decades. On the 15th March 1939 it perished or rather was destroyed as an independent state. It became a protectorate of Germany. The circumstances attending its expiry were of a very bewildering nature. Her death was brought about by the very powers which had given it birth. By signing the Munich Pact on 30th September 1938—of which the Protectorate was an inevitable consequence, Great Britain, France and Italy assisted Germany, their former enemy of the Great War, to conquer Czechoslovakia, their former ally. All the work of the Czechs of the past century to gain freedom had been cancelled out. They were once more to be the slaves of thier former German overlords.

III

What are the reasons for the disruption of Turkey ?

Lord Eversely in his Turkish Empire* has attempted to give reasons for the decay of Turkey, some internal, some external. Among the internal causes there were two. First the degeneracy of the Othman dynasty. The supreme power fell into the hands either of the Vaziers of the Sultans or more often in the hands of women of the harem of the Sultan. The harem was always in antagonism to the official administration of the Porte, which ostensibly carried on the administration of the state under the direction of the Sultan. The harem was the centre from which corruption spread throughout the Turkish Empire, as officials of every degree, from the highest to the lowest, found it expedient to secure their interests with its inmates by heavy bribes, with the result that the sale of offices civil and military became universal. The second main cause of the decadence of the Turkish Empire was the deterioration of its armies due to two causes. During the last 300 years the army had lost the elan and the daring by which the Ottomans won their many victories in the early period of their career. The loss of this elan and daring by the Turkish Army was due to the composition of army, recruitment to which was restricted to Turks and Arabs and also to the diminution of opportunities of plunder and the hope of acquiring lands for distribution among the soldiers as an incentive to victory and valour in the latter period when the Empire was on the defensive and when it was no longer a question of making fresh conquests, but of retaining what had already been won.

As an external cause of the disruption of Turkey the chief one is the rapacity of the European nations.

All this of course is true. But this analysis omits to take note of the true cause. The true and the principal cause of the disruption of Turkey was underminded by the growth of the spirit of nationalism among its subject peoples. The Greek revolt, the revolt of the Serbs, Bulgarians and other Balkans against the Turkish authority was no doubt represented as a conflict between Christianity and Islam. That is one way of looking at it. But only a superficial way of looking at it. These revolts, were simply the manifestations of the spirit of nationalism by which they were generated. These revolts had no doubt for their immediate causes Turkish misrule, Christian antipathy to Islam and the machinations of European nations. But all this is a superficial way of looking at the phenomenon. The real motive force was the spirit of nationalism by which they were actuated and their revolts were only a manifestation of this inner urge brought on by nationalism.

That it was nationalism which had brought about the disruption of Turkey is proved by the revolt of the Arabs in the last war and their will to be independent. Here there was no conflict between Islam and Christianity. Nor there was the relationship between the two that of the oppressor and the oppressed. Yet, the Arab claimed to be freed from the Turkish Empire. Why? Because he was moved by Arab nationalism and preferred to be an Arab nationalist to being a Turkish subject.

What is the cause of the destruction of Czechoslovakia?

The general impression is that it was the result of German aggression. To some extent that is true. But it is not the whole truth. If Germany was the only enemy of Czechoslovakia all that she would have lost was the fringe of her borderland which was inhabited by the Sudetan Germans. German aggression need have cost her nothing more. Really speaking the destruction of Czechoslovakia was brought about by an enemy within her own borders. That enemy was the intransigent nationalism of the Slovaks who were out to break up the unity of the state and secure the independence of Slovakia.

The union of the Slovaks with the Czechs as units of a single state was based upon certain assumptions. First the two were believed to be so closely akin as to be one people, and that the Slovaks were only a branch of Czechoslovaks. Second that the two spoke a single 'Czechoslovak' language. Third there was no separate Slovak national consciousness. Nobody examined these assumptions at the time, because the Slovaks themselves desired this union, expressing their wish in 1918 by formal declaration of their representatives at the Peace Conference. This was of course a superficial and hasty view of the matter. As Prof. Mackartney points out ...." the central political fact which emerges from the consideration of this history (of the relations between the Czechs and Slovaks) for the purposes of the present age is the final crystallization of a Slovak national consciousness.........". The genuine and uncompromising believers in a single indivisible Czechoslovak language and people were certainly never so large, at least in Slovakia, as they were made to appear. Today they have dwindled to a mere handful, under the influence of actual experience of the considerable differences which exist between the Czechs and the Slovaks.   At present Slovak is in practice recognized by the Czechs themselves as the official language of Slovakia   The political and national resistance has been no less tenacious and to-day the name of 'Czechoslovakia' is practically confined to official documents and to literature issued for the benefit of foreigners.   During many weeks in the country I only remember hearing one person use the term for herself ; this was a half-German, half-Hungarian girl, who used it in a purely political sense, meaning that she thought irredentism futile.   No Czech and no Slovak feels or calls himself, when speaking naturally, anything but a Czech or a Slovak as the case may be."

This national conciousness of the Slovaks, which was always alive began to burst forth on seeing that the Sudetan Germans had made certain demands on Czechoslovakia for autonomy. The Germans sought to achieve their objective by the application of gangster morality to international politics, saying "Give us what we ask or we shall burst up your shop." The Slovaks followed suit by making their demands for autonomy but with a different face.   They did not resort to gangster methods and modulated their demands to autonomy only.   They had eschewed all idea of independence and in the Proclamation issued on October 8 by Dr. Tiso, the leading man in the autonomist movement in Slovakia, it was said "We shall proceed in the spirit of our motto, for God and the Nation, in a Christian and national spirit."   Believing in their *bona fides* and desiring to give no room to the *Gravaminpolitik* of which the Slovaks were making full use to disturb the friendly relations between the Czechs and the Slovaks, the National Assembly in Prague passed an Act in November 1938 — immediately after the Munich Pact — called the "Constitutional Act on the Autonomy of Slovakia "   Its provisions were of a far reaching character.   There was to be a separate Parliament for Slovakia and this Parliament was to decide the Constitution of Slovakia within the framework of the legal system of the Czechoslovak Republic.   An alteration in the territory of Slovakia was to be with the consent of the two-third majority in the Slovak Parliament.   The consent of the Slovak Parliament was made necessary for international treaties which

27

exclusively concerned Slovakia. Officials of the Central State administration in Slovakia were to be primarily Slovaks. Proportional representation of Slovakia was guaranteed in all central institutions, councils, commissions and other organizations. Similarly, Slovakia was to be proportionally represented on all international organizations in which the Czechoslovak Republic was called upon to participate. Slovak soldiers, in peace time, were to be stationed in Slovakia as far as possible. As far as legislative authority was concerned all subjects which were strictly of common concern were assigned to the Parliament of Czechoslovakia. By way of guaranteeing these rights to the Slovaks, the Constitution Act provided that the decision of the National Assembly to make constitutional changes shall be valid only if the majority constitutionally required for such changes includes also a proportionate majority of the members of the National Assembly elected in Slovakia. Similarly, the election of a President of the Republic required the consent not merely of the constitutionally determined majority of the Members of the Parliament, but also of a proportionate majority of the Slovak Members. Further to emphasize that the Central Government must enjoy the confidence of the Slovaks it was provided by the Constitution that one-third of the Slovak Members of the Parliament may propose a motion of 'No Confidence.'

These constitutional changes introduced a hyphen between the Czechs and the Slovaks which did not exist before much against the will of the Czechs. But it was done in the hope that, once the relatively minor quarrels between the two were got out of the way, the very nationalism of the Slovaks was more likely to bring them closer to the Czechs than otherwise. With the constitutional changes guaranteeing an independent status to Slovakia and the fact that the status so guaranteed could not be changed without the consent of the Slovaks themselves, there was no question of the Slovaks ever losing their national identity through submergence by the Czechs. The autonomy however introduced a hyphen which did not exist before. It separated the cultural waters and saved the Slovaks from losing their colour.

The first Slovak Parliament elected under the new constitution was opened on January 18, 1939 and Dr. Martin Sokol, the President of the Parliament declared "The period of the Slovak's struggle for freedom is ended. Now begins the period of national rebirth ". Other speeches made on the occasion indicated that now that Slovakia had its autonomy the Slovaks would never feel animosity towards the Czechs again and that both would loyally abide by the Czecho-Slovak State.

But not even a month had elapsed since the inauguration of the Slovak Parliament before the Slovak politicians had begun their battle against the hyphen and for complete separation. They made excited speeches in which they attacked the Czechs, talked about Czech oppression, and demanded a completely independent Slovakia. By the beginning of March the various forms of separatism in Slovakia were seriously threatening the integrity of the Czecho-Slovak State. On March 9 it was learnt that Tiso the Slovak Premier had decided to proclaim the independence of Slovakia. On the 10th in anticipation of such an act troops were moved in Slovakia and Tiso, the Prime Minister, was dismissed along with other Slovak Ministers by the President of the Republic, Dr Hacha. On the next day Tiso, supposed to be under police supervision, telephoned to Berlin and asked for help. On Monday Tiso and Hitler met and had an hour and a half's talk in Berlin. Immediately after the talk with Hitler Tiso got on the phone to Prague and passed on the German orders.

They were :—

(i) All Czech troops to be withdrawn from Slovakia ;

(ii) Slovakia to be an independent state under German protection ;

(iii) The Slovak Parliament to be summoned by President Hacha to hear the proclamation of independence.

There was nothing that President Hacha and the Prague Government could do except say—yes, for they knew very well that dozens of divisions of German troops were massed round the defenceless frontiers of Czechoslovakia ready to march in at any moment if the demands made by Germany in the interest of and at the instance of Slovakia were refused. Thus ended the new state of Czechoslovakia.

IV

What is the lesson to be drawn from the story of these two countries ?

There is some difference as to how the matters should be put. Mr. Sydney Brooks would say that the cause of these wars of disruption is nationalism, which according to him is the enemy of the universal peace.   Mr. Norman Angell on the other hand would say it is not nationalism but the threat to nationalism which is the cause. To Mr. Robertson nationalism is an irrational instinct if not a positive hallucination and the sooner humanity got rid of it the better for all.

In whatever way the matter is put and howsoever ardently one may wish for the elimination of nationalism, the lesson to be drawn is quite clear.   That nationalism is a fact which can neither be eluded nor denied.   Whether one calls it an irrational instinct or a positive hallucination, the fact remains that it is a potent force which has a dynamic power to disrupt empires.   Whether nationalism is the cause or the threat to nationalism is the cause they are differences of emphasis only.   The real thing is to recognize as does Mr. Toynbee that " nationalism is strong enough to produce war inspite of us. It has terribly proved itself to be no outworn creed, but a vital force to be reckoned with." As was pointed out by him "the right reading of nationality has become an affair of life and death. "   It was not only so for Europe.   It was so for Turkey.   It was so for Czechoslovakia.   And what was a question of life and death to them could not but be one of life and death to India.   Prof. Toynbee pleaded of as was done before him, by Gizot, the recognition of nationality as the necessary foundation of European peace.   Could India ignore to recognize this plea ?   If she does, she will be acting so at her own peril. That nationalism is a disruptive force is not the only lesson to be learnt from the history of these two countries.   Their experience embodies much else of equal if not of greater significance.   What that is, will be evident if certain facts are recalled to memory.

The Turks were by no means as illiberal as they are painted. They allowed their minorities a large measure of autonomy.   The Turks had gone far towards solving the problem of how people of different communities with different social heritages are to live in harmony together when they are geographically intermingled. The Ottoman Empire had accorded, as a matter of course to the Non-Muslim and Non-Turkish communities within its frontiers a degree of territorial as well as cultural autonomy which had never been dreamt of in the political philosophy of the West. Ought not the Christian subjects to have been satisfied with this ? Say what one may, the nationalism of Christain minorities was not satisfied with this local autonomy. It fought for complete freedom and in that fight Turkey was slit open.

The Turks were bound to the Arabs by the tie of religion. The religious tie of Islam is the strongest known to humanity. No social confederacy can claim to rival the Islamic brotherhood in point of solidarity. Add to this the fact that while the Turk treated his Christian subjects as his inferior he acknowledged the Arab as his equal. In the Ottoman Army all non-Muslims were excluded. But the Arab soldiers and officers served side by side with Turks and Kurds. The Arab officer class, educated in Turkish schools, served in military and civil capacities on the same terms as the Turks. There was no derogating distinction between the Turk and the Arab and there was nothing to prevent the Arab from rising to the highest rank in the Ottoman services. Not only politically but even socially the Arab was treated as his equal by the Turk and Arabs married Turkish wives and Turks married Arab wives Ought not the Arabs to have been satisfied with this Islamic brotherhood of Arabs and Turks based on fraternity, liberty and equality ? Say what one may, the Arabs were not satisfied. Arab nationalism broke the bonds of Islam and fought against his fellow Muslim, the Turk, for its independence. It won but Turkey was completely dismantled.

As to Czechoslovakia, she began with the recognition that both the Czechs and the Slovaks were one people. Within a few years the Slovaks claimed to be a separate nation. They would not even admit that they were a branch of the same stock as the Czechs. Their nationalism compelled the Czechs to recognize the fact that they were a distinct people. The Czechs sought to pacify the nationalism of the Slovaks by drawing a hyphen as a mark indicating distinctness.   In place of Czechoslovakia they agreed to have Czecho—Slovakia.   But even with the hyphen the Slovak nationalism remained non-content.   The act of antonomy was both a hyphen separating them from the Czechs as well as a link joining them with the Czechs.   The hyphen as making separation was welcome to the Slovaks but as making a link with the Czechs was very irksome to them.   The Slovaks accepted the autonomy with its hyphen with great relief and promised to be content and loyal to the State.   But evidently this was only a matter of strategy. They sought the autonomy with the hyphen which had the effect of separating them and not as an ultimate end.   They accepted it because they thought that they could use it as a vantage ground for destroying the hyphen which was their main aim   The nationalism of the Slovaks was not content with a hyphen.   It wanted a bar in place of the hyphen.   Immediately the hyphen was introduced they began their battle to replace the hyphen between the Czechs and the Slovaks by a bar.   They did not care what means they should employ.   Their nationalism was so wrong-headed and so intense that when they failed they did not hesitate to call the aid of the Germans.

Thus a deeper study of the disruption of Turkey and Czechoslovakia shows that neither local autonomy nor the bond of religion is sufficient to withstand the force of nationalism, once it is set on the go.

This is a lesson which the Hindus will do well to grasp.   They should ask themselves if the Greek, Balkan and Arab nationalism has blown up the Turkish State and if Slovak nationalism has caused the dismantling of Czechoslovakia what is there to prevent Muslim nationalism from disrupting the Indian State ?   If experience of other countries teaches that this is the inevitable consequence of pent-up nationalism, why not profit by their experience and avoid the catastrophe by agreeing to divide India into Pakistan and Hindustan ?   Let the Hindus take the warning that if they refuse to divide India into two before they launch on their career as a free people they will be sailing in those shoal waters in which Turkey, Czechoslovakia and many others have foundered.   If they wish to avoid ship-wreck in mid-ocean they must lighten the draught by throwing overboard all superfluous cargo.   They will ease the course of their voyage considerably if they—to use the language of Prof. Toynbee—reconcile themselves to making jetsam of less cherished and more combustible cargo.

V

Will the Hindus really lose if they agree to divide India into two, Pakistan and Hindustan ?

With regard to Czechoslovakia it is instructive to note the real feelings of its Government on the loss of their territory caused by the Munich Pact. They were well expressed by the Prime Minister of Czechoslovakia in his message to the people of Czechoslovakia. In it he said :—

"Citizens and soldiers . . . . I am living through the hardest hour of my life ; I am carrying out the most painful task, in comparison with which death would be easy. But precisely because I have fought and because I know under what conditions a war is won, I must tell you frankly . . . . that the forces opposed to us at this moment compel us to recognize their superior strength and to act accordingly . . . . .

"In Munich four European Great Powers met and decided to demand of us the acceptance of new frontiers, according to which the German areas of our State would be taken away. We had the choice between desperate and hopeless defence, which would have meant the sacrifice not only of the adult generation but also of women and children, and the acceptance of conditions which in their ruthlessness, and because they were imposed by pressure without war, have no parallel in history. We desired to make a contribution to peace ; we would gladly have made it. But not by any means in the way it has been forced upon us.

"But we were abandoned, and were alone . . . . Deeply moved, all your leaders considered, together with the army and the President of the Republic, all the possibilities which remained. *They recognized that in choosing between narrower frontiers and the death of the nation it was their sacred duty to save the life of our people, so that we may not emerge weakened from these terrible times, and so that we may remain certain that our nation will gather itself together again, as it has done so often in the past. Let us all see that our State re-establishes itself soundly within its new frontiers, and that its population is assured of a new life of peace and fruitful labour.* With your help we shall succeed. We rely upon you, and you have confidence in us."

It is evident that the Czechs refused to be led by the force of historic sentiment. They were ready to have narrower frontiers and a smaller Czechoslovakia to the ultimate destruction of their people.

With regard to Turkey the prevalent view was the one that was expressed in 1853 by the Czar Nicholas I, during a conversation with the British Ambassador in St. Petersburg in which he said "We have on our hands a sick man—a very sick man......He may suddenly die upon our hands." From that day the imminent decease of Turkey, the sick man of Europe, was awaited by all his neighbours. The shedding of the territories was considered as the convulsions of a dying man who is alleged to have breathed his last by affixing his signature to the treaty of Severs.

Is this really a correct view to take of Turkey in the process of dissoultion ? It is instructive to note the comments of Arnold Toynbee on this view. Referring to the Czar's description of Turkey as the sick man who may suddenly die, he says .—

"In this second and more sensational part of his diagnosis Czar Nicholas went astray because he did not understand the nature of the symptoms. If a person totally ignorant of natural history stumbled upon a snake in course of shedding its skin, he would pronounce dogmatically that the creature could not possibly recover. He would point out that when a man (or other mammal) has the misfortune to lose his skin, he is never known to survive. Yet while it is perfectly true that the leopard cannot change his spots nor the Ethiopian his skin, a wider study would have informed our amateur naturalist that a snake can do both and does both habitually. Doubtless, even for the snake, the process is awkward and uncomfortable. He becomes temporarily torpid, and in this condition he is dangerously at the mercy of his enemies. Yet, if he escapes the kites and crows until his metamorphosis is complete, he not only recovers his health but renews his youth with the replacement of his mortal coils. This is the recent experience of the Turk, and "moulting snake" is better simile than "Sick man" for a description of his distemper."

In this view the loss of her possessions by Turkey is the removal of an anomalous excrescence and the gain of a new skin. Turkey is certainly homogeneous and she has no fear of any disruption from within.

Pakistan is an anomalous excrescence on Hindustan and Hindustan is an anomalous excrescence on Pakistan. Tied together they will make India the sickman of Asia. Pakistan and Hindustan put together make a most heterogeneous Unit. It is obvious that if Pakistan has the demerit of cutting away parts of India it has also one merit namely of introducing homogeneity.

Severed into two, each becomes a more homogeneous Unit. This homogeneity of each is obvious enough Each has a cultural unity. Each has a religious unity Pakistan has a linguistic unity. If there is no such unity in Hindustan it is possible to have it without any controversy as to whether the common language should be Hindustani, Hindi or Urdu. Separated, each can become a strong and well-knit state. India needs a strong Central Government. But it cannot have it so long Pakistan remains a part of India. Compare the structure of the Federal Government as embodied in the Government of India Act, 1935 and it will be found that the Central Government as constituted under it is an effete ramshakle thing with very little life in it * As has already been pointed out this weakening of the Central Government is brought about by the desire of Muslim Provinces to be independent of the authority of the Central Government on the ground that the Central Government is bound to be predominantly Hindu in character and composition. When Pakistan comes into being these considerations can have no force. Hindustan can then have a strong Central Government a homogeneous population which are necessary elements and neither of which will be secured unless there is severance of Pakistan from Hindustan.

----

* For further discussion on this topic see my Tract on *Federation vs Freedom.*

PART IV

PAKISTAN AND THE MALAISE

The Hindu-Moslem Problem has two aspects to it. In its first aspect the problem that presents itself is the problem of two separate communities facing each other and seeking adjustment of their respective rights and privileges. In its other aspect the problem is the problem of the reflex influences which this separation and conflict produces upon each of them. In the course of the foregoing discussion we have looked at the project of Pakistan in relation to the first of the two aspects of the Hindu-Moslem problem. We have not examined the project of Pakistan in relation to the second aspect of that problem. Yet such an examination is necessary because that aspect of the Hindu-Moslem problem is not unimportant. It is a very superficial if not an incomplete view to stop with the problem of the adjustment of their claims. It cannot be overlooked that their lot is cast together : as such they have to participate in a course of common activity whether they like it or not. And if in this common activity they face each other as two combatants do, then their actions and reactions are worth study, for they affect both and produce a state of affairs which if it is a deceased state, the question of escape from it must be faced. A study of the situation shows that the actions and reactions have produced a malaise which exibits itself in there ways (1) Social Stagnation, (2) Communal Aggression and (3) National Frustration of Political Destiny. This malaise is a grave one Will Pakistan be remedy for the malaise ? Or, will it aggravate the malaise ? The following chapters are devoted to the consideration of Pakistan as a remedy for the malaise

CHAPTER X
SOCIAL STAGNATION

I

The Social evils which characterize the Hindu Society have been well known. The publication of 'Mother India' by Miss Mayo gave these evils the widest publicity. But while Mother India served the purpose of exposing these evils and calling their authors at the Bar of the world to answer for their sins, it created the unfortunate impression throughout the world that while the Hindus were grovelling in the mud of these social evils and were conservative, the Muslims in India were free from them, and as compared to the Hindus were a progressive people. That, such an impression should prevail, is of course surprizing to those who know the Muslim Society in India at close quarters.

One may well ask if there is any social evil which is found among the Hindus and is not found among the Muslims?

Take child marriage. The Secretary of the Anti-child-marriage Committee, constituted by the All-India Women's Conference published a bulletin which gives the extent of the evils of child-marriage in the different communities in the country. The figures which were taken from the Census Report of 1931 are as follows :—

TABLE.

Married Females aged 0-15 per 1000 Females of that age.

		Hindus	Muslims	Jains	Sikhs.	Christians
1881	.	208	153	189	170	33
1891	.	193	141	172	143	37
1901	.	186	131	164	101	38
1911	..	184	123	130	88	39
1921	..	170	111	117	72	32
1931	..	199	186	125	80	43

Can the position of the Musalmans so far as child—marriage is considered better than the position of Hindus ?

Take the position of women. It is insisted by Muslims that the legal rights given to Moslem women ensure them a measure of independence greater than that of some other Eastern women, for example, Hindus and also in excess of the rights of women in some Western countries. Reliance is placed on some of the provisions of the Muslim Law.

Firstly it is said the Muslim Law does not fix any age for marriage, and recognizes the right of a girl to marry any time. Further except where the marriage is celebrated by the father or grand-father a Muslim girl if given in marriage in childhood has the power to repudiate her marriage on attaining puberty.

Secondly marriage among the Musalmans is a contract. Being a contract the husband has a right to divorce his wife and the Muslim Law has provided ample safeguards for the wife which, if availed of, would place the Muslim wife on the same footing as the husband in the matter of divorce. For, the wife under the Muslim Law can, at the time of the marriage, or even thereafter in some cases, enter into a contract by which she may under certain circumstances obtain a divorce

Thirdly the Mahomedan Law requires that a wife can claim from her husband, by way of consideration for the surrender of her person, a sum of money or other property — known as her ' Dower '. The dower may be fixed even after marriage and if no amount is fixed the wife is entitled to proper dower. The amount of dower is usually split into two parts, one is called "prompt" which is payable on demand, and other "deferred" which is payable on dissolution of marriage by death or divorce. Her claim for dower will be treated as a debt against the husband's estate. She has complete dominion over her dower which is intended to give her economic independence. She can remit it or she can appropriate the income of it as she pleases.

Granting all these provisions of law in her favour, the Muslim woman is the most helpless person in the world. To quote an Egyptian Moslem leader —

"Islam has set its seal of inferiority upon her, and given the sanction of religion to social customs which have deprived her of the full opportunity for self-expression and development of personality."

No Muslim girl has the courage to repudiate her marriage although it may be open to her on the ground that she was a child and that it was brought about by persons other than her parents. No Muslim wife will think it proper to have a clause entered into her marriage contract reserving her the right to divorce. In that event her fate is 'once married, always married' She cannot escape the marriage tie however irksome it may be. While she cannot repudiate the marriage the husband can always do it without having to show any cause. Utter the word *'Tallak'* and observe continance for three weeks and the woman is cast away The only restraint on his caprice is the obligation to pay dower. If the dower has already been remitted his right to divorce is a matter of his sweet will.

This latitude in the matter of divorce destroys that sense of security which is so fundamental for a full, free and happy life for a woman. This insecurity of life to which a Muslim woman is exposed is greatly augmented by the right of polygamy and concubinage, which the Muslim law gives to the husband.

Mahomedan Law allows a Muslim to marry four wives at a time It is not unoften said that this is an improvement over the Hindu Law which places no restrictions on the number of wives a Hindu can have at any given time. But it is forgotten that in addition to the four legal wives the Muslim Law permits, a Mahomedan to cohabit with his female slaves. In the case of female slaves nothing is said as to the number. They re allowed to him without any restriction whatever and without any obligation to marry them.

No words can adequately express the great and many evils of polygamy and concubinage and especially as a source of misery to a Muslim woman. It is true that because polygamy and concubinage are sanctioned one must not suppose they are indulged in by the generality of Muslims ; still the fact remains that they are previleges which are easy for a Muslim to abuse to the misery and unhappiness of his wife.   Mr. John J. Pool, no enemy of Islam, observes* .—

"This latitude in the matter of divorce is very greatly taken advantage of by some Mohammedans.   Stobart, commenting on this subject in his book, 'Islam, and its Founder,' says : "Some Mohammedans make a habit of continually changing their wives. We read of young men who have had twenty and thirty wives, a new one every three months ; and thus it comes about that women are liable to be indefinitely transferred from one man to another, obliged to accept a husband and a home whenever they can find one, or in case of destitution, to which divorce may have driven them, to resort to other more degrading means of living." Thus while keeping the strict letter of the law, and possessing only one or certainly not more than four wives, unscrupulous characters may yet by divorce obtain in a lifetime as many wives as they please.

"In another way also a Mohammedan may really have more than four wives, and yet keep within the law.   This is by means of living with concubines, which the Koran expressly permits.   In that *sura* which allows four wives, the words are added, "or the slaves which ye shall have acquired."   Then, in the 70th *sura*, it is revealed that it is no sin to live with slaves.   The very words are : "The slaves which their right hands possess, as to them they shall be blameless." At the present day, as in days past, in multitudes of Mohammedan homes, slaves are found ; and as Muir say, in his ' Life of Mahomet ' "so long as this unlimited permission of living with their female slaves continues, it cannot be expected that there will be any hearty attempt to put a stop to slavery in Mohammedan countries," Thus the Koran, in this matter of slavery, is the enemy of the mankind. And women, as usual, are the greatest sufferers."

Take the caste system.   Islam speaks of brotherhood.   Everybody infers that Islam must be free from slavery and caste.   Regarding slavery nothing needs to be said.   It stands abolished now by law· But while it existed much of its support was derived from Islam and Islamic countries.†   While the prescriptions by the Prophet regarding the just and humane treatment of slaves   contained in

---

* Studies in Mahomedanism pp. 34 35.

† Studies in Mahomedanism. Chapter XXXIX.

the Koran are praiseworthy, there is nothing whatever in Islam that lends to the abolition of this curse. As Sir W. Muir has well said* :—

"... . rather, while lightening, he rivetted the fetter .... There is no obligation on a Moslem to release his slaves .... "

But if slavery has gone, caste has remained. As an illustration one may take the conditions prevalent among the Bengal Muslims. The Superintandent of the Census for 1901 for the Province of Bengal records the following interesting facts regarding the Muslims of Bengal .—

" The conventional division of the Mahomedans into four tribes-Sheikh, Saiad, Moghul and Pathan — has very little application to this Province (Bengal). The Mahomedans themselves recognize two main social divisions, (1) Ashraf or Sharaf and (2) Ajlaf. Ashraf means 'noble' and includes all undoubted descendants of foreigners and converts from high caste Hindus. All other Mahomedans including the occupational groups and all converts of lower ranks, are known by the contemptuous terms, ' Ajlaf', "wretches" or "mean people" : they are also called Kamina or Itar, 'base' or Rasil, a corruption of Rizal, 'worthless'. In some places a third class, called Arzal or ' lowest of all' is added. With them no other Mahomedan would associate, and they are forbidden to enter the mosque or to use the public burial ground.

" Within these groups there are castes with social precedence of exactly the same nature as one finds among the Hindus.

I. Ashraf—or better class Mahomedans.

   (1) Saiads.
   (2) Sheikhs.
   (3) Pathans.
   (4) Moghul.
   (5) Mallik.
   (6) Mirza.

II. *Ajlaf* or lower class Mohamedans.

   (1) Cultivating Sheiks, and others who were originally Hindus but who do not belong to any functional group, and have not gained admittance to the Ashraf Community e. g. Pirali and Thakrai.

---

* The Coran, its Composition and Teaching p. 58.

(2) Darzi, Jolaha, Fakir, and Rangrez.

(3) Barhi, Bhathiara, Chik, Churihar, Dai, Dhawa, Dhunia, Gaddi, Kalal, Kasai, Kula Kunjara, Laheri, Mahifarosh, Mallah, Naliya, Nikari.

(4) Abdal, Bako, Bediya, Bhat, Chamba, Dafali, Dhobi, Hajjam, Mucho, Nagarchi, Nat, Panwaria, Madaria, Tuntia.

III. *Arzal* or degraded class.

Bhanar, Halalkhor, Hijra, Kasbi, Lalbegi Maugta, Mehtai."

The Census Superintendent mentions another feature of the Muslim Social system, namely, the prevalence of the "panchayet system, he states " :—

"The authority of the panchayet extends to social as well as trade matters and.........marriage with people of other communities is one of the offences of which the governing body takes cognizance The result is that these groups are often as strictly endogamous as Hindu castes. The prohibition on inter-marriage extends to higher as well as to lower castes, and a Dhuma, for example, may marry no one but a Dhuma. If this rule is transgressed, the offender is at once hauled up before the panchayet and ejected ignominously from his community. A member of one such group cannot ordinarily gain admission to another, and he retains the designation of the community in which he was born even if he abandons its distinctive occupation and takes to other means of livelihood......... .thousands of Jolahas are butchers, yet they are still known as Jolahas."

Similar facts from other Provinces of India could be gathered from their respective Census Reports and those who are curious may refer to them. But the facts for Bengal are enough to show that the Mahomedans observe not only caste but also untouchability.

There can thus be no manner of doubt that the Muslim Society in India is afflicted by the same social evils which afflict the Hindu Society. Indeed the Muslims have all the social evils of the Hindus and something more. That something more is the compulsory system of Purdah for Muslim women.

As a consequence of the Purdah system a segregation of the Muslim women is brought about. The ladies are not expected to visit the outer rooms, varandahs or gardens their quarters are in the backyard.   All of them, young and old, are confined in the same room ; No male servant can work in their presence.   Women are allowed to see only their sons, brothers, father, uncles and husband, or any other near relation who may be admitted to a position of trust.   The cannot go even to the mosque to pray and must wear *burka* (veil) whenever they have to go out.   These *burka* women walking in the streets is a one of the most hideous sights one can witness in India.   Such seclusion cannot but have its deteriorating effects, upon the physical constitution of Muslim women.   They are usually victims to anaemia, tuberculosis and pyorrhoea.   Their bodies are deformed, with their backs bent, bones protruded, hands and feet crooked.   Ribs, joints and nearly all their bones ache.   Heart palpitation is very often present in them.   The result of this pelvic deformity is untimely death at the time of delivery.   Purdah deprives Muslim women of mental and moral nourishment.   Being deprived of healthy social life, the process of moral degeneration must and does set in.   Being completely secluded from the outer world they engage their minds in petty family quarrels with the result that they became narrow and restricted in their out-look.

They lag behind their other sisters, cannot take part in any out-door activity and are weighed down by a slavish mentality and an inferiority complex.   They have no desire for knowledge, because they are taught not to be interested in anything outside the four walls of the house.   Purdah women in particular become helpless, timid, and unfit for any fight in life.   Considering the large number of purdah women among Muslims in India, one can easily understand the vastness and seriousness of the problem of purdah.*

The physical and the intellectual effects of purdah are nothing as compared with its effects on morals.   The origin of purdah lies of course in the deep-rooted suspicion of sexual appetites in both sexes and the purpose is to check them by segregating the sexes.   But far from achieving the purpose, purdah has adversely affected the morals of Muslim men.   Owing to purdah a Muslim has no contact with any woman outside those who belong to his own household.   Even with them his contact extends only to occasional conversation.   For a male there is no company of and

---

* For the position of Muslim women see "Our Cause" edited by Shyam Kumari Nehru.

no comingling with the females except those who are children or aged. This isolation of the males from females is sure to produce bad effects on the morals of men. It requires no psychoanalyst to say that a social system which cuts off all contact between the two sexes produces an unhealthy tendency towards sexual excesses and unnatural and other morbid habits and ways.

The evil consequences of purdha are not confined to the Muslim community only. It is responsible for the social seggrega- tion of Hindus from Muslims which is the bane of public life in India. This argument may appear for fetched and one is inclined to attribute this seggregation to the unsociability of the Hindus rather than to purdah among the Muslims. But the Hindus are right when they say that it is not possible to establish social contact between Hindus and Muslims because such contact can only mean contact between women from one side and men from the other.*

Not that purdah and the evils consequent thereon are not to be found among certain sections of the Hindus in certain parts of the country. But the point of distinction is that among the Muslims, purdah has a religious sanctity which it has not with the Hindus The evil of purdah has deeper roots among the Muslims than it has among the Hindus and can only be removed by facing the inevitable conflict between religious injunctions and social needs. The problem of purdah is a real problem with the Muslims — apart from its origin — which it is not with the Hindus. But, of any attempt by the Muslims to do away with it, there is no evidence.

There is thus a stagnation in the social life of the Muslims. But there is also a stagnation in the political life of the Muslim community of India. The Muslims have no interest in politics as such. Their predominant interest is religion. This can be easily seen by the terms and conditions that a Muslim constituency makes for its support to a candidate fighting for a seat. The Muslim constituency does not care to examine the programme of the candidate. All that the constituency wants from the candidate is that he should agree to replace the old lamps of the masjid by

---

* The Europeans who are accused by Indians for not admitting them to their clubs use the same argument · "we bring our women to the clubs. If you agree to bring your women to the club you can be admitted. We can't expose our women to your company if you deny us the company of your women. Be ready to go fifty fifty, then ask for entry in our clubs."

supplying new ones as his cost, to provide a new carpet for the masjid because the old one is torn, to repair the masjid because it has become dilapidated.   In some places a Muslim constituency is quite satisfied if the candidate agrees to give a sumptuous feast and in other places if he agrees to buy votes for so much a piece.   With the Muslims election is a mere matter of money and is very seldom a matter of social programme of general improvement.   Muslim politics takes no note of purely secular categories of life, namely, the differences between rich and poor, capital and labour, landlord and tenant, priest and laymen, reason and superstition.   Muslim politics is essentially clerical and recognizes only one difference namely that existing between Hindus and Muslims.   None of the secular categories of life have any place in the politics of the Muslim community and if they do find a place — and they must because they are irrepressible — they are subordinated to one and the only governing principle of the Muslim political universe, namely, religion.

II

The existence of these evils among the Muslims is distressing enough   But far more distressing is the fact that there is no organized movement of social reform among the Mussalmans of India on a scale sufficient to being about their eradication   The Hindus have their social evils.   But there is this relieving feature about them — namely that some of them are conscious of their existence and a few of them are actively agitating for their removal. But the Muslims on the other hand do not realize that they are evil and consequently do not agitate for their removal.   On the other hand they oppose any change in their existing practices.   It is noteworthy that the Muslims opposed the Child Marriage Bill brought in the Central Assembly in 1930, whereby the age for marriage of a girl was raised to 14 and of a boy to 16 on the ground that it was opposed to the Muslim cannon law.   Not only did they oppose the bill at every stage but that when it became law they started a compaign of Civil Disobedience against that Act.   Fortunately the Civil Disobedience campaign of the Muslims against the Act did not swell and was submerged in the Congress Civil Disobedience campaign which synchronized with it.   But the fact remains that the Muslims are opposed to social reform.

The question may be asked why are the Muslims opposed to social reform ?

The usual answer given is that the Muslims all over the world are an unprogressive people. This view no doubt accords with the facts of history. After the first spurts of their activity — the scale of which was undoubtedly stupendous leading to the foundations of vast Empires — the Muslims suddenly fell into a strange condition of torpor, from which they never seemed to have become awake. The cause assigned for this torpor by those who have made a study of their condition is said to be the fundamental assumption made by all Muslims that Islam is a world religion, suitable for all peoples, for all times and for all conditions. It has been contended that :—

"The Mussalman, remaining faithful to his religion, has not progressed ; he has remained stationary in a world of swiftly moving modern forces. It is indeed, one of the salient features of Islam that it immobilizes in the native barbarism the races whom it enslaves. It is fixed in a crystallization, inert and impenetrable. It is unchangeable ; and political, social or economic changes have no repercussion upon it.

"Having been taught that outside Islam there can be no safety ; outside its law no truth and outside its spiritual massage there is no happiness, the Muslim has become incapable of conceiving any other condition than his own, any other mode of thought than the Islamic thought. He firmly believes that he has arrived at any unequalled pitch of perfection , that he is the sole possessor of true faith, of the true doctrine, the true wisdom , that he alone is in possession of the truth — no relative truth subject to revision, but absolute truth.

"The religious law of the Muslims has had the effect of imparting to the very diverse individuals of whom the world is composed, a unity of thought, of feeling, of ideas of judgment."

It is urged that this uniformity is deadening and is not merely imparted to the Muslims, but is imposed upon them by a spirit of intolerance which is unknown anywhere outside the Muslim world for its severity and its violence and which is directed towards the suppression of all rational thinking which is in conflict with the teachings of Islam. As Renan observes :—

"Islam is a close union of the spiritual and the temporal ; it is the reign of. a dogma, it is the heaviest chain that humanity has ever borne......Islam has its beauties as a religion ;......But to the human reason Islamism has only been injurious. The minds that it has shut from the light were, no doubt, already closed in their own internal limits ; but it has persecuted free thought, I shall not say more violently than other religions, but more effectually. It has made of the countries that it has conquered a closed field to the rational culture of the mind. What is, in fact essentially distinctive of the Musalman is his hatred of science, his persuation that research is useless, frivolous, almost impious — the natural sciences, because they are attempts at rivalry with God ; the historical sciences, because since they apply to times anterior to Islam, they may revive ancient heresies....." Renan concludes by saying "Islam, in treating science as an enemy, is only consistent, but it is a dangerous thing to be consistent. To its own misfortune Islam has been successful. By slaying science it has slain itself ; and is condemned in the world to a complete inferiority."

But this obvious answer cannot be the true answer. If it were the true answer how are we to account for the stir and ferment that is going on in all Muslim countries outside India where the spirit of inquiry, the spirit of change and the desire to reform is noticeable in every walk of life. Indeed the social reforms which have taken place in Turkey have been of the most revolutionary character. If Islam has not come in the way of the Muslims of these countries, why should it come in the way of the Muslims of India? There must be some special reason for the social and political stagnation in the Muslim community of India.

What that special reason can be ? It seems to me that the reason for the absence of the spirit of change in the Indian Mussalman is to be sought in the peculiar position he occupies in India. He is placed in a social environment which is predominantly Hindu. That Hindu environment is always silently but surely encroaching upon him. He feels that it is de-mussalmanizing him. As a protection against this gradual weaning out he is led to insist on preserving everything that is Islamic without caring to examine whether it is helpful or harmful to his society. Secondly, the Muslims in India are placed in a political environment which is also predominantly Hindu. He feels that he will be suppressed and that political suppression will make the Muslims a depressed class. It is this consciousness that he has to save himself from being submerged by the Hindus socially and politically which to my mind is the primary cause why the Indian Muslims as compared with their fellows outside are backward in the matter of social reform. Their energies are directed to maintaining a constant struggle against the Hindus for seats and posts in which there is no time, no thought and no room for questions relating to social reform. And if there is any, it is all overweighed and suppressed by the desire, generated by pressure of communal tension, to close the ranks and offer a united front to the menace of Hindus and Hinduism by maintaining their socio-religious unity at any cost.

The same is the explanation of the political stagnation in the Muslim community of India. Muslim politicians do not recognize secular categories of life as the basis of their politics because to them it means the weakening of the community in its fight against the Hindus. The poor Muslims will not join the poor Hindus to get justice from the rich. Muslim tenants will not join Hindu tenants to prevent the tyranny of the land-lords. Muslim labourers will not join Hindu labourers in the fight of labour against capital. Why? The answer is simple. The poor Muslim sees that if he joins in the fight of the poor against the rich he may be fighting against a rich Muslim The Muslim tenant feels that if he joins in the campaign against the land-lord he may have to fight against a Muslim land-lord. A Muslim labourer feels that if he joins in the onslaught of labour against capital he will be injuring a Muslim mill-owner. He is conscious that any injury to a rich Muslim, to Muslim landlord or to a Muslim millowner is a disservice to the Muslim Community for it weakens the Community in its struggle against the Hindu Community.

How Muslim politics has become perverted is shown by the attitude of the Muslim leaders to the political reforms in the Indian States. The Muslims and their leaders carried on a great agitation for the introduction of representative government in the Hindu State of Kashmere. The same Muslims and their leaders are deadly opposed to the introduction of representative governments in other Muslim States. This is somewhat difficult to understand. But the reason for this strange attitude is quite simple. The determining question with the Muslims is how will that affect the Muslims. If representative government can help the Muslims they will demand it and fight for it. In the State of Kashmere the ruler is a Hindu but the majority of its subjects are Muslims. The Muslims fought for representative government in Kashmere because representative government in Kashmere means the transfer of power from a Hindu king to the Muslim masses. In other Muslim States the ruler is a Muslim but the majority of his subjects are Hindus. In such States representative government means the transfer of power from a Muslim Ruler to the Hindu masses and that is why the Muslims support the introduction of representative government in one case and oppose it in the other case. The dominating consideration with the Muslims is not democracy. The dominating consideration is how will democracy affect the Muslims in their struggle against the Hindus. Will it strengthen them or will it weaken them ? If democracy weakens them they will not have democracy. They will rather prefer the rotten state to continue in the Muslim States than weaken the Muslim Ruler in his hold upon his Hindu subjects.

The political and social stagnation in the Muslim community can be explained by one and only one reason. The Muslims think that the Hindus and Muslims must perpetually struggle, the Hindus, to establish their dominance over the the Muslims and the Muslims to establish their historical position as the ruling community — that in this struggle the strong will win and to ensure strength they must suppress or put in cold storage everything which causes dissension in their ranks.

If the Muslims in other countries have undertaken the task of the reform of their society and the Muslims of India have refused to do so, it is because the former are free from the communal and political clashes with rival communities while the latter are not.

III

It is not that this blind spirit of conservatism which does not recognize the need of repair to the social structure has taken hold of the Muslims only. It has taken hold of the Hindus also. The Hindus at one time did recognize that without social efficiency no
30

permanent progress in the other fields of activity was possible, that owing to the mischief wrought by the evil customs Hindu Society was not in a state of efficiency and that ceaseless efforts must be made to eradicate these evils. It was due to the recognition of this fact that the birth of the National Congress was accompanied by the foundation of the Social Conference. While the Congress was concerned with defining the weak points in the political organisation of the country, the Social Conference was engaged in removing the weak points in the social organisation of the Hindu Society. For some time the Congress and the Conference worked as two wings of one common activity and they held their annual sessions in the same pandal. But soon the two wings developed into two parties, a Political Reform Party and a Social Reform Party, between whom there raged a fierce controversy. The Political Reform Party supported the National Congress and Social Reform Party supported the Social Conference. The two bodies thus became two hostile camps. The point at issue was whether social reform should precede political reform. For a decade the forces were evenly balanced and the battle was fought without victory to either side. It was however evident that the fortunes of the Social Conference were ebbing fast. The gentlemen who presided over the sessions of the Social Conference lamented that the majority of the educated Hindus were for political advancement and indifferent to social reform and that while the number of those who attended the Congress was very large and the number who did not attend but who sympathized with it even larger, the number of those who attended the Social Conference was very much smaller. This indifference, this thinning of its ranks was soon followed by active hostility from the politicians, like the late Mr. Tilak. Thus, in course of time the party in favour of political reform won and the Social Conference vanished and was forgotten.* And with it also vanished from the Hindu Society the urge for social reform. Under the leadership of Mr. Gandhi the Hindu society if it did not become a political mad-house certainly became mad after politics. Non-Cooperation, Civil Disobedience, and a cry for Swaraj took the place which social reform once had in the minds of the Hindus. In the din and dest of political agitation the Hindus

---

* For a more detailed Statement see my tract on *Annihilation of Caste.*

do not even know that there are any evils to be remedied. Those who are conscious of it do not believe that social reform is as important as political reform, and when forced to admit its importance argue that there can be no social reform unless first political power is achieved. They are so eager to possess political power that they are impatient even of propaganda in favour of social reform as so much time and energy deducted from political propaganda. A correspondent of Mr. Gandhi put the point of view of the Nationalists very appropriately if bluntly when he wrote* to Mr. Gandhi, saying :—

"Don't you think that it is impossible to achive any great reform without winning political power ? The present economic structure has got to be tackled ? No reconstruction is possible without political reconstruction and I am afraid all this talk of polished and unpolished rice, balanced diet and so on and so forth is mere moonshine."

The Social Reform party, led by Ranade and Gokhale, died leaving the field to the Congress. There has grown up among the Hindus another party which is also a rival to the Congress. It is the Hindu Maha Sabha. One would expect from its name that it was a body for bringing about the reform of Hindu Society. But it is not. Its rivalry with the Congress has nothing to do with the issue of social reform vs. political reform. Its quarrel with the Congress has its origin in the pro-Muslim policy of the Congress. It is organized for the protection of Hindu rights against Muslim enchroachment. Its plan is to organize the Hindus, for offering a common front to the Muslims. As a body organized to protect Hindu rights it is all the time engaged in keeping an eye on political movements on seats and posts. It cannot spare any thought for social reform. As a body keen on bringing about a common front of all Hindus it cannot afford to create dissensions among its elements as would be the case if it undertook to bring about social reforms. For the sake of the consolidation of the Hindu rank and file the Hindu Maha Sabha is ready to suffer all social evils to remain as they are. For the sake of consolidation of the Hindus it is prepared to welcome the Federation as devised by the Act of 1935 inspite of its many inequities and defects. For the same purpose the Hindu

---

* Harijan—11th January 1936.

Maha Sabha favours the retention of the Indian States with their administration as it is. 'Hands off the Hindu States' has been the battle cry of its President. This attitude is stranger than that of the Muslims. Representative government in Hindu States cannot do harm to the Hindus. Why then should the President of the Hindu Mahasabha oppose it ? Probably because it helps the Muslims which he cannot tolerate.

IV

To what length this concern for the conservation of their forces can lead the Hindus and the Musalmans cannot be better illustrated than by the Dissolution of Muslim Marriage Act VIII of 1939 passed by the Indian Legistature. Before 1939 the law was that apostasy of a male or female married under the Muslim Law *ipso facto* dissolved the marriage with the result that if a Muslim married woman changed her religion she was free to marry any person professing her new religion. This was the rule of law enforced by the courts all throughout India at any rate for the last 60 years*

This law was annulled by the Act VIII of 1939, section 4 of which reads as follows :—

" The renunciation of Islam by a married Muslim woman or her conversion to a faith other than Islam shall not by itself operate to dissolve her marriage .

Provided that after such renunciation, or conversion the woman shall be entitled to obtain a decree for the dissolution of marriage on any of the grounds mentioned in Section 2 :

Provided further that the provisions of this section shall not apply to a woman converted to Islam from some other faith who re-embraces her former faith."

According to this Act the marriage of a Muslim married woman is not dissolved by reason of her conversion to another religion. All that she gets is a right of divorce. It is very intriguing to find that section 2 does not refer to conversion or apostasy as a ground for divorce. The effect of the law is that a Muslim married woman

---

* The earliest reported decision was that given by the High Court of the North West Province in 1870 in the case of *Zabaroast Khan vs. His wife.*

has no liberty of conscience and is tied for ever to her husband whose religious faith may be quite abhorent to her.

The grounds urged in support of this change are well worth attention. The mover of the Bill Quazi Kazmi, M.L A. adopted a very ingenious line of argument in support of the change. In his speech * on the motion to refer the Bill he said :—

Apostasy was considered by Islam, as by any other religion, as a great crime, almost amounting to a crime against the State. It is not novel for the religion of Islam to have that provision. If we look up the older Acts of any nation, we will find that similar provision also exists in other Codes as well. For the male a severer punishment was awarded, that of death, and for females, only the punishment of imprisonment was awarded. This main provision was that because it was a sin, it was a crime, it was to be punished, and the woman was to be deprived of her status as wife. It was not only this status that she lost, but she lost all her status in society, she was deprived of her propety and civil rights as well. But we find that as early as 1850 an Act was passed here, called the Caste Disabilities Removal Act of 1850, Act XXI of 1850......

".... by this Act, the forfeiture of civil rights that could be imposed on a woman on her apostasy has been taken away. She can no longer be subjected to any forfeiture of property or her right of inheritance or anything of the kind. The only question is that the Legislature has come to her help, it has given her a certain amount of liberty of thought, some kind of liberty or religion to adopt any faith she likes, and has removed the forfeiture clause from which she could suffer, and which was a restraint upon her changing the faith. The question is how far we are entitled after that to continue placing the restriction on her status as a wife. Her status as a wife is of some importance in society. She belongs to some family, she has got children, she has got other connections too. If she has got a liberal mind, she may not like to continue the same old religion. If she changes her religion, why should we, according to our modern ideas, inflict upon her a further penalty that she will cease to be the wife of her husband. I submit, in these days when we are advocating freedom of thought and freedom of religion, when we are advocating inter-marriages between different communities, it would be inconsistent for us to support a provision that a mere change of faith or change of religion would entail forfeiture of her rights as the wife of her husband.

* Legislative Assembly Debates 1938, Vol. V, pages 1098—1101

So, from a modern point of view, I have got no hesitation in saying that we cannot, in any way, support the contrary proposition that apostasy must be allowed to finish her relationship with her husband. But that is only one part of the argument.

"Section 32 of the Parsi Marriage and Divorce Act, 1936, is to the effect that a married woman may sue for divorce on the grounds "that the defendant has ceased to be a Parsi....

"There are two things apparent from this. The first is, that it is a ground for dissolution, not from any religious idea or religious sentiment, because, if two years have passed after the conversion and if plaintiff does not object, then either the male or female has no right to sue for dissolution of marriage. The second thing is, that it is the plaintiff who has got the complaint that the other party has changed the religion, who has got the right of getting the marriage dissolved .... In addition to this Act, as regards other communities we can have an idea of the effect of conversion on marriage tie from the Native Converts' Marriage Dissolution Act, Act XXI of 1866......... It applies to all the communities of India, and this legislation recognises the fact that mere conversion of an Indian to Christianity would not dissolve the marriage but he will have the right of going to a law court and saying that the other party, who is not converted, must perform the marital duties in respect of him .... then they are given a year's time and the judge directs that they shall have an interview with each other in the presence of certain other persons to induce them to resume their conjugal relationship, and if they do not agree, then on the ground of desertion the marriage is dissolved. The marriage is dissolved no doubt, but not on the ground of change of faith,....... So, every community in India has got this accepted principle that conversion to another religion cannot amount to a dissolution of marriage."

Syed Gulam Bikh Nairang another Muslim member of the Assembly and a protagonist of the Bill was brutally frank. In support of the principle of the Bill he said[*] :—

. " For a very long time the courts in British India have held without reservation and qualification that under all circumstances apostasy automatically and immediately puts an end to the married state without any judicial proceedings, any decree of court, or any other ceremony. That has been the position which was taken up by the Courts. Now, there are three distinct views of *Hanafi juris* on the

---

[*] Legislative Assembly Debates 1938, Vol. V 1953-55.

point. One view which is attributed to the Bokhara jurists was adopted and even that not in its entirety but in what I may call mutilated and maimed condition. What that Bokhara view is has been already stated by Mr. Kazmi and some other speakers. The Bokhara jurists say that marriage is dissolved by apostasy. In fact, I should be more accurate in saying — I have got authority for that—that it is, according to the Bokhara view, not dissolved but suspended. The marriage is suspended but the wife is then kept in custody or confinement till she repents and embraces Islam again and then, she is induced to marry the husband, whose marriage was only suspended and not put an end to or cancelled. The second view is that on apostasy a married Muslim ceases to be the wife of her husband but becomes his bond woman. One view, which is a sort of corollary to this view, is that she is not necessarily the bond woman of her ex-husband but she becomes the bond woman of the entire Muslim community and anybody can employ her as a bond woman. The third view, that of the Ulema of Samarkand and Balkh is that the marriage tie is not affected by such apostasy and that the woman still continues to be the wife of the husband. These are the three views. A portion of the first view, the Bokhara view, was taken hold of by the Courts and rulings after rulings were based on that portion.

" This house is well aware that it is not only in this solitary instance that judicial error is sought to be corrected by legislation, but in many other cases, too, there have been judicial errors or conflicts of judicial opinion or uncertainties and vagueness of law. Errors of judicial view are being constantly corrected by legislation. In this particular matter there has been an error after error and a tragedy of errors. To show me those rulings is begging the question. Surely, it should be realised that it is no answer to my Bill that because the High Courts have decided against me, I have no business to come to this House and ask it to legislate this way or that way."

Having regard to the profundity of the change, the arguments urged in support of it were indeed very insubstantial. Mr. Kazmi failed to realize that if there was a difference between the divorce law relating to Parsis, Christians and Muslims, once it is established that the conversion is genuine, the Muslim law was in advance of the Parsee and the Christian law and instead of making the Muslim law to retrograde, the proper thing ought to have been to make the Parsi and the Christian law progress. Mr. Nairang did not stop to inquire that if there were different schools of thought among the Muslim jurists whether it was not more in consonance with justice to adopt the more enlightened view which recognized the freedom of the Muslim woman and not to replace it by the barbaric one which made her a bondswoman.

Be that as it may, the legal arguments had nothing to do with the real motive underlying the change. The real motive was to put a stop to the illicit conversion of women to alien faiths followed by immediate and hurried marriages with some one professing the faith she happened to have joined with a view to lock her in the new community and prevent her from going back to the community to which she originally belonged. The conversion of Muslim women to Hinduism and of Hindu women to Islam looked at from social and political point of view cannot but be fraught with tremendous consequences. It means a disturbance in the numerical balance between the two communities. As the disturbance was being brought about by the abduction of women it could not be overlooked. For woman is at once the seed of and the hop-house for nationalism more than man can ever be.* These conversions of women and their subsequent marriages were therefore regarded, and rightly, as series of depradations practised by Hindus against Muslims and by Muslims against Hindus with a view to bring about a change in their relative numerical strength. This practice of woman-lifting, in addition to being as bad, had become as common as cattle lifting and with its obvious danger to cattle-lifting had to be stopped. That this was the real reason can be seen from the two provisos to Section 4 of the Act. In Proviso I the Hindus concede to the Musalmans that if they convert a woman who was originally a Muslim she will remain bound to her former Muslim husband notwithstanding her conversion. By Proviso 2 the Muslims concede to the Hindus that if they convert a Hindu married woman and she is married to a Musalman, her marriage will be deemed to be dissolved if she renounces Islam and she will be free to return to her Hindu fold. Thus what underlies the change in law is the desire to keep the numerical balance and it is for this purpose that the rights of women were sacrificed.

---

* The part played by woman in sustaining nationalism has not been sufficiently noticed. See the observations of Rennan on this point in his Essay on Nationality.

There are two other features of this malaise which have not been sufficiently noted.

The jealousy with which one of them looks upon any reform by the other in its social system, if the effect of such reform is to give it increase of strength for resistance, is one such feature.

Swami Shradhanand relates a very curious incident which well illustrates this attitude. Writing in the Liberator* his recollections he refers to this incident. He says :—

" Mr. Ranade was there.........to guide the Social Conference to which the title of " National" was for the first and last time given. It was from the beginning a Hindu Conference in all walks of life. The only Mahomedan delegate who joined the National Social Conference was a Muftisaheb of Barreily. Well ! The Conference began when the resolution in favour of remarriage of child-widows was moved by a Hindu delegate and by me. Sanatanist Pandits opposed it. Then the Mufti asked permission to speak. The late Baijnath told Muftisaheb that as the resolution concerned the Hindus only, he need not speak. At this the Mufti flared up.

" There was no loophole left for the President and Muftisaheb was allowed to have his say. Muftisaheb's argument was that as Hindu Shastras did not allow remarriage, it was a sin to press for it. Again, when the resolution about the reconversion of those who had become Christians and Mussalmans came up, Muftisaheb urged that when a man abandoned the Hindu religion he ought not to be allowed to come back."

Another illustration would be the attitude of the Muslims towards the problem of the Untouchables. The Muslims have always been looking at the Depressed Classes with a sense of longing and much of the jealousy between Hindus and Muslims arises out of the fear of the latter that the former might become stronger by assimilating the Depressed Classes. In 1909 the Muslims took the bold step of suggesting that the Depressed Classes should not be enrolled in the Census as Hindus. In 1923 Mr. Mahomed Ali in his address as the President of the Congress went much beyond the position taken by the Muslims in 1909. He said —

" The quarrels about ALAMS and PIPAL trees and musical processions are truly childish ; but there is one question which can easily furnish a ground for complaint of unfriendly action if communal activities are not amicably adjusted. It is the question of the conversion of the Suppressed Classes, if Hindu society does not speedily

* 26th April 1926.

absorb them.   The Christian missionary is already busy and no one quarrels with him.   But the moment some Muslim Missionary Society is organized for the same purpose there is every likelihood of an outcry in the Hindu Press.   It has been suggested to me by an influential and wealthy gentleman who is able to organize a Missionary Society on a large scale for the conversion of the Suppressed Classes, that it should be possible to reach a settlement with leading Hindu gentlemen and divide the country into separate areas where Hindu and Muslim Missionaries could respectively work, each community preparing for each year, or longer unit of time if necessary, an estimate of the numbers it is prepared to absorb or convert   These estimates would, of course, be based on the number of workers and funds each had to spare, and tested by the actual figures of the previous period. In this way each community would be free to do the work of absorption and conversion, or rather, of reform without chances of collision with one another.   I cannot say in what light my Hindu brethren will take it and I place this suggestion tentatively in all frankness and sincerity before them.   All that I say for myself is that I have seen the condition of the " Kali Praja " in the Baroda State and of the Gonds in the Central Provinces and I frankly confess it is a reproach to us all.   If the Hindus will not absorb them into their own society, others will and must, and then the orthodox Hindu too will cease to treat them as untouchables.   Conversion seems to transmute them by a strong alchemy.   But does this not place a premium upon conversion ? "

The other feature is the " preparations " which the Muslims and Hindus are making against each other without abatement.   It is like a race in armaments between two hostile nations.   If the Hindus have the Benares University, the Musalmans must have the Aligarh University.   If the Hindus start Shudhi movement, the Muslims must launch the Tablig movement.   If the Hindus start Sangathan, the Muslims must meet it by Tanjim.   If the Hindus have the R. S. S.*, the Muslims must reply by organizing the Khaksars.†   This race in social armament and equipment is run with the determination and apprehension characteristic of nations which are on the war path.   The Muslims fear that the Hindus are subjugating them.   The Hindus feel that the Muslims are engaged in reconquering them.   Both appear to be preparing for war and each is watching the " preparations " of the other.

* Short for the Rashtriya Swayam Sevaka Sangh which is a Hindu volunteer corps.
† Khaksar is a Muslim volunteer corps.

Such a state of things cannot but be ominous. It is a vicious circle. If the Hindus make themselves stronger, the Musalmans feel menaced. The Muslims endeavour to increase their forces to meet the menace and the Hindus then do the same to equalize the position. As the preparations proceed so does the suspicion, the secrecy, and the plotting. The possibilities of peaceable adjustment are poisoned at the source and precisely because every one is fearing and preparing for it that "war" between the two tends to become inevitable But in the situation in which they find themselves, for the Hindus and Muslims not to attend to anything, except to prepare themselves to meeting the challenge of the one by the other, is quite natural. It is a struggle for existence and the issue that counts is survival and not the quality or the plane of survival.

Two things must be said to have emerged from this discussion. One is that the Hindus and Muslims regard each other as a menace. The second is that to meet this menace, both have suspended the cause of removing the social evils with which they are infested. Is this a desirable state of things ? If it is not a desirable state of things, how can it be ended ?

No one can say that to have the problems of social reform put aside, is a desirable state of things. Wherever there are social evils the health of the body politic requires that they shall be removed before they become the symbols of suffering and injustice. For it is the social and economic evils which everywhere are the parent of revolution or decay. Whether social reform should precede political reform or political reform should precede social reform may be a matter of controversy. But there can be no two opinions on the question that the sole object of political power is the use to which it can be put in the cause of social and economic reform. The whole struggle for political power would be a barren and a bootless labour, if it was not justified by the feeling that, because of the want of political power, urgent and crying social evils are eating into the vitals of society and are destroying it. But suppose Hindus and Muslims somehow come into possession of political power, what hope is there that they will use it for purposes of social reform ? There is hardly any hope in that behalf. So long as the Hindus and Muslims regard each other as a menace, their attention will be engrossed in preparations, for meeting the menace. The exigencies of a common front will generate that conspiracy of silence which will not brook any call for reform. So long as the menace is there, the spirit of conservativism will continue to dominate the thoughts and actions of both. The situation will be a heaven for the haves and a hell for the have-nots.

How long will this menace last ? It is sure to last as long as the Hindus and Muslims are required to live as members of one country under the mantle of a single constitution. For it is the fear of the single constitution with the possibility of the shifting of the balance—for nothing can keep the balance at the point originally fixed by the Constitution—which makes the Hindus a menace to the Muslims and the Muslims a menace to the Hindus. If this is so, Pakistan is the obvious remedy. It certainly removes the chief condition which makes for the menace. Pakistan liberates both the Hindus and the Muslims from the fear of enslavement of and encroachment against each other. It removes, by providing a separate constitution for each, Pakistan and Hindustan, the very basis which leads to this perpetual struggle for keeping a balance of power in the day to day life and frees them to take into hand those vital matters of urgent social importance which they are now forced to put aside in cold storage and improve the lives of their people, which after all is the main object of this fight for Swaraj.

Without some such arrangement the Hindus and Muslims will act and react as though they were two nations, one about to be conquered by the other. Preparations will always have precedence over social reform, so that the social stagnation which has set in will continue. This is quite natural and no one need be surprized at it. For, as Bernard Shaw pointed out :—

" A conquerred nation is like a man with cancer ; he can think of nothing else . . . . A healthy nation is as unconscious of its nationality as a healthy man of his bones. But if you break a nation's nationality it will think of nothing else but getting it set again. It will listen to no reformer, to no philosopher, to no preacher, until the demand of the nationalist is granted. It will attend to no businesss, however vital, except the business of unification and liberation. "

Unless there is unification of the Muslims who wish to separate from the Hindus and unless there is liberation of each from the fear of domination by the other, this malaise of social stagnation will not be set right.

CHAPTER XI

COMMUNAL AGGRESSION

Even a superficial observer cannot fail to notice that a spirit of aggression underlies the Hindu attitude towards the Muslim and the Muslim attitude towards the Hindu. The Hindu's spirit of aggression is a new phase which he has just begun to cultivate. The Muslim's spirit of aggression is his native endowment and is very much ancient as compared with that of the Hindu. It is not that the Hindu, if given time, will not pick up and overtake the Muslim. But as matters stand to-day the Muslim in this exhibition of the spirit of aggression leaves the Hindu far behind.

Enough has been said about the social aggression of the Muslims in the chapter dealing with communal riots. It is necessary to speak briefly of the political aggression of the Muslims. For this political aggression has created a malaise which cannot be overlooked.

Three things are noticeable about this political aggression of the Muslims.

First is the ever-growing catalogue of the Muslim's political demands. Their origin goes back to the year 1892.

In 1885 the Indian National Congress was founded. It began with a demand for good government as distinguished from self-government. In response to this demand the British Government felt the necessity of altering the nature of the Legislative Councils, Provincial and Central, established under the Act of 1861. In that nascent stage of Congress agitation the British Government did not feel called upon to make them fully popular. It thought it enough to give them a popular colouring. Accordingly the British Parliament passed in 1892 what is called the Indian Councils Act. This Act is memorable for two things. It was in this Act of 1892 that the British Government for the first time accepted the semblance of the principle of popular representation as the basis for the constitution of the Legislatures in India. It was not a principle of election. It was a principle of nomination, only it was qualified by the requirement that before nomination a person must be selected by important public bodies such as municipalities, district boards, universities and the associations of merchants etc. Secondly it was in the Legislatures that were constituted under this Act that the principle of separate representation for Musalmans was for the first time introduced in the political constitution of India.

The introduction of this principle is shrouded in mystery. It is a mystery as to why it was introduced so silently and stealthily. The principle of separate representation does not find a place in the Act   The Act says nothing about it   It was in the directions —but not in the Act — issued to those charged with the duty of framing Regulations as to the classes and interests to whom representation was to be given that the Muslims were named as a class to be provided for.

It is a mystery as to who was responsible for its introduction. This scheme of separate representation was not the result of any demand put forth by any organized Muslim Association. In whom did it then originate ? It is suggested* that it originated with the Viceroy Lord Dufferin who, as far back as the year 1888 when dealing with the question of representation in the Legislative Councils, emphasized the necessity that in India representation will have to be, not in the way representation is secured in England, but representation by interests. Curiosity leads to a further question namely what could have led Lord Dufferin to propose such a plan ? It is suggested† that the idea was to wean‡ away the Musalmans from the Congress

---

* See the speech of Sir Mahomad Shafi in the Minorities Sub-Committee of the first R. T. C. (Indian Edition) p 57

† See the speech of Raja Narendranath *Ibid.*, p. 65

‡ The Musalmans had already been told by Sir Sayad Ahamad not to join the Congress in the two speeches one delivered at Lucknow on 28th December 1887, and the other at Meerut on 16th March 1888 Mr. Mahamed Ali in his presidential address speaks of them as historic speeches.

which had already been started three years before. Be that as it may it is certain that it is by this Act that separate representation for Muslims became, for the first time, a feature of the Indian Constitution. It should however be noted that neither the Act nor the Regulations conferred any right of selection upon the Muslim community and nor did it give the Muslim community a right to claim a fixed number of seats. All that it did was to give the Muslims the right to separate representation

Though, to start with, the suggestion of separate representation came from the British, the Muslims did not fail to appreciate the social value of separate political rights with the result that when in 1909 the Muslims came to know that the next step in the reform of the Legislative Councils was contemplated they waited of their own accord in deputation* upon the Viceroy, Lord Minto and placed before him the following demands —

(i) Communal representation in accordance with their numerical strength, social position and local influence, on district and municipal boards.

(ii) An assurance of Muhammadan representation on the gorverning bodies of Universities

(iii) Communal representation on provincial councils, election being by special electoral colleges composed of Muhammadan landlords, lawyers, merchants, and representatives of other important interests, University graduates of a certain standing and members of district and municipal boards.

(iv) The number of Muhammadan representatives in the Imperial Legislative Council should not depend on their numerical strength, and Muhammadan should never be in an ineffective minority. They should be elected as far as possible (as opposed to being nominated), election being by special Muhammadan colleges composed of landowners, lawyers merchants, members of provincial councils, Fellows of Universities etc.

---

* Mr Mahomad Ali in his speech as the President of the Congress said that this deputation was a command performance".

These demands were granted and given effect to in the Act of 1909. Under this Act the Muhammadans were given (1) the right to elect their representatives, (2) the right to elect their representatives by separate electorates, (3) the right to vote in the general electorates as well and (4) the right to weightage in representation. The following table shows the proportion of representation secured to the Muslims in the Legislatures by the Act of 1909 and the Regulations made thereunder ·—

Composition of Legislative Councils under   Act of 1909 showing Com.   Proportion between Hindus and Muslims

Province.	Maximum number of Additional Members prescribed by the Act of 1909	Maximum of Additional Members allowed by the Regulations columns 5 and 12	Ex-officio Members	Elected Members.			Nominated Members.						Total strength columns 4, 5, 12.
				Total	Non-Muslims	Muslims	Officials		Non-Officials	Experts.	Total		
							Law Officers	Others.*					
1	2	3	4	5	6	7	8	9	10	11	12		13
India	60	60	8	27	22	5		28	5		33		68
Madras	50	45	4	21	19	2	1	16	5	2	24		49
Bombay	50	45	4	21	17	4	1	14	7	2	24		49
Bengal	50	50	4	28	23	5		16	4	2	22		54
Bihar	50	41	4	21	17	4		15	4	1	20		45
U. P.	50	49	1	21	17	4	.	20	6	2	28		50
Punjab	30	26	1	8	8	none	.	10	6	2	18		27
Burma	30	17	1	1	1	none	..	6	8	2	16		18
Assam	30	25	1	11	9	2	..	9	4	1	14		25

Strength of the Councils under the Regulations

* The numbers in column 9 represent the maximum of Official Members permitted under the Regulations.

The provisions were applied to all Provinces except the Punjab and C. P. It was not applied to Punjab because such special protection was considered unnecessary for the Muhammadans of the Punjab and it was not applied to C. P. because it had no Legislative Council at the time.*

In October 1916, 19 members of the Imperial Legislative Council presented the Viceroy (Lord Chelmsford) a memorandum demanding a reform of the Constitution. Immediately the Muslims came forward with a number of demands on behalf of the Muslim community. These were :—

(i) The extension of the principle of separate representation to the Punjab and the C. P.

(ii) Fixing the numerical strength of the Muslim representatives in the Provincial and Imperial Legislative Councils.

(iii) Safegaurd against legislation affecting Muslims, their religion and religious usages.

The negotiations following upon these demands resulted in an agreement between the Hindus and the Muslims and which is known as the Lucknow Pact. It may be said to contain two clauses. One ralated to legislation. By it it was agreed that—

"No Bill, nor any clause thereof, nor a resolution introduced by a non-official affecting one or other community (which question is to be determined by the member of that community in the Legislative Council concerned) shall be proceeded with, if threefourths of the members of that community in the particular Council, Imperial and Provincial, oppose the Bill or any clause thereof or the resolution."

The other clause related to the proportion of Muslim representation. With regard to the Imperial Legislative Council the Pact provided :—

"That one-third of the Indian elected members should be Muhammadans, elected by separate electorates in the several Provinces, in the proportion, as nearly as might be, in which they were represented on the provincial legislative councils by separate Muhammadan electorates."

* The C. P. Legislative Council was established in 1914,

In the matter of Muslim representation in the provincial legislative councils it was agreed that the proportion of Muslim representation should be as follows* :—

			Percentage of elected Indian Members
Punjab	...	..	50
United Provinces	...	.	30
Bengal	...		40
Bihar and Orissa	...	..	25
Central Provinces	..	...	15
Madras	..	...	15
Bombay	...	...	33½

While allowing this proportion of seats to the Muslims the right to a second vote in the general electorates which they had under the arrangement of 1909 was taken way

The Lucknow Pact was adversely criticized by the Montagu—Chelmsford Report. But being an agreement between the parties Government did not like to reject it and substitute in its place its own decision. Both clauses of the agreement were accepted by Government and embodied in the Government of India Act of 1919. The clause relating to legislation was given effect to but in a different form. Instead of leaving it to the members of the Legislature to oppose it, it was provided † that legislation affecting the religion or religious rites and usages of any class of British subjects in India shall not be introduced at any meeting of either Chamber of the Indian Legislature without the previous sanction of the Governor-General.

The clause relating to representation was accepted by the Government though in the opinion of the Government, the Punjab and Bengal Muslims were not fairly treated.

The effect of these concessions can be seen by reference to the composition of the Legislatures constituted under the Government of India Act 1919 which was as follows :—

* For some reason the Pact did not settle the proportion of Muslim representation in Assam.

† Government of India Act 1919, Section 67 (2) (b).

Composition of the Legislatures.

1	Statutory Minimum	Elected Members.			Nominated Members.		Actual Total.
		Total	Muslims	Non-Muslims	Officials	Non-Officials	
	2	3	4	5	6	7	8
Legislative Assembly	145	104	52	52	26	15	145
Council of State	60	33	11	22	17	10	60
Madras Provincial Council	118	98	13	85	11	23	132
Bombay Provincial Council	111	86	27	59	19	9	114
Bengal Provincial Council	125	114	39	75	16	10	140
U. P Provincial Council	118	110	29	71	17	6	123
Punjab Provincial Council	83	71	32	39	15	8	94
Bihar Provincial Council	98	76	18	58	15	12	103
C. P. Provincial Council	70	55	7	48	10	8	73
Assam Provincial Council	53	39	12	27	7	7	53

The extent of representation secured by the Muslims by the Lucknow Pact can be seen from the following table* .—

Legislative Body	Percentage of Moslems to total population of the electrol area (1921 Census)	Percentage of Moslem members to total No. of members	Percentage of Moslem elected members to total No of elected Indian members.	Percentage of Moslem members to total members in seats filled by election from Indian general (communal) constituencies	Lucknow Pact percentage.
	1	2	3	4	5
Punjab	55 2	40	48 5	50	50
United Provinces	14 3	25	30	32 5	30
Bengal .	54 6	30	40 5	46	40
Bihar and Orissa	10 9	18 5	25	27	25
Central Provinces	4·4	0·5	13	14 5	15
Madras ..	6·7	10 5	14	16 5	15
Bombay	19·8	25 5	35	37	33 3
Assam . .	32·3	30	35·5	37·5	No provision.
Legislative Assembly	24·0	26	34	38	33·3

* Statutory Commission 1929 Report Vol. I page 189.

† Column 3 includes Indians elected by special constituencies, e.g. Commerce, whose communal proportions may of course vary slightly from time to time   Similarly column 2, including also officials and nominated non-officials, will show slightly different results at different periods.

This table does not show quite clearly the weightage obtained by the Muslims under the Lucknow Pact It was worked out by the Government of India in their despatch* on the Report of Franchise Committee of which Lord Southborough was the chairman. The following table is taken from that despatch which shows that the the Muslims got a weightage under the Lucknow Pact far in excess of what Government gave them in 1909.

	Muslim per centage of Population	Percentage of Muslim seats proposed	Percentage (2) of (1).
	1	2	3
Bengal	52 0	40	76
Bihar and Orissa	10 5	25	238
Bombay	20 1	33 3	163
Central Provinces	4 3	15	349
Madras	6 5	15	231
Punjab	54 8	50	91
United Provinces	14 0	30	214

In 1927 the British Government announced the appointment of the Simon Commission to examine the working of the Indian Constitution and to suggest further reforms. Immediatly the Muslims came forward with further political demands. These demands were put forth from various Muslim platforms, such as the Muslim League, All-India Muslim Conference, All Parties Muslim Conference, Jamait-ul-Ulema and the Khilafat Conference. The demands were substantially the same. It would suffice to state those that were formulated by Mr. Jinnah † on behalf of the Muslim League.

They were in the following terms .—

1. The form of the future Constitution should be federal with residuary powers vested in the provinces.

2. A uniform measure of autonomy should be granted to all provinces.

---

* Fifth despatch on Indian Constitutional Reforms (Franchises) dated 23rd April 1919 para 21.

† The demands are known as Mr Jinnah's 14 points As a matter of fact they are 15 in number and were formulated at a meeting of Muslim leaders of all shades of opinion held at Delhi in March 1927 and were known as the Delhi Proposals. For Mr Jinnah's explanation of the origin of his 14 points see All India Register 1929 Vol. I p. 367.

3. All legislatures in the country and other elected bodies should be reconstituted on the definite principle of adequate and effective representation of minorities in every province without reducing the majority of any province to a minority or even equality.

4. In the Central Legislature Muslim representation should not be less than one-third.

5. The representation of communal groups should continue to be by means of separate electorates as at present, provided that it should be open to any community at any time to abandon its separate electorate in favour of joint electorates.

6 Any territorial redistribution that might at any time be necessary shold not in any way affect the Muslim majority in the Punjab, Bengal and North-West Frontier Province.

7. Full religious liberty, that is, liberty of belief, worship, observances, propaganda, association and education should be guaranteed to all communities

8. No bill or resolution, or any part thereof, should be passed in any legislature or any other elected body if three-fourths of the members of any community in that particular body oppose such a bill or resolution or part thereof on the ground that it would be injurious to the interests of that community or, in the alternative, such other method as may be devised or as may be found feasible and practicable to deal with such cases.

9. Sind should be separated from the Bombay Presidency.

10. Reforms should be introduced in the North-West Frontier Province and Baluchistan on the same footing as in other provinces.

11. Provision should be made in the Constitution giving the Muslims an adequate share along with other Indians in all the Services of the State and in self-governing bodies, having due regard to the requirements of efficiency.

12   The constitution should embody adequate safeguards for the protection of Muslim religion, culture and personal law, and the promotion of Muslim education, language, religion, personal laws, Muslim charitable institutions, and for their due share in grants-in-aid given by the State and by self-governing bodies.

13.   No cabinet, either Central or Provincial, should be formed without there being a proportion of Muslim Ministers of at least one-third.

14.   No change to be made in the Constitution by the Central Legislature except with the concurrence of the States constituting the Indian Federation

15   That in the present circumstances the representation of Musalmans in the different legislatures of the country and of the other elected bodies through separate electorates is inevitable, and, further, Government being pledged not to deprive the Musalmans of this right, it cannot be taken away without their consent, and so long as the Musalmans are not satisfied that their rights and interests are safeguarded in the manner specified above (or herein) they would in no way consent to the establishment of joint electorates with or without conditions.

Note —The question of excess representation of Musalmans over and above their population in the provinces where they are in minority to be considered hereafter.

This is a consolidated statement of Muslim demands. In it there are some which are old, and there are some which are new. The old ones are included because the aim is to retain the advantages accruing therefrom.   The new ones are added in order to remove the weaknesses in the Muslim position   The new ones are five in number : (1) Representation in proportion to population to Muslim majorities in the Punjab and Bengal. (2) One-third representation to Muslims in the cabinets both Central and Provincial. (3) Adequate   representation   of   Muslims   in   the   Services, (4) Separation of Sind from the Bombay Presidency and the raising of N. W. F. and Baluchistan to the status of self-governing provinces. and (5) Vesting of residuary powers in the Provinces and not in the Central Government.

These demands are self-explanatory except perhaps 1, 4 and 5. The object of demands 1 and 4 was to place, in four provinces, the Muslim community in a statutory majority where it had only communal majority, as a force counteracting the six provinces in which the Hindu community happened to be in a majority. This was insisted upon on the ground that it would in itself constitute a guarantee of good treatment by both the communities of its minorities. The object of demand No. 5 was to guarantee Muslim rule in Sind. N. W. F., the Punjab and Bengal. But a Muslim majority rule in these Muslim Provinces it was feared would not be effective if they remained under the control of the Central Government which could not but be in the hand of the Hindus. To free the Muslim Provinces from the control of the Hindu Government at the Centre was the object for which demand No. 5 was put forth.

These demands were opposed by the Hindus. There may not be much in this. But what is significant is that they were also rejected by the Simon Commission The Simon Commission, which was by no means unfriendly to the Muslims, gave some very cogent reasons for rejecting the Muslim demands. It said* .—

"This claim goes to the length of seeking to preserve the full security for representation now provided for Moslems in these six provinces and at the same time to enlarge in Bengal and the Punjab the present proportion of seats secured to the community by separate electorates to figures proportionate to their ratio of population. This would give Muhammadans a fixed and unalterable majority of the "general constituency" seats in both provinces. We cannot go so far. The continuance of the present scale of weightage in the six provinces could not — in the absence of a new general agreement between the communities — equitably be combined with so great a departure from the existing allocation in Bengal and the Punjab.

"It would be unfair that Muhammadans should retain the very considerable weightage they enjoy in the six provinces, and that there should at the same time be imposed, in face of Hindu and Sikh opposition, a definite Moslem majority in the Punjab and Bengal unalterable by any appeal to the electorate..... ......"

But not withstanding the opposition of the Hindus and the Sikhs and the rejection by the Simon Commission, the British

---

* Report Vol. II page 71

Government when called upon to act as an arbiter granted the Muslims all their demands old and new.

By a Notification* in the Gazette of India dated 25th January 1932 the Government of India, in exercise of the powers conferred by sub-section (2) of section 52 A of the Government of India Act 1919, declared that the N. W. F. Province shall be treated as a Governor's Province†. By an Order in Council, issued under the provisions contained in sub-section (1) of section 289 of the Government of India Act of 1935, Sind was separated from Bombay as from 1st April 1936 and declared to be a Governor's Province to be known as the Province of Sind. By the Resolution issued by the Secretary of State for India and published on 7th July 1934 the Muslim share in the public services was fixed at 25 per cent of all appointments Imperial and Provincial*. With regard to residuary powers, it is true that the Muslim demand that they should be vested in the Provinces was not accepted. But in another sense the Muslim demand in this respect must be deemed to have been granted. The essence of the Muslim demand was that the residuary powers should not be vested in the Centre, which, put in different language, meant that it should not be in the hands of the Hindus. This is precisely what is done by section 104 of the Government of India Act 1935 which vests the residuary powers in the Governor General to be exercised in his discretion. With regard to the demand for 33⅓ per cent. representation in the cabinets Central and Provincial the same was not given effect to by a legal provision in the Act. But if convention counts for anything then not only the right of Muslims to representation in the cabinets was accepted by the British Government but provision for giving effect to it was made in the instruments of Instructions issued to the Governors and Governor General. As to the remaining demand which related to a statutory majority in the Punjab and Bengal the demand was given effect to by the Communal Award.

---

* Notification No F 173/31- It in the Gazette of India Extraordinary dated 25th January 1932

† The Simon Commission had rejected the claim saying ' We entirely share the view of the Bray Committee that provision ought now to be made for the constitutional advance of the N W F. P   But we also agree that the situation of the Province and its intimate relation with the problem of Indian defence are such that special arrangements are required. It is not possible, therefore, to apply to it automatically proposals which may be suited for provincial areas in other parts of India." They justified it by saying: "The inherent right of a man to smoke a cigarette must necessarily be curtailed if he lives in a powder magazine — Report Vol II, paras. 120-121.

True, a statutory majority over the whole House, has not been given to the Muslims and could not be given having regard to the necessity for providing representation to other interests. But a statutory majority as against Hindus has been given to the Muslims of Punjab and Bengal without touching the weightages obtained by the Muslim minorities under the Lucknow Pact.

These political grants to the Muslim community by the British Government lacked security and it was feared by the Muslims that pressure might be brought upon them or upon His Majesty's Government by the Hindus to alter the terms of the grants to the prejudice of the Muslims. This fear was due to two reasons. One was the success of Mr Gandhi in getting that part of the Award which related to the Depressed Classes revised by means of the pressure of fast unto death *. Some people encouraged by this success actually agitated for a revision of that part of the Award which related to the Muslims and some Muslims were even found to be in favour of entering into such negotiations †. This alarmed the Muslim Community. The other reason for the fear of revision of the terms of the grants arose out of certain amendments in the clauses in the Government of India Bill which were made in the House of Commons permitting such revision under certain conditions. To remove these fears and to give complete security to the Muslims against hasty and hurried revision of the grants His Majesty's Government authorized the Government of India to issue the following communique ‡ —

" It has come to the notice of His Majesty's Government that the impression is prevalent that what is now Clause 304 of the Government of India Bill (numbered 285 in the Bill as first introduced and 299 in the Bill as amended by the Commons in Committee) has been amended during the passage of the Bill through the Commons in such a way as to give His Majesty's Government unfettered power to alter at any time they may think fit the constitutional provisions based upon what is commonly known as Government's Communal Award.

* This resulted in the Poona Pact which was signed on 24th September 1932.

† For the efforts to get the Muslim part of the Award revised *See* All-India Register 1932 Vol. II pp. 281—315

‡ The Communique is dated Simla July 2, 1935

" His Majesty's Government think it desirable to give the following brief explanation both of what they consider is the practical effect of Clause 304 in relation to any change in the Communal Award and of their own policy in relation to any such change.

" Under this Clause there is conferred on the Governments and Legislatures in India, after the expiry of ten years, the right of initiating a proposal to modify the provisions and regulating various matters relating to the constitution of the Legislature, including such questions as were covered by the Communal Award.

" The Clause also imposes on the Secretary of State the duty of laying before Parliament from the Governor General or the Governor as the case may be his opinion as to the proposed amendment and in particular as to the effect which it would have on the interests of any minority and of informing Parliament of any action which he proposed to take.

" Any change in the constitutional Provisions resulting from this procedure can be effected by an Order in Council, but this is subject to the proviso that the draft of the proposed Order has been affirmatively approved by both Houses of Parliament by a resolution. This condition is secured by Clause 305 of the Bill.

" Before the expiry of ten years there is no similar constitutional initiative residing in the Governments and the Legislatures of India. Power is, however, conferred by the Clause to make such a change by an Order in Council (always with the approval of both Houses of Parliament) even before the end of ten years, but within the first ten years (and indeed subsequently, if the initiative has not come from the Legislatures of India) it is incumbent upon the Secretary of State to consult the Governments and the Legislatures of India who will be affected (unless the change is of a minor character) before any Order in Council is laid before Parliament for its approval.

" The necessity for the powers referred to in the preceding paragraph is due to such reasons as the following :—

" (a) It is impossible to foresee when the necessity may arise for amending minor details connected with the franchise and the constitution of legislatures, and for such amendment it will be clearly disadvantageous to have no method available short of a fresh amending Act of Parliament, nor is it practicable statutorily to separate such details from the more important matter such as the terms of the Communal Award ;

" (b) It might also become desirable, in the event of a unanimous agreement between the communities in India, to make a modification in the provisions based on the Communal Award ; and for such an agreed change it would also be disadvantageous to have no other method available than an amending Act of Parliament.

" Within the range of the Communal Award His Majesty's Government would not propose, in the exercise of any power conferred by this Clause, to recommend to Parliament any change unless such changes had been agreed to between the communities concerned.

" In conclusion, His Majesty's Government would again emphasise the fact that none of the powers in Clause 304 can, in view of the provisions in Clause 305, be exercised unless both Houses of Parliament agreed by an affirmative resolution. "

After taking into account what the Muslims demanded at the R.T.C. and what was conceded to them any one could have thought that the limit of Muslim demands was reached and that the 1932 settlement was a final settlement.   But it appears that even with this the Musalmans are not satisfied.   A further list of new demands for safeguarding the Muslim position seems to be ready.   In the controversy that went on between Mr. Jinnah and the Congress in the year 1938 Mr. Jinnah was asked to disclose his demands which he refused to do.   But these demands have come to the surface in the correspondence that passed between Pandit Nehru and Mr. Jinnah in the course of the controversy and they have been tabulated by Pandit Nehru in one of his letters to Mr. Jinnah.   His tabulation gives the following as items in dispute and requiring settlement* —

(1) The fourteen points formulated by the Muslim League in 1929.

(2) The Congress should withdraw all opposition to the Communal Award and should not describe it as a negation of nationalism.

(3) The share of the Muslims in the state services should be definitely fixed in the constitution by statutory enactment.

(4) Muslim personal law and culture should be guaranteed by statute

---

* Indian Annual Register 1938 Vol. I p. 369.

(5) The Congress should take in hand the agitation in connection with the Sahidganj Mosque and should use its moral pressure to enable the Muslims to gain possession of the Mosque.

(6) The Muslims' right to call Azan and perform their religious ceremonies should not be fettered in any way.

(7) Muslims should have freedom to perform cow-slaughter.

(8) Muslim majorities in the provinces, where such majorities exist at present, must not be affected by any territorial re-distribution or adjustments

(9) The 'Bande Mataram' song should be given up.

(10) Muslims want Urdu to be the national language of India and they desire to have statutory guarantees that the use of Urdu shall not be curtailed or damaged

(11) Muslim representation in the local bodies should be governed by the principles underlying the Communal Award, that is, separate electorates and population strength.

(12) The tricolour Flag should be changed or alternately the flag of the Muslim League should be given equal importance.

(13) Recognition of the Muslim League as the one authoritative and representative organization of Indian Muslims

(14) Coalition Ministries should be formed.

With this new list there is no knowing where the Muslims are going to stop in their demands. Within one year, that is between 1938 and 1939, one more demand and that too of a substantial character namely 50 per cent. share in everything has been added to it In this catalogue of new demands there are some which on the face of them are extravagant and impossible, if not irresponsible. As an instance, one may refer to the demand for fifty fifty and the demand for the recognition of Urdu as the national language of India. In 1929 the Muslims insisted that in alloting seats in Legislatures a majority shall not be reduced to a minority or equality.* This principle, enunciated by themselves, it is new demanded, shall be abandoned and a majority shall be reduced to equality. The Muslims in 1929 admitted that the other minorities required protection and that they must have it in the same manner as the Muslims. The only distinction made between the Muslims and other minorities was as to the extent of the protection. The Muslims claimed a higher degree of protection than was conceded to the other minorities on the ground of there political importance. But as to the necessity and adequacy of protection for the other minorities the Muslims never denied it But with this new demand of 50 per cent. the Muslims are not only seeking to reduce the Hindu majority to a minority but they are also cutting into the political rights of the other minorities. The Muslims are now speaking the language of Hitler and claiming a place in the Sun which Hitler has been claiming for Germany. For their demand for 50 per cent. is nothing but a counterpart of the German claims for *Deuchland Uber Alles* and *Lebensraum* for themselves, irrespective of what happens to other minorities.

Their claim for the recognition of Urdu as to the national language of India is equally extravagant Urdu is not only not spoken all over India but it is not even the language of all the Musalmans of India. Of the 68 millions of Muslims† only 28 millions speak Urdu. The proposal of making Urdu a national language means that the language of 28 millions of Muslims is to be imposed particularly upon 40 millions of Musalmans or generally upon 322 millions of Indians

It will thus be seen that every time a proposal for the reform of the constitution comes forth, the Muslims are there, ready with some new political demand or demands. The only check upon such indefinite expansion of Muslim demands is the power of the British Government, which must be the final arbiter in any dispute between the Hindus and the Muslims. But who can confidently say that the decision of the British will not be in favour of the Muslims if the dispute relating to these new demands was referred to them for arbitration ? Just as the Muslim demands

---

* See point No 3 in Mr. Jinnah's 14 points
† These figures relate to the Census of 1921.

are endless so also, the British seem to be becoming powerless to put a curb on them.   At any rate past experience shows that the British have been inclined to give the Muslims more than what the Muslims had themselves asked.   Two such instances can be cited.

One of these relates to the Lucknow Pact.   The question was whether the British Government should accept the Pact.   The author of the Montagu—Chelmsford Report were disinclined to accept it for reasons which were very weighty.   Speaking of the weightages granted to the Muslims by the Lucknow Pact the authors of the Joint-Report observed* .—

"Now a privileged position of this kind is open to the objection, that if any other community hereafter makes good a claim to separate representation, it can be satisfied only by deduction from the Non-Muslim seats, or by a rateable deduction from both Muslim and Non-Muslim, and Hindu and Muslim opinions are not likely to agree which process should be adopted   While, therefore, for reasons that we explain subsequently we assent to the maintenance of separate representation for Muhammadans, we are bound to reserve our approval of the particular proposals set before us, until we have ascertained what the effect upon other interests will be, and have made fair provision for them

Notwithstanding   this grave flaw in the Lucknow Pact the Government of India, in its despatch referred to above, recommended that the terms of the Pact should be improved in so far as it related to the Muslims of Bengal.   Its reasons make a strange reading.   It argued that —

"The Muhammadan representation which they [the authors of the Pact] propose for Bengal is manifestly insufficient.†   It is questionable whether the claims of the Muhammadan population of Eastern Bengal were adequately pressed when the Congress-League compact was in the making.   They are conspicuously a backward and impoverished community.   The repartition of the presidency in 1912 came as a severe disappointment to them, and we should be very loath to fail in seeing that their interests are now generously secured.   In order to

* Montagu—Chelmsford Report 1918 para. 163

† The Government of India also felt that injustice was done to Punjab as well.   But as there was no such special reason as there was in the case of Bengal namely the unsettling of the partition they did not propose any augmentation in its representation as settled by the Pact.

give the Bengal Muslims a representation proportionate to their numbers, and no more, we should allot them 44 instead of 34 seats [due to them under the Pact]."

This enthusiasm for the Bengal Muslims shown by the Government of India was not shared by the British Government. It felt that as the number of seats given to the Bengal Muslims was the result of an agreement, any interference to improve the bargain when there was no dispute about the genuineness of the agreement, could not but create the impression that the British Government was in some special sense and for some special reason the friend of the Muslims. In suggesting this augmentation in the seats the Government of India forgot to take note of the reason why the Muslims of Punjab and Bengal were not given by the Pact seats in proportion to their population. The Lucknow Pact was based upon the principle, now thrown to the winds, that a community as such was not entitled to political protection. A community was entitled to protection when it was in a minority. That was the principle underlying the Lucknow Pact. The Muslim Community in the Punjab and Bengal was not in a minority and therefore was not entitled to the same protection which it got in other Provinces where it was in a minority. Notwithstanding their being in a majority the Muslims of Punjab and Bengal felt the necessity of separate electorates. According to the principle underlying the Pact they could qualify themselves for this only by becoming a minority which they did by agreeing to a minority of seats. This is the reason why the Muslims of Bengal and the Punjab did not get the majority of seats they were entitled to on the population basis.*

The proposal of the Government of India to give to the Bengal Muslims more than what they had asked for did not go through. But the fact that they wanted to do so remains as evidence of their inclinations.

*There is no doubt that this was well understood by the Muslims who were parties to the Pact. This is what Mr. Jinnah said as a witness appearing before the Joint Select-Committee appointed by Parliament on the Government of India Bill 1919 in reply to question No 3808 "The position of Bengal was this In Bengal the Moslems are in a majority, and the argument was advanced that any section or any community which is in the majority cannot claim a separate electorate separate electorate is to protect the minority. But the counter-argument was perfectly true that numerically we are in a majority but as voters we are in the minority in Bengal, because of poverty, and backwardness and so on. It was said Very well, then fix 40 per cent, because if you are really put to test you will not get 40 per cent, because you will not be qualified as voters, Then we had the advantage in other Provinces."

The second occasion when the British Government as an arbiter gave the Muslims more than they asked for was when the Communal Decision was given in 1932. Sir Muhammad Shafi made two different proposals in the Minorities Sub-Committee of the R. T. C. In his speech on January 6th, 1931 Sir Muhammad Shafi put forth the following proposal in the interest of communal settlement* .—

"We are prepared to accept joint electorates on the conditions named by me . Firstly, that the rights at present enjoyed by the Musalmans in the minority Provinces should be continued to them ; that in the Punjab and in Bengal they should have two joint electorates and representation on a population basis ; that there should be the principle of reservation of seats coupled with Moulana Mahommad Ali's condition.† "

In his speech on 14th January 1931 before the same committee he made a different offer.   He said‡ .—

"To-day I am authorized to make this offer : that in the Punjab the Musalmans should have through communal electorates 49 per cent. of the entire number of seats in the whole House, and should have liberty to contest the special constituencies which it is proposed to create in that Province . so far as Bengal is concerned that Musalmans should have through communal electorates 46 per cent. representation in the whole House, and should have the liberty to contest the special constituencies which it is proposed to create in that Province , in so far as the Minority Provinces are concerned, the Musalmans should continue to enjoy the weightage which they have at present through separate electorates, similar weightage to be given to our Hindu brethren in Sind, and to our Hindu and Sikh brethren in the North-West Frontier Province.   If at any time hereafter two-thirds of the representatives of any community in any Provincial Legislative Council or in the Central Legislative Council desire to give up communal electorates and to accept joint electorates then thereafter the system of joint electorates, should come into being."

---

* Report of the Minorities Sub Committee of the first R T C. (Indian Edition) p. 96.

† Mr Mahamad Ali's formula was for joint electorates and reserved seats with this proviso that no candidate shall be declared elected unless he had secured at least 40 per cent of the votes of his own community and at least 5 or 10 per cent of the votes of the other community.

‡ Ibid p. 123.

34

The difference between the two proposals was clear. Joint electorates, if accompanied by statutory majority. If statutory majority is refused, then a minority of seats with separate electorates. The British Government took statutory majority from the first demand and separate electorates from the second demand and gave the Muslims both when they had not asked for both.

The second thing that is noticeable among the Muslims is the spirit of exploiting the weaknesses of the Hindus. If the Hindus object to anything then the Muslim policy seems to be to insist upon it and give it up only when the Hindus show themselves ready to offer a price for it by giving the Muslims some other concessions. As an illustration of this one can refer to the question of separate and joint electorates. The Hindus have been to my mind utterly foolish in fighting over joint electorates especially in Provinces in which the Muslims are in a minority. Joint electorates can never suffice for a basis for nationalism. Nationalism is not a matter of political nexus or cash nexus, for the simple reason that union cannot be the result of calculation of mere externals. Where two communities live a life which is exclusive and self-inclosed for five years they will not be one because they are made to come together on one day in five years for the purposes of voting in an election. Joint electorates may produce the enslavement of the minor community by the major community but by themselves they cannot produce nationalism. Be that as it may, because the Hindus have been insisting upon joint electorates the Muslims have been insisting upon separate electorates. That this insistance is a matter of bargain only can be seen from Mr. Jinnah's 14 points* and the Resolution† passed in the Calcutta Session of the All-India Muslim League held on 30th December 1927. Therein it was stipulated that only when the Hindus agreed to the separation of Sind and to the raising of the N. W. F. to the status of a self-governing Province that the Musalmans would consent to give up separate electorates.‡ The Musalmans evidently did not regard separate

---

* See point No 15 in Mr. Jinnahs' points

† For the Resolution and the speech of Mr. Barkat Ali thereon see the Indian Quartely Register 1927 Vol. II page 447-48.

‡ The unfortunate thing for the Hindus is that they did not get joint electorates although the Musalmans got the concessions,

electorates as vital. They regarded them as a good *quid pro quo* for obtaining their other claims. If this is not a bargain it is difficult to find one which is.

An other illustration of this spirit of exploitation is furnished by the Muslim insistance upon cow-slaughter and the stoppage of music before mosque.   Islamic law does not insist upon the slaughter of the cow for sacrificial purposes and no Musalman when he goes to Haj sacrifices the cow in Mecca or Medina.   But in India they will not be content with the sacrifice of any other animal.   Music before mosque is played in all Muslim countries without any objection.   Even in Afghanistan which is not a secularized country no objection is taken to music before mosque.   But in India the Musalmans must insist upon its stoppage because the Hindus claim a right to it.

The third thing that is noticeable is the adoption by the Muslims of the gangsters' methods in politics.   The riots are a sufficient indication that gangsterism has become a settled part of their strategy in politics.   They seem to be consciously and deliberately imitating the Sudeten Germans in the means employed by them against the Czechs.*   So long the Muslims were the aggressors.   The Hindus were passive and in the conflict they suffered more than the Muslims did.   But this is no longer true.   The Hindus have learned to retaliate and no longer feel any compunction in knifing a Musalman.   This spirit of retaliation bids fare to produce the ugly spectacle of gangsterism against gangsterism.

How to meet this problem must exercise the minds of·all concerned.   There are the simple-minded Hindu Maha Sabha patriots who believe that the Hindus have only to make up their minds to swipe the Musalmans and they will be brought to their senses. On the other hand there are the Congress Hindu Nationalists whose policy is to tolerate and appease the Musalmans by political and other concessions, because they believe that they cannot reach their cherished goal of independence unless the Musalmans back their demand.   The Hindu Maha Sabha plan is no way to unity.

---

* In the Karachi Session of the All-India Muslim League both Mr. Jinnah and Sir Abdullah Haroon compared the Muslims of India as the " Studeten " of the Muslim world and capable of doing what the Studeten Germans did to Czechoslovakia.

On the contrary it is a sure block to progress. The slogan of the Hindu Maha Sabha President — Hindustan for Hindus — is not merely arrogant but is arrant nonsense. Question however is, is the Congress way the right way? It seems to me that the Congress has failed to realize two things. The first thing which the Congress has failed to realise is the fact that there is a difference between appeasement and settlement and that the difference is an essential one. Appeasement means to offer to buy off the aggressor by conciving at or collaborating with him in the rape, murder and arson on innocent Hindus who happen for the moment to be the victims of his displeasure. On the other hand settlement means laying down the bounds which neither party to it can transgress. Appeasement sets no limits to the demands and aspirations of the aggressor. Settlement does. The second thing the Congress has failed to realize is that the policy of concession has increased their aggressiveness and what is worse the Muslims interpret these concessions as a sign of defeatism on the part of the Hindus and the absence of will to resist. This policy of appeasement will involve the Hindus in the same fearful situation in which the Allies found themselves as a result of the policy of appeasement which they adopted towards Hitler. This is another malaise, no less acute than the malaise of social stagnation. Appeasement will surely aggravate it. The only remedy for it is settlement. If Pakistan is a settlement then as a remedy it is worth consideration. For as a settlement it will do away with this constant need of appeasement and ought to be welcomed by all those who prefer the peace and tranquility of a settlement to the insecurity of a growing political appetite shown by the Muslims in their dealings with the Hindus.

CHAPTER XII

NATIONAL FRUSTRATION

I

Suppose an Indian was asked, what is the highest destiny you wish for your county, what would be his answer ? The question is important and the answer cannot but he instructive.

There can be no doubt that other things being equal, a hundred percent Indian, proud of his country, would say "An integral and independent India is my ideal of Indias destiny " But it will be equally true to say that unless this destiny was accepted by both, Hindus as well as Muslims the ideal can only convey a pious wish. It cannot take a concrete form. Is it only a pious wish of some or is it cherished by all ?

So far as profession of political aims go, all parties seem to be in agreement in as much as all of them have declared that the goal of India's political evolution is Independence. The Congress was the first to announce that its aim was to achieve political independence for India. In its Madras Session, held in December 1927, the creed of the Congress was defined in a special resolution to the effect that the goal of the Indian people was complete national independence. The Hindu Maha Sabha until 1932 was content to have Responsible Government as the goal of India's political evolution. It made no change in its political creed till 1937 when in its session held at Ahamadabad it declared that the Hindu Maha Sabha believed in " Poorna Swaraj " that is, absolute political independence for India. The Muslim League declared its political creed in 1912 to be the establishment of Responsible Government in India. In 1937 it made a similar advance by changing its creed from Responsible

Government to Independence and thereby brought itself in line with the Congress and the Hindu Maha Sabha.

This independence defined by the three political bodies means freedom from British Imperialism. But an agreement on freedom from the yoke of British Imperialism is not enough. There must be an agreement upon maintaining an Independent India. For this there must be an agreement that India shall not only be free and independent of the British but that her freedom and independence shall be maintained as against any other foreign power. Indeed the obligation to maintain her freedom is more important than merely winning freedom from the British. But on this more important obligation there does not seem to be the same unanimity. At any rate the attitude of the Muslims on this point has not been very assuring. Indeed it is obvious from the numerous utterances of Muslim leaders that they do not accept the obligation to maintain India's freedom   I give below two such utterances.

In a meeting held in Lahore in 1925 Dr. Kitchlew said[*] .—

"The Congress was lifeless till the Khilafat Committee put life in it. When the Khilafat Committee joined it, it did in one year what the Hindu Congress had not done in 40 years. The Congress also did the work of uplifting the seven crores of untouchables. This was purely a work for the Hindus, and yet the money of the Congress was spent on it. Mine and my Musalman brethren's money was spent on it like water. But the brave Musalmans did not mind. Then why should the Hindus quarrel with us when we Musalmans take up the Tanzim work and spend on it money that belongs neither to the Hindus nor to the Congress ? "

" If we remove British rule from this country and establish Swaraj, and if the Afghans or other Muslims invade India, then we Moslems will oppose them and sacrifice all our sons in order to save the country from the invasion. But one thing I shall declare plainly. Listen, my dear Hindu brothers, listen very attentively ! If you put obstacles in the path of our Tanzim movement, and do not give us our rights, we shall make common cause with Afghanistan or some other Musalman power and establish our rule in this country. "

Maulana Azad Sobhani in his speech[†] made on the 27th January 1939 at Sylhet expressed sentiments which are worthy of attention.

---

[*] " Through Indian Eyes." Times of India dated   14-3-25

[†] The Bengali version of the speech appeared in the Anand Bazar Patrika. The English version of it given here is a translation made for me by the Editor of the Hindustan Standard.

In reply to the question of a Maulana, Maulana Azad Sobhani said, " If there is any eminent leader in India who is in favour of driving out the English from this country, then I am that leader. Inspite of this I want that there should be no fight with the English on behalf of the Moslem League. Our big fight is with the 22 crores of our Hindu enemies, who constitute the majority. Only 4½ crores of Englishmen have practically swallowed the whole world by becoming powerful. And if these 22 crores of Hindus who are equally advanced in learning, intelligence and wealth as in numbers, if they become powerful, then these Hindus will swallow Moslem India and gradually even Egypt, Turkey, Kabul, Mecca, Medina and other Moslem principalities, like Yajuj-Majuj (it is so mentioned in the Koran that before the destruction of the world, they will appear on the earth and will devour whatever they will find)

" The English are gradually becoming weak.. . .they will go away from India in the near future So if we do not fight the greatest enemies of Islam, the Hindus, from now on and make them weak, then they will not only establish *Ramrajya* in India but also gradually spread all over the world. It depends on the 9 crores of Indian Moslems either to strengthen or to weaken them (the Hindus). So it is the essential duty of every devout Moslem to fight on by joining the Moslem League so that the Hindus may not be established here and a Moslem rule may be established in India as soon as the English depart.

Though the English are the enemies of the Moslems, yet for the present our fight is not with the English. At first we have to come to some understanding with the Hindus through the Moslem League. Then we shall be easily able to drive out the English and establish Moslem rule in India.

Be careful ! Don't fall into the trap of Congress Maulvis ; because the Moslem world is never safe in the hands of 22 crores of Hindu enemies. " He then narrated various imaginary incidents of oppressions on Moslems in Congress provinces. He said that when the Congress accepted ministry after the introduction of Provincial Autonomy, he felt that Moslem interests were not safe in the hands of the Hindu-dominated Congress ; but the Hindu leaders felt indifferently and so he left the Congress and joined the League. What he had feared has been put in reality by the Congress ministers. This forestalling of the future is called politics. He was, therefore, a great politician. He was again thinking that before India became independent some sort of understanding had to be arrived at with the

Hindus either by force or in a friendly way. Otherwise, the Hindus who had been the slaves of the Moslems for 700 years, would enslave the Moslems. "

The Hindus are aware of what is passing in the mind of the Muslims and dread the possibility of Muslims using independence to enslave them. As a result Hindus are lukewarm towards making independence as the goal of India's political evolution. These are not the fears of those who are not qualified to judge. On the contrary the Hindus who have expressed their apprehensions as to the wisdom of heading for independence are those who are eminently qualified by their contact with Muslim leaders to express an opinion.

Mrs. Annie Besant says* .—

"Another serious question arises with regard to the Muhammadans of India. If the relation between Muslims and Hindus were as it was in the Lucknow days, this question would not be so urgent, though it would even then have almost certainly arisen, sooner or later, in an Independent India But since the Khilafat agitation, things have changed and it has been one of the many injuries inflicted on India by the encouragement of the Khilafat crusade, that the inner Muslim feeling of hatred against "unbelievers" has sprung up, naked and unashamed, as in years gone by. We have seen revived, as guide in practical politics, the old Muslim religion of the sword, we have seen the dragging out of centuries of forgetfulness, the old exclusivenss, claiming the Jazirut-Arab, the island of Arabia, as a holy land which may not be trodden by the polluting foot of a non-Muslim ; we have heard Muslim leaders declare that if the Afghans invaded India, they would join their fellow believers, and would slay the Hindus who defended their motherland against the foe ; we have been forced to see that the primary allegiance of Mussalmans is to Islamic countries, not to our motherland ; we have learned that their dearest hope is to establish the "Kingdom of God ", not God as Father of the world, loving all his creatures, but as a God seen through Mussalman spectacles resembling in his command through one of the prophets, as to the treatment of unbeliever—the Mosaic *JEHOVA* of the early Hebrews, when they were fighting as did the early Muslims, for freedom to follow the religion given to them by their prophet. The world has gone beyond such so-called

* The Future of Indian Politics, pages 301—305,

theocracies, in which, God's commands are given through a man. The claim now put forward by Mussalman leaders that they must obey the laws of their particular prophet above the laws of the State in which they live, is subversive of civic order and the stability of the State , it makes them bad citizens for their centre of allegiance is outside the Nation and they cannot, while they hold the views proclaimed by Moulana Mahomed Ali and Shaukat Ali, to name the most prominent of these Muslim leaders, be trusted by their fellow citizens. If India were independent the Muslim part of the population—for the ignorant masses would follow those who appealed to them in the name of their prophet—would become an immediate peril to India's freedom. Allying themselves with Afghanistan, Baluchistan, Persia, Iraq, Arabia, Turkey and Egypt and with such of the tribes of Central Asia who are Mussalmans, they would rise to place India under the Rule of Islam—those in "British India" being helped by the Muslims in Indian States—and would establish Mussalman rule. We had thought that Indian Mussalmans were loyal to their Motherland, and indeed, we still hope that some of the educated class might strive to prevent such a Mussalman rising ; but they are too few for effective resistance and would be murdered as apostates. Malabar has taught us what Islamic rule still means, and we do not want to see another specimen of the "Khilafat Raj" in India. How much sympathy with the Moplas is felt by Muslims outside Malabar has been proved by the defence raised for them by their fellow believers, and by Mr Gandhi himself, who stated that they had acted as they believed that there religion taught them to act. I fear that that is true ; but there is no place in a civilised land for people who believe that their religion teaches them to murder, rob, rape, burn, or drive away out of the country those who refuse to apostatise from their ancestral faiths, except in its schools, under surveillance, or in its goals. The Thugs believed that their particular form of God commanded them to strangle people— especially travellers with money Such "Laws of God" cannot be allowed to override the laws of a civilised country, and people living in the twentieth century must either educate people who hold these Middle Age views, or else exile them. Their place is in countries sharing their opinions, where they can still use such arguments against any who differ from them—as indeed, Persia and with the Parsis long ago, and the Bahaists in our own time. In fact, Muslim sects are not safe in a country ruled by orthodox Muslims. British rule in India has protected the freedom of all sects : Shiahs, Sunnis, Sufis, Bahaists, live in safety under her sceptre, although it cannot protect

35

any of them from social ostracism, where it is in a minority. Mussalmans are more free under British rule, than in countries where there are Muslim rulers. In thinking of an independent India, the menace of Mohamedan rule has to be considered."

Similar fear was expressed by Lala Lajpatrai in a letter* to Mr. C. R. Das :—

"There is one point more which has been troubling me very much of late and one which I want you to think carefully and that is the question of Hindu-Mohamedan unity. I have devoted most of my time during the last six months to the study of Muslim history and Muslim Law and I am inclined to think, it is neither possible nor practicable. Assuming and admitting the sincerity of the Mohamedan leaders in the Non- co-operation movement, I think their religion provides an effective bar to anything of the kind. You remember the conversation, I reported to you in Calcutta, which I had with Hakim Ajmalkhan and Dr. Kitchlew. There is no finer Mohamedan in Hindustan than Hakimsaheb but can any other Muslim leader override the Quran ? I can only hope that my reading of Islamic Law is incorrect, and nothing would relieve me more than to be convinced that it is so. But if it is right then it comes to this that although we can unite against the British, we cannot do so to rule Hindusthan on British lines, we cannot do so to rule Hindustan on democratic lines. What is then the remedy ? I am not afraid of seven crores in Hindusthan but I think the seven crores of Hindustan plus the armed hosts of Afghanistan, Central Asia, Arabia, Mesopotamia and Turkey will be irresistible. I do honestly and sincerely believe in the necessity or desirability of Hindu-Muslim Unity. I am also fully prepared to trust the Moslem leaders, but what about the injunctions of the Quran and Hadis ? The leaders cannot override them. Are we then doomed ? I hope not. I hope your learned mind and wise head will find some way out of this difficulty."

In 1924 the editor of a Bengalee paper had an interview with the poet Dr. Ravindra Nath Tagore. The report of this interview states† :—

"..... ...... another very important factor which, according to the Poet, was making it almost impossible for the Hindu-Mohamedan unity to become an accomplished fact was that the Mohamedans

---

* Quoted in Life of Savarkar by Indra Prakash.
† Quoted in " Through Indian Eyes " in the Times of India dated 18-4-24.

could not confine their patriotism to any one country............The poet said that he had very frankly asked many Mohamedans whether, in the event of any Mohamedan power invading India, they would stand side by side with their Hindu neighbours to defend their common land. He could not be satisfied with the reply he got from them. He said that he could definitely state that even such men as Mr. Mahomed Ali had declared that under no circumstances was it permissible for any Mohamedan, whatever his country might be, to stand against any other Mohamedan."

II

If independence is impossible then the destiny acceptable to a hundred per cent. Indian as the next best would be for India to have the status of a Dominion within the British Empire. Who would be content with such a destiny? I feel certain that left to themselves the Musalmans will not be content with Dominion Status while the Hindus most certainly will. Such a statement is sure to jar on the ears of Indians and Englishmen. The Congress being loud and vociferous in its insistance on independence the impression prevails that the Hindus are for independence and the Muslims are for Dominion Status. Those who were present at the R. T. C. could not have failed to realize how strong a hold this impression had taken of the English mind and how the claims and interests of the Hindus suffered an injury because of the twin cries raised by the Congress, namely, independence and repudiation of debts. Listening to these cries Englishmen felt that the Hindus were the enemies of the British and the Muslims who did not ask either for independence or repudiation were their friends. But this impression, however true it may be in the light of the avowed plans of the Congress, is a false impression created by false propoganda. For there can be no doubt that the Hindus are at heart for Dominion Status and that the Muslims are at heart for Independence. If proof is wanted there is abundance of it.

The question of independence was first raised in 1921. In that year the Indian National Congress, the All-India Khilafat Conference and the All-India Muslim League held their annual

Sessions in the city of Ahmadabad.   In the Session of every one of
them a resolution in favour of Independence was moved.   It is
interesting to note the fate which the Resolution met at the hands of
the Congress, the Khilafat Conference and the Muslim League.

The President of the Congress was Hakim Ajmal Khan who
acted for Mr. C. R. Das who though duly elected could not preside
owing to his having been arrested by Government before the
Session commenced   In the Session of the Congress, Moulana
Hasrat Mohani moved a resolution pressing for a change in
the creed of the Congress.   The following is the summary of the
proceedings* relating to the resolution :—

"Moulana Hasrat Mohani in proposing his resolution on complete
independence made a long and impassioned speech in Urdu.   He
said, although they had been promised Swaraj last year, the redress of
the Khilafat and Punjab wrongs within a year, they had so far
achieved nothing of the sort.   Therefore it was no use sticking to the
programme.   If remaining within the British Empire or the British
Commonwealth they could not have freedom, he felt that, if necessary,
they should not hesitate to go out of it.   In the words of Lok. Tilak
" liberty was their birth-right, " and any Government which denied
this elementary right of freedom of speech and freedom of action did
not deserve allegiance from the people.   Home Rule on Dominion
lines or Colonial Self-Government could not be a substitute to them
for their inborn liberty.   A Government which could clap into jail
such distinguished leaders of the people as Mr. Chitta Ranjan Das,
Pandit Motilal Nehru, Lala Lajpat Rai and others, had forfeited all
claim to respect from the people.   And since the end of the year did not
bring them Swaraj nothing should prevent them from taking the only
course left open to them now, that of winning their freedom free from
all foreign control.   The resolution reads as follows :—

" The object of the Indian National Congress is the attainment of
Swaraj or complete independence free from all foreign control by the
people of India by all legitimate and peaceful means. "

After several delegates had spoken in favour of it, Mr. Gandhi
came forward to opposed the Resolution.   In opposing the
Resolution, Mr. Gandhi said :—

" Friends, I have said only a few words in Hindi in connection with
the proposition of Mr. Hasrat Mohani.   All I want to say to you in

English is that the levity with that proposition which has been taken by some of you has grieved me. It has grieved me because it shows lack of responsibility. As responsible men and women we should go back to the days of Nagpur and Calcutta and we should remember what we did only an hour ago. An hour ago we passed a resolution which actually contemplates a final settlement of the Khilafat and the Punjab wrongs and transferrence of the power from the hands of the bureaucracy into the hands of the people by certain definite means. Are you going to rub the whole of that position from your mind by raising a false issue and by throwing a bombshell in the midst of the Indian atmosphere? I hope that those of you who have voted for the previous resolution will think fifty times before taking up this resolution and voting for it. We shall be charged by the thinking portion of the world that we do not know really where we are. Let us understand too our limitations. Let Hindus and Musalmans have absolute, indissoluable unity. Who is here who can say today with confidence : " Yes, Hindu-Muslim Unity has become an indissoluble factor of Indian Nationalism ? " Who is here who can tell me that the Parsis and the Sikhs and the Christians and the Jews and the untouchables about whom you heard this afternoon — who will tell me that those very people will not rise against any such idea ? Think therefore fifty times before you take a step which will rebound not to your credit, not to your advantage, but which may cause you irreparable injury. Let us first of all gather up our strength ; let us first of all sound our own depths. Let us not go into waters whose depts we do not know, and this proposition of Mr. Hasrat Mohani lands you into depths unfathomable. I ask you in all confidence to reject that proposition, if you belive in the proposition that you passed only an hour ago. The proposition now before you rubs off the whole of the effect of the proposition that you passed only a moment ago. Are creeds such simple things like clothes which a man can change at will ? For creeds people die, and for creeds people live from age to age. Are you going to change the creed which with all deliberation, and after great debate in Nagpur, you accepted ? There was no limitation of one year when you accepted that creed. It is an extensive creed ; it takes in all, the weakest and the strongest, and you will deny yourselves the privilege of clothing the weakest amongst yourselves with protection if you accept this limited creed of Maulana Hasrat Mohani, which does not admit the weakest of your brethren. I therefore ask you in all confidence to reject his proposition."

The Resolution when put to vote was declared to be lost.

The session of the All-India Khilafat Conference was presided over also by Hakim Ajmal Khan. A Resolution in favour of Independence was also moved in the subjects committee of this Conference. What happened to the Resolution is clear from the following summary of its proceedings. The Report of the proceedings says* :—

" Before the Conference adjourned at eleven in the night till the next day the President, Hakim Ajmalkhan, announced that the Subjects Committee of the Conference had, on the motion of Mr. Azad Sobhani, supported by Mr. Hasrat Mohani, by a majority resolved to ask all Mohamedans and other communities to endeavour to destroy British imperialism and secure complete independence.

This resolution stated that whereas through the persistent policy and attitude of the British Government it cannot be expected that British Imperialism would permit the Jazirat-Ul-Arab and the Islamic world to be completely free from the influence and control of non-Muslims, which means that the Khilafat cannot be secured to the extent that the Shariat demands its safety, therefore, in order to secure permanent safety of the Khilafat and the prosperity of India, it is necessary to endeavour to destroy British Imperialism. This Conference holds the view that the only way to make this effort is, for the Muslims, conjointly with other inhabitants of India, to make India completely free, and that this Conference is of opinion that Muslim opinion about Swaraj is the same, that is, complete independence, and it expects that other inhabitants of India would also hold the same point of view.

On the Conference resuming its sitting on the second day, December 27th, 1921, a split was found to have taken place in the camp over this resolution about independence. When Mr. Hasrat Mohani was going to move his resolution declaring as their goal independence and the destruction of British Imperialism, objection was taken to its consideration by a member of the Khilafat Subjects Committee on the ground that according to their constitution no motion which contemplated a change in their creed could be taken as adopted, unless it was voted for in the Subjects Committee by a majority of two-third.

---

* The Indian Annual Register 1922 Appendix pages 133-34.

The President, Hakim Ajmal Khan, upheld this objection and ruled the independence motion out of order.

Mr. Hasrat Mohani strongly protested and pointed out that the President had disallowed a similar objection by the same member in the Subjects Committee, while he had allowed it in the open Conference. He said that the President had manoeuvred to rule his motion out of order in order to stand in their way of declaring from that Conference that their Swaraj meant complete independence.

The President of the All-India Muslim League was Maulana Hasrat Mohani. A Resolution for independence also came before the League. The Report of the proceedings of the League bearing on the Resolution says* ——

" The Moslem League met at 9 p. m. on 31st December 1921. After it had passed some non-contentious resolutions the President Hasrat Mohani made an announcement amidst applause that he proposed that the decision of the Subjects Committee rejecting his resolution regarding the attainment of independence and destruction of British Imperialism would be held as final and representing the opinion of the majority in the League, but that in view of the great importance of the subject he would allow a discussion on that resolution without taking any vote.

Mr. Azad Sobhani who had moved the resolution in the Subjects Committee, also moved it in the League. He said he believed in Hindu-Moslem unity as absolutely essential, in non-violent non-co-operation as the only way to fight their battle and Mr. Gandhi was fully deserving the dictatorship which had been invested on him by the Congress, but that he also believed that British Imperialism was the greatest danger to India and the Moslem world and must be destroyed by placing before them an ideal of independence.

Mr. Azad Sobhani was followed by several speakers who supported him in the same vein.

The Hon'ble Mr. Raza Ali announced that the reason for the ruling of the President was that the League did not want to take a step which the Congress had not taken. He warned them against saying big things without understanding them and reminded the audience that India was at present not ready for maintaining liberty even if it was attained.

He asked, who would, for instance, be their Commander-in-Chief if the British left tomorrow. (A voice, " Enver Pasha ").

*Ibid Appendix page 78

The speaker emphatically declared that he would not tolerate any foreigner.   He wanted an Indian Commander-in-Chief. "

In 1923 the question of Independence was again raised in the Congress Session held in Madras but with no success.

In 1924 Mr. Gandhi presiding over the Congress Session held in Belgaum said .—

In my opinion, if the British Government mean what they say and honestly help us to equality, it would be a greater triumph than a complete severance of the British connection.   I would therefor strive for Swaraj within the Empire but would not hesitate to sever all connection if it became a necessity through Britain's own fault. I would thus throw the burden of separation on the British people. "

In 1925 Mr. C. R. Das again took up the theme.   In his address to the Bengal Provincial conference held in May of that year he, with the deliberate object of giving a deadly blow to the idea of independence, took particular pains to show the inferiority of the idea of Independence as compared with that of Dominion Status :—

"............ Independence, to my mind, is a narrower ideal than that of Swaraj.   It implies, it is true, the negation of dependence ; but by itself it gives us no positive ideal.   I do not for a moment suggest that independence is not consistent with Swaraj.   But what is necessary is not mere independence but the establishment of Swaraj.   India may be independent tomorrow in the sense that the British people may leave us to our destiny but that will not necessarily give us what I understand by 'Swaraj'.   As I pointed out in my Presidential address at Gaya, India presents an interesting but a complicated problem of consolidating the many apparently conflicting elements which go to make up the Indian people.   This work of consolidation is a long process, may even be a weary process ; but without this no Swaraj is possible...........

"Independence, in the second place, does not give you that idea of order which is the essence of Swaraj.   The work of consolidation which I have mentioned means the establishment of that order. But let it be clearly understood that what is sought to be established must be consistent with the genius, the temperament and the traditions of the Indian people. ·To my mind, Swaraj implies, firstly, that we must have the freedom of working out the consolidation of the diverse elements of the Indian people ; secondly, we must proceed with this work on National lines, not going back two thousand years ago, but going forward in the light and in the spirit of our national genius and temperament...........

"Thirdly, in the work before us, we must not be obstructed by any foreign power.   What then we have to fix upon in the matter of ideal is what I call Swaraj and not mere Independence which may be the negation of Swaraj.   When we are asked as to what is our national ideal of freedom, the only answer which is possible to give is Swaraj. I do not like either Home Rule or Self-Government.   Possibly they come within what I have described as Swaraj.   But my culture somehow or other is antagonistic to the word 'rule' — be it Home Rule or Foreign Rule.

*   *   *   *   *   *   *   *

"Then comes the   question as   to whether this ideal is to be realised within the Empire or outside ?   The answer which the Congress has always given is ' within the Empire if the Empire, will recognise our right' and 'outside the Empire, if it does not.   We must have opportunity to live our life, — opportunity for self-realization, self-development, and self-fulfilment.   The question is of living our life.   If the Empire furnishes sufficient scope for the growth and development of our national life the Empire idea is to be preferred.   If, on the contrary, the Empire like the Car of Jagannath crushes our life in the sweep of its imperialistic march, there will be justification for the idea of the establishment of Swaraj outside the Empire.

"Indeed, the Empire idea gives us a vivid sense of many advantages. Dominion Status is in no sense servitude.   It is essentially an alliance by consent of those who form part of the Empire for material advantages in the real spirit of co-operation.   Free alliance necessarily carries with it the right of separation.   Before the War it is generally believed that it is only as a great confederation that the Empire or its component parts can live.   It is realised that under modern conditions no nation can live in isolation and the Dominion Status, while it affords complete protection to each constituent composing the great Commonwealth of Nations called the British Empire, secures to each the right to realise itself, develop itself and fulfil itself and therefore it expresses and implies all the elements of Swaraj which I have mentioned."

"To me the idea is specially attractive because of its deep spiritual significance.   I believe in world peace, in the ultimate federation of the world ; and I think that the great Commonwealth

36

of Nations called the British Empire — a federation of diverse races, each with its distinct life, distinct civilization, its distinct mental outlook — if properly led with statesmen at the helm is bound to make lasting contribution to the great problem that awaits the statesman, the problem of knitting the world into the greatest federation the mind can conceive, the federation of the human race. But if only properly led with statesman at the helm ; — for the development of the idea involves apparent sacrifice on the part of the constituent nations and it certainly involves the giving up for good the Empire Idea with its ugly attribute of domination. I think it is for the good of India, for the good of the world that India should strive for freedom within the Commonwealth and so serve the cause of humanity."

Mr. Das not only insisted that Dominion Status was better than Independence but he went further and got the Conference to pass the following Resolution on the goal of India's political evolution.

" 1. This Conference declares that the National ideal of Swaraj involves the right of the Indian Nation to live its own life, to have the opportunity of self-realization, self-development and self-fulfilment and the liberty to work for the consolidation of the diverse elements which go to make up the Indian Nation, unimpeded and unobstructed by any outside domination.

2. That if the British Empire recognises such right and does not obstruct the realisation of Swaraj and is prepared to give such opportunity and undertakes to make the necessary sacrifices to make such rights effective, this Conference calls upon the Indian Nation to realise its Swaraj within the British Commonwealth."

It may be noted that Mr. Gandhi was present throughout the session. But there was no word of dissent coming from him. On the contrary he approved of the stand taken by Mr. Das.

With these facts, who can doubt that the Hindus are for Dominion Status and the Muslims are for Independence ? But if there be any doubt still remaining, the repurcussions in Muslim quarters over the Nehru Committee's Report in 1928 must dissolve it completely. The Nehru Committee appointed by the Congress to frame a constitution for India accepted Dominion Status as the basis for India's constitution and rejected independence.

It is instructive to note the attitude adopted by the Congress and the Muslim political organizations in the country towards the Nehru Report.

The Congress in its session held at Lahore in 1928 passed a resolution moved by Mr. Gandhi which was in the following terms :—

" This Congress, having considered the constitution recommended by the All-Parties' Committee Report, welcomes it as a great contribution towards the solution of India's political and communal problems, and congratulates the Committee on the virtual unanimity of its recommendations and, whilst adhering to the resoluion relating to complete independance passed at the Madras Congress approves of the constitution drawn up by the Committee as a great step in political advance, especially as it represents the largest measure of agreement attained among the important parties in the country.

"Subject to the exigencies of the political situation this Congess will adopt the constitution in its entirety if it is accepted by the British Parliament on or before December 31, 1929, but in the event of its non-acceptance by that date or its earlier rejection, Congress will organise a non-violent non-co-operation by advising the country to refuse taxation in such other manner as may be decided upon. Consistently with the above, nothing in this resolution shall interfere with the carrying on, in the name of the Congress, of the propaganda for complete independence."

This shows that Hindu opinion is not in favour of Independence but in favour of Dominion Status. Some will take exception to this statement. It may be asked what about the Congress Resolution of 1927 ? It is true that the Congress in its Madras Session held in 1927 did pass the following resolution moved by Pandit Jawaharlal Nehru :—

" This Congress declares the goal of the Indian people to be complete National Independence."

But there is enough evidence to support the contention that this resolution did not and does not speak the real mind of the Hindus in the Congress.

PAKISTAN AND THE MALAISE

The resolution came as a surprise. There was no indication of it in the speech of Dr. Ansari * who presided over the 1927 Session. The Chairman† of the Reception Committee only referred to it in passing not as an urgent but a contingent line of action.

There was no forethought about the resolution. It was the result of a coup and the coup was successful because of three factors.

In the first place there was then a section in the Congress which was opposed to the domination of Pandit Motilal Nehru and Mr.Gandhi, particularly the former. This group was led by Mr.Srinivas Iyengar who was a political rival of Pandit Motilal. They were searching for a plan which would destroy the power and prestige of Pandit Motilal and Mr. Gandhi. They knew that the only way to win people to their side was to take a more extreme position and to show that their rivals were really moderates and as moderation was deemed by the people to be a sin they felt that this plan was sure to succeed. They made the goal of India the battle ground, and knowing that Pundit Motilal and Gandhi who were for Dominion Status, put forth the goal of Independence. In the second place there was a section in the Congress which was led by Mr. Vallabhbhai Patel. This section was in touch with the Irish Sinn Fein party and was canvassing its help in the cause of India. The Irish Sinn Fein party was not willing to render any help unless the Indians declared that their goal was Independence. This section was anxious to change the goal from Dominion Status to Independence in order to secure Irish help. To these two factors was added a third, namely, the speech made by Lord Birkenhead, the then Secretary of State for India

* This is all that Dr. Ansari said about the subject in his speech .

" Whatever be the final form of the constitution, one thing may be said with some degree of certainly, that it will have to be on federal lines providing for a United States of India with existing Indian States as autonomous units of the Federation taking their proper share in the defence of the country, in the regulation of the nation's foreign affairs and other joint and common interests." — The Indian Quarterly Register 1927 Vol. II page 372

† Mr. Muthuranga Mudliar said :

" We ought to make it known that if Parliament continues in its present insolent mood, we must definitely start on an intensive propoganda for the severance of India from the Empire. Whenever the time may come for the effective assertion of Indian nationalism, Indian aspriation will then be towards free nationhood, untramelled even by the nominal suzerainty of the king of England. It behoves English statesmanship to take careful note of this fact. Let them not drive us to despair" — Ibid page 356.

on the occasion of the appointment of the Simon Commission when
he taunted the Indians on their incapacity to produce a constitution.
The speech was regarded as a great insult by Indian politicians. It is
the combination of these three factors which was responsible for the
passing of this resolution. Indeed the resolution was passed more
from the motive* of giving a fitting reply to Lord Birkenhead than
from the motive of defining the political goal of the country and it
is because of the bad temper created by Lord Birkenhead that forced
Mr. Gandhi and Pandit Motilal to bow to the storm rather than
engage upon the task of sweeping it off which they would have
otherwise done

That this resolution did not speak the real mind of the
Hindus in the Congress is beyond doubt. Otherwise it is not possible
to explain how the Nehru Committee which was appointed a year
after could have flouted the Madras resolution of 1927 by adopting
Dominion Status as the basis of the constitutional structure framed by it.
Nor is it possible to explain how the Congress adopted Dominion
Status in 1928 if it had really accepted† independence in 1927 as the
resolution says. The clause in the Resolution that the Congress would
accept Dominion Status if given before 31st December 1929, if not,
it would change its faith from Dominion Status to Independence
was only a facet-saving device and did not connote a real change
of heart. For time can never be of essence in a matter of so deep
a concern such as the political destiny of the country.

That notwithstanding the resolution of 1927 the Congress
continued to believe in Dominion Status and did not believe in
Independence is amply borne out by the pronouncements made from
time to time by Mr. Gandhi who is the oracle of the Congress.
Anyone who studies Mr. Gandhi's pronouncements on this subject
from 1929 onwards cannot help feeling that Mr. Gandhi was not
happy about the resolution on Independence and that he felt it
necessary to wheel the Congress back to Dominion Status. He
began with the gentle process of interpreting it away. The goal was

* Mr Sambamurti in seconding the resolution said . " The Resolution is the only reply
to the arrogant challenge thrown by Lord Birkenhead."—The Indian Quarterly Register 1927,
Vol II p 381.

† Pandit Jewhar Nehru in moving the Resolution said :—

" It declares that the Congress stands to-day for complete Independence. Nonetheless
it leaves the doors of the Congress open to such persons as may perhaps be satisfied with
a lesser goal "—Ibid p.381.

first reduced from Independence to substance of Independence. From substance of Independence it was reduced to equal partnership and from equal partnership it was brought back to its original position. The wheel completed the turn when Mr. Gandhi in 1937 gave the following letter to Mr. Pollock for the information of the English people :—

" Your question is whether I retain the same opinion as I did at the Round Table Conference in 1931. I said then, and repeat now, that, so far as I am concerned, if Dominion Stutus were offered to India in terms of the Statute of Westminster, i. e., the right to secede at will, I would unhesitatingly accept*"

Turning to the pronouncements of Muslim political organizations the fact is that they too rejected the Nehru Report. But the reasons given by them for its rejection are wholly different. No doubt some Muslim organizations such as the Muslim League rejected the Report because it recommended the abolition of separate electorates. But that was certainly not the reason why it was condemned by the Khilafat Conference or the Jamiat-ul-Ulema — the two Muslim organizations which went with the Congress through the same firey ordeal of non-co-operation and civil disobedience and whose utterances expressed far more truly the real opinion of Muslim masses on the issues relating to the political affairs of the country than did the utterances of any other Muslim organization.

Maulana Mohamad Ali gave his reasons for the rejection of the Nehru Report in his Presidential address to the All-India Khilafat Conference held in Calcutta in 1928. He said† :—

" [I] was a member of the Indian National Congress, its Working Committee, the All-India Muslim League and [I] have come to the Khilafat Conference to express (my views) on the important political issues of the time, which should have the serious attention of the whole Moslem Community.

*　　　　*　　　　*　　　　*

"In the All-Parties Convention he had said that India should have complete independence and there was no communalism in it. Yet he was being heckled at every moment and stopped during his speech at every step.

*　　　　*　　　　*　　　　*

* Times of India 1-2-37. In view of this the declaration made by the National Convention—consisting of the members elected to the new Provincial Legislatures under the new constitution — on the 20th March 1937 at Delhi in favour of independence has no significance.

† The Indian Quarterly Register 1928 Vol. II pages 402-403.

"The Nehru Report had as its preamble admitted the bondage of servitude................Freedom and Dominion Status were widely divergent things....................

　　　*　　　　　*　　　　　*　　　　*

"I ask, when you boast of your nationalism and condemn communalism, show me a country in the world like your India — your nationalist India.

"You make compromises in your constitution every day with false doctrines, immoral conceptions and wrong ideas but you make no compromise with our communalists — with separate electorates and reserved seats. Twenty-five per cent, is our portion of population and yet you will not give us 33 per cent in the Assembly. You are a Jew, a Bania. But to the English you give the status of your dominion."

The Conference passed a short resolution in the following pithy terms :—

"This Conference declares once more that complete independence was our goal."

Maulana Hasrat Mohani, as President of the Jamiat-ul-Ulema Conference held in Allahabad in 1931, gave the same reasons for condemning the Nehru Report in words more measured but not less scathing. Said* the Maulana . —

"My political creed with regard to India is now well known to everybody. I cannot accept anything short of complete independence, and, that too, on the model of the United States of America or the Soviet Russia which is essentially (1) democratic, (2) federal and (3) centrifugal, and in which the rights of Muslim minorities are safeguarded.

"For some time the Jamiat-ul-Ulema of Delhi held fast to the creed of complete independence and it was mostly for this reason that it repudiated the Nehru Report which devised a unitary constitution instead of a federal one. Besides, when, after the Lahore session, the Congress, at the instance of Mahatma Gandhi, declared the burial of the Nehru Report on the banks of the Ravi and the resolution of complete independence was unanimously agreed upon, the Delhi Jamiat ventured to co-operate with the Congress and its programme of civil disobedience simply because it was the duty of every Indian, Hindu or Muslim, to take part in the struggle for independence.

---

* Ibid 1931 Vol. II pages 238-39.

"But unfortunately Gandhiji very soon went back upon his words and (1) while yet in jail he told the British journalist Mr. Slocombe that by complete independence he meant only the substance of independence, (2) besides, when he was released on expressing his inclination for compromise he devised the illusory term of Purna Swaraj in place of complete independence and openly declared that in " *Purna Swaraj*" there was no place for severance of the British connection, (3) by making a secret pact with Lord Irwin he definitely adopted the ideal of Dominion Status under the British Crown.

"After this change of front by Gandhiji the Delhi Jamiat ought to have desisted from blindly supporting the Mahtma and like the Nehru Report it should have completely rejected this formula of the Congress Working Committee by which the Nehru Report was sought to be revived at Bombay.

"But we do not know what unintelligible reasons induced the Delhi Jamiat-ul-Ulema to adopt "Purna Swaraj" as their ideal, in spite of the knowledge that it does not mean complete independence but something even worse than complete independence. And the only explanation for adopting this creed is said to be that, although Gandhiji has accepted Dominion Status, he still insists that Britain should concede the right of cessation from the British Empire to the Indians.

"Although it is quite clear that insistence on this right has no better worth than the previous declaration of complete independence, in other words, just as Gandhiji insisted on complete independence with the sole object of forcing the British Government to accede to the demand of Dominion Status, which was the sole ultimate aim of the Mahatma, in the same way the leaders of the Congress insisted upon the right of secession with the object of extorting the largest measure of political rights from the British people who might not go beyond a certain limit in displeasing them. Otherwise Gandhiji and his followers know it full well that even if this right of secession is given to Indians it would perhaps be never put into practice.

"If some one considers this contention of mine to be based on suspicion and contends that the Congress will certainly declare for secession from the Empire whenever there is need of it, I will ask him to let me know what will be the form of Indian Government after the British connection is withdrawn. It is clear that no one can conceive of a despotic form and a democratic form whether it be unitary or federal but centripetal, will be nothing more than Hindu Raj which the Musalmans can in no circumstances accept. Now remains only one form viz, after complete withdrawal of the British connection India with its autonomous Provinces and States forms into united centrifugal democratic Government on the model of the United States Republic or Soviet Russia. But this can never be acceptable to the Mahasabhite Congress or a lover of Britain like Mahatma Gandhi.

"Thus the Jamiat-ul-Ulema of Delhi after washing its hands of complete independence has stultified itself, but thank God the Ulemas of Cawnpore, Lucknow, Badaun, etc., still hold fast to their pledge and will remain so, God willing. Some weak-kneed persons urge against this highest ideal that, when it is not possible for the present to attain it, there is no use talking about it. We say to them that it is not at all useless but rather absolutely necessary, for if the highest ideal is not always kept before view it is liable to be forgotten.

"We must, therefore, oppose Dominion Status in all circumstances as this is not the half-way house or part of our ultimate aim, but its very negation and rival. If Gandhiji reaches England and the Round Table Conference is successfully concluded, giving India Dominion Status of any kind, with or without safeguards, the conception of complete Independence will completely vanish or at any rate will not be thought of for a very long time to come."

The All-India Khilafat Conference and the Jamiat-ul-Ulema were of course extremist bodies avowedly Anti-British. But the All-Parties Muslim Conference was not at all a body of extremists or anti-British Musalmans. Yet the U. P. Branch of it in its session held at Cawnpore on 4th November 1928 passed the following resolution —

"In the opinion of the All-Parties U. P. Moslem Conference, Mussalmans of India stand for the goal of complete independence, which shall necessarily take the form of a federal republic."

In the opinion of the mover, Islam always taught freedom, and for the matter of that the Moslems of India would fail in their religious duty, if they were against complete independence. Though Indian Moslems were poor yet they were, the speaker was sure, devoted to Islam more than any people on earth.

In this Conference an incident* of some interest occurred in the Subjects Committee when Maulana Azad Sobhani proposed that the Conference should declare itself in favour of complete independence.

---

* *See* The Indian Quarterly Register 1928 Vol. II page 425.

Khan Bahadur Masoodul Hassan and some other persons, objected to such declaration, which, in their opinion, would go against the best interests of Mussalmans.

Upon this, a number of women from their purdah gallery sent a written statement to the President saying that if men had not the courage to stand for complete independence, women would come out of purdah, and take their place in the struggle for independence.

III

Notwith-standing this difference in their ultimate destiny, an attempt is made to force the Hindus and Muslims to live in one country, as one people, bound by the political ties of a single constitution.   Assuming that this is done and that the Muslims are some-how manœuvred into it what guarantee is there that the constitution will not break down ?

The successful working of a Parliamentary Government assumes the existence of certain conditions.   It is only when these conditions exist that Parliamentary Government can take roots. One such condition was pointed out by the late Lord Balfour when in 1925 he had an occasion to discuss the political future of the Arab peoples in conversation with his niece Blanche Dugdale.

In the course of this convention he said* —

"It is partly the fault of the British nation — and of the Americans ; we can't exornate them from blame either — that this idea of "representative government" has got into the heads of nations who haven't the smallest nation of what its basis must be.   It's difficult to explain, and the Anglo-Saxon races are bad at exposition.   More-over we know it so well ourselves that it does not strike us as necessary to explain it.   I doubt if you would *find it* written in any book on the British Constitution that the whole essence of British Parliamentary Government lies in the *intention to make the thing work*.   We take that for granted.   We have spent hunderds of years in elaborating a system that rests on that alone.   It is so deep in us that we have lost sight of it.   But it is not so obvious to others.   These pepoles — Indians, Egyptians, and so on — study our learning. They read our history, our philosophy, an politics.   "They learn about our parliamentary methods of obstruction, but nobody explains to them that when it comes to the point all our

---

* Dugdale's Balfour (Hutchinson) Vol. II pp. 363—64.

parliamentary parties are determined that the machinery stan't stop.
"The king's government must go on" as the Duke of Wellington said.
But their idea is that the function of opposition is to stop the machine.
Nothing easier, of course, but hopeless."

Asked why the opposition in England does not go to the length
of stopping the machine he said —

"Our whole political machinery presupposes a people . . .
fundamentally at one"

Lasky has well summarized these observations of Balfour on the
condition necessary for the successful working of Parliamentary
Government when he says .*

"The strength of Parliamentary Government is exactly measured
by the unity of political parties upon its fundamental objects."

Having stated the condition — necessary for the successful
working of the machinery of representative Government it will be
well to examine whether these conditions are present in India.

How far can there be said to be an intention in the Hindus and
Muslims to make representative government work ?   To prove the
futility and unworkability of representative and responsible government it is enough even if one of the two parties shows an intention
to stop the machinary of government.   If such an intention is
enough, then it does not matter much whether it is found in the
Hindus or in the Muslims   The Muslims being more outspoken
than the Hindus one gets to know their mind more than one gets
to know the mind of the Hindus.   How the Muslim mind will work
and by what factors it is likely to be swayed will be clear if the
fundamental tenets of Islam which dominate Muslim politics and the
views expressed by prominent Muslims having a bearing on Muslim
attitude towards an Indian Government are taken into consideration.
Certain of such religious tenets of Islam and the views of some of the
Muslim leaders are given below to enable all those who are capable
of looking at things dispassionately to judge for themselves whether the
condition postulated by Balfour can be said to exist in India.

Among the tenets the one that calls for notice is the tenet of
Islam which says that in a country which is not under Muslim Rule

* Parliamentary Government in England page 37.

wherever there is a conflict between Muslim law and the law of the land the former must prevail over the latter and a Muslim will be justified in obeying the Muslim Law and defying the law of the land.

What the duty of the musalmans is in such cases was well pointed out by Maulana Mahomad Ali in the course of his statement made in 1921 before the Committing Magistrate of Karachi in answer to the charges for which he was prosecuted by the Government. The prosecution arose out of a resolution passed at the session of the All-India Khilafat Conference held in Karachi on 8-7-21 at which Mr. Mahomad Ali presided and introduced the resolution in question.

The reslution was as follows :—

" This meeting clearly proclaims that it is in every way religiously unlawful for a Musalman at the present moment to continue in the British Army, or to enter the Army, or to induce others to join the Army. And it is the duty of all Musalmans in general and of the Ulemas in particular to see that these religious commandments are brought home to every Musalman in the Army. "

Along with Maulana Mahomad Ali other six persons* were prosecuted under Sections 120-B read with Sec 131 I. P. C. and under Sec 505 or 505 read with Sec 114 and Section 505 read with 117 I. P. C. Maulana Mahomad Ali in justification of his plea of not guilty said† :—

" After all what is the meaning of this precious prosecution. By whose convictions are we to be guided, we the Musalmans and the Hindus of India ? Speaking as a Musalman, if I am supposed to err from the right path, the only way to convince me of my error is to refer me to the Holy Koran or to the authentic traditions of the last Prophet — on whom be peace and God's benediction — or the religious pronoucements of recognized Muslim divines, past and present, which purport to be based on these two original sources of Islamic authority demands from me in the present circumstances, the precise action for which a Government that does not like to be called Satanic, is prosecuting me to-day.

If that which I neglect, becomes by my neglect a deadly sin, and is yet a crime when I do not neglect it how am I to consider myself safe in this country ?

---

*Strange enough one of them was the Shankaracharya of Sharada Peeth.
†The Trial of Ali Brothers by R. V. Thadani pages 69-71.

I must either be a sinner or a criminal..............................Islam·
recognizes one sovereignty alone, the sovereignty of God, which is
supreme and unconditional, indivisible and inalienable.............

*   *   *   *   *   *   *   *

The only allegiance a Musalman, whether civilian or soldier,
whether living under a Muslim or under a non-Muslim administration,
is commanded by the Koran to acknowledge his allegiance to God,
to his prophet and to those in authority from among the Musalmans
chief among the last mentioned being of course that Prophet's successor
or commander of the faithful.. ....
This doctrine of unity is not a mathematical formula elaborated by
abstruse thinkers but a work-a-day belief of every Musalman learned
or unlettered....... ....Musalmans have before this also and elsewhere
too, lived in peaceful subjection to non-Muslim administrations. But
the unalterable rule is and has always been that as Musalmans they
can obey only such laws and orders issued by their secular rulers as do
not involve disobedience to the commandments of God who in the
expressive language of the Holy Koran is " the all-ruling ruler."
These very clear and rigidly definite limits of obedience are not laid
down with regard to the authority of non-Muslim administrations only.
On the contrary they are of universal application and can neither be
enlarged nor reduced in any case "

This must make any one wishing for a stable Government
very apprehensive. But this is nothing as compared with the
second fact to be noted. It relates to Muslim tenets which prescribe
when a country is a motherland to the Muslim and when it is not.

According to Muslim Cannon law the world is divided into two
camps, Dar-ul-Islam (abode of Islam) and Dar-ul-Harb (abode of
war). A country is Dar-ul-Islam when it is ruled by Muslims.
A country is Dar-ul-Harb when Muslims only reside in it but
are not rulers of it. That being the Cannon Law of the Muslims,
India cannot be the common motherland of Hindus *and* Musalmans.
It can be the land of Musalmans — but it cannot be the land of
' Hindus and Muslmans living as equal. ' Further, it can be the
land of the Musalmans only when it is governed by the Muslims.
The moment the land becomes subject to the authority of
a non-Muslim power it ceases to be the land of the Muslims. Instead
of being Dar-ul-Islam it becomes Dar-ul-Harb.

It must not be supposed that this view is only of an academic interest. For it is capable of becoming an active force capable of influencing the conduct of the Muslims. It did greatly influence the conduct of the Muslims when the British occupied India. The British occupation raised no qualms in the minds of the Hindus. But so far as the Muslims were concerned, it at once raised the question whither India was any longer a suitable place of residence for Muslims A discussion was started in the Muslim community, which Dr. Titus says lasted for half a century, as to whether India was Dar-ul-Harb or Dar-ul-Islam. Some of the more zealous elements, under the leadership of Sayyed Ahmed, actually did declare a holy war, preached the necessity of emigration (*Hijrat*) to lands under Muslim rule, and carried their agitation all over India.

It took all the ingenuity of Sir Sayyed Ahmad the founder of the Aligarh movement to persuade the Indian Musalmans not to regard India under the British as Dar-ul-Harb merely because it was not under Muslim rule. He urged upon the Muslims to regard it as Dar-ul-Islam, because the Muslims were perfectly free to exercise all the essential rites and ceremonies of their religion The movement for Hijrat for the time being died down. But the doctrine that India was Dar-ul-Harb had not been given up. It was again preached by Muslim patriots during 1920 21, when the Khilafat agitation was going on. The agitation was not without response from the Muslim masses and there were a goodly number of Muslims who not only showed themselves ready to act in accordance with the Muslim Cannon Law but actually abandoned their homes in India and crossed over to Afghanistan.

It might also be mentioned that Hijrat is not the only way of escape to Muslims who find themselves in a Dar-ul-Harb. There is another injunction of Muslim Cannon Law called Jihad by which it becomes " incumbent on a Muslim ruler to extend the rule of Islam until the whole world shall have been brought under its sway The world, being divided into two camps, Dar-ul Islam (abode of Islam), and Dar-ul-Harb (abode of war), all countries come under one category or the other. Technically, it is the duty of the Muslim ruler, who is capable of doing so, to transform Dar-ul Harb into Dar-ul-Islam." And just as there are instances of the

Muslims in India resorting to Hijrat there are instances showing that they have not hesitated to proclaim Jihad. The curious may examine the history of the Mutiny of 1857 and if he does, he will find that in part at any rate it was really a Jihad proclaimed by the Muslims against the British, and that the Mutiny so far as the Muslims were concerned was a recrudesence of revolt which had been fostered by Syyed Ahmad who preached to the Musalmans for several decades that owing to the occupation of India by the British the country had become a Dar-ul-Harb. The Mutiny was an attempt by the Muslims to re-convert India into a Dar-ul-Islam. A more recent instance was the invasion of India by Afghanistan in 1919. It was engineered by the Musalmans of India who led by the Khilafatists, antipathy to the British Government sought the assistance of Afghanistan to emancipate India * Whether the invasion would have resulted in the emancipation of India or whether it would have resulted in its subjugation, it is not possible to say because the invasion failed to take effect. Apart from this the fact remains that India if not exclusively under Muslim rule is a Dar-ul-Harb and the Musalmans according to the tenets of Islam are justified in proclaiming a Jihad

Not only they can proclaim Jihad but they can call the aid of a foreign Muslim power to make his Jihad a success or if the foreign Muslim power intends to proclaim a Jihad, help that power in making its endeavour a success This was clearly explained by Mr. Mahomad Ali in his address to the Jury in the Session Court. Mr. Mahomad Ali said —

"But since the Government is apparently uninformed about the manner in which our Faith colours and is meant to colour all our actions, including those which, for the sake of convenience, are generally characterised as mundane, one thing must be made clear, and it is this : Islam does not permit the believer to pronounce an adverse judgment against another believer without mere convincing proof ; and we could not, of course, fight against our Moslem brothers without making sure that they were guilty of wanton aggression, and did not take up arms in defence of their faith. " (This was in relation to the war that was going on between the British and the Afghans in

*This interesting and awful episode has been examined in some details, giving the part played therein by Mr. Gandhi in a series of articles in the *Maratha*, 1940 by Mr. Karandikar.

1919). " Now our position is this. Without better proof of the Amir's malice or madness we certainly do not want Indian soldiers, including the Mussalamans, and particularly with our own encouragement and assistance, to attack Afghanistan and effectively occupy it first, and then be a prey to more perplexity and perturbation afterwards. "

" But if on the contrary His Majesty the Amir has no quarrel with India and her yeople and if his motive must be attributed, as the Secretary of State has publicly said, to the unrest which exists throughout the Mahomedan world and unrest with which he openly professed to be in cordial sympathy, that is to say, if impelled by the same religious motive that has forced Muslims to contemplate Hijrat, the alternative of the weak, which is all that is within our restricted means, His Majesty has been forced to contemplate Jihad, the alternative of those comparatively stronger, which he may have found within his means , if he has taken up the challenge of those who believed in force and yet more force, and he intends to try conclusions with those who require Mussalmans to wage war against the Khalifat and those engaged in Jehad , who are an wrongful occupation of the Jazirut-ul-arab and the holy places ; who aim at the weaking of Islam ; discriminate against it ; and deny to us full freedom to advocate its cause ; then the clear law of Islam requires that in the first place, in no case whatever should a Musalman render any one any assistance against him ; and in the next place if the Jihad approaches my region every Musalman in that region must join the Mujahidin and assist them to the best of his or her power."

"Such is the clear and undisputed law of Islam ; and we had explained this to the Committee investigating our case when it had put to us a question about the religious duty of a Moslem subject of a non-Moslem power when Jihad had been declared against it, long before there was any notion of trouble on the Fronties, and when the late Amir was still alive."

A third tenet which calls for notice as being relevant to the issue is that Islam does not recognize territorial affinities. Its affinities are social and religious and therefore extra-territorial. Here again Maulana Mahomad Ali will be the best witness. When he was committed to the Sessions Court in Karachi Mr. Mahomad Ali addressing the Jury said :—

" One thing has to be made clear as we have since discovered that the doctrine to which we shall now advert is not so generally known in Non-Moslem and particularly in official circles as it ought to be. A Mussalman's faith does not consist merely in believing in a set of doctrines and living up to that belief himself ; he must also exert himself to the fullest extent of his power, of course without resort to any compulsion, to the end that others also conform to the prescribed belief and practices.   This is spoken of in the Holy Koran as "Amrbil-maroof" and "Nahi anilmunkar ; and certain distinct chapters of the Holy Prophets, traditions relate to this essential doctrine of Islam. A Mussalman cannot say : "I am not my brother's keeper," for in a sense he is and his own salvation cannot be assured to him unless he exhorts others also to do good and dehorts them against doing evil. If therefore any Mussalman is being compelled to wage war against the Mujahid of Islam, he must not only be a conscientious objector himself, but must, if he values his own salvation, persuade his brothers also at whatever risk to himself to take similar objection.   Then and not until then, can he hope for salvation.   This is our belief as well as the belief of every other Mussalman and in our humble way we seek to live up to it ; and if we are denied freedom to inculcate this doctrine we must conclude that the land where this freedom does not exist is not safe for Islam."

This is the basis of Pan-Islamism.   It is this which leads every Mussalman in India to say that he is a Muslim first and Indian afterwards.   It is this sentiment which explains why the Indian Muslim has taken so small a part in the advancement of India but has spent himself to exhaustion* by taking up the cause of Muslim countries and why Muslim countries occupy the first place and India occupies a second place in his thoughts.

His Highness the Aga Khan justifies it by saying .—

"This is a right and legitimate Pan-Islamism to which every sincere and believing Mahomedan belongs — that is, the theory of the spiritual brotherhood and unity of the children of the Prophet.   It is a deep, perennial element in that Perso-Arabian culture, that great family of civilization to which we gave the name Islamic in the first chapter.   It cannotes charity and goodwill towards fellow-believers everywhere from China to Morocco, from the Volga to Singapore. It means an abiding interest in the literature of Islam, in her beautiful arts, in her lovely architecture, in her entrancing poetry.   It also

---

* Between 1912 when the first Balkan war began and 1922 when Turkey made peace with the European powers the Indian Muslims did not bother about Indian politics in the least.   They were completely absorbed in the fate of Turkey and Arabia.

means a true reformation — a return to the early and pure simplicity of the faith, to its preaching by persuation and argument, to the manifestation of a spiritual power in individual lives, to beneficient activity of mankind. This natural and worthy spiritual movement makes not only the Master and His teaching but also His children of all climes and object of affection to the Turk or the Afghan, to the Indian or the Egyptian. A famine or a desolating fire in the Moslem quarters of Kashgar or Sarajevo would immediately draw the sympathy and material assistance of the Mahomedan of Delhi or Cairo. The real spiritual and cultural unity of Islam must ever grow, for to the follower of the Prophet it is the foundation of the life of the soul."

If this spritual Pan-Islamism seeks to issue forth in political Pan-Islamism it cannot be said to be unatural. It is perhaps that feeling which was in the mind of the Aga Khan when he said —

"It is for the Indian patriot to recognise that Persia, Afghanistan and possibly Arabia must sooner or later come within the orbit of some Continental Power — such as Germany, or what may grow out of the break-up of Russia — or must throw in their lot with that of the Indian Empire, with which they have so much more genuine affinity. The world forces that move small States into closer contact with powerful neighbours, though so far most visible in Europe, will inevitably make themselves felt in Asia. Unless she is willing to accept the prospect of having powerful and possibly inimical neighbours to watch, and the heavy military burdens thereby entailed, India cannot afford to neglect to draw her Mahomedan neighbour States to herself by the ties of mutual interest and goodwill."

"In a word, the path of beneficent and growing union must be based on a federal India, with every member exercising her individual rights, her historic peculiarities and natural interests, yet protected by a common defensive system and customs union from external danger and economic exploitation by stronger forces. Such a federal India would promptly bring Ceylon to the bosom of her natural mother, and the further developments we have indicated would follow. We can build a great South Asiatic Federation by now laying the foundations wide and deep on justice, on liberty, and on recognition for every race, every religion, and every historical entity."

"A sincere policy of assisting both Persia and Afghanistan in the onward march which modern conditions demand, will raise two natural ramparts for India in the North-West that neither German nor Slav, Turk nor Mongol, can ever hope to destroy. They will be drawn of their own accord towards the Power which provides the object lesson of a healthy form of federalism in India, with real autonomy for each province, with the internal freedom of principalities assured, with a revived and liberalised kingdom of Hyderabad, including the Berars, under the Nizam. They would see in India freedom and order, autonomy and yet Imperial union, and would appreciate for themselves the advantages of a confederation assuring the continuance of internal self-government buttressed by goodwill, the immense and unlimited strength of that great Empire on which the sun never sets. The British position in Mesopotamia and Arabia also, whatever its nominal form may be, would be infinitely strengthened by the policy I have advocated."

This South Asiatic Federation was more for the good of the Muslim countries such as Arabia, Messapotemia and Afghanistan than for the good of India.* This shows how very naturally the thoughts of Indian Mussalmans are occupied by considerations of Muslim countries other than those of India

Government is based on obedience to authority. But those who are eager to establish self-government of Hindus and Muslims do not seem to have stopped to inquire on what such obedience depends and how far such obedience would be forthcoming in the usual course and in moments of crisis. This is a very important question. For, if obedience fails self-government must fail. It is no use arguing that representative government means working together and not working under That may be so in an ideal sense. But in the practical and work-a-day world, if the elements brought under one representative government are disproportionate in numbers, the

---

* What a terrible thing it would have been if this South Asiatic Federation had come into being. Hindus would have been reduced to the position of a distressed minority, The "Indian Annual Register" says "Supporters of British Imperialism in the Muslim Community of India have also been active trying by the organization of an Anglo-Muslim alliance to stabilize the rule of Britain in Southern Asia, from Arabia to the Malaya Archipelago, wherein the Muslims will be junior partners in the firm at present, hoping to rise in time to the senior partnership. It was to some such feeling and anticipation that we must trace the scheme adumbrated by His Highness the Aga Khan in his book-'India in Transition' published during the war years. The scheme had planned for the setting up of a South Western Asiatic Federation of which India might be a constituent unit. After the War when Mr. Winston Churchill was Secretary of State for the Colonies in the British Cabinet he found in the Archives of the Middle Eastern Department a scheme ready-made of a Middle Eastern Empire" – 1938 Vol. II Section on India in Home Polity p. 48.

minor section will have to work under the major section and whether it works under the major section or not will depend upon how far it is disposed to obey the authority of the government carried on by the major section. So important is this factor in the success of self-government that Balfour may be said to have spoken only part of the truth when he made its success dependent upon parties being fundamentally at one. He failed to note that willingness to obey the authority of Government is a factor equally necessary for the success of any scheme of self-government.

The importance of this second condition the existence of which is necessary for a successful working of parliamentary government has been discused by * by James Bryce. While dealing with the basis of political cohesion Bryce points out that while force may have done much to build up States, force is only one among many factors and not the most important. In creating moulding, expanding and knitting together political communities with more important than force is obedience. This willingness to obey and comply the sanctions of a government depends upon certain psychological attibutes of the individual citizens and groups. According to Bryce the attitude which produces obedience are indolence, deference, sympathy, fear and reason. All are not of the same value. Indeed they are relative in their importance as causes producing a disposition to obey. As formulated by Bryce, in the sum total of obedience the percentage due to fear and to reason respectively is much less than that due to indolence and less also than that due to deference or sympathy. According to this view deference and sympathy are therefore the two most powerful factors which predispose a people to obey the authority of its Government.

Willingness to render obedience to the authority of the Government is as essential for the stability of Government as the unity of political parties on the fundamentals of the state. It is impossible for any sane person to question the importance of obedience in the maintainance of the state To believe in civil disobedience is to believe in anarchy.

---

* Studies in History and Jurisprudence, Vol. II Essay I

How far will Muslims obey the authority of a Government manned and controlled by the Hindus ?   The answer to this question need not call for much inquiry.   To the Muslims a Hindu is a Kaffir.*   A Kaffir is not worthy of respect.   He is low born and without status.   That is why a country which is ruled by a Kaffir is Dar-ul-Harb to a Mussalman.   Given this, no further evidence seems to be necessary to prove that the Muslims will not obey a Hindu Government.   The basic feelings of deference and sympathy which predispose persons to obey the authority of Government do not simply exist.   But if proof is wanted there is no dearth of it.   It is so abundant that the problem is what to tender and what to omit.

In the midst of the Khilafat agitation when the Hindus were doing so much to help the Mussalmans, the Muslims did not forget that as compared with them the Hindus were a low and an inferior race.   A Mussalman wrote† in the Khilafat paper called '*Insaf*'

"What is the meaning of Swami and Mahatma ?   Can Muslims use in speech or writing these words about non-Muslims ?"   He says that Swami means 'Master', and 'Mahatma' means 'possessed of the highest spiritual powers' and is equivalent to 'Ruh-i-aazam', and the supreme spirit."

He asked the Muslim divines to decide by an authoritative *fatwa* whether it was lawful for Muslims to call Non-Muslims by such deferential and reverential titles.

A remarkable incident was reported‡ in connection with the celebration of Mr Gandhi's release from goal in 1924 at the Tibbi College of Yunani medicine run by Hakim Ajmal Khan at Delhi. According to the report a Hindu student compared Mr. Gandhi to Hazarat Isa (Jesus) and at this sacrilege to the Mussalman sentiment all the Mussalman students flared up and threatened the Hindu student with violence, and, it is alleged, even the Mussalman professors joined with their co-religionists in this demonstration of their outraged feelings.

* The Hindus have no right to feel hurt at being called Kaffirs   They call the Muslims *Mlenchas*-persons not fit to associate with.

† See "Through Indian Eyes" Times of India dated 11-3-24

‡ Ibid dated 21-3-24.

In 1923 Mr. Mahommad Ali presided over the session of the Indian National Congress. In this address he spoke of Mr. Gandhi in the following terms :—

"Many have compared the Mahatma's teachings, and laterly his personal sufferings, to those of Jesus (on whom be peace)............... When Jesus contemplated the world at the outset of his ministry he was called upon to make his choice of the weapons of reform......... The idea of being all-powerful by suffering and resignation, and of triumphing over force by purity of heart, is as old as the days of Abel and Cain, the first progeny of man. . .. .

Be that as it may, it was just as peculiar to Mahatma Gandhi also ; but it was reserved for a christian Government to treat as felon the most christ-like man of our times (*Shame, Shame*) and to penalize as a disturber of the public peace the one man engaged in public affairs who comes nearest to the Prince of Peace The political conditions of India just before the advent of the Mahatma resembled those of Judea on the eve of the advent of Jesus, and the prescription that he offered to those in search of a remedy for the ills of India was the same that Jesus had dispensed before in Judea. Self-purification through suffering, a moral preparation for the responsibilities of Government ; self-discipline as the condition precedent of Swaraj— this was Mahatma's creed and conviction ; and those of us who have been privileged to have lived in the glorious year that culminated in the Congress session at Ahmedabad have seen what a remarkable and rapid change he wrought in the thoughts, feelings and actions of such large masses of mankind."

A year after, Mr. Mahommad Ali speaking at Aligarh and Ajmere said :—

"However pure Mr. Gandhi's character may be, he must appear to me from the point of view of religion inferior to any Mussalman, even though he be without character."

The statement created a great stir. Many did not believe that Mr. Mahommad Ali who testified to so much veneration for Mr. Gandhi was capable of entertaining such ungenerous and contemptuous sentiments above him. When Mr. Mahommad Ali was speaking at a meeting held at Aminabad Park in Lucknow he was asked whether the sentiments attributed to him were true. Mr. Mahommad Ali without any hesitation or compunction replied* :—

"Yes, according to my religion and creed, I do hold an adulterous and a fallen Mussalman to be better than Mr. Gandhi."

---

* Ibid dated 21-3.24.

It was suggested* at the time that Mr. Mahommad Alı had to recant because the whole of the orthodox Muslim community had taken offence for his havıng shown such deference to Mr. Gandhi, who was a Kaffir, as to put him on the same pedastal as Jesus. Such praise of a Kaffir, they felt, was forbidden by the Muslim cannon law.

In a mainfesto† on Hindu Moslem Relations issued ın 1928 Khwaja Hasan Nızami declared .—

"Mussalmans are separate from Hindus , they cannot unite wıth the Hındus. After bloody was the Mussalmans conquered India, and the English took India from them. The Mussalmans are one united nation and they alone will be masters of India. They will never give up their individuality. They have ruled India for hundreds of years, and hence they have a prescriptıve right over the country. The Hındus are a minor community ın the woıld. They are never free from internecine quarrels ; they belıeve ın Gandhı and worshıp the cow : They are polluted by takıng other people's water. The Hındus do not care for self-government ; they have no tıme to spare for it . let them go on wıth theıı ınternal squabbles. What capacıty have they for rulıng over men ? The Mussalmans dıd rule, and the Mussalmans will rule."

Far from renderıng obedıence to Hındus the Muslıms seem to be ready to try conclusions wıth the Hındus again. In 1925 there arose a controversy as to who really won the thırd battle of Panipat, fought ın 1761. It was contended for the Muslims that it was a great victory for them because Ahamad Sha Abdali had 1 lakh of soldiers while the Marathas had 4 to 6 lakhs. The Hindus replıed that it was a victory to them — a vıctory to the vanquıshed — because ıt stemmed the tide of Muslım invasions. The Muslıms were not prepared to admit defeat at the hands of the Hındus and claimed that they wıll always prove superior to the Hindus. To prove the eternal superiority of Muslıms over Hındus ıt was proposed by one Maulana Akabar Shah Khan of Najıbabad ın all seriousness, that the Hindus and Muslims should fight, under test condıtıons, a fourth

<hr/>

* Ibid dated 26-4-24.

† " Through India Eyes " Tımes of Indıa dated 14-3-28.

battle on the some fateful plain of Panipat. The Maulana accordingly issued* a challenge to Pandit Madan Mohan Malviya in the following terms :—

"If you, Malviyaji are making efforts to falsify the result at Panipat, I shall show you an easy and an excellent way (of testing it). Use your well-known influence and induce the British Government to permit the fourth battle of Panipat to be fought out without hindrance from the authorities. I am ready to provide .....a comparative test of the valour and fighting spirit of the Hindus and the Mussalmans.. . . As there are seven crores of Musalmans in the India, I shall arrive on a fixed date on the plain of Panipat with 700 Mussalmans representating the seven crores of Moslem in India and as there are 22 crores of Hindus I allow you to come with 2,200 Hindus. The proper thing is not to use cannon, machine guns or bombs : only swords and javelins and spears, bows and arrows and daggers should be used. If you cannot accept the post of generalissimo of the Hindu host, you may give it to any descendent of Sadashivrao† or Vishwasrao† so that there scions may have on opportunity to avenge the defeat of their ancestors in 1761. But any way do come as a spectator, for on seeing the result of this battle you will have to change your views, and I hope there will be then an end of the present discord and fighting in the country. .... In conclusion I beg to add that among the 700 men that I shall bring there will be no Pathans or Afghans as you are mortally afraid of them. So I shall bring with me only Indian Mussalmans of good family who are staunch adherents of shariat."

IV

Such are the religious beliefs, social attitudes and ultimate destinies of the Hindus and Muslims and their communal and political manifestations. These religious beliefs, social attitudes and veiws regarding ultimate destinies constitute the motive force which determines the lines of their action, whether they will be cooperative or conflicting. Past experience shows that they are too irreconcilable and too incompatible to permit Hindus and Muslims

---

* Quoted in "Through Indian Eyes" Times of India dated 20-6-25.

† They were the Military Commanders on the side of the Hindus in the third battle of Panipat.

ever forming one single nation or even two harmonious parts of one whole. These differences have the sure effect not only of keeping them asunder but also of keeping them at war. The differences are permanent and the Hindu-Moslem problem bids fare to be eternal. To attempt to solve it on the footing that Hindus and Muslims are one or if they are not one now they will be one hereafter is bound to be a barren occupation — as barren as it proved to be in the case of Czechoslovakia. On the contrary time has come when certain facts must be admitted as beyond dispute, however unpleasant such admissions may be.

In the first place it should be admitted that every possible attempt to bring about union between Hindus and Muslims has been made and that all of them have failed.

The history of these attempts may be said to begin with the year 1909. The demands of the Muslim deputation, if they were granted by the British, were assented to by the Hindus, prominent amongst whom was Mr. Gokhale. He has been blamed by many Hindus for giving his consent to the principle of separate electorates. His critics forget that witholding consent would not have been part of wisdom. For, as has been well said by Mr. Mahommad Ali :—

"...... .... paradoxical as it may seem, the creation of separate electorates was histening the advent of Hindu-Muslim unity. For the first time a real franchise, however restricted, was being offered to Indians, and if Hindus and Mussalmans remained just as divided as they had hitherto been since the commencement of the British rule, and often hostile to one another, mixed electorates would have provided the best battle-ground for inter-communal strifes, and would have still further widened the gulf separating the two communities. Each candidate for election would have appealed to his own community for votes and would have based his claims for preference on the intensity of his ill-will towards the rival community, however disguised this may have been under some such formula as "the defence of his community's interests". Bad as this would have been, the results of an election in which the two communities were not equally matched would have been even worse, for the community that failed to get its representative elected would have inevitably borne a yet deeper grudge against its successful rival. Divided as the two

39

communities were, there was no chance for any political principles coming into prominance during the elections. The creation of separate electorates did a great deal to stop this inter-communal warfare, though I am far from oblivious of the fact that when inter-communal jealousies are acute the men that are more likely to be returned even from communal electorates are just those who are noted for the ill-will towards the rival community."

But the concession in favour of separate electorates made b the Hindus in 1909 did not result in Hindu-Moslem unity. The came the Lucknow compact in 1916. Under it the Hindu gave satisfaction to the Muslims on every count. Yet it did no produce any accord between the two   Six years later anothe attempt was made to bring about Hindu-Moslem unity. Th All-India Moslem League at its annual session held a Lucknow in March 1923 passed a resolution * urging th establishment of a national pact to ensure unity and harmon among the various communities and sects in India and appointe a committee to colloberate with committees to be appointed b other organizations. The Indian National Congress in its specia session held in September 1923 at Delhi under the Presidentship c Maulana Abdul Kalam Azad passed a resolution reciprocating th sentiments expressed by the League. The Congress resolved t appoint two committees (1) to revise the constitution and (2) t prepare a draft of a national pact. The report† of the committe on the Indian National Pact was signed by Dr. Ansari an Lala Lajpat Rai and was presented at the session of the Congres held at Coconada in 1923. Side by side with the making of the term of the Indian National Pact there was forged the Bengal Pact ‡ b the Bengal Provincial Congress committee with the Bengal Muslim under the inspiration of Mr. C. R. Das. Both the Indian Nationa Pact and the Bengal Pact came up for discussion§ in the subjects com mittee of the Congress. The Bengal Pact was rejected by 678 vote

* For the full text of the Resolution of the League see Indian Annual Register 1923 Vol. I pp. 935-36.

† For the Report and the draft terms of the Pact see the Indian Annual Register 1923 Vol. II supplement pp. 104-108.

‡ For the terms of the Bengal Pact see Ibid p. 127.

§ For the debate on these two Pacts see Ibid pp 121-127.

against 458.   With regard to the Indian National Pact the Congress resolved* that the Committee do call for further opinions on the draft of the Pact prepared by them and submit their report by 31 March 1924 to the A. I. C. C. for its consideration.   The Committee however did not proceed any further in the matter.   This was because the feeling among the Hindus against the Bengal Pact was so strong that according to Lala Lajpat Rai † it was not considered opportune to proceed with the Committee's labours.   Moreover Mr. Gandhi was then released from jail and it was thought that he would take up the question. Dr. Ansari therefore contented himself with handing over to the A. I. C. C. the material he had collected.

Mr. Gandhi took up the threads as soon as he came out of the gaol   In November 1924 informal discussions were held in Bombay. As a result of these discussions an All-Parties Conference was constituted and a committee was appointed to deal with the question of bringing about unity.   The Conference was a truly All-Parties Conference in as much as the representatives were drawn from the Congress, the Hindu Maha Sabha, the Justice Party, Liberal Federation, Indian Christians, Muslim League etc.   On the 23rd January 1925 a meeting of the Committee ‡ appointed by the All-Parties Conference was held in Delhi at the Western Hotel. Mr. Gandhi presided.   On the 24th January the Committee appointed a representative Sub-Committee consisting of 40 members (a) To frame such recommendations as would enable all parties to join the Congress (b) To frame a scheme for the representation of all communities, races and sub-divisions on the legislative and other elective bodies under Swaraj and recommend the best method of securing the just and proper representation of the communities in the services with due regard to efficiency and (c) To frame a scheme of Swaraj that will meet the present needs of the country.   The Committee was instructed to report on or before the 15th February. In the interest of expediting the work some members formed themselves into a smaller committee for drawing up a scheme of

* For the Resolution see Ibid p 122.

† See his statement on the All Parties Conference held in 1925 in the Indian Quarterly Register 1925 Vol. I, p. 70.

‡ For the Proceedings of the Committee see the Indian Quarterly Register 1925 Vol. I, pp 66-77.

Swaraj leaving the work of framing the scheme of communal representation to the main committee.

The Swaraj Sub-Committee under the chairmanship of Mrs. Besant succeeded in framing its report on the constitution and submitted the same to the General Committee of the All-Parties Conference. But the Sub-Committee appointed to frame a scheme of communal representation met at Delhi on the 1st March and adjourned *sine die* without coming to any conclusion. This was due to the fact that Lala Lajpat Rai and other representatives of the Hindus would not attend the meeting of the Sub-Committee. Mr. Gandhi and Pandit Motilal Nehru issued the following statement* :—

"Lala Lajpat Rai had asked for a postponement by reason of the inability of Messrs. Jayakar, Srinivas Iyengar and Jai Ram Das to attend. We were unable to postpone the meeting on our own responsibility. We therefore informed Lala Lajpat Rai that the question of postponement be placed before the meeting. This was consequently done but apart from the absence of Lala Lajpat Rai and of the gentlemen named by him the attendance was otherwise also too meagre for coming to any decision. In our opinion there was moreover no material for coming to any definite conclusions nor is there likelihood of any being reached in the near future. . .."

There is no doubt that this statement truly summed up the state of mind of the parties concerned. The late Lala Lajpat Rai the spokesman of the Hindus on the Committee, had already said in an article in the '*Leader*' of Allahabad that there was no immediate hurry for a fresh pact and that he declined to accept the view that a Hindu majority in some provinces and a Muslim majority in others was the only way to Hindu-Moslem Unity.

The question of Hindu-Moslem Unity was again taken up in 1927. This attempt was made just prior to the Simon Commission inquiry, in the hope that it would be as successful as the attempt made prior to the Montagu-Chelmsford inquiry in 1917 and which had fructified in the Lucknow Pact. As a preliminary, a Conference of leading Muslims was held in Delhi on the 20th March 1927 at which certain proposals† for safeguarding the interest of the Muslims

---

* Ibid p. 77.

† These proposals will be found in the Indian Quarterly Register 1927 Vol. I, p. 3. These proposals subsequently became the basis of Mr. Jinnah's 14 points.

These proposals which were known as the Delhi proposals wer considered by the Congress at its session held in Madras i December 1927. At the same time the Congress passed a resolution authorizing its working Committee to confer with similar committee to be appointed by other organizations to draft a Swaraj constitutio for India. The Liberal Federation and the Muslim League passe similar resolutions appointing their representatives to join in th deliberations. Other organizations were also invited by the Congres working Committee to send their spokesmen. The All parties Cor vention † as it came to be called met on 12th February 19₂8 an appointed a Committee to frame a constitution. The Committe prepared a Report with a draft of the constitution — which is know as the Nehru Report. The Report was placed before the All-Partie Convention which met under the presidentship of Dr. Ansari o 22nd December 1928 at Calcutta just prior to the Congress sessio On the 1st January 1929 the Convention adjourned 'sine die without coming to any agreement, on any question, not even on th Communal question.

This is rather surprizing because the points of difference between the Muslim proposals and the proposals made in the Nehr Committee's Report were not substantial. That this is so is quit obvious from the speech‡ of Mr. Jinnah in the All-Parties Conventio in support of his amendments. Mr. Jinnah wanted four amendment to be made in the Report of the Nehru Committee. Speaking o his first amendment relating to the Muslim demand for $33\frac{1}{3}$ per cer representation in the Central Legislature Mr. Jinnah said:—

"The Nehru Report has stated that according to the scheme which they propose the Muslims are likely to get one-third in the Central Legislature and perhaps more, and it is argued that the Punjab and Bengal will get much more than their population proportion. What we feel is this. If one third is going to be obtained by Muslims then the method which you have adopted is not quite fair to the provinces where the Muslims are in a minority because the Punjab and Bengal will obtain more than their population basis in the Central Legislature.

' For the Resolution of the Congress on these proposals see Ibid 1927 Vol II, pp. 397-9

† For the origin, history and composition of the All Parties Convention and for the tex of the Report Ibid 1928 Vol. I, pp. 1 142.

‡ See the Indian Quarterly Register 1928 Vol. I, pp. 123-24.

You are going to give to the rich more and keeping the poor according to population. It may be sound reasoning but it is not wisdom.......

"Therefore, if the Muslims are, as the Nehru Report suggest, to get one-third, or more, they cannot give the Punjab or Bengal more, but let six or seven extra seats be distributed among provinces which are already in a very small minority, such as, Madras and Bombay, because, remember, if Sind is separated, the Bombay Province will be reduced to something like for 8 per cent. There are other provinces where we have small minorities. This is the reason why we say, fix one-third and let it be distributed among Muslims according to our own adjustment."

His second amendment related to the reservation of seats on population basis in the Punjab and in Bengal i.e. the claim to a statutory majority. On this Mr. Jinnah said :—

"You remember that originally proposals emanated from certain Muslim leaders in March 1927 known as the "Delhi Proposals." They were dealt with by the A. I. C. C. in Bombay and at the Madras Congress and the Muslim League in Calcutta last year substantially endorsed at least this part of the proposal. I am not going into the detailed arguments. It really reduces itself into one proposition, that the voting strength of Mahomedans in the Punjab and Bengal, although they are in a majority, is not in proportion to their population. That was one of the reasons. The Nehru Report has now found a substitute and they say that if adult franchise is established then there is no need for reservation, but in the event of its not being established we want to have no doubt that in that case there shoud be reservation for Muslims in the Punjab and Bengal, according to their population, but they shall not be entitled to additional seats."

His third amendment was in regard to residuary powers which the Nehru Committee had vested in the Central Government. In moving his amendment that they should be lodge in the Provincial Governments Mr. Jinnah pleaded :—

"Gentlemen, this is purely a constitutional question and has nothing to do with the Communal aspect. We strongly hold — I know Hindus will say Muslims are carried away by communal consideration and Muslims will say Hindus are carried away by communal consideration — we strongly hold the view that, if you examine this question carefully, we submit that the residuary powers should rest with the provinces."

His fourth amendment was concerned with the separation c Sind. The Nehru Committee had agreed to the separation of Sin but had subjected it to one priviso namely that the separation shoul come "only on the establishment of the system of Governmen outlined in the report." Mr. Jinnah in moving for the deletion c the proviso said .—

"We feel this difficulty.. .. ..Suppose the Government choose, within the next six months, or a year or two years, to separate Sind before the establishment of a Government under this constitution. Are the Mahomedans to say, ' we do not want it '............So long as this clause stands its meaning is that Mahomedans should oppose its separation until simultaneously a Government is established under this constitution. We say delete these words and I am supporting my argument by the fact that you do not make such a remark about the N. W. F. Provinces.............. The Committee says it cannot accept it as the resolution records an agreement arrived at by parties who signed at Lucknow. With the utmost deference to the members of the Committee I venture to say that that is not valid ground.......... Are we bound, in this convention, bound because a particular resolution was passed by an agreement between certain persons."

These amendments show that the gulf between the Hindus and Muslims was not in any way a wide one. Yet there was no desire to bridge the same. It was left to the British Government to do which the Hindus and Muslims failed to do and it did it by the Communal Award.

The Poona Pact between the Hindus and the Depressed classes gave another spurt to the efforts to bring about unity* During the months of November and December 1932 Muslims and Hindus did their best to come to some agreement. Muslims met in their All-Parties Conferences, Hindus, Muslims and Sikhs met in Unity Conferences. Proposals and counter proposals were made. But nothing came out of these negotiations to replace the Award by a Pact and were in the end abandoned after the Committee had held 23 sittings.

Just as attempts were made to bring about unity on political questions similarly attempts were also made to bring about unity on social and religious questions.

*For an account of these efforts see the Indian Quarterly Register 1932 Vol. 11, p. 296 et seq.

The social and religious differences arise over three questions (1) Cow slaughter, (2) Music before Mosque and (3) Conversions. Attempts to bring about unity over these questions were also made. The first attempt in this direction was made in 1923 when the Indian National Pact was proposed. It failed. Mr. Gandhi was then in gaol. Mr. Gandhi was released from gaol on the 5th February 1924. Stunned by the destruction of his work for Hindu-Moslem Unity Mr. Gandhi decided to go on a twenty-one days' fast, holding himself morally responsible for the murderous riots that had taken place between Hindus and Muslims. Advantage was taken of the fast to gather leading Indians of all communities at a Unity Conference*, which was attended also by the metropolitan of Calcutta. The Conference held prolonged sittings from September 26th to October 2nd, 1924. The members of the Conference pledged themselves to use their utmost endeavours to enforce the principles of freedom of conscience and religion and condemn any deviation from them even under provocation. A Central National Panchayet was appointed with Mr Gandhi as the chairman. The Conference laid down certain fundamental rights relating to liberty of holding and expressing religious beliefs and following religious practices, sacredness of places of worship, cow slaughter, and music before mosques, with a statement of the limitations they must be subject to. This Unity Conference did not produce peace between the two communities. It only produced a lull in the rioting which had become the order of the day. Between 1925 and 1926 rioting was renewed with an intensity and malignity unknown before. Shocked by this rioting Lord Irwin, the then Viceroy of India, in his address to the Central Legislature on 29th August 1927 made an appeal to the two communities to stop the rioting and establish amity. Lord Irwin's extortation to establish amity was followed by another Unity Conference which was known as the Simla Unity Conference†. This Unity Conference met on the 30th August 1927 and issued an appeal beseeching both the communities to support the leaders in their efforts to arrive at a satisfactory settlement. The Conference appointed a Unity

---

* Pattabhi Sitarammaya — History of the Congress page 532.

† For the proceedings of this conference see the Indian Quarterly Register Vol. II, pp. 39-50.

Committee which sat in Simla from 16th to 22nd September under chairmanship of Mr. Jinnah. No conclusions were reached on any of the principal points involved in the cow and music questions and others pending before the committee were not even touched. Some members felt that the committee might break up The Hindu members pressed that the committe should meet again on some future convenient date. The Muslim members of the committee were first divided in their opinion, but at last agreed to break up the committee and the President was requested to summon a meeting if he received a requisiton within six weeks from eleven specified members. Such a requision never came and the committe never met again.

The Simla Conference having failed Mr. Srinivas Iyengar the then President of the Congress called a special conference of Hindus and Muslims which sat in Calcutta between the 27th and 28th October 1927. It came to be known as the Calcutta Unity Conference*. The Conference passed certain resolutions on the three burning questions. But the resolution had no support behind them as neither the Hindu Mahasabha nor the Muslim League was represented at the Conference.

At one time it was possible to say that Hindu-Moslem Unity was an ideal which not only must be realized but could be realized and leaders were blamed for not making sufficient efforts for its realization. Such was the view expressed in 1911 even by Maulana Mahommed Ali who had not then made any particular efforts to achieve Hindu-Moslem Unity. Writing in the *Comrade* of 14th January 1911 Mr. Mahommad Ali said† :—

> " We have no faith in the cry that India is united. If India was united where was the need of dragging the venerable President of this year's Congress from a distant home ? The bare imagination of a feast will not dull the edge of hunger We have less faith still in the sanctimoniousress that transmutes in its subtle alchemy a rapacious monopoly into fervent patriotism. ... .the person we love best, fear the most, and I trust the least is the impatient idealist. Geothe said of Byron that he was a prodigious poet, but that when

---

* For the proceedings of the Conference see Ibid pp 50-58

† Quoted in his Presidential address at Coconada Session of the Congress 1923.

40

he reflected he was a child. Well, we think no better and no worse of the man who combines great ideals and a greater impatience. So many efforts, well meaning as well as ill-begotten, have failed in bringing unity to this distracted land, that we cannot spare even cheap and scentless flowers of sentiment for the grave of another ill-judged endeavour. We shall not make the mistake of guming together pieces of broken glass, and then cry over the unsuccessful result, or blame the refractory material. In other words we shall endeavour to face the situation boldly, and respect facts, howsoever ugly and ill-favoured. It is poor statesmanship to slur over inconvenient realities, and not the least important success in achieving unity is the honest and frank recognition of the deep-seated prejudices that hinder it and the yawning differences that divide."

Looking back on the history of these 30 years one can well ask whether Hindu-Moslem Unity has been realized ? Whether efforts have not been made for its realization ? And whether any efforts remains to be made ? The history of the last 30 years shows that Hindu-Moslem Unity has not been realised. On the contrary there now exists the greatest disunity between them : that efforts — sincere and persistent — have been made to achieve it and that nothing new remains to be done to achieve it except surender by one party to the other. If any one who is not in the habit of cultivating optimism where there is no justification for it said that the pursuit of Hindu-Moslem Unity is like a mirage and that the idea must now be given up no one can have the courage to call him a pessimist or an impatient idealist It is for the Hindus to say how long they will engage themselves in this vain pursuit inspite of the tragic end of all their past endeavours or give up the pursuit of unity and try for a settlement on another basis.

In the second place it must be admitted that the Muslim point of view has undergone a complete revolution. How great is the revolution can be seen by reference to the past pronouncements of some of those who insist on the two nation theory and believe that Pakistan is the only solution of the Hindu Moslem problem. Among these Mr. Jinnah, of course, must be accepted as the foremost. The revolution in his views on Hindu Moslem question is striking, if it is not staggering. To realize the nature, character

and vastness of this revolution it is necessary to know his pronouncements in the past relating to the subject so that they may be
compared with those he is making now.

A study of his past pronouncement may well begin with the
year 1906 when the leaders of the Muslim Community waited upon
Lord Minto and demanded separate electorates for the Muslim Community.   It is to be noted that Mr Jinnah was not a member of the
deputation.   Whether he was not invited to join the deputation or
whether he was invited to join but he declined is not known.   But
the fact remains that he did not lend his support to the Muslim claim
to separate representation when it was put forth in 1906.

In 1918 Mr. Jinnah resigned his membership of the Imperial
Legislative Council as a protest against the Rowlatt Bill.*.   In
tendering his resignation Mr. Jinnah said —

"I feel that under the prevailing conditions, I can be of no use to
my people in the Council, nor consistently with one's self-respect is
co-operation possible with a Government that shows such utter
disregard for the opinion of the representatives of the people at the
Council Chamber and the feelings and the sentiments of the people
outside."

In 1919 Mr. Jinnah gave evidence before the Joint Select
Committee appointed by Parliament on the Government of India
Reform Bill, then on the anvil.   The following views were expressed
by him in answer to questions put by members of the Committee
on the Hindu-Moslem question.

EXAMINED BY MAJOR ORSMBY-GORE.

Q.   3806—You appear on behalf of the Moslem League — that
is, on behalf of the only widely extended Mohammedan organisation
in India ?   Yes.

Q.   3807.—I was very much struck by the fact that neither in
your answers to the questions nor in your opening speech this
morning did you make any reference to the special interest of the
Mohammedans in India : is that because you did not wish to say
anything ? — No, but because I take it the Southborough Committees
have accepted that, and I left it to the members of the Committee to

* The Bill notwithstanding the protest of the Indian members of the Council was
passed into law and became Act XI of 1919 as " The Anarchical and Revolutionary
Crimes Act."

put any questions they wanted to. I took a very prominent part in the settlement of Lucknow. I was representing the Mussalmans on that occasion.

Q. 3809.—On behalf of the All-India Moslem League, you ask this Committee to reject the proposal of the Government of India — ? I am authorised to say that — to ask you to reject the proposal of the Government of India with regard to Bengal [i.e. to give the Bengal Muslims more representation than was given to them by the Lucknow Pact].

Q. 3810.—You said you spoke from the point of view of India. You speak really as an Indian Nationalist ?—I do.

Q. 3811.—Holding that view, do you contemplate the early disappearance of separate communal representation of the Mohammedan community ?—I think so.

Q. 3812.—That is to say, at the earliest possible moment you wish to do away in political life with any distinction between Mohammedans and Hindus ?—Yes Nothing will please me more than when that day comes

Q. 3813.—You do not think it is true to say that the Mohammedans of India have many special political interests, not merely in India but outside India, which they are always particularly anxious to press as a distinct Mohammedan community ?—There are two things. In India the Mohammedans have very few things really which you can call matters of special interest for them — I mean secular things.

Q. 3814.—I am only referring to them, of course ?—And therefore that is why I really hope and expect that the day is not very far distant when these separate electorates will disappear.

Q. 3815.—It is true, at the same time, that the Mahomedans in India take a special interest in the foreign policy of the Government of India ? They do . a very, — No, because what you propose to do is to frame very keen interest and the large majority of them hold very strong sentiments and very strong views.

Q. 3816.—Is that one of the reasons why you, speaking on behalf of the Mahommedan community, are so anxious to get the Government of India more responsible to an electorate ?—No

Q. 3817.—Do you think it is possible, consistently with remaining in the British Empire, for India to have one foreign policy and for His Majesty, as advised by his Ministers in London, to have another ?—Let me make it clear. It is not a question of foreign policy at all.   What the Moslems of India feel is that it is a very difficult position for them.   Spiritually, the Sultan or the Khalif is their head.

Q, 3818.—Of one community ?—Of the Sunni sect, but that is the largest ; it is in an overwhelming majority all over India.   The Khalif is the only rightful custodian of the Holy Places according to our view, and nobody else has a right.   What the Moslems feel very keenly is this, that the Holy Places should not be severed from the Ottoman Empire — that they should remain with the Ottoman Empire under the Sultan.

Q. 3819.—I do not want to get away from the Reform Bill on to foreign policy — I say it has nothing to do with foreign policy. Your point is whether in India the Moslems will adopt a certain attitude with regard to foreign policy in matters concerning Moslem all over the world

Q. 3820.—My point is, are they seeking for some control over the Central Government in order to impress their views on foreign policy on the Government of India ?—No ,

EXAMINED BY MR BENNET.

Q. 3853 — . . . . Would it not be an advantage in the case of an occurrence of that kind [i.e. a communal riot] if the maintenance of law and order were left with the executive side of the Government ? I do not think so, if you ask me, but I do not want to go into unpleasant matters, as you say.

Q. 3854 —It is with no desire to bring up old troubles that I ask the question ; I would like to forget them ? — If you ask me, very often these riots are based on some misunderstanding, and it is because the police have taken one side or the other, and that has enraged one side or the other.   I know very well that in the Indian States you hardly ever hear of any Hindu-Mohammedan riots, and I do not mind telling the Committee, without mentioning the name, that I happened to ask one of the ruling Princes, "How do you account for this ?" and he told me, "As soon as there is some trouble we have invariably traced it to the police, through the police taking one side or the other, and the only remedy we have found is that as soon as we come to know we move that the police officer from that place, and there is an end of it."

Q. 3855.—That is a useful piece of information, but the fact remains that these riots have been inter-racial, Hindu on the one side and Mohammedan on the other.   Would it be an advantage at a time like that the Minister, the representative of one community or the other, should be in charge of the maintenance of law and order ? — Certainly.

Q. 3856.—It would ? — If I thought otherwise I should be casting a reflection on myself. If I was the Minister I would make bold to say that nothing would weigh with me except justice, and what is right.

Q. 3857.—I can understand that you would do more than justice to the other side ; but even then, there is what might be called the subjective side. It is not only that there is impartiality, but there is the view which may be entertained by the public, who may harbour some feeling of suspicion ? — With regard to one section or the other, you mean they would feel that an injustice was done to them, or that justice would not be done ?

Q. 3858.—Yes : that is quite apart from the objective part of it ? — My answer is this . That these difficulties are fast disappearing. Even recently, in the whole district of Thana, Bombay, every officer was an Indian officer from top to bottom, and I do not think there was a single Mohammedan — they were all Hindus — and I never heard any complaint. Recently that has been so. I quite agree with you that ten years ago there was that feeling what you are now suggesting to me, but it is fast disappearing.

Examined by Lord Islington

Q. 3892.—........................... You said just now about the communal representation, I think in answer to Major Ormsby-Gore, that you hope in a very few years you would be able to extinguish communal representation, which was at present proposed to be established and is established in order that Mahomedans may have their representation with Hindus. You said you desired to see that. How soon do you think that happy state of affairs is likely to be realised ? — I can only give you certain facts : I cannot say anything more than that : I can give you this, which will give you some idea : that in 1913, at the All-India Moslem League Sessions at Agra, we put this matter to the test whether separate electorates should be insisted upon or not by the Mussalmans, and we got a division, and that division is based upon Provinces ; only a certain number of votes represent each Province, and the division came to 40 in favour of doing away with the separate electorate, and 80 odd — I do not remember the exact number — were for keeping the separate electorate. That was in 1913. Since then I have had many opportunities of discussing this matter with various Mussalmans leaders; and they are changing their angle of vision with regard to this matter. I cannot give you the period, but I think it cannot last very long. Perhaps the next Inquiry may hear something about it.

Q. 3893.—You think at the next Inquiry the Mahommedans will ask to be absorbed into the whole ? — Yes, I think the next Inquiry will probably hear something about it

Although Mr Jinnah appeared as a witness on behalf of the Muslim League he did not allow his membership of the League to come in the way of his loyalty to other political organizations in the country. Besides being a member of the Muslim League, Mr. Jinnah was a member of the Home Rule League and also of the Congress. As he said in his evidence before the Joint Parliamentary Committee he was a member of all three bodies although he openly disagreed with the Congress, with the Muslim League and that there were some views which the Home Rule League held which he did not share That he was an independent but a nationalist is shown by his relationship with the Khilafatist Mussalmans. In 1920 the Mussalmans organized the Khilafat Conference. It become so powerful an organization that the Muslim League went underground and lived in a state of suspended animation till 1924. During these years no Muslim leader could speak to the Muslim masses from a Muslim platform unless he was a member of the Khilafat Conference. That was the only platform for a Muslim to meet Muslims. Even then Mr. Jinnah refused to join the Khilafat Conference. This was no doubt due to the fact that then he was only a statutory Mussalman with none of the religious fire of the orthodox which he now says is burning within him. But the real reason why he did not join the Khilafat was because he was opposed to the Indian Mussalmans engaging themselves in extra-territorial affairs relating to Muslims outside India.

After the Congress accepted non-co-operation, civil disobedience and boycott of Councils Mr. Jinnah left the Congress. He became its critic but never accused it of being a Hindu body. He protested when such a statement was attributed to him by his opponents. There is a letter by Mr. Jinnah to the editor of the Times of India written about the time which puts in a strange contrast the present opinion of Mr. Jinnah about the Congress and his opinion in the past. The letter* reads as follows :—

To the Editor of "The Times of India"

Sir, — I wish again to correct the statement which is attributed to me and to which you have given currency more than once and now again repeated by your correspondent "Banker" in the second column of your issue of the 1st October that I denounced the Congress as "a Hindu Institution." I publicly corrected this misleading report of my speech in your columns soon after it appeared ; but it did not find a place in the columns of your paper and so may I now request you to publish this and oblige "

After the Khilafat storm had blown over and the Muslims had shown a desire to return to the internal politics of India the Muslim League was resusciated. The session of the League held in Bombay on 30th December 1924 under the Presidentship of Mr. Raza Ali was a lively one. Both Mr. Jinnah and Mr. Mahommad Ali took part in it†.

In this session of the League a resolution was moved which affirmed the desirability of representatives of the various Muslim Associations of India representing different shades of polititical thought meeting in a Conference at any early date at Delhi or at some other central place with a view to develope " a united and sound practial activity ' to supply the needs of the Muslim Community. Mr. Jinnah in explaining the Resolution said‡ :—

"The object was to organize the Muslim Community, not with a view to quarrel with the Hindu Community, but with a view to unite and co-operate with it for their motherland. He was sure once they had organized themselves they would join hands with the Hindu Mahasabha and declare to the world that Hindus and Mahomedans are brother."

---

* Published in the Times of India of 3-10-25

† Mr. Mahommad Ali in his presidential address to the Congress at Cocanada humourously said " Mr. Jinnah would soon come back to us (cheers) I may mention that an infidel becomes a Kaffir and a Kaffir becomes an infidel ; likewise, when Mr. Jinnah was in the Congress I was not with him in those days, and when I was in the Congress and in the Muslim League he was away from me. I hope some day we would reconcile (Laughter)

‡ From the Report in the Times of India 1st January 1925

The League also passed another resolution in the same session for appointing a Committee of 33 prominent Mussalmans to formulate the political demands of the Muslim Community. The resolution was moved by Mr. Jinnah. In moving the resolution Mr. Jinnah* —

" Repudiated the charge that he was standing on the platform of the League as a communalist. He assured them that he was, as ever, a nationalist. Personally he had no hesitation. He wanted the best and the fittest men to represent them in the Legislatures of the land (Hear, Hear and Applause). But unfortunately his Muslim compatriots were not prepared to go as far as he. He could not be blind to the situation. The fact was that there was a large number of Muslims who wanted representation separately in Legislatures and in the countrys' Services. They were talking of communal unity, but where was unity ? It had to be achieved by arriving at some suitable settlement. He knew, he said amidst deafening cheers, that his fellow-religionists were ready and prepared to fight for Swaraj, but wanted some safeguards. Whatever his view, and they knew that as a practical politician he had to take stock of the situation, the real block to unity was not the communities themselves, but a few mischief makers on both sides."

And he did not hesitate to tell the mischief makers in the following stern language which could only emanate from an earnest nationalist. He said† to them in his capacity as the President of the session of the League held in Lahore on 24th May 1924 .—

" If we wish to be free people, let us unite, but if we wish to continue slaves of Bureaucracy, let us fight among ourselves and gratify petty vainty over petty matters, Englishmen being our arbiters."

In the two All-Parties Conferences, one held in 1925 and the other in 1928, Mr Jinnah was prepared to settle the Hindu-Moslem question on the basis of joint electorates. In 1927 he openly said‡ from the League platform :—

" I am not wedded to separate electorates, although I must say that the overwhelming majority of the Mussalmans firmly and honestly believe that it is the only method by which they can be sure."

*The Indian Quarterly Register 1924 Vol. II p. 481.
†See the Indian Quarterly Review 1924 Vol. I, p. 658.
‡The Indian Quarterly Register 1927 Vol I, p. 37.

In 1928 Mr. Jinnah joined the Congress in the boycott of the Simon Commission. He did so even though the Hindus and Muslims had failed to come to a settlement and he did so at the cost of splitting the League into two.

Even when the ship of the Round Table Conference was about to break on the communal rock Mr. Jinnah resented being named as a communalist who was responsible for the result and said that he preferred an agreed solution of the communal problem to the arbitration of the British Government. Addressing* the U. P. Muslim Conference held at Allahabad on 8th August 1931 Mr. Jinnah said :—

" The first thing that I wish to tell you is that it is now absolutely essential and vital that Muslims should stand united. For Heaven's sake close all your ranks and files and stop this internecine war. I urged this most vehemently and I pleaded to the best of my ability before Dr. Ansari, Mr. T. A. K. Sherwani, Maulana Abul Kalam Azad and Dr. Syed Mahmud. I hope that before I leave the shores of India I shall hear the good news that whatever may be our differences, whatever may be our convictions between ourselves, this is not the moment to quarrel between ourselves.

' Another thing I want to tell you is this. There is a certain section of the press, there is a certain section of the Hindus, who constantly misrepresent me in various ways. I was only reading the speech of Mr. Gandhi this morning and Mr. Gandhi said that he loves Hindus and Muslims alike. I again say standing here on this platform that although I may not put forward that claim but I do put forward this honestly and sincerely that I want fair play between the two communities."

Continuing further Mr. Jinnah said : " As to the most important question, which to my mind is the question of Hindu-Muslim settlement — all I can say to you is that I honestly believe that the Hindus should concede to the Muslims a majority in the Punjab and Bengal and if that is conceded, I think, a settlement can be arrived at in a very short time.

' The next question that arises is one of separate-*vs.*-joint electorates. As most of you know, if a majority is conceded in the Punjab and Bengal, I would personally prefer a settlement on the basis of joint electorate. (Applause). But I also know that there is a large body of Muslims — and I believe a majority of Muslims — who are holding on to separate electorate. My position is that I would rather have a settlement even on the footing of separate electorate, hoping and trusting that when we work our new constitution and when both Hindus and Muslims get rid of distrust, suspicion and fears and when they get their freedom, we would rise to the occasion and probably separate electorate will go sooner than most of us think.

'Therefore, I am for a settlement and peace among the Muslims first ; I am for a settlement and peace between the Hindus and Mahommedans. This is not a time for argument, not a time for propaganda work and not a time for embittering feelings between the two communities, because the enemy is at the door of both of us and I say without hesitation that if the Hindu-Muslims question is not settled, I have no doubt that the British will have to arbitrate and that he who arbitrates will keep to himself the substance of power and authority. Therefore, I hope they will not vilify me. After all, Mr. Gandhi himself says that he is willing to give the Muslims whatever they want, and my only sin is that I say to the Hindus give to the Muslims only 14 points, which is much less than the " blank cheque " which Mr. Gandhi is willing to give. I do not want a blank cheque, why not concede the 14 points ? When Pandit Jawaharlal Nehru says · " Give us a blank cheque " when Mr. Patel says : " Give us a blank cheque and we will sign it with a Swadeshi pen on a Swadeshi paper " they are not communalists and I am a communalist ! I say to Hindus not to misrepresent everybody. I hope and trust that we shall be yet in a position to settle the question which will bring peace and happiness to the millions in our country.

'One thing more I want to tell you and I have done. During the time of the Round Table Conference, — it is now an open book and anybody who cares to read it can learn for himself — I observed the one and the only principle and it was that when I left the shores of Bombay I said to the people that I would hold the interests of India sacred, and believe me — if you care to read the proceedings of the Conference, I am not bragging because I have done my duty — that I have loyally and faithfully fulfilled my promise to the fullest extent and I venture to say that if the Congress or Mr. Gandhi can get anything more than I fought for, I would congratulate them.'

Concluding Mr. Jinnah said that they must come to a settlement, they must become friends eventually and he, therefore, appealed to the Muslims to show moderation, wisdom and conciliation, if possible in the deliberation that might take place and the resolution that might be passed at the conference."

As an additional illustration of the transformation in Muslim ideology I propose to record the opinions once held by Mr. Barkat Ali who is now a follower of Jinnah and a staunch supporter of Pakistan.

When the Muslim League split into two over the question of cooperation with the Simon Commission, one section led by Sir Mahommad Shafi favouring cooperation and another section led by Mr. Jinnah supporting the Congress plan of boycott, Mr. Barkat Ali belonged to the Jinnah section of the League.   The two wings of the League held their annual sessions in 1928 at two different places. The Shafi wing met in Lahore and the Jinnah wing met in Calcutta. Mr. Barkat Ali who was the Secretary of the Punjab Muslim League attended the Calcutta session of the Jinnah wing of the League and moved the resolution relating to the communal settlement.   The basis of the settlement was joint electorates.   In moving the resolution Mr. Barkat Ali said * :—

" For the first time in the history of the League there was a change in its angle of vision.   We are offering by this change a sincere hand of fellowship to those of our Hindu countrymen who have objected to the principle of separate electorates."

In 1928 there was formed a Nationalist Muslim Party under the leadership of Dr. Ansari†.   The Nationalist Muslim Party was a step in advance of the Jinnah wing of the Muslim League and was prepared to accept the Nehru Report, as it was, without any amendments — not even those which Mr. Jinnah was insisting upon.   Mr. Barkat Ali who in 1927 was with the Jinnah wing of the League left the same as not being nationalistic enough and joined the Nationalist Muslim Party of Dr. Ansari.   How great a nationalist Mr. Barkat Ali then was can be seen by his trenchent and vehement attack on Sir Muhammad Iqbal for his having put forth in his presidential address to the annual session of the All-India Muslim League held at Allahabad in 1930 a scheme ‡ for the division

---

* The Indian Quarterly Register 1927 Vol. II, p. 448.
† The Indian Quarterly Register 1929, Vol. II, p 350.
‡ For his speech see The Indian Annual Register 1930, Vol. II, pp. 334–345.

of India which is now taken up by Mr. Jinnah and Mr. Barkat Ali and which goes by the name of Pakistan. In 1931 there was held in Lahore the Punjab Nationalist Muslim Conference and Mr. Barkat Ali was the Chairman of the Reception Committee. The views he then expressed on Pakistan are worth recalling.* Reiterating and reaffirming the conviction and the political faith of his party, Malik Barkat Ali, Chairman of the Reception Committee of the Conference, said :—

"We believe, first and foremost in the full freedom and honour of India. India, the country of our birth and the place with which all our most valued and dearly cherished associations are knit, must claim its first place in our affection and in our desires. We refuse to be parties to that sinister type of propaganda which would try to appeal to ignorant sentiment by professing to be Muslim first and Indian afterwards. To us a slogan of this kind is not only bare, meaningless cant, but downright mischievous. We cannot conceive of Islam in its best and last interests as in any way inimical to or in conflict with the best and permanent interests of India. India and Islam in India are identical, and whatever is to the detriment of India, must, from the nature of it, be detrimental to Islam whether economically, politically, socially or even morally. Those politicians, therefore, are a class of false prophets and at bottom the foes of Islam, who talk of any inherent conflict between Islam and the welfare of India. Further, howsoever much our sympathy with our Muslim brethren outside India i. e. the Turks and the Egyptians or the Arabs, — and it is a sentiment which is at once noble and healthy, — we can never allow that sympathy to work to the detriment of the essential interests of India. Our sympathy, in fact, with those countries can only be valuable to them, if India as the source, nursery and fountain of that sympathy' is really great. And if ever the time comes, God forbid, when any Muslim Power from across the Frontier chooses to enslave India and snatch away the liberties of its people, no amount of pan-Islamic feeling, whatever it may mean, can stand in the way of Muslim India fighting shoulder to shoulder with non-Muslim India in defence of its liberties.

Let there be, therefore, no misgivings of any kind in that respect in any non-Muslim quarters. I am conscious that a certain class of narrow-minded Hindu politicians is constantly harping on the bogey of

*Indian Annual Register 1931, Vol. II, pp. 234-235.

an Islamic danger to India from beyond the N. W. Frontier passes, but I desire to repeat that such statements and such fears are fundamentally wrong and unfounded. Muslim India shall as much defend India's liberties as non-Muslim India, even if the invader happens to be a follower of Islam.

Next, we not only believe in a free India but we also believe in a united India — not the India of the Muslim, not the India of the Hindu or a the Sikh, not the India of this community or of that community but the India of all. And as this is our abiding faith, we refuse to be parties to any division of the India of the future into a Hindu or a Muslim India. However much the conception of a Hindu and a Muslim India may appeal and send into frenzied ecstasies abnormally orthodox mentalities of their party, we offer our full throated opposition to it, not only because it is singularly unpractical and utterly obnoxious but because it not only sounds the death-knell of all that is noble and lasting in modern political activity in India, but is also contrary to and opposed to India's chief historical tradition.

India was one in the days of Asoka and Chandragupta and India remained one even when the sceptre and rod of Imperial sway passed from Hindu into Moghal or Muslim hands. And India shall remain one when we shall have attained the object of our desires and reached those uplands of freedom, where all the light illuminating us shall not be reflected glory but shall be light proceeding direct as it were from our very faces.

The conception of a divided India, which, Sir Mohammad Iqbal put forward recently in the course of his presidential utterence from the platform of the League at a time when that body had virtually become extinct and ceased to represent free Islam — I am glad to be able say that Sir Mohammad Iqbal has since recanted it — must not therefore delude anybody into thinking that is Islam's conception of the India to be. Even if Dr. Sir Mohammad Iqbal had not recanted it as something which could not be put forward by any sane person, I should have emphatically and unhesitatingly repudiated it as something foreign to the genius and the spirit of the rising generation of Islam, and I really deem it a proud duty to affirm today that not only must there be no division of India into communal provinces but that both Islam and Hinduism must run coterminously with the boundaries of India and must not be cribbed, cabined and confined within any shorter bounds. To the same category as Dr. Iqbal's conception of a Muslim India and a Hindu India, belongs the sinister proposals of some Sikh communalists to partition and divide the Punjab.

With a creed so expansive, namely a free and united India with its people all enjoying in equal measure and without any kinds of distinctions and disabilities the protection of laws made by the chosen representatives of the people on the widest possible basis of a true democracy, namely, adult franchise, and though the medium of joint electorates—and an administration charged with the duty of an impartial execution of the laws, fully accountable for its actions, not to a distant or remote Parliament of foreigners but to the chosen representatives of the land, — you would not expect me to enter into the details and lay before you, all the colours of my picture. And I should have really liked to conclude my general observations on the aims and objects of the Nationalist Muslim Party here, were it not that the much discussed question of joint or separate electorates, has today assumed proportions where no public man can possibly ignore it.

Whatever may have been the value or utility of separate electorates at a time when an artificially manipulated high-propertied franchise had the effect of converting a majority of the people in the population of a province into a minority in the electoral roll, and when communal passions and feelings ran particularly high, universal distrust poisoning the whole atmosphere like a general and all-pervading miasma, — we feel that in the circumstances of today and in the India of the future, separate electorates should have no place whatever."

Such were the views which Mr. Jinnah and Mr. Barkat Ali held on Nationalism, on Separate Electorates and on Pakistan and which are so diametrically opposed to the views now held by them on these very problems.

In the third place it must be realized that this Muslim demand for Pakistan which is the result of this revolutionary Muslim ideology is not devoid of justification acceptable to political philosophers. Many people are under the impression that there is no moral justification for it. It is however a great mistake.

The philosophical justification for Pakistan rests upon the distinction between a Community and a Nation. With regard to this distinction two things must be noted. In the first place it is recognized comparatively recently. Political philosophers for a long time were concerned, mainly, with the controversy summed up in the two questions, how far the right of a mere majority to rule the minority be accepted as a rational basis for Government and how far the legitimacy of a Government be said to depend upon the consent of the governed.   Even those who insisted, that the legitimacy of a Government depended upon the consent of the governed remained content with a victory for their proposition and did not care to probe further into the matter.   They did not feel the necessity for making any distinctions within the category of the " governed."   They evidently thought that it was a matter of no moment whether those who were included in the category of the governed formed a Community or a Nation.   Force of circumstances have, however, compelled political philosophers to accept this distinction.   In the second place it is not a mere distinction without a difference.   It is a distinction which is substantial and the difference is consequentially fundamental.   That this distinction between a Community and a Nation is fundamental, is clear from the difference in the political rights which political philosophers are prepared to permit to a Community and those they are prepared to allow to a Nation, against the Government established by law.   To a Community they are prepared to allow the right of insurrection only.   But to a Nation they are willing to concede the right of disruption.   The distinction between the two is as obvious as it is fundamental.   A right of insurrection is restricted only to insisting on a change in the mode and manner of government.   The right of disruption is greater than the right of insurrection and extends to the secession of a group of the members of a State with a secession of the portion of the State's territory in its occupation.   One wonders what must be the basis of this difference.   Unfortunately, those writers on political philosophy who have discussed this subject have given their reasons for the justification of a Community's right to insurrection* and of a Nation's right to

* Sidgwick justifies it in these words "   ..   the evils of insurrection may reasonably be thought to be outweighed by the evils of submission, when the question at issue is of vital importance   an insurrection may sometimes induce redress of grievances, even when the insurgents are clearly weaker in physical force , since it may bring home to the majority the intensity of the sense of injury aroused by their actions.   For similar reasons, again a conflict in prospect may be anticipated by a compromise , in short, the fear of provoking disorder may be a salutory check on the persons constitutionally invested with supreme power under a democratic as under other forms of Government   .I conceive, then that a moral right of insurrection must be held to exist in the most popularity governed community " — *Elements of Politics* (1929) pp. 646-47.

to demand disruption*. The difference comes to this a community has a right to safeguards, a nation has a right to demand separation. The difference is at once clear and crucial But they have not given any reasons why the right of one is limited to insurrection and why that of the other extends to disruption. They have not even raised such a question. Nor are the reasons apparent on the face of them. But it is both interesting and instructive to know why this difference is made. To my mind the reasons for this difference pertain to questions of ultimate destiny. A State either consists of a series of communities or it consists of a series of nations. In a State which is composed of a series of communities one community may be arrayed against another community and the two may be opposed to each other. But in the matter of their ultimate destiny they feel they are one But in a State which is composed of a series of nations when one nation rises against the other the conflict is one as to differences of ultimate destiny. This is the distinction between communities and nations and it is this distinction which explains the difference in their political rights There is nothing new or original in this explanation. It is merely another way of stating why the community has one kind of right and the nation another of quite a different kind. A community has a right of insurrection because it is satisfied with it. All that it wants is a change in the mode and form of Government. Its quarrel is not over any difference of ultimate

---

* This is what Sidgwick has to say on the right to disruption "   some of those who hold that a government to be legitimate, must rest on the consent of the governed, appear not to shrink from drawing this inference they appear to qualify the right of the majority of members of a state to rule by allowing the claim of a minority that suffers from the exercise of this right to secede and form a new state, when it is in a majority in a continuous portion of its old state's territory   and I conceive that there are cases in which the true interests of the whole may be promoted by disruption. For instance, where two portions of a State's territory are separated by a long interval of sea, or other physical obstacles, from any very active intercommunication, and when, from differences of race or religion, past history, or present social conditions, their respective inhabitants have divergent needs and demands in respect of legislation and other governmental interference, it may easily be inexpedient that they should have a common Government for internal affairs ; while if, at the same time, their external relations, apart from their union, would be very different, it is quite possible that each part may lose more through the risk of implication in the other's quarrels, than it is likely to gain from the aid of its military force. Under such conditions as these, it is not to be desired that any sentiment of historical patriotism, or any pride in the national ownership of an extensive territory, should permanently prevent a peaceful dissolution of the incoherent whole into its natural parts "— Ibid pp. 648-49.

43

destiny. A nation has to be accorded the right of disruption because
it will not be satisfied with mere change in the form of Government·
Its quarrel is over the question of ultimate destiny. If it will not
be satisfied unless the unnatural bond that binds them is dissolved
their produce and even ethics demands that the bond shall be
dissolved and they shall be freed each to purpose its own destiny.

V

While it is necessary to admit that the efforts at Hindu-Moslem
unity have failed and that the Muslim ideology has undergone
a complete revolution it is equally necessary to know the precise
causes which have produced these effects. The Hindus say that the
British policy of divide and rule is the real cause of this failure and
of this ideological revolution. There is nothing surprising in this.
The Hindus having cultivated the Irish mentality to have no other
politics except that of being always against the Government are
ready to blame the Government for everything including bad
weather. But time has come to discard this facile explanation so
dear to the Hindus. For it fails to take into account two very
important circumstances. In the first place it overlooks the fact that
the policy of divide and rule, allowing that the British do resort to it,
cannot succeed unless there are elements which make division possible,
and further if the policy succeeds for such a long time it means that the
elements which divide are more or less permanent and irreconsilable
and are not transitory or superficial. Secondly it forgets that
Mr. Jinnah who represents this ideological transformation can never
be suspected of being a tool in the hands of the British, even by the
worst of his enemies. He may be too self-opinionated, an
egotist without the mask and has perhaps a degree of arrogance
which is not compensated by any extraordinary intellect or
equipment. It may be that on that account he is unable to reconcile
himself to a second place and work with others in that capacity for
a public cause. He may not be overflowing with ideas although he
is not, as his critics make him out to be, an empty headed dandy

living upon the ideas of others. It may be that his fame is built up more upon art and less on substance. At the same time it is doubtful if there is a politician in India to whom the adjective incorruptible can be more fittingly applied. Any one who knows what his relations with the British Government have been will admit that he has always been their critic, if indeed, he has not been their adversary. No one can buy him. For it must be said to his credit that he has never been a soldier of fortune. Sheer common sense would suggest that the customary Hindu explanation must fail to account for the ideological transformation of Mr. Jinnah.

What is then the real explanation of these tragic phenomena, this failure of the efforts for unity, this transformation in the Muslim ideology ?

The real explanation of this failure of Hindu-Moslem Unity lies in the failure to realize that what stands between the Hindus and Muslims is not a mere matter of difference. It is an antagonism as distinguished from mere difference and that this antagonism is not to be attributed to material causes. It is spiritual in its character. It is formed by causes which take their origin in historical, religious, cultural and social antipathy of which political antipathy is only a reflection. These form one deep river of discontent which, being regularly fed by these sources, keeps on mounting to a head and overflowing its ordinary channels. Any current of water running from another spring, when it joins it, instead of altering the colour or diluting its strength becomes lost in the main stream. The silt of this antagonism which this current has deposited, has become permanent and deep. So long as this silt keeps on accumulating and so long as this antagonism lasts it is unnatural to expect this antipathy between Hindus and Moslems to give place to unity.

Like the Christians and Moslems in the Turkish Empire the Hindus and Moslems of India have met as enemies on many fields, and the result of the struggle has often brought them into the relation of conquerors and conquered. Whichever party has triumphed, a great gulf has remained fixed between the two and their enforced political union either under the Moghals or the British instead of passing over, as in so many other cases, into organic unity, has only accentuated their mutual antipathy. Neither religion nor social code can bridge this gulf. The two faiths are mutually exclusive and at their core and centre are irreconcilable. There seems to be an inherent antagonism between the two which centuries have not been able to dissolve. Notwithstanding the efforts made to bring the creeds together by the of Reformers like Akbar and Kabir, the ethical realities behind each have still remained, to use a mathematical phrase, surds which nothing can alter or make integers capable of having a common denominator. A Hindu can go from Hinduism to Christianity without causing any commotion or shock. But he cannot pass from Hinduism to Islam without causing a communal riot, certainly not without causing qualms. That shows the depth of the antagonism which divides the Hindus from the Musalmans.

If Islam and Hinduism keep Muslims and Hindus apart in the matter of their faith they also prevent their social assimilation. That Hinduism prohibits intermarriage between Hindus and Muslims is quite well known. But this narrow-mindedness is not the vice of Hinduism only. Islam is equally narrow in its social code. It also prohibits intermarriage between Muslims and Hindus. With these social laws there can be no social assimilation and consequently no socialization of ways, modes and outlooks, no blunting of the edges and no modulation of age old angularities.

There are other defects in Hinduism and in Islam which are responsible for keeping the sore between Hindus and Muslims an open and a running sore. Hinduism is said to divide people and in contrast Islam is said to bind people together. But this is only a half truth. For Islam divides as inexhorably as it binds. Islam is a close corporation and the distinction that it makes between Muslims and Non-Muslims is a very real, very positive and very alienating distinction. The brotherhood of Islam is not the universal brotherhood of man. It is a brotherhood of Muslims for Muslims only. There is a fraternity but its benefit is confined to those within that corporation. For those who are outside the corporation there is nothing but contempt and enmity. The second defect of Islam is that it is a system of *social* self-government and is incompatible with *local* self-government, because the allegiance of a Muslim does not rest on his domicile in the country which is his but on the faith to which he belongs. To the Moslem *ibi bene ibi patria* is unthinkable. Wherever there is the rule of Islam there is his own country. In other words Islam can never allow a true Muslim to adopt India as his motherland and regard a Hindu as his kith and kin. That is probably the reason why Maulana Mohammad Ali a great Indian but a true Muslim preferred to be buried in Jerusalem rather than in India.

The real explanation of the ideological transformation of the Muslim leaders is not to be attributed to any dishonest drift in their opinion. It appears to be the dawn of a new vision pointing to a new destiny symbolized by a new name, Pakistan. The Muslims appear to have started a new worship of a new destiny for the first time. But this is really not so. The worship is new because the sun of their new destiny which was so far hidden in the clouds has only now made its appearance in full glow. The magnetism of this new destiny cannot but draw the Muslims towards it. Its magnetism is so great that even men like Mr. Jinnah have been violently shaken and have not been able to resist its force. This destiny spreads itself out in a concrete form over the map of India. No one who just looks at the map can miss it. It lies there as though it is deliberately planned by Providence as a separate National State for Muslims. Not only is this new destiny capable of being easily worked out and put in concrete shape, it is also catching because it opens up the possibilities of realizing the Muslim idea of linking up all the Muslim kindred in one Islamic State and thus avert the danger of Muslims in different countries adopting the nationality of the country to which they belong and thereby bring about the disintegration of the Islamic brotherhood*. With the separation of Pakistan from Hindustan there is nothing to prevent Pakistan from joining Afghanistan, Iran, Iraq, Arabia, Turkey and Egypt and forming a federation of Muslim countries constituting one Islamic State extending from Constantinople down to Lahore. A Mussalman must be really very stupid if he is not attracted by the glamour of this new destiny and be completely transformed in his view of the place of Muslims in the Indian cosmos.

* Sir Mahommad Iqbal strongly condemned nationalism in Mussalmans of any non-Muslim country including Indian Mussalmans in the sense of an attachment to the mother country.

So obvious is the destiny that it is somewhat surprising that the Muslims should have taken so long to own it up. There is evidence that some of them knew this to be the ultimate destiny of the Muslims as early as 1923. In support of this reference may be made to the evidence of Khan Saheb Sardar M. Gulkhan who appeared as a witness before the North-West Frontier Committee appointed in that year by the Government of India under the Chairmanship of Sir Dennis Bray, to report upon the administrative relationship between the Settled Districts of the N. W. F. Province and the Tribal Area and upon the amalgamation of the Settled Districts with the Punjab. The importance of his evidence was not realized by any member of the Committee except Mr. N. M. Samarth who was the one member who drew pointed attention to it in his Minority Report. Extract from his Report illuminates a dark corner in history of the evolution of this new destiny. Says Mr. Samarth :—

" There was not before the Committee another witness who could claim to speak with the authority of personal knowledge and experience of not only the North-West Frontier Province and Independent Territory but Baluchistan, Persia and Afghanistan, which this witness could justly lay claim to. It is noteworthy that he appeared before the Committee as a witness in his capacity as " President, Islamic Anjuman, Dera Ismail Khan." This witness (Khan Saheb Sardar Muhammad Gul Khan) was asked by me . "Now suppose the Civil Government of the Frontier Province is so modelled as to be on the same basis as in Sind, then this Province will be part and parcel of the Punjab as Sind is of the Bombay Presidency. What have you to say to it ?"' He gave me, in the course of his reply, the following straight answer : "As far as Islam is concerned and the Mahomedan idea of the League of Nations goes, I am against it." On this answer, I asked him some further questions to which he gave me frank, outspoken replies without mincing matters. I extract the pertinent portions below :—

" Q.—The idea at the back of your Anjuman is the Pan-Islamic idea which is that Islam is a League of Nations and as such amalgamating this Province with the Punjab will be detrimental, will be prejudicial, to that idea. That is the dominant idea at the back of those who think with you ? Is it so ?

---

* Report of the North-West Frontier Inquiry Committee 1924 pages 122-23.

A.—It is so, but I have to add something. Their idea is that the Hindu-Moslem Unity will never become a fact, it will never become a *faith accompli*, and they think that this Province should remain separate and a link between Islam and Brittanic Commonwealth. In fact, when I am asked what my opinion is — I, as a member of the Anjuman, am expressing his opinion — we would very much rather see the separation of the Hindus and Muhammadans, 23 crores of Hindus to the South and 8 crores of Muslims to the North. Give the whole portion from Raskumari* to Agra to Hindus and from Agra to Peshawar to Muhammadans, I mean trans-migration from one place to the other. This is an idea of exchange. It is not an idea of annihilation. Bolshevism at present does away with the possession of private property. It nationalizes the whole thing and this is an idea which of course appertains to only exchange. This is of course impracticable. But if it were practicable, we would rather want this than the other.

Q.—That is the dominant idea which compels you not to have amalgamation with the Punjab ?   A — Exactly.

Q.—When you referred to the Islamic League of Nations, I believe you had the religious side of it more prominently in your mind than the political side ?

A.—Of course, political. Anjuman is a political thing. Initially, of course, anything Muhammadan is religious, but of course Anjuman is a political Association.

Q.—I am not referring to your Anjuman but I am referring to the Musalmans. I want to know what the Musalmans think of this Islamic League of Nations, what have they most prominently in mind, is it the religious side or the political side ?

A.—Islam, as you know, is both religious and political.

*   *   *   *

Q.—Therefore politics and religion are intermingled ?

A.—Yes, certainly."

Mr. Samarth used this evidence for the limited purpose of showing that to perpetuate a separate Pathan Province by refusing to amalgamate the N. W. F. with the Punjab was dangerous in view

---

* This is as in the original. It is probably a misprint for Kanya Kumari.

of the Pathan's affiliations with Afghanistan and with other Muslim countries outside India. But this evidence also shows that the idea underlying the scheme of Pakistan had taken birth sometime before 1923.

In 1924 Mr. Mahommed Ali speaking on the Resolution on the extension of the Montagu-Chelmsford Reforms to the N. W. F. Province which was moved in the session of the Muslim League held in Bombay in that year is said to have suggested* that the Mahommedans of the Frontier Province should have the right of self-determination to choose between an affiliation with India or with Kabul. He also quoted a certain Englishman who had said that if a straight line be drawn from Constantinople to Delhi, it will disclose a Mohammedan corridor right up to Shaharanpur It is possible that Mr. Mahommad Ali knew the whole scheme of Pakistan which came out in the evidence of the witness referred to by Mr. Samarth and in an unguarded moment gave out what the witness had failed to disclose, namely, the ultimate linking of Pakistan to Afghanistan.

Nothing seems to have been said or done by the Muslims about this scheme between 1924 and 1930. The Muslims appear to have buried it and conducted negotiations with the Hindus for safeguards, as distinguished from partition, on the basis of the traditional one nation theory. But in 1930 when the Round Table Conference was going on certain Muslims had formed themselves into a Committee with head quarters in London for the purpose of getting the R. T. C. to entertain the project of Pakistan. Leaflets and circulars were issued by the Committee and sent round to members of the R. T. C. in support of Pakistan Even then nobody took any interest in it, and even the Muslim members of the R. T. C. did not countenance it in any way†.

* For reference see Lala Lajpatrai's Presidential address to the Hindu Maha Sabha session held at Calcutta on 11th April 1925 in the Indian Quarterly Register 1925 Vol I p. 379

† If opposition to one Common Central Government be taken as a principal feature of the scheme of Pakistan then the only member of the R. T. C. who may be said to have supported it without mentioning it by name was Sir Mahommad Iqbal who expressed the view at the third session of the R T. C. that there should be no Central Government for India and that the provinces should be autonomous and independent dominions in direct relationship to the Secretary of State in London.

It is possible that the Muslims in the beginning, thought that this destiny was just a dream incapable of realization. It is possible that later on when they felt that it could be a reality they did not raise any issue about it because they were not sufficiently well organized to compel the British as well as the Hindus to agree to it. It is of course difficult to explain why the Muslims did not press for Pakistan at the R. T. C. Perhaps they knew that the scheme would offend* the British and as they had to depend upon them for a decision on the 14 points of dispute between them and the Hindus, the Musalmans, perfect statesmen as they are and knowing full well that politics, as Bismark said, was always the game of the possible, preferred to wait and not to show their teeth till they had got a decision from the British in their favour on the 14 points of dispute.

There is another explanation of this delay in putting forth the scheme of Pakistan. It is far more possible that the Muslim leaders did not until very recently know the philosophical justification for Pakistan. After all, Pakistan is no small move on the Indian political chess-board. It is the biggest move ever taken for it involves the disruption of the State. Any Mahommedan if he had ventured to come forward to advocate it, was sure to have been asked what moral and philosophical justification he had in support of so violent a project. The reason why they had not so far discovered what the philosophical justification for Pakistan is, is equally understandable. The Muslim leaders were, heretofore, speaking of the Mussalmans of India as a community or a minority. They never spoke of the Muslims as a nation. The distinction between a community and a nation is rather thin and even if it is otherwise it is not so striking in all cases. Every State is more or less a composite State and there is, in most of them, a great diversity of populations, of varying languages, religious codes and social traditions, forming a congeries of loosely associated groups. No State is ever a single society, an inclusive and permeating body of thought and action. Such being the case, a group may mistakenly call itself a community even when it has in it the elements of being a nation. Secondly, as has been pointed out earlier, a people may not be

* It is said that it was privately discussed with the British authorities who were not in favour of it. It is possible that the Muslims did not insist on it for fear of incurring their displeasure-

43

possessed of a national consciousness although in every sense of the term they are a nation.

Again from the point of view of minority rights and safeguards this differnce is unimportant. Whether the minority is a community or a nation both are minorities and the safeguards for the protection of a minor nation cannot be very different from the safeguards necessary for the protection of a minor community. The protection asked for is against the tyranny of the majority and once the possibility of such a tyranny of the majority over a minority is established it matters very little whether the minority driven to ask for safeguards is a community or is a nation· Not that there is no distinction between a community and a nation or if there is it makes no real difference. The difference indeed is very great. It may be summed up by saying that a community, however different·from and however opposed to other communities major or minor it may be, is one with the rest in the matter of the ultimate destiny of all. A nation on the other hand is not only different from other components of the State but it believes in and cherishes a different destiny totally antagonistic to the destiny entertained by other component elements in the State. The difference appears to me so profound that speaking for myself I would not hestitate to adopt it as a test to distinguish a community from a nation. A people who notwithstanding their differences accept a common destiny for themselves as well as for their opponents are a community. A people who are not only different from the rest but who refuse to accept for themselves the same destiny which others do, are a nation. It is this difference in the acceptance and non-acceptance of a common destiny which alone can explain why the Untouchables, the Christians and the Parsis are in relation to the Hindus only communities and why the Muslims are a nation. Thus from the point of view of harmony in the body politic the difference is of the most vital character as the difference is one of ultimate destiny. The dynamic charactor of this difference is undeniable. If it persists, it cannot but have the effect of rending the State in fragments. But so far as safegaurds are concerned, there cannot be any radical difference between a minor nation and a minor community, where both are prepared to live under one single constitution,

The delay in discovering the philosophical justification for Pakistan is due to the fact that the Muslims leaders had become habituated to speaking of Muslims as a community and as a minority. The use of this terminology took them in a false direction and brought them to a dead end. As they acknowledged themselves to be a minority community they felt that there was nothing else open to them except to ask for safeguards which they did and with which they concerned themselves for practically half a century. If it had struck them that they need not stop with acknowledging themselves to be a minority but that they could proceed further to distinguish a minority which is a community from a minority which is a nation they might have been led on to the way to discover this philosophical justification for Pakistan. In that case Pakistan would have in all probability come much earlier than it has done.

Be that as it may, the fact remains that the Muslims have undergone a complete transformation and that the transformation is brought about not by any criminal inducement but by the discovery of what is their true and ultimate destiny. To some this suddenness of the transformation may give a shock. But those who have studied the course of Hindu-Moslem politics for the last twenty years cannot but admit to a feeling that this transformation, this parting of the two was on the way. For the course of Hindu-Muslim politics has been marked by a tragic and ominous parallelism. The Hindus and Moslems have trodden parallel paths. No doubt they went in the same direction But they never travelled the same road. In 1885 the Hindus started the Congress to vindicate the political rights of Indians as against the British. The Moslems refused to be lured by the Hindus in the Congress posing for and speaking in the name of all Indians. Between 1885 to 1906 the Muslims kept out of this stream of Hindu politics. In 1906 they felt the necessity for the Muslim community taking part in political activity. Even then they dug their own separate channel for the flow of Muslim political life. The flow was to be controlled by a separate political organization called the Muslim League Ever since the formation of the Muslim League the waters of Muslim politics have flown in this separate channel. The Congress and the League have lived apart and have worked apart. Their aims and objects have not always been the same. They have even avoided holding their annual sessions at one and the same place, lest the shadow of one should fall upon the other. It is not that the League and the Congress have not met. The two have met but only for negotitations, a few times with success and most times without success. They met in 1915 at Lucknow and their efforts were crowned with success. In 1925 they met but without success. In 1928 a section of the Muslims were prepared to meet the Congress. Another section refused to meet. It rather preferred to depend upon the British. The point is they have met but have never merged. Only during the Khilafat agitation did the waters of the two channels leave their appointed courses and flow as one stream in one channel. It was believed that nothing would separate the waters which God was pleased to join. But that hope was belied. It was found that there was something in the composition of the two waters which would compel their separation Within a few years of their confluence but as soon as the substance of the Khilafat cause vanished — the water from the one stream reacted violently to the presence of the other, as one does to a foreign substance entering one's body. Each began to show a tendency to throw out and separate from the other. The result was that when the waters did separate they did with such impatient velocity and determined violence — if one can use such language in speaking of water — against each other that thereafter they have been flowing in channels far deeper and far more distant from each other than those existing before. Indeed the velocity and violence with which the two waters have burst out from the pool in which they had temporarily gathered have altered the direction in which they were flowing. At one time their direction was parallel. Now they are opposite. One is flowing towards the east as before. The other has started to flow in the opposite direction towards the west. Apart from any possible objection to the particular figure of speech, I am sure, it cannot be said that this is a wrong reading of the history of Hindu-Moslem politics. If one bears this parallelism in mind he will know that there is nothing sudden about the transformation. For if the transformation is a revolution the parallelism in Hindu-Moslem politics marks the evolution of that revolution. That Moslem politics should have run a parallel course and should never have merged in the Hindu current of politics is a strange fact of modern Indian History.   In so seggregating themselves the Muslims were influenced by some mysterious feeling, the source of which they could not define and guided by a hidden hand which they could not see but which was all the same directing them to keep apart from Hindus.   This mysterious feeling and this hidden hand was no other than their pre-appointed destiny, symbolized by Pakistan, which, unknown to them, was working within them.   Thus viewed, there is nothing new or nothing sudden in the idea of Pakistan.   The only thing that has happened is that, what was indistinct appears now in full glow, and what was nameless has taken a name.

VI

Summing up the whole discussion it appears that an integral India is incompatible with an independent India or even with India as a dominion.   On the footing that India is to be one integral whole there is a frustration of all her hopes of freedom writ large on her future.   There is frustration if the national destiny is conceived in terms of independence, because the Hindus will not follow that path.   They have reasons not to follow it. They fear that that way lies the establishment of the domination of the Muslims over the Hindus.   The Hindus see that the Muslim move for independence is not innocent.   It is strategy.   It is to be used only to bring the Hindus out of the protecting shield of the British Empire in the open and then by alliance with the neighbouring Muslim countries and by their aid subjugate them.   For the Muslims independence is not the end.   It is only a means to establish Muslim Raj.   There is frustration if the national destiny is conceived of in terms of Dominion Status because the Muslims will not agree to abide by it.   They fear that under Dominion Status the Hindus will establish Hindu Raj over them by taking benefit of the principle of one man one vote and one vote one value and that however much the benefit of the principle is curtailed by weightage to Muslims the result cannot fail to be a Government of the Hindus, by the Hindus and therefore for the Hindus. Complete frustration of her destiny therefore seems to be the fate of India if it is insisted that India shall remain as one integral whole.

It is a question to be considered whether integral India is an ideal worth fighting for. In the first place even if India remained as one integral whole it will never be an organic whole. India may in name be continued to to be known as one country but in reality it will be two separate countries—Pakistan and Hindustan — joined together by a forced and artificial union. This will be specially so under the stress of the two nation theory. As it is, the idea of unity has had little hold on the Indian world of fact and reality, little charm for the common Indian, Hindu or Muslim, whose vision is bounded by the valley in which he lives. But it did appeal to the imaginative and unsophisticated minds on both sides. The two-nation theory will not leave room even for the growth of that sentimental desire for unity. The spread of that virus of dualism in the body politic must some day create a mentality which is sure to call for a life and death struggle for the dissolution of this forced union. If by reason of some superior force the dissolution does not take place, one thing is sure to happen to India — namely that this continued union will go on sapping her vitality, loosening its cohesion, weakning its hold on the love and faith of her people and preventing the use, if not retarding the growth, of its moral and material resources. India will be an anæmic and sickly state inefective, a living corpse, dead though not buried.

The second disadvantage of this forced union will be the necessity of finding a basis for Hindu-Moslem settlement. How difficult it is to reach a settlement no one needs to be told. What more can be offered — short of dividing India into Pakistan and Hindustan — to bring about a settlement, than what has aleady been conceded without injury to the other interests in the country, it is difficult to conceive. But whatever the difficulties be, it cannot be gainsaid that if this forced union continues there can be no political advance for India unless it is accompanied by Communal Settlement. Indeed a Communal Settlement — rather an international settlement for now and hereafter Hindus and Muslims must be treated as two nations—will remain under this scheme of forced ʿunionʾ a condition precedent for every inch of political progress.

There will be a third disadvantage of this forced political union. It cannot eliminate the presence of a third party. In the first place the constitution, if one comes in existence, will be a federation of mutually suspicious and unfriendly states. They will of their own accord want the presence of a third party to appeal to in cases of dispute. For their suspicious and unfriendly relationship towards each other will come in the way of the two nations reaching satisfaction by the method of negotiation. India will not have in future even that unity of opposition to the British which used to gladden the hearts of so many in the past. For the two nations will be more opposed to each other than before, ever to become united against the British. In the second place the basis of the constitution will be the settlement between the Hindus and the Muslims and for the successful working of such a constitution the presence of a third party and be it noted, with sufficient armed force, will be necessary to see that the settlement is not broken.

All this of course means the frustration of the political destiny which both Hindus and Muslims profess to cherish and the early consumation of which they so devoutly wish What else, however, can be expected if two warring nations are locked in the bosom of one Country and one Constitution ?

Compare with this dark vista, the vista that opens out if India is divided into Pakistan and Hindustan. The partition opens the way to a fulfilment of the destiny each may fix for itself. Muslims will be free to choose for their Pakistan independence or dominion status whatever they think good for themselves. Hindus will be free to choose for their Hindustan independence or dominion status, whatever they may think wise for their condition. The Muslims will be freed from the nightmare of Hindu Raj and Hindus will save themselves from the hazard of a Muslim Raj. Thus the path of political progress becomes smooth for both. The fear of the object being frustrated gives place to the hope of its fulfilment. With Pakistan separated from Hindustan, Communal Settlement must remain a necessary condition precedent, if India, as one integral whole, desires to make any political advance. But Pakistan and Hindustan are free from the rigourous trammels of such a condition precedent and even if a communal settlement with minorities remained to be a condition precedent it will not be difficult of fulfilment. The path of each is cleared of this obstacle. There is another advantage of Pakistan which must be mentioned. It is generally admitted that there does exist a kind of antagonism between Hindus and Muslims which if not dissolved will prove ruinous to the peace and progress of India. But it is not realized that the mischief is caused not so much by the existence of mutual antagonism as by the existence of a common theatre for its display It is the common theatre which calls this anatonism in action. It cannot but be so. When the two are called to participate in acts of common concern what else can happen except a display of that antagonism which is inherent in them. Now this scheme of Pakistan has this advantage, namely, that it leaves no theatre for the play of that social antagonism which is the cause of disaffection among Hindus and Muslims. There is no fear of Hindustan and Pakistan suffering from that disturbance of peace and tranquility which has torn and shattered India for so many years. Last, but by no means least, is the elemination of the necessity of a third party to maintain peace. Freed from the trammels which one imposes upon the other by reason of this forced union — Pakistan and Hindustan can each grow into a strong stable State with no fear of disruption from within. As two separate entities, they can reach respective destinies which as parts of one whole they never can.

Those who want an integral India must note what Mr. Mahomad Ali as President of the Congress in 1923 said. Speaking about the unity of among Indians Mr. Mahomad Ali said—

" Unless some new force other than the misleading unity of opposition unites this vast continent of India it will remain a geographical misnomer."

Is there any new force which remains to be harnessed ? All other forces having failed the Congress, after it became the Government of the day, saw a new force in the plan of *mass contact.* It was intended to produce political unity between Hindu and Muslim masses by ignoring or circumventing the leaders of the Muslims. In its essence, it was the plan of the British Conservative Party to buy

Labour with "Tory Gold."   The plan was as mischievous as it was futile.   The Congress forgot that there are things so precious that no owner who knows their value will part with them and any attempt to cheat him to part with it is sure to cause resentment and bitterness.   Political power is the most precious thing in the life of a community especially if its position is constantly being challenged and is required to maintian it by meeting the challenge.   Political power is the only means by which it can sustain its position.   To attempt to make it part with it by false propoganda, by misrepresentation or by the lure of office or of gold is equivalent to disarming the community, to silencing its guns and to making it ineffective and servile.   It may be a way of producing unity.   But the way is despicable for it means suppressing the opposition by a false and an unfair way.   It cannot produce any unity.   It can only create exasperation, bitterness and hostility*.   This is precisely what the *"mass contact"* plan of the Congress did.   For there can be no doubt that this mad plan of mass contact has had a great deal to do with the emergence of Pakistan.

It might be said that it was unfortunate that mass contact was conceived and employed as a political lever and that it might have been used as a force for social unity with greater success.   But could it have succeeded in breaking the social wall which divides the Hindus and the Muslims ?   It cannot but be a matter of the deepest regret to every Indian that there is no social tie to draw them together.   There is no interdining and no intermarriage between the two.   Can they be introduced ?   Their festivals are different.   Can the Hindus

---

* So sober a person as Sir Abdur Rahim in his presidential address to the session of the Muslim League held in Aligarh on 30th December 1925 gave expression to this bitterness caused by Hindu tactics wherein he "deplored the attacks on the Muslim community in the form of Shuddhi, Sangathan and Hindu Mahasabha movements and activities led by politicians like Lala Lajpat Rai and Swami Shradhanand" and said "some of the Hindu leaders had spoken publicly of driving out Muslims from India as Spaniards expelled Moors from Spain. Mussalmans would be too big a mouthful for their Hindu friends to swallow.   Thanks to the artificial conditions under which they lived they had to admit that Hindus were in a position of great advantage and even the English had learned to dread their venomous propoganda.   Hindus were equally adept in the art of belittling in every way possible the best Mussalmans in public positions excepting only those who had subscribed to the Hindu political creed.   They had in fact by their provocative and aggressive conduct made it clearer than ever to Muslims that the latter could not entrust their fate to Hindus and must adopt every possible measure of self-defence." — All-India Register 1925 Vol. II page 356.

be induced to adopt them or join in them ? Their religious notions are not only divergent but repugnant to each other so that on a religious platform the entry of the one means the exit of the other. Their cultures are different ; their literatures and their histories are different. Not only different, they are so distasteful to each other, that they are sure to cause aversion and nausea. Can any one make them drink from the same fount of these perrenial sources of life ? No common meeting ground exists. None can be cultivated. There is not even sufficient physical contact, let alone their sharing a common cultural and emotional life. They do not even live together. Hindus and Muslim live in a separate world of their own. Hindus live in villages and Muslims in towns in those provinces where the Hindus are in a majority. Muslims live in villages and Hindus in towns in those provinces where the Muslims are in a majority. Wherever they live, they live apart. Every town, every village has its Hindu quarters, and Muslim quarters which are quite separate from each other. There is no common continuous cycle of participation. They meet to trade or they meet to murder· They do not meet to befriend one another. When there is no call to trade or when there is no call to murder, they cease to meet. When there is peace, the Hindu quarters and the Muslim quarters appear like two alien settlements. The moment war is declared, the settlements become armed camps. The periods of peace and the periods of war are brief. But the interval is one of continuous tension. What can mass contact do against such barriers ? It cannot even get over on the other side of the barrier, much less can it produce organic unity.

Epilogue

Here I propose to stop. For I feel that all that can be said about the subject has been said. It is true I have not given any finding. But I may state that it was never my intention to give a finding. To use legal language my object was to draw the pleadings and to state the issues.. This I may claim to have done at sufficient length. In doing so I have adopted that prolix style of pleadings so dear to the Victorian lawyers, under which the two sides plied one another with plea and replication, rejoinder and rebutter, surrejoinder and surrebutter and so on. I have done this deliberately with the object of letting a full statement of the case for and against Pakistan be made. The foregoing pages contain the pleadings. The facts contained therein are true to the best to my knowledge and belief. It only remains for me to state the issues and to invite Hindus and Muslims to give their findings such as they may think correct and well founded.

It seems to me that the following issues necessarily arise on the pleadings.

(1) Is Hindu-Moslem Unity necessary for India's political advancement ? If necessary, is it still possible of realization notwithstanding the new ideology of Hindus and Muslims being two different nations ?

(2) If Hindu-Moslem Unity is possible should it be reached by appeasement or by settlement ?

(3) If it is to be achieved by appeasement, what are the new concessions that can be offered to the Muslims to obtain their willing co-operation, without prejudice to other interests ?

(4) If it is to be achieved by a settlement what are the terms of that settlement ? If there are only two alternatives (i) Division of India into Pakistan and Hindustan or (ii) Fifty-fifty share in Legislature, Executive and the Services which alternative is preferable ?

(5) Whether India, if she remained one integral whole, can rely upon both Hindus and Mussalmans to defend her independence, assuming it is won from the British?

(6) Having regard to the prevailing antagonism between Hindus and Mussalmans and having regard to the new ideology demarcating them as two distinct nations and postulating an opposition in their ultimate destinies, whether a single constitution for these two nations can be built in the hope that they will show an intention to work it and not to stop it ?

(7) On the assumption that the two-nations theory has come to stay, does not India become an incoherent body without organic unity, incapable of developing into a strong united nation bound by a common faith in a common destiny and therefore likely to remain as a feeble and a sickly country, easy to be kept in perpetual subjection either of the British or of any other foreign power ?

(8) If India cannot be one united country is it not better that Indians should help India in the peaceful dissolution of this incoherent whole into its natural parts, namely Pakistan and Hindustan ?

(9) Whether it is not better to provide for the growth of two independent and separate nations, a Muslim nation inhabiting Pakistan and a Hindu nation inhabiting Hindustan, rather than pursue the vain attempt of keeping India as one undivided country in the vain hope that Hindus and Muslims will some day be one and occupy it as the members of one nation and sons of one motherland ?

Nothing can come in the way of an Indian getting to grips with these issues and reaching his own conclusions with the help of the material contained in foregoing pages except three things : (1) A false sentiment of historical patriotism, (2) a false conception of the exclusive ownership of territory and (3) absence of willingness to think for himself. Of these obstacles the last is the most difficult to get over. Thought is rare all over the world and free thought is rarer still. The victories, won in the battles over freedom of thought, have not produced free thinking. As Sir Herbert Grierson in in his *Essays and Addresses* observes :—

" A much more obvious fact is the almost pathetic readiness of the mass of men to accept leadership in things political, intellectual, and spiritual. We in educational circles are always declaring that the end of education is to teach people to think for themselves. But can the majority ever do so ? My experience is that eighty per cent. of a class do not want to think for themselves, or are incapable of doing so. The man who can does so from the beginning. The majority want to be taught what to think, and the practice of Communist Russia and Fascist Italy points to the same conclusion. Men can and must be taught what to think. So the Catholic Church has always taught, and so the Communist and Fascist insist today."

This is particularly true of the people of India. A great number of Indians being illiterate and uninformed are incapable of thought. Those who are informed and therefore capable of thought desire to be taught what to think. By their social affiliations they have become disposed to accept one particular ideology without examination and cannot free themselves from a servile submission to that ideology. If they can free themselves from this servile mentality then, the other two obstacles, namely a false sentiment of historical patriotism and a false conception of exclusive ownership of territory, will not come in the way of their arriving at right conclusions on the issues which arise.

A large part of the argument of this book has been addressed to the Hindus. There is an obvious reason for this, which would be patent to any one. The Hindus are in a majority. Being in majority their view point must count. There is not much possibility of peaceful solution if no attempt is made to meet their objections, rational or sentimental. But there are special reasons which has led me to address so large a part of the argument to them which may not be quite so obvious to others. I feel that those Hindus who are guiding the destinities of their fellows have lost what Carlyle calls " the Seeing Eye " and are walking in the glamour of certain vain illusions, the consequences of which must, I fear, be terrible for the Hindus.

The Hindus will not realize, although it is now a matter of experience, that the Hindus and Muslims are neither one in temparament, nor in spiritual experience, nor in the desire for political union ; and even at the few moments when they approached a kind of cordiality their relations were uneasy. Yet the Hindus will continue to cherish the illusion that notwithstanding this past experience there is still left a sufficient stock of broad and real community of aim, sentiments and policy to enable Hindus and Muslims to come together.

The Hindus will not realize that Mr. Jinnah has engaged himself in mobilizing all his forces for battle. Mr. Jinnah was never a man for the masses. He distrusted them. To exclude them from political power he was always for a high franchise. Mr. Jinnah was never known to be a very devout, pious or a professing Muslim. Besides kissing the Holy Koran as and when he was sworn as an M. L. A. he does not appear to have bothered much about its contents or its special tenents. It is doubtful if he frequented any Mosque either out of curiosity or religious fervour. Mr. Jinnah was never found in the midst of Muslim mass congregations, religious or political. To-day one finds a complete change in Mr. Jinnah. He has become a man of the masses. He is no longer above them. He is among them. Having come among them they have raised him above themselves and call him their Qaide-Azam. He has not only become a believer in Islam. He is prepared to die for Islam. To-day he knows more of Islam than mere *Kalama*. To-day he goes to the Mosque to here *Khutba* and takes delight in joining the Id congregessional prayers. Dongri and Nulbazar once knew Mr. Jinnah by name. To-day they know him by his presence. No Muslim meeting in Bombay begins or ends without Alla-ho-Akabar and Long Live Qaide' Azam. In spite of all this the Hindus will not give up the illusion that Pakistan is only the fancy of Mr. Jinnah and that it has no support from the Muslim masses or other Muslim Leaders. They are hugging to this illusion because Sir S. Hayat Khan and Mr. Fazulal Haq are not openly supporting Mr. Jinnah. As to Mr. Jinnah's mixing among the Muslim masses the Hindus are only amused. For they see in it nothing but Mr. Jinnah exchanging his reason for the superstition of his followers.

When one hears these things from the Hindu camp one wonders what has made the Hindu intellect so weak and so dull. They fail to see that both Sir Sikandar and Mr. Fazlul Haque were opposed to the formation of branches of the Muslim League in their

Provinces when Mr. Jinnah tried to revive it in 1937. **Notwith-standing** their opposition the branches of **the** League **were** formed in the Punjab as well as in Bengal and within one **year** both were compelled to join them. It is a case of those coming to scoff remaining to pray. No more cogent proof seems to be necessary to prove the victory of the League. Besides, if they are really opposed to Pakistan it is easy for them to denounce it. But so far they have not done so. All this is so obvious. Still the Hindus will keep on saying that Muslim leaders do not support Mr. Jinnah. In Mr. Jinnah's contact with the Muslim masses there is undoubtedly more than a mere exchange of reason for superstition. In this Mr. Jinnah has merely followed King Henry IV of France — the unhappy father-in-law of the English King Charles I. Henry IV was a Huguenot by faith. But he did not hesitate to attend mass in a Catholic Church in Paris. He believed that to change his Huguenot faith and go to mass was an easy price to pay for the powerful support of Paris. As Paris became worth a mass to Henry IV, so have Dongri and Nullbazar became worth a mass to Mr. Jinnah and for the same reason. It is strategy ; it is mobilization. But even if it is viewed as the sinking of Mr. Jinnah from reason to superstition he is sinking with his ideology which by his very sinking is spreading into all the different strata of Muslim Society and is becoming part and parcel of its mental make-up. This is as clear as any thing could be. But the Hindus will not see it in that light.

Further the Hindus will not care to understand the implications of the European War. To them this war is simply an occasion to put forward their national demand. As their demand has failed to draw any response they have become cynical in temperament and have cultivated that peculiar type of patriotism which spends itself in chuckling over British reverses and laughing at the European peoples for the mad slaughter which they seem to have made their business. It cannot be denied that this war has lessons for those who care to note the causes of this commerce in death. Undoubtedly they are two and they are distinct. (1) The problem of the domination of a race calling itself superior to other races which it is pleased to regard as its inferior. (2) The struggle of a minority seeking its freedom from the yoke of the majority. The former is typified by Germany. Czechoslovakia furnishes an instance of the latter. Every Hindu ought to know that these are the very problems which they will have to face, before India is free and even after India is free. But the Hindus simply will not cease laughing at Europe, will not consider that the exercise of the right to present a national demand is not the only proper use of this occasion of war and that the war throws upon them the far more important duty to know if the problems which brought about the war are among those which they are heir to and whether they can solve them without the blood price that Europe is paying.

These are the reasons why I have addressed so a large part of the argument to the Hindus. A thick and impervious wall of false sentiments and false illusions has prevented the Hindu from receiving fresh light. It is because of this that I felt the grave necessity of applying my batteries. I do not know how far I have succeeded in making breeches in the wall to let in light in the dark places. I am satisfied that I have done my duty. If the Hindus don't do theirs they will be plagued by the very consequences for which they are laughing at Europe and they will perish in the same way in which Europe is perishing.

I APPENDICES

II MAPS

(1) Hindu and Muslim Area in the Punjab

(2) Hindu and Muslim Area in Bengal and Assam.

(3) India as divided into Pakistan and Hindustan.

APPENDIX I

PUNJAB

PROPORTION OF MUSLIM POPULATION BY DISTRICTS

	Districts where Muslims are above 50 per cent	Actual Proportion of Muslims		Districts where Muslims are below 50 per cent.	Actual Proportion of Muslims.
1	Lahore	59·9	1	Hissar	27·6
2	Sialkot	62·1	2	Rohtak	17 1
3	Gujaranwalla	70 7	3	Gurgaon	32·1
4	Shaikupura	84 8	4	Karnal	30 5
5	Gujrat	63 7	5	Ambala	30 6
6	Shahpur	82 8	6	Simla	15 8
7	Jhelum	89	7	Kangra	5
8	Rawalpindi	82·8	8	Hoshyarpur	32 8
9	Attock	91	9	Jullunder	44 3
10.	Mianwali	87	10	Ludhiana	35 1
11	Montgomeri	69 1	11	Ferozpur	44·8
12	Lyallpur	62 5	12	Amritsar	46·9
13.	Jhang	83·1	13	Gurudaspur	50·0
14	Muzaffarpur	86 5			
15	Dera Gazikhan	86 1			
16.	Biloch Transfrontier Track.	99 9			
17.	Multan	80·2			

APPENDIX II

BENGAL

PROPORTION OF MUSLIM POPULATION BY DISTRICTS

	Districts where Muslims are above 50 per cent.	Actual Proportion of Muslims		Districts where Muslims are below 50 per cent.	Actual Proportion of Muslims.
1	Nadia	61·6	1	Burdwan	18·9
2.	Murshidabad	55 5	2	Birbhum	26 6
3.	Jessore	62 0	3	Bankura	4 7
4	Rajashahi	75 7	4.	Midnapur	7·5
5	Rangpur	71·0	5	Hoogly	17·0
6.	Bogra	83 5	6	Howrah	21 1
7.	Pabna	76 9	7.	Howrah City	21 3
8.	Malda	54·2	8	24 Parganahas	34 6
9	Dacca	69 8	9	Dacca City	41 3
10.	Mymensing	76·6	10	Calcutta	25 9
11	Faridpur	65 1	11	Calcutta Suburbs	19·
12	Bakar Gunj	72·4	12.	Khulna	49 3
13	Tippera	76 0	13	Jalpaiguri	23 9
14	Naokhali ...	76 5	14	Darjeeling	2 5
15.	Chittagong	76 7	15	Dinajpur	50·5

APPENDIX III

ASSAM

PROPORTION OF MUSLIM POPULATION BY DISTRICTS

Districts where Muslims are above 50 per cent.	Actual Proportion of Muslims	Districts where Muslims are below 50 per cent	Actual Proportion of Muslims.
Sylhet	59 2	Cachar	33·1
		Khasi and Jamtia Hills	8
		Naga Hills	3
		Lushi Hills	·06
		Goalpara	42 8
		Kamrup	24 9
		Daurang	11 3
		Nowgang	31 1
		Sibsagar	4 6
		Lakhmipur	5 4
		Garo Hills	5 2
		Ladhya Frontier Tracks	15·2
		Balipara Frontier	1·4

APPENDIX IV

SIND

Proportion of Muslim Population by Districts

District.	Total Population	Total Muslims	Percentage of Muslims to Total.	Total Non-Muslims.	Percentage of Non-Muslims to Total
Karachi	650,240	465,785	71·3	184,455	28 7
Hyderabad	662,924	460,920	69 5	202,004	30·5
Nawabshah	496,612	377,746	76 0	118,866	24 0
Larkhana	693,735	577,899	83·3	115,836	16 7
Sukkur	623,779	440,148	70 0	183,631	30·0
Thar Parkar	468,010	245,964	52·5	223,067	47 5
ɔd Frontier	291,740	262,338	89 9	29,402	10 1
Total	3,887,070	2,830,800	73·2	1,057,261	26·8

APPENDIX V

N. W. F.

PROPORTION OF MUSLIM POPULATION BY DISTRICTS

District	Total Population	Total Muslim Population	Percentage of Muslim Population to Total.	Total Non-Muslim Population.	Percentage of Non-Muslims to Total.
Hazara	670,106	636,794	95·0	33,312	5 0
Peshawar	974,249	898,683	92 2	75,586	7·8
Kohat	236,273	218,445	92 4	17,828	7 6
Banu ...	270,301	237,674	87 9	32,627	12 1
ail Khan .	274,064	235,707	86·0	38,357	14·0
Total	2,424,993	2,227,303	90 7	197,690	9 3

APPENDIX VI

SIND

PROPORTION OF MUSLIM TO NON-MUSLIM POPULATION IN TOWNS

Towns by Districts.	Total Population.	Total Muslim Population	Percentage of Muslims to Total	Total Non-Muslim Population	Percentage of Non-Muslims to Total
Hyderabad					
1. Hala	7,304	4,745	64·9	2,559	35 1
2. Hyderabad	96,021	27,116	29 2	68,905	70 8
3 Matiari	6,692	4,886	73·0	1,806	27 0
4. Narsapur	4,254	2,744	64 5	1,510	35 5
5. Taudo Alahyar	5,146	1,745	33 9	3,400	66 1
6. Taudo Mahomed-khan	6,625	2,938	44 3	3,688	55 7
Karachi.					
7 Karachi	247,791	118,412	46 9	129,379	53 1
8 Ketibunder	1,655	833	50 3	822	49·7
9. Kotri	10,033	6,058	60 3	3,975	39 7
10 Manjhand	2,746	1,253	45 6	1,493	54 4
11. Tatta	9,635	5,170	53 6	4,465	46·4
Larkana					
12. Bubak	3,002	1,300	43 3	1 702	56 7
13 Dadu	7,328	4,199	57 2	3,129	42 8
14 Kambar	9,717	6,255	62 3	3,462	37 7
15. Larkana	26,841	10,945	40 8	15,896	59 2
16 Rato Dero	7,285	2,582	35 4	4,703	64·6
17 Shewan	5,795	3,753	64 7	2,042	35 3
Nawabsha.					
18 Nawabsha	7,023	2,468	35 1	5,555	64 9
19. Shahadadpui	8,847	2,960	33 4	5,887	66 6
20 Taudo Adam	13,469	3,204	23 7	10,265	76 3
Sukkar					
21. Ghotki	4,826	1 668	34 5	3,158	65 5
22. Gahriyassin	7,370	2,971	40 3	4,409	52 7
23. Rohri	16,900	6,804	40 2	10,099	59 8
24. Shikarpur	62,505	22,654	36 2	39 513	63 8
25. Sukkur	69,277	27,642	39 9	41,625	60 1
Thar Parkar.					
26. Mirpurkhas	10,178	2,769	27 2	7,409	72 8
27 Umarkot	3,841	947	24 6	2,894	75 4
Upper Sind Frontier.					
28. Jacobabad	15,748	7,783	49 4	7,965	50 6

APPENDIX VII

N. W. F.

Proportion of Muslim to Non-Muslim Population in Towns

	Towns by Districts	Total Population	Total Muslim Population	Percentage of Muslims to Total	Total Non-Muslim Population	Percentage Non-Muslim to Total
	Hazara District					
1	Abottabad Cantt	8,527	1,712	20 0	6,815	80·0
2	Abottabad Municipl	7,638	5,314	69 4	2,324	30 6
3	Haripur	7,653	4,253	55 2	3,400	54·8
4	Batla N A	7,257	6,409	55 5	1,848	44 5
5	Nawanshar	5,130	3,884	75 7	1,246	24 3
6	Manshera	5,780	4,217	72 9	1,563	27 1
	Peshawar District					
7	Peshawar Municipl	87,440	69,893	79 9	17,547	20 1
8	Peshawar Cantt	34,426	16,476	47 8	17,950	52 2
9	Mardan Municipl	23,848	18,588	77 8	5,260	22 2
10	Mardan Cantt	2,431	991	40 8	1,440	59 2
11	Nowshera N A	12,829	12,126	94 5	703	5 5
12	Nowshera Cantt	16,137	7,536	46 6	8,601	53 4
13	Charsada	11,537	10,703	93 0	834	7 0
14	Parang	10,227	10,211	99 9	16	0 1
15	Tangi	8,689	8,320	96 5	369	3 5
16	Risalpur Cantt	8,016	2,380	28 6	5,636	71 4
17	Cherat Cantt	843	896	46 4	447	53 6
	Kohat District					
18	Kohat Municipl	25,100	20,655	80 0	4,445	20 0
19	Kohat Cantt	9,250	3,733	40 2	5,517	59 8
	Bannu District					
20	Bannu	24,980	8,296	33 3	16,784	66 7
21	Bannu Cantt	5,559	2,311	41 8	3,248	58 2
22	Lakki N A	7,703	4,630	60 0	3,073	40 0
	Dera Ismail Khan					
23	Dera Ismail Khan Municipl	38,956	21,709	55 2	17,247	44·8
24	Dera Ismail Khan Cantt	1,375	612	44 5	763	55 5
25	Kulachi N A	8,425	6,115	72 7	2,310	27 3
26	Tank N A.	6,421	3,929	69 1	2,492	30 9

APPENDIX VIII

DISTRIBUTION OF MUSLIM POPULATION IN BRITISH INDIA

	inces	Total Population	Muslim Population.	Percentage of Muslims to Total.
1	Ajmere—Merwara	560,292	97,133	17 3
2.	Andaman and Nicobar Islands	29,463	6,719	20·6
3.	Assam	8,622,251	2,755,914	31 4
4.	British Baluchistan	463,508	405,309	87 0
5.	Bengal	50,114,002	27,497,624	54 1
6.	Bihar	25,727,500	3,689,954	12 0
7.	Orissa	5,306,142	124,463	1 9
8.	Chhotta Nagpur	6,643,934	450,373	6 1
9	Bombay	17,916,318	1,583,259	8 3
10.	Central Provinces	15,507,723	682,854	3 8
	C P	12,065,885	383,174	2·5
	Berar	3,441,838	299 680	8 7
11	Coorg	163,327	13,777	6 1
12	Delhi	636,246	206 960	33 0
13	Madras	46,740,107	3,305,937	6 2
14.	N W F	2,425,076	2,227,303	65 8
15.	Punjab	23,580,852	13,332,460	56 5
16.	Sind	3,887,070	2,830,809	73 7
17.	United Provinces	48,408,763	7,181,927	14 1
	Agra	35,613,784	5,318,077	14 1
	Audh	12,794,979	1,863,850	8 0
	Total	256,732,574	66,442,766	25 9

APPENDIX IX

DISTRIBUTION OF MUSLIM POPULATION IN INDIAN STATES

	Indian States and Agencies	Total Population.	Muslims Population	Percentage of Muslims to Total.
1	Assam States	625,606	21,600	3·3
2	Baluchistan States	405,109	392,782	97 5
3	Baroda	2,443,007	182,630	7 2
4	Bengal States	973,336	312,476	32 1
5	Bihar and Orissa States	4,652,007	19,516	4 1
6	Bombay	4,468,396	414,931	9·0
7	Central India Agency	6,632,790	376,637	4·6
8	Central Provinces States	2,483,214	23,254	9 4
9	Gwalior	3,523,070	204,297	5·9
10	Hyderabad	14,436,148	1,534,660	10·4
11	Jammu and Kasmir	3,646,243	2,817636	77 7
12	Madras States Agency	6,754,484	467,396	6 0
	Cochin	1,205,016	87,902	6 8
	Travancore	5,095,973	353,274	6 0
	Other Madras States	453,495	26,220	4 5
13.	Mysore	6,557,302	398,628	6 1
14	N W F Agencies	46,451	23,086	50·0
15	Punjab States	437,787	40,845	9 1
16	Punjab States Agency	4,472,218	1,556,591	35·2
17	Rajputana Agency	11,225,712	1,069,325	9 7
18	Sikim	109,808	104	0 1
19	United Provinces States	1,206,070	352,131	25 0
20	Western India States Agency	3,999,250	545,569	13·0
	Total	79,098,008	10,657,102	12·7

APPENDIX X*

CONGRESS—MUSLIM PACT

MUSLIM DELEGATION TO THE ROUND TABLE CONFERENCE

Tel. Victoria 2360

Telegrams : " Courtlike " London.

Queen's House,

57, St James's Court,
Buckingham Gate,
LONDON, S.W.1.

6th October, 1931.

The following proposals were discussed by Mr. Gandhi and the Muslim Delegation at 10 p.m. last night They are divided into two parts — the proposals made by the Muslims for safeguarding their rights, and the proposals made by Mr. Gandhi regarding the Congress policy. They are given herewith as approved by Mr Gandhi, and placed for submission to the Muslim Delegation for their opinion.

MUSLIM PROPOSALS

1. In the Punjab and Bengal bare majority of one per cent of Musalmans, but the question of whether it should be by means of joint electorates and reservation of 51 per cent of the whole house, or separate electorates with 51 per cent seats in the whole house should be referred to the Musalman voters before the new constitution comes into force and their verdict should be accepted.

2. In other provinces where the Musalmans are in a minority the present weightage enjoyed by them to continue, but whether the seats should be reserved to a joint electorates, or whether they shold have separate electorates should be determined by the Musalman voters by a referendum under the new constitution, and their verdict should be accepted.

3. That the Musalman representatives to the Central Legislature in both the houses should be 26 per cent. of the total number of the

---

* This document is coming to light for the first time It embodies the efforts made by Mr Gandhi at the Second R T. C to bring about a communal settlement with the Muslims. It was circulated among the Muslim delegates The author was able to secure a copy from a Hindu delegate who was acting with the Muslim Delegates at the R. T. C. Mr. Gandhi failed to reach an agreement with the Muslims All the same the document is both interesting and instructive It reveals the ways and means adopted by Mr. Gandhi to reach an agreement with the Muslims. Proposal No 2 of Mr Gandhi is very significant. It shows that Mr Gandhi was prepared to give every thing to the Muslims on condition that the Muslims agreed to side with him in opposing the claims of the Depressed Classes, the Indian Christians and the Anglo-Indians for special representation Heretofore people only knew of the Minorities Pact tendered to the R. T C which was decried as being anti-national. They did not know that Mr. Gandhi was also engaged in forging a pact the object of which was to defeat with the help of the Muslims the just claims of the smaller minorities

British India representatives, and 7 per cent. at least by convention should be Musalmans, out of the quota that may be assigned to Indian States, that is to say, one-third of the whole house when taken together

4. That the residuary power should vest in the federating Provinces of British India.

5. That the other points as follows being agreed to —

   1. Sindh.
   2. N. W, F. P
   3. Services.
   4. Cabinet.
   5. Fundamental rights and safeguards for religion and culture.
   6. Safeguards against legislation affecting any community.

MR. GANDHI'S PROPOSALS.

1 That the Franchise should be on the basis of adult suffrage.

2. No special reservations to any other community save Sikhs and Hindu minorities.

3. The Congress demands .—

   A. Complete independence
   B Complete control over the defence immediately.
   C. Complete control over external affairs
   D. Complete control over finance.
   E. Investigation of public debts and other obligations by an independent tribunal.
   F. As in the case of a partnership, right of either party to terminate it.

APPENDIX XI.

COMMUNAL AWARD

In the statement made by the Prime Minister on 1st December last on behalf of His Majesty's Government at the close of the second session of the Round Table Conference, which was immediately afterwards endorsed by both Houses of Parliament, it was made plain that if the communities in India were unable to reach a settlement acceptable to all parties on the communal questions which the Conference had failed to solve His Majesty's Government were determined that India's constitutional advance should not on that account be frustrated, and that they would remove this obstacle by devising and applying themselves a provisional scheme.

2. On the 19th March last His Majesty's Government, having been informed that the continued failure of the communities to reach agreement was blocking the progress of the plans for the framing of a new Constitution, stated that they were engaged upon a careful re-examination of the difficult and controversial questions which arise. They are now satisfied that without a decision of at least some aspects of the problems connected with the position of minorities under the new Constitution, no further progress can be made with the framing of the Constitution.

3. His Majesty's Government have accordingly decided that they will include provisions to give effect to the scheme set out below in the proposals relating to the Indian Constitution to be laid in due course before Parliament. The scope of this scheme is purposely confined to the arrangements to be made for the representation of the British Indian communities in the Provincial Legislatures, consideration of representation in the Legislature at the Centre being deferred for the reason given in paragraph 20 below. The decision to limit the scope of the scheme implies no failure to realise that the framing of the Constitution will necessitate the decision of a number of other problems of great importance to minorities, but has been taken in the hope that once a pronouncement has been made upon the basic questions of method and proportions of representation the communities themselves may find it possible to arrive at a *modus vivendi* on other communal problems, which have not as yet received the examination they require.

4. His Majesty's Government wish it to be most clearly understood that they themselves can be no parties to any negotiations which may

Parliamentary Paper Command 4147 of 1932. Officially it is spoken of as *Communal Decision.*

be initiated with a view to the revision of their decision, and will not be prepared to give consideration to any representation aimed at securing the modification of it which is not supported by all the parties affected. But they are most desirous to close no door to an agreed settlement should such happily be forthcoming. If, therefore, before a new Government of India Act has passed into law, they are satisfied that the communities who are concerned are mutually agreed upon a practicable alternative scheme, either in respect of any one or more of the Governors' Provinces or in respect of the whole of the British India, they will be prepared to recommend to Parliament that that alternative should be substituted for the provisions now outlined.

5 Seats in the Legislative Councils in the Governors' Provinces, or in the Lower House if there is an Upper Chamber, will be allocated as shown in the annexed table.*

6 Election to the seats allotted to Muhammadan, European and Sikh constituencies will be by voters voting in separate communal electorates covering between them the whole area of the Province (apart from any portions which may in special cases be excluded from the electoral area as " backward").

Provision will be made in the Constitution itself to empower a revision of this electoral arrangement (and the other similar arrangements mentioned below) after 10 years with the assent of the communities affected, for the ascertainment of which suitable, means will be devised.

7. All qualified electors, who are not voters either in a Muhammadan Sikh, Indian Christian (see paragraph 10 below), Anglo-Indian (see paragraph 11 below) or European constituency, will be entitled to vote in a general constituency.

8. Seven seats will be reserved for Mahrattas in certain selected plural member general constituencies in Bombay.

9 Members of the " depressed classes" qualified to vote will vote in a general constituency. In view of the fact that for a considerable period these classes would be unlikely, by this means alone, to secure any adequate representation in the Legislature, a number of special seats will be assigned to them as shown in the table. These seats will be filled by election from special constituencies in which only members of the " depressed classes" electorally qualified will be entitled to vote Any person voting in such a special constituency will, as stated above, be also entitled to vote in a general constituency.

* See page 370.

It is intended that these constituencies should be formed in selected areas where the depressed classes are most numerous, and that, except in Madras, they should not cover the whole area of the Province.

In Bengal it seems possible that in some general constituencies a majority of the voters will belong to the Depressed Classes. Accordingly, pending further investigation, no number has been fixed for the members to be returned from the special Depressed Class constituencies in that Province. It is intended to secure that the Depressed Classes should obtain not less than 10 seats in the Bengal Legislature.

The precise definition in each Province of those who (if electorally qualified) will be entitled to vote in the special Depressed Class constituencies has not yet been finally determined. It will be based as a rule on the general principles advocated in the Franchise Committee's Report. Modification may, however, be found necessary in some Provinces in Northern India where the application of the general criteria of untouchability might result in a definition unsuitable in some respects to the special conditions of the Province

His Majesty's Government do not consider that these special Depressed Classes constituencies will be required for more than limited time. They intend that the Constitution shall provide that they shall come to an end after 20 years if they have not previously been abolished under the general powers of electoral revision referred to in paragraph 6.

10. Election to the seats allotted to Indian Christians will be by voters voting in separate communal electorates. It seems almost certain that practical difficulties will, except possibly in Madras, prevent the formation of Indian Christian consituencies covering the whole area of the Province, and that accordingly special Indian Christian constituencies will have to be formed only in one or two selected areas in the Province. Indian Christian voters in these areas will not vote in a general constituency. Indian Christian voters outside these areas will vote in a general constituency. Special arrangements may be needed in Bihar and Orissa, where a considerable proportion of the Indian Christian community belong to the aboriginal tribes.

11. Election to the seats allotted to Anglo-Indians will be by voters voting in separate communal electorates. It is at present intended, subject to investigation of any practical difficulties that may arise, that the Anglo-Indian constituencies shall cover the whole area

of each Province, a postal ballot being employed ; but no final decision has yet been reached.

12. The method of filling the seats assigned for representatives from backward areas is still under investigation, and the number of seats so assigned should be regarded as provisional pending a final decision as to the constitutional arrangements to be made in relation to such areas.

13. His Majesty's Government attach great importance to securing that the new Legislatures should contain at least a small number of women members. They feel that at the outset this object could not be achieved without creating a certain number of seats specially allotted to women. They also feel that it is essential that women members should not be drawn disproportionately from one community. They have been unable to find any system which would avoid this risk, and would be consistent with the rest of the scheme for representation which they have found it necessary to adopt, except that of limiting the electorate for each special women's seat to voters from one community.* The special women's seats have accordingly been specifically divided, as shown in the table, between the various communities. The precise electoral machinery to be employed in these special constituencies is still under consideration.

14. The seats allotted to "Labour" will be filled from non-communal constituencies. The electoral arrangements have still to be determined, but it is likely that in most Provinces the Labour constituencies will be partly trade union and partly special constituencies as recommended by the Franchise Committee.

15. The special seats alloted to Commerce and Industry, Mining and Planting will be filled by election through Chambers of Commerce and various Associations. The details of the electoral arrangements for these seats must await further investigation.

16. The special seats allotted to Landholders will be filled by election by special Landholders' constituencies.

17. The method to be employed for election to the University seats is still under consideration.

18. His Majesty's Government have found it impossible in determining these questions of representation in the Provincial Legislatures to avoid entering into considerable detail. There remains, nevertheless, the determination of the constituencies. They intend that this task should be undertaken in India as early as possible.

---

* Subject to one exception, see note (e) to Table.

It is possible that in some instances delimitation of constituencies might be materially improved by slight variations from the numbers of seats now given. His Majesty's Government reserve the right to make such slight variations, for such purpose, provided that they would not materially affect the essential balance between communities. No such variations will, however, be made in the case of Bengal and Punjab.

19. The question of the composition of Second Chambers in the Provinces has so far received comparatively little attention in the constitutional discussions and requires further consideration before a decision is reached as to which Provinces shall have a Second Chamber or a scheme is drawn up for their composition.

His Magesty's Government consider that the composition of the Upper House in a Province should be such as not to disturb in any essential the balance between the communities resulting from the composition of the Lower House.

20. His Majesty's Government do not propose at present to enter into the question of the size and composition of the Legislature at the Centre, since this involves among other questions that of representation of the Indian States which still needs further discussion. They will, of course, when considering the composition, pay full regard to the claims of all communities for adequate representation therein.

21. His Majesty's Government have already accepted the principle that Sind should be constituted a separate Province, if satisfactory means of financing it can be found. As the financial problems involved still have to be reviewed in connection with other problems of federal finance, His Majesty's Government have thought it preferable to include, at this stage, figures for a Legislature for the existing Province of Bombay, in addition to the schemes for separate Legislatures for Bombay Presidency proper and Sind.

22. The figures given for Bihar and Orissa relate to the existing Province. The question of constituting a separate Province of Orissa is still under investigation.

23. The inclusion in the table of figures relating to a Legislature for the Central Provinces including Berar does not imply that any decision has yet been reached regarding the future constitutional position of Berar.

LONDON,
4th August, 1932.

ALLOCATION OF SEATS IN PROVINCIAL LEGISLATURES (LOWER HOUSE ONLY)

Province	General	Depressed Classes	Representatives from Backward Areas	Sikh	Muhammadan	Indian Christian	Anglo-Indian	European	Commerce and Industry, Mining and Planting, Special (a)	Landholders, Special	University, Special	Labour, Special	Total
Madras	134 (including 6 women)	18	1	0	29 (including 1 woman)	9 (inc 1 woman)	2	3	6	6	1	6	215
Bombay (including Sind)	97 (b) (including 5 women)	10	1	0	63 (including 1 woman)	3	2	4	8	3	1	8	200
Bengal	80 (c) (including 2 women)	(c)	0	0	119 (including 2 women)	2	4 (inc. 1 woman)	11	19	5	2	8	250
United Provinces	132 (including 4 women)	12	0	0	66 (including 2 women)	2	1	2	3	6	1	3	228
Punjab	43 (including 1 woman)	0	0	32 (including 1 woman)	86 (including 2 women)	2	1	1	1	5 (d)	1	3	175
Bihar and Orissa	99 (including 3 women)	7	8	0	42 (including 1 woman)	2	1	2	4	5	1	4	175
Central Provinces (including Berar)	77 (including 3 women)	10	1	0	14	0	1	1	2	3	1	2	112

Assam	44 (including 1 woman)(e)	4	9	0	34	1	1	0	1	11	0	0	4	108
North-West Frontier Province.	9	0	0	3	36	0	0	0	0	0	2	0	0	50
Bombay (without Sind).	109 (b) (including 5 women)	10	1	0	30 (including 1 woman)	3	2	3	7	2	1	7	175
Sind	19 (including 1 woman)	0	0	0	34 (including 1 woman)	0	2	2	2	2	0	1	60

(a) The composition of the bodies through which election to these seats will be conducted, though in most cases neither predominantly European or predominantly Indian, will not be statutorily fixed. It is, accordingly, not possible in each Province to state with certainty how many Europeans and Indians respectively will be returned. It is, however, expected that, initially, the numbers will be approximately as follows:—Madras, 4 Europeans, 2 Indians; Bombay (including Sind), 5 Europeans, 3 Indians; Bengal, 14 Europeans, 5 Indians; United Provinces, 2 Europeans, 1 Indian; Punjab, 1 Indian; Bihar and Orissa 2 Europeans, 2 Indians; Central Provinces including Berar, 1 European, 1 Indian; Assam, 8 Europeans, 3 Indians; Bombay without Sind, 4 Europeans, 3 Indians; Sind, 1 European, 1 Indian.

(b) Seven of these seats will be reserved for Mahrattas.

(c) As explained in paragraph 9 of the statement, the number of special Depressed Class seats in Bengal—which will not exceed 10—has not yet been fixed. The number of General seats will be 80, less the number of special Depressed Class seats.

(d) One of these seats is a Tumandar's seat. The four Landholder's seats will be filled from special constituencies with joint electorates. It is probable, from the distribution of the electorate, that the members returned will be one Hindu, one Sikh, and two Muhammadans.

(e) This woman's seat will be filled from a non-communal constituency at Shillong.

APPENDIX XII

SUPPLEMENTARY COMMUNAL AWARD *

" Then there was the question of the representation of communities in the Centre, particularly of the Moslem community. There, I think, I can say, definitely—I think I have said it indirectly very often before—that the Government consider that the Moslem community should have a representation 33⅓ per cent. in the Federal Centre. As far as Indian India is concerned that must be a matter for arrangement between the communities affected and the princes, but, so far as the British Government has any part in the question we will, at any time, give our good offices to making it as easy as possible for the arrangement between those parties with regard to the future allocation of seats.

* The Communal Award of His Majesty's Government (Appendix XI) did not give any decision regarding the Muslim claim for 33⅓ per cent representation in the Central Government. The decision of His Majesty's Government on this claim was announced by the Secretary of State for India on 24th December 1932 in the course of his statement to the Third Round Table Conference.

APPENDIX X III

POONA PACT *

(1) There shall be seats reserved for the Depressed Classes out of the general electorate seats in the Provincial Legislatures as follows :

Madras 30 : Bombay with Sind 15 ; Punjab 8 ; Bihar and Orissa 18 ; Central Provinces 20 ; Assam 7 ; Bengal 30 ; United Provinces 20 ; Total 148.

These figures are based on the total strength of the Provincial Councils, announced in the Prime Minister's decision.

(2) Election to these seats shall be by joint electorates subject, however, to the following procedure :

All the members of the Depressed Classes registered in the general electoral roll in a constituency will form an electoral college, which will elect a panel of four candidates belonging to the Depressed Classes for each of such reserved seats, by the method of the single vote ; the four persons getting the highest number of votes in such primary election, shall be candidates for election by the general electorate.

(3) Representation of the Depressed Classes in the Central Legislature shall likewise be on the principal of joint electorates and reserved seats by the method of primary election in the manner provided for in Clause two above, for their representation in the Provincial Legislatures.

(4) In the Central Legislatures, eighteen per cent of the seats allotted to the general electorate for British India in the said legislature shall be reserved for the Depressed Classes.

(5) The system of primary election to a panel of candidates for election to the Central and Provincial Legislatures, as hereinbefore mentioned, shall come to an end after the first ten years, unless terminated sooner by mutual agreement under the provision of Clause six below.

(6) The system of representation of the Depressed Classes by reserved seats in the Provincial and Central Legislatures as provided for in Clauses 1 and 4 shall continue until determined by mutual agreement between the communities concerned in the settlement.

(7) Franchise for the Central and Provincial Legislatures for the Depressed Classes shall be as indicated in the Lothian Committee Report.

---

* Signed on 25th September 1932.

(8) There shall be no disabilities attaching to any one on the ground of his being a member of the Depressed Classes in regard to any elections to local bodies or appointment to the Public Services. Every endeavour shall be made to secure fair representation of the Depressed Classes in these respects, subject to such educational qualifications as may be laid down for appointment to the Public Services.

(9) In every province out of the educational grant, an adequate sum shall be earmarked for providing educational facilities to the members of the Depressed Classes.

APPENDIX XIV

Communal Representation in Services.

RESOLUTION.*

Establishments.

the 4th July 1934.

Section I—General.

No. F. 14/17-B./33, — In accordance with undertakings given in the Legislative Assembly the Government of India have carefully reviewed the results of the policy followed since 1925 of reserving a certain percentage of direct appointments to Government service for the redress of communal inequalities. It has been represented that though this policy was adopted mainly with the object of securing increased representation for Muslims in the public services, it has failed to secure for them their due share of appointments and it has been contended that this position cannot be remedied unless a fixed percentage of vacancies is reserved for Muslims. In particular, attention has been drawn to the small number of Muslims in the Railway services, even on those railways which run through areas in which Muslims form a high percentage of the total population.

The review of the position has shown that these complaints are justified, and the Government of India are satisfied by the enquiries they have made that the instructions regarding recruitment must be revised with a view to improving the position of Muslims in the services.

2. In considering this general question the Government of India have also to take into account the claims of Anglo-Indians and Domiciled Europeans and of the depressed classes. Anglo-Indians have always held a large percentage of appointments in certain branches of the public service and it has been recognised that in view of the degree to which the community has been dependent on this employment steps must be taken to prevent in the new conditions anything in the nature of a rapid displacement of Anglo-Indians from their existing positions, which might occasion a violent dislocation of the economic structure of the community. The instructions which follow in regard to the employment of Anglo-Indians and Domiciled Europeans in certain departments are designed to give effect to this policy.

* Gazette of India Part I July 7, 1934,

3. In regard to the depressed classes it is common ground that all reasonable steps should be taken to secure for them a fair degree of representation in the public services. The intention of caste Hindus in this respect was formally stated in the Poona Agreement of 1932 and His Majesty's Government in accepting that agreement took due note of this point. In the present state of general education in these classes the Government of India consider that no useful purpose will be served by reserving for them a definite percentage of vacancies out of the number available for Hindus as a whole, but they hope to ensure that duly qualified candidates from the depressed classes are not deprived of fair opportunities of appoiniment merely because they cannot succeed in open competition

4. The Government of India have also considered carefully the position of minority communities other than those mentioned above and are satisfied that the new rules will continue to provide for them, as at present, a reasonable degree of representation in the services.

Section II—Scope of Rules.

5. The Government of India propose to prescribe annual returns in order to enable them to watch the observance of the rules laid down below.

6. The general rules which the Government of India have with the approval of the Secretary of State adopted with the purpose of securing these objects are explained below. They relate only to direct recruitment and not to recruitment by promotion which will continue to be made as at present solely on merit. They apply to the Indian Civil Service, the Central Services, Class I and Class II, and the Subordinate services under the administrative control of the Government of India with the exception of a few services and posts for which high technical or special qualifications are required, but do not apply to recruitment for these Services in the province of Burma. In regard to the Railways, they apply to all posts other than those of inferior servants or labourers on the four State-managed Railways, and the administrations of the Company-managed railways will be asked to adopt similar rules for the services on these railways.

Section III—Rules for Services recruited on an All-India basis.

7. (1) For the Indian Civil Service and the Central and Subordinate services to which recruitment is made on an All-India basis, the following rules will be observed :—

(i) 25 percent. of all vacancies to be filled by direct recruitment of Indians, will be reserved for Muslims and 8 1/3 per cent. for other minority communities.

48

(ii) When recruitment is made by open competition, if Muslims or the other minority communities obtain less than these percentages, these percentages will be secured to them by means of nomination ; if, however, Muslims obtain more than their reserved percentage in open competition, no reduction will be made in the percentage reserved for other minorities, while if the other minorities obtain more than their reserved percentage in open competition, no reduction will be made in the percentage reserved for Muslims.

(iii) If members of the other minority communities obtain less than their reserved percentage in open competition and if duly qualified candidates are not available for nomination, the residue of the 8 1/3 per cent. will be available for Muslims.

(iv) The percentage of 8 1/3 reserved for the other minorities will not be distributed among them in any fixed proportion.

(v) In all cases a minimum standard of qualification will be imposed and the reservations are subject to this condition.

(vi) In order to secure fair representation for the depressed classes duly qualified members of these classes may be nominated to a public service, even though recruitment to that service is being made by competition. Members of these classes, if appointed by nomination, will not count against the percentages reserved in accordance with clause (1) above.

(2). For the reasons given in paragraph 2 of this Resolution, the Government of India have paid special attention to the question of Anglo-Indians and Domiciled Europeans in the gazetted posts on the Railways for which recruitment is made on an All-India basis. In order to maintain approximately their present representation in these posts the Anglo-Indian and Domiciled community will require to obtain about 9 per cent. of the total vacancies available to members of Indian communities. The Government of India have satisfied themselves that at present the community is obtaining by promotions to these gazetted posts and by direct recruitment to them more than 9 per cent. of these vacancies. In these circumstances, it has been decided that no special reservation is at present required. If and when the community is shown to be receiving less than 9 per cent. of the vacancies, it will be considered what adjustments in regard to direct recruitment may be required to safeguard their legitimate interests.

Secton IV—Rules for Services recruited

(3) In the case of all services to which recruitment is made by local areas and not on an All-India basis, e.g., subordinate posts in the Railways, posts and Telegraphs Department, Customs Service, Income-tax Department, etc., the general rules prescribed above apply subject to the following modifications :—

(1) The total reservation for India as a whole of 25 per cent. for Muslims and of 8 1/3 per cent. for other minorities will be obtained by fixing a percentage for each Railway or local area or circle having regard to the population ratio of Muslims and other minoritiy communities in the area and the rules for recruitment adopted by the local Government of the area concerned ;

(2) In the case of the Railways and Posts and Telegraphs Department and Customs Service in which the Anglo-Indian and Domiciled European community is at present principally employed special provisions described in the next paragraph are required in order to give effect to the policy stated in paragraph 2 above.

9. (1) (a) The Anglo-Indian and Domiciled European community at present holds 8.8 per cent. of the subordinate posts on the railways. To safeguard their position 8 per cent. of all vacancies to be filled by direct recruitment will be reserved for members of this community. This total percentage will be obtained by fixing a separate percentage (1) for each railway having regard to the number of members of this community at present employed, (ii) for each branch or department of the Railway service, so as to ensure that Anglo-Indians continue to be employed in those branches in which they are at present principally employed, e.g , the Mechanical Engineering, Civil Engineering and Traffic Departments. No posts in the higher grades of the subordinate posts will be reserved, and promotion to these grades will be made, as at present solely on merit.

(b) the reservation of 25 per cent. for Muslims and 8 per cent for Anglo-Indians makes it necessary to increase the reservation of 33⅓ per cent. hitherto, adopted for all minority communities, in order to safeguard the interests of minorities other than Muslims and Anglo-Indians. It has been decided, therefore, to reserve for them 6 per cent. of vacancies filled by direct recruitment, which is approximately the percentage of posts held by members of these communities at present. This total reservation will be obtained in the manner prescribed in paragraph 8 (1) of this Resolution and will not be further sub-divided among the minority communities.

(2) In the Posts and Telegraphs Department the same principles will be followed as in the case of the Railways for safeguarding the interests of the Anglo-Indian and Domiciled European community which at present holds about 2·2 per cent. of all subordinate posts. It has been ascertained that if a reservation is made for this community of 5 per cent. of the vacancies in the branches, departments or categories which members of this community may reasonably be expected to enter, it will result in securing for them a percentage equal to slightly less than the percentage of subordinate posts which they at present hold. In the departments or branches in which a special reservation is made for Anglo-Indians the reservation of vacancies for other minorities will be fixed so as to be equal approximately to the percentage of subordinate posts at present held by them. The total reservation for Anglo-Indians and other minority communities, other than Muslims, will in any case be not less than 8¾ per cent.

(3) Anglo-Indians are at present largely employed in subordinate posts in the Appraising Department and in the Superior Preventive Service at the major ports. For the former department special technical qualifications are required, and in accordance with the general principles indicated in paragraph 6 of this Resolution it will be excluded from the operation of these rules. In the Preventive Service special qualifications are required, and the present system of recruitment whereby posts are reserved for Anglo-Indians will be maintained.

ORDER.—Ordered that this Resolution be communicated to all Local Government and Administrations and the several Departments of the Government of India, for information (and guidance) and that it be also published in the Gazette of India.

M. G. Hallett,
Secretary to the Government of India.

Lightning Source UK Ltd.
Milton Keynes UK
UKOW04f0003260117

292918UK00011B/532/P